The Manasseh Hill Country Survey

Culture and History of the Ancient Near East

Founding Editor

M.H.E. Weippert

Editor-in-Chief

Jonathan Stökl

Editors

Eckart Frahm
W. Randall Garr
Baruch Halpern
Theo P.J. van den Hout
Leslie Anne Warden
Irene J. Winter

VOLUME 21.6

The titles published in this series are listed at *brill.com/chan*

The Manasseh Hill Country Survey

Volume VI: The Eastern Samaria Shoulder, from Nahal Tirzah (Wadi Far'ah) to Ma'ale Ephraim Junction

By

Shay Bar
Adam Zertal

BRILL

LEIDEN | BOSTON

The Library of Congress Cataloging-in-Publication Data is available online at http://catalog.loc.gov
LC record available at http://lccn.loc.gov/2004045595

Typeface for the Latin, Greek, and Cyrillic scripts: "Brill". See and download: brill.com/brill-typeface.

ISSN 1566-2055
ISBN 978-90-04-46322-6 (hardback)
ISBN 978-90-04-46323-3 (e-book)

Copyright 2021 by Shay Bar. Published by Koninklijke Brill NV, Leiden, The Netherlands.
Koninklijke Brill NV incorporates the imprints Brill, Brill Hes & De Graaf, Brill Nijhoff, Brill Rodopi, Brill Sense, Hotei Publishing, mentis Verlag, Verlag Ferdinand Schöningh and Wilhelm Fink Verlag.
Koninklijke Brill NV reserves the right to protect this publication against unauthorized use. Requests for re-use and/or translations must be addressed to Koninklijke Brill NV via brill.com or copyright.com.

This book is printed on acid-free paper and produced in a sustainable manner.

1. The Manasseh Hill Country Survey team, left to right, Upper picture: Daniel Zohar, Isaac Bejarano, Shay Bar, Meir Adar, Shoshi Lotan, Leah Tramer, Amatsia Halevi and Evgeny Kaminsky (photo M. Einav; 2018). Lower picture: Isaac Bejarano, Noga Goldring, Amatsia Halevi, Meir Adar, the late Shraga Hashman, Osnat Avizel Gadir, the late Adam Zertal and Oren Cohen. Missing: Dror Ben-Yosef, Moshe Einav, Ari Levi and Lital Shtern (photo S. Bar; 2012).

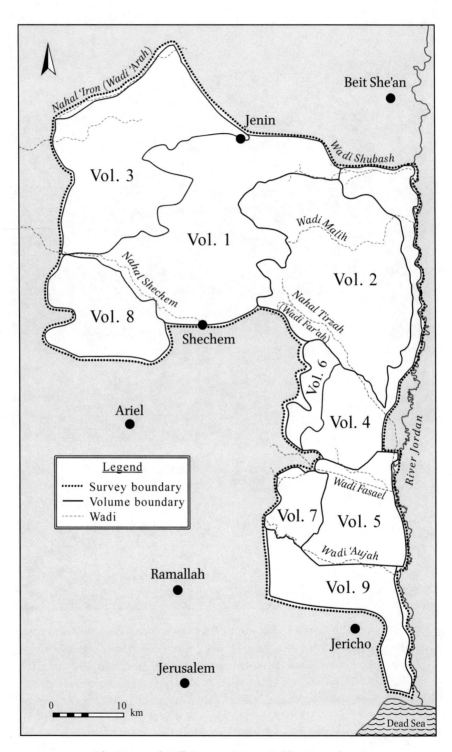

2. The Manasseh Hill Country Survey: Publication volumes.

CONTENTS

Abbreviations ix
Preface 1

PART ONE: INTRODUCTION

CHAPTER ONE
Geographical and Settlement Data 7
   A. History of Research and Historical Sources 7
      1. Ancient Sources 7
   B. The Geography of the Eastern Samaria Shoulder 10
      1. Boundaries 10
      2. Geology and Geomorphology 12
      3. Climate, Water, Soil and Vegetation 15
      4. Roads 18

CHAPTER TWO
The Landscape Units 27

CHAPTER THREE
The Settlement by Periods 37

CHAPTER FOUR
Outline of the History of the Region 73

CHAPTER FIVE
Methodological Comments on the Survey 83

PART TWO: DESCRIPTION OF THE SITES

CHAPTER SIX
Samaria Mountain Slopes from Nahal Tirzah to Wadi Ahmar - Landscape Unit 34 89

CHAPTER SEVEN
The Valley of Gittit - Landscape Unit 35 263

BIBLIOGRAPHY 449

PART THREE: APPENDICES AND INDICES

APPENDIX A
Excavation of a Middle Roman Period Tower in Mras ed-Din, by Nofar Shamir and Shay Bar...457

INDICES
1. List of Springs and Other Water Sources 469
2. List of Roads.. 470
3. Agricultural Installations and Other Features 471
4. Site Index 486
5. List of Sites by Period... 492

Volume 6 map 494

ABBREVIATIONS

a.s.a. - above surrounding area
a.s.l. - above sea level
b.s.a. - below surrounding area
b.s.l. - below sea level
BCE, B.C.E. - Before Common Era
bl - blue
blk - black
brn - brown
bs - body sherd
burn - burnish/ed
Byz - Byzantine period
CE, C.E. - Common Era
Chal - Chalcolithic period
clr - colouring
CP - cooking pot
dec - decorated, decoration
drk/dk - dark
EB, EBA - Early Bronze Age
EM - Early Moslem period
eng - engraved
EP, E.P. - Elevation point
ER - Early Roman period
gls - glass
gr - grey
grn - green
ha - hectare
Hel - Hellenistic period
HM - holemouth (jar)
IA, Ir - Iron Age
IB, IBA - Intermediate Bronze Age
ill. - illustration
imp - impression/impressed
inc - incision/incised
Kh. - Khirbeh (t)

km - kilometre
LB, LBA - Late Bronze Age
lt - light
LR - Late Roman period
LU - landscape unit/s
m - metre, metres
MA - Middle Ages, Medieval period
MB, MBA - Middle Bronze Age
Med - Medieval
MHCS - Manasseh Hill Country Survey
misc - miscellaneous
Mod - modern
No., nos - number, numbers
org - orange
orn - ornamentation
Ott - Ottoman period
PEF - Palestine Exploration Fund
Pers - Persian period
pk - pink
pl – plastic
PPNB - Pre-Pottery Neolithic B period
rd - red
Rom - Roman
sq. km - square kilometres
sq. m - square metres
SWP - Survey of Western Palestine
Tal. - Talmud
T.F. - threshing floor
vt - violet
wh - white
yel - yellow

PREFACE

A year has elapsed since Volume 5 of The Manasseh Hill Country Survey (MHCS) was published (Zertal and Bar 2019). We are happy to introduce Volume 6 in the series to researchers, students and interested readers. The preceding volumes of the survey have long been an important publication and significant database in the research of the Land of Israel, and a fundamental source for the study of Samaria and the Jordan Valley.

In this Volume, we reach the heart of the arable land to the east of the Samaria Mountains, an area bounded by the Alon road in the east and the Aqraba-Yanun mountain escarpment in the west. Thus, we supplement gaps west of the surveyed area included in Volume 4 (Zertal and Bar 2017), and south of the area surveyed and described in Volume 2 (Zertal 2008).

Similarly to the former volumes, this one presents information concerning an area which was almost *terra incognita* as regards archaeological research. Only 15 of the 181 sites presented here had previously been discovered and received scientific attention. In other words, this is the first comprehensive record of the ancient history of this region.

As is our *modus operandi* of the survey, the region was not explored in one sequence. The work started in the mid-1990s, and continued with lengthy intervals until the summer of 2016.

The region is divided into two separate landscape units: LU 34 – the Samaria Mountain slopes from Nahal Tirzah to Wadi Ahmar, and LU 35 – the Gittit Valley.

The entire area was explored systematically and thoroughly on foot.

We open with the introductory chapters, where the properties of the landscape units are presented broadly: history of research, geography of the eastern Samaria Shoulder, boundaries of the region, geology and geomorphology, climate, water, soil, vegetation, roads, description of the landscape units, habitation in the various periods, and outline of the region's history.

Following the Introductions is a special chapter of updates and changes which developed in methodology in the 40 years of the survey, as presented in Volume 1 (Zertal 2004a).

The 181 sites that we found are presented and described according to their places in the two landscape units. As was our custom in the previous volumes, most sites were measured and their plans were drawn. Each site that we discovered has descriptions of its geographical, ecological and archaeological features, accompanied by graphical descriptions of finds and plans of the remains in the field, and aerial photographs for some of the sites.

The Bibliography and Indices follow.

To this Volume is annexed a report on the excavation of a Middle Roman period tower in Mras ed-Din (Site 173).

The reader's attention is drawn to the Agricultural Installations and Other Features list, which is one of the indices which comprises 255 additional archaeological features discovered in the survey. The list refers to man-made remains, not defined by us as sites, most of which are not datable. They include agricultural installations, cisterns, caves, hewn items and places, walls, road remains, etc. All these contribute to a broader view of ancient human activity in the area.

During the fieldwork for the current Volume, Professor Adam Zertal, the initiator and leader of the project for the last 40 years, passed away. Adam was the living spirit and leading researcher in the survey, a teacher for all of us, and a dear friend. It is a great honour for us to follow in his footsteps, continuing his lifetime's undertaking in the field and elsewhere, and producing a scholarly publication. During the publication of this Volume, two other dear friends of the MHCS passed away: Amnon Rotem, an enthusiastic supporter of the volunteers' association operating the Survey, offering and promoting new ideas and venues for its advancement; and Shraga Hashman, one of the first volunteers of the MHCS, who spent more than 30 years in the field with us. May their memory be blessed.

We wish to acknowledge the survey participants who have been involved through the years in the research of the eastern Samaria Shoulder: Shoshi and Meir Adar-Lotan, Osnat Avizel-Gadir, Isaac Bejerano, Dror Ben-Yosef, Oren Cohen, Moshe Einav, Noga Goldring, Amatsia Halevi, Shraga Hashman, Ari Levi, Leah Tramer and others. This devoted and indefatigable team is the heart of the operation.

Thanks are due to all those who carried out the task of publishing this Volume: to Oren Cohen, in charge of gathering and organizing the information, and for the processing of the ceramic data; Osnat Avizel-Gadir for drawing some of the plans; Sapir Haad for the pagination of the book, drawing and sketching the finds and part of the plans; Sonia Pinski for processing the flint finds; Amatsia Halevi for the logistic and administrative management and the translation of this book into English; John Tresman for the English editing; photographers Isaac Bejerano and Moshe Einav, and Asaf Solomon, Aaron Lipkin and Nizan Eshed for the aerial photographs.

We also wish to thank those assisting and providing financial and logistic support: the Scandinavian Fund headed by Gro and Bruno Venske, and the Jordan Valley Regional Council headed by David Elhiyani.

PREFACE

Many thanks are also due to our academic mainstay, the Zinman Institute of Archaeology at the University of Haifa.

And last, but not least, to our friends in the Jordan Valley: the Atidya, Cooper and Leibe families, and to many others who contributed and assisted in accomplishing this goal.

Shay Bar, April 2020

PART ONE
INTRODUCTION

CHAPTER ONE

GEOGRAPHICAL AND SETTLEMENT DATA

A. HISTORY OF RESEARCH AND HISTORICAL SOURCES

1. Ancient Sources

The eastern Samaria Shoulder has been investigated less than any other region in the Land of Israel, and very little is known about it. The region is outside the usual areas of interest of researchers and surveyors: it contains no recognized historical places, and only a handful of archaeological sites have been marked on the various maps.

The researchers and travellers of the first half of the 19th century followed a fixed and regular route via the mountain watershed and the places known from the Bible: Shechem – Shomron (Sebastia) – Jenin – Dothan (Ben-Aryeh 1970). There are no reports of deviations eastwards in the direction of the eastern Samaria Shoulder.

The first mention of the region and references to it are from the second half of the 19th century:

- The Dutch researcher Van de Velde visited the Land in 1851–1852, and was the first to describe this region. On his tour, he set out from Juraish (a village south-west of Aqraba), along the valley of Gittit, in the direction of Wadi Ahmar. In his descriptions, he mentioned Mras ed-Din (Sites 172-173) and the fertile wheatfields in the area (de Velde 1854: 315).
- The French researcher Victor Guérin (1874: chapter 30) toured the area and three sites are mentioned in his account. He observed Khirbet Juraish (Site 64) from a distance, and noted that its name was Khirbet ed-Dowara; He described Khirbet Mras ed-Din (Sites 172-173) as a ruined village, and did not visit it either; and he mentions the stone walls of the structure (fort?) at es-Sireh (1) (Site 133), which he called Zireh, and wondered whether it was a military or agricultural structure.
- The explorers of the SWP worked in the area in 1887. Their main contribution was a preliminary mapping of the area, and particularly the recording of its ancient road system. Only three sites were noted in their research, with a single sentence dedicated to each: the Iron Age fort at Khirbet er-Risa (1) was described as "traces of ruins" (Conder and Kitchener 1882: 391); the fort at Khirbet Tawil (1) (Tuweiyil) was described as "foundations" (Conder

and Kitchener 1882: 395); and the site at Mras ed-Din as "foundations of a building, and cisterns" (Conder and Kitchener 1882: 394); (Sites 94, 171, and 172-173 respectively). It is very odd that the British explorers and cartographers, who mapped the region with precision, did not discover the most

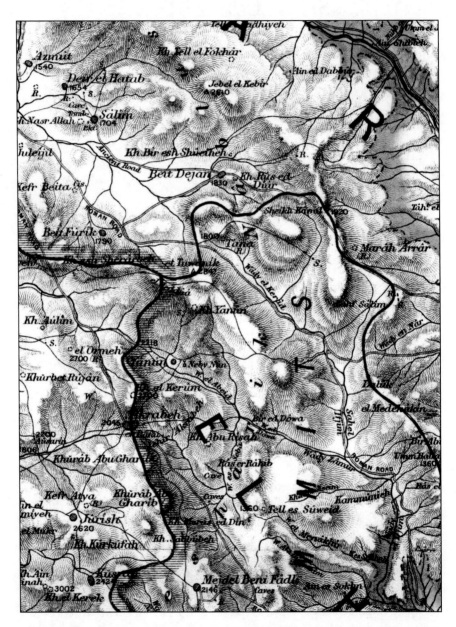

3. A section from the British Survey map (sheet XII) presenting the territory in this volume.

prominent site in the eastern Samaria Shoulder – the Roman-Byzantine city at Khirbet Tana et-Tahta (Site 47).

The eastern side of Samaria was neglected and forgotten for over 80 years, and only after 1967 was research interest in it renewed:
- The Emergency Survey (Kochavi 1972) was carried out in 1967–1968. A team headed by Pesach Bar-Adon was sent to the eastern Samaria Shoulder. Bar-Adon (1972: 92) grumbled that the short time allowed was not enough to survey the whole area allocated to them, and indeed, not a single archaeological site was reported in that survey in the eastern Samaria Shoulder.
- The Samaria Survey B by Yosef Porath, a supplementary survey of the Emergency Survey, took place in 1968. The report has not yet been published, but the manuscript is available to researchers. Porath reported five sites: 1. The fortified Bronze and Iron Age city at Khirbet Juraish (Site 64); 2. The Iron Age fort at Khirbet er-Risa (1) (Site 94) – as stated, the fort had already been recorded by the SWP; 3. The fort at Khirbet et-Tawil (1) (Site 171), also mentioned in the SWP; 4. Mras ed-Din (Sites 172-173), mentioned in the SWP; and 5. Khirbet Bani Fadil (Site 181). These sites are amongst the most important of those of the eastern Samaria Shoulder.
- Ilan's book (1973) was the first to discuss the Samarian desert. Although he did not present any new research, he took care to compile all the preceding data, and to represent it in an orderly manner.
- The Southern Samaria Survey (Finkelstein et al. 1997) was the last one to survey the area prior to the MHCS. His main work was done south-west and west of the eastern Samaria Shoulder, but also reached the southern and eastern bounds of the shoulder. This survey revisited sites discovered during previous surveys, and added six new ones (Sites 43, 102, 142, 144, 176-177).

The few researchers who toured the region later did not conduct a comprehensive survey or regional research, and only referred to specific research topics or to accidental discoveries at several sites. Among them are:
- Ilan and Damati (1975) surveyed the Roman road system in the Sartaba area, and as part of that operation, also some of the roads in the eastern Samaria Shoulder.
- Campbell (1991: 37-41) managed a survey in Shechem region, reached the edges of the eastern Samaria Shoulder, and produced an account of the Roman-Byzantine city at Khirbet Tana et-Tahta (Site 47).
- The Staff Officer of Archaeology for Judea and Samaria also conducted research activity in the region. As part of this activity, Kagan (2009) headed a salvage excavation at Gittit Quarry (Site 124) – the only archaeological excavation in the whole of the eastern Samaria Shoulder prior to the MHCS.

The above review of the research history shows that until the MHCS reached the eastern Samarian Shoulder, only 15 sites were known in the region. Currently we know 181 sites, which are presented here. These numbers prove the importance of meticulous and detailed survey, and we can show for the first time an almost complete archaeological-historical picture of the settlement in the region.

B. THE GEOGRAPHY OF THE EASTERN SAMARIA SHOULDER

1. Boundaries

The boundaries of the eastern Samaria Shoulder match the region's natural borders and other prominent features: roads and main routes (see Fig. 4).

The northern boundary runs along the slopes from the line Beit Dajan–Mekhora north-eastwards to Nahal Tirzah (Wadi Far'ah). The boundary goes from E.P. 708 in the north-west to E.P. 254, and from there south-east via E.P. 274 to 'Iraq Labadeh and the Alon road.

The eastern boundary passes along the Alon road from Iraq Labadeh in the north to Khirbet Bani Fadil in the south. In the middle of the Alon road, in the area of Sahel Afjeam, the area broadens eastwards from the road to the valley south-west of the Jebel el-Mahjarah ridge, between Mahjarath el-Ramdath and es-Sunah. This area is annexed to this Volume as a supplement to Volume 4 of the MHCS (Zertal and Bar 2017).

The southern boundary passes along the Alon road between Wadi Kamoneh and Khirbet Bani Fadil, and then north-west to the bottom of the high ridge east of Majdal Bani Fadil.

The western boundary comprises several geographically separate sections, described below from north to south.

From E.P. 708 in the north-west, the boundary descends south via E.P. 572, and thence via a ridge north of Wadi Juni and Wadi Qard. From the confluence of Wadi Qard and Wadi et-Tal'ah the boundary descends southward along the foot of the steep eastern slope of E.P. 685 (Fig. 5). It then climbs south-west along Wadi Sha'ab es-Saiyakh, and from there turns south to the spurs of Jaffa en-Nun, and further south-east to the deep Wadi Ahmar. The boundary then ascends north-west along the Wadi Ahmar channel up to the prominent hilltops of Khirbet Juraish and Khirbet er-Risa (1). From there it descends south to the western spurs above Wadi Zamor to Khallet el-Hashbeh. The boundary continues southward on the low eastern part of the steep escarpment, descending westwards from the ridges of Aqraba and Majdal Bani Fadil, and terminating at the southernmost of the survey boundaries – Khirbet Bani Fadil.

GEOGRAPHICAL AND SETTLEMENT DATA

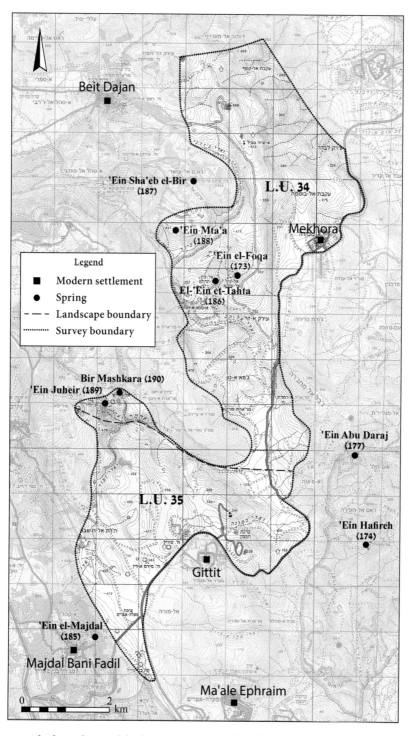

4. The boundaries of the landscape units and the locations of water sources.

5. The steep eastern escarpment of E.P. 685, part of the western boundary of this Volume (S. Bar).

2. *Geology and Geomorphology*

The region and its landscape have been affected by geological faulting and folding. Concerning folding, the eastern Samaria Shoulder is located in the eastern wing of the central anticline of the Land of Israel. The central components of the structure are the Fari'a (Far'ah – Tirzah) anticline (the northern extensions of the Judean Hills anticlines), and the Sartaba syncline to the east of it. The Fari'a anticline is situated between two major bends. The eastern one is the 'Aujah monocline – the strata of which are inclined up to 40 degrees – which influences the eastern Samaria Shoulder area. The Sartaba syncline stretches north-north-east from the Fari'a anticline to the Jordan Valley.

The effects of faulting (rifting) have almost totally obliterated the ancient folding structure. The whole of eastern Samaria is cleft by cross-faults, forming horsts, grabens and bent massifs. The outcome is a landscape of high ridges with cross-valleys among them, and an array of terraces.

In the north, in Landscape Unit 34, the Beit Furiq fault, which depressed the north-eastern side by about 450 m from the Yanun land block eastwards, is dominant, forming the region of the high spurs of Jaffa en-Nun and the western boundary of the present survey area. In the northern part of LU 34 are the

6. The ridge between Aqraba and Majdal Bani Fadil, which is the southern boundary of the survey (A. Solomon).

slopes to the Fari'a graben – the broad valley of Nahal Tirzah, which is about 700 m lower than its surroundings. The survey boundary passes through the northern slopes descending to this valley.

In Landscape Unit 35 are a) the prominent Majdal Bani Fadil fault, which depresses the inclined land block of Gittit about 200 m to its east; and b) the terrace of Gittit, which is an inclined land block to the east, cut by many short faults (see below in the elevation cross-section of LU 35).

In southern Samaria, the mountain is built uniformly of Cenomanian chalk and dolomite as far as the vicinity of Aqraba (the western boundary of the survey territory). There the mountain 'breaks', and north of it a line of parallel ridges and valleys orientated from north-west to south-east is visible (Hoter 1971). The combination of ridges and valleys forms the unique landscape of the eastern Samaria Shoulder.

The following ridges and valleys are especially prominent in the survey area (from south to north):
- The high ridge of the mountains between Aqraba and Majdal Bani-Fadil is 700–800 m a.s.l. The south-western boundary of the survey territory passes its eastern foot (Fig. 6).
- The Gittit Valley. This fertile 10 sq. km valley is crossed by secondary low ridges fanning out from north-west to south-east (Fig. 7). In the broad valleys between the ridges are cultivated plots.

- The high rocky ridge bounding the Gittit Valley to the east – its summits are E.P. 337 and E.P. 338. To the north stretches the deep channel of Wadi Ahmar, which is the border between the two landscape units of this Volume.
- The small fertile valley of Sahel Afjeam spreads from the north of the ridge mentioned above, west of Jebel el-Mahjarah ridge, and east of the ridges and spurs of Jaffa en-Nun. Its total area is about 4.5 sq. km.
- The spurs of Jaffa en-Nun: The eastern part of the high eastern Samaria mountains (the land block of Yanun: Nebi Yanun, E.P. 777 and the 'Three Seas Lookout'). The area is mountainous and cut by narrow ravines. The western boundary of the survey passes through its eastern slopes. To the north-east, outside the survey boundary, are the towering ridges of Beit Dajan.
- The long narrow rocky ridge of E.P. 667, Sheikh Kamel, E.P. 557 and E.P. 394. It is nearly 6 km long and never more than 1 km wide. This is the final terrace of the Samaria mountain range before the steep slopes descending north and east towards Nahal Tirzah.
- The small fertile cultivated valley of Mekhora, which stretches east of the ridge mentioned above. Its total area is about 5.5 sq km. The valley is the last flat terrace suitable for cultivation before the Nahal Tirzah Valley.

7. Gittit Valley, view to north-west. The valley is crossed by low rocky ridges, among which are cultivated fields (A. Solomon).

Between these ridges and valleys are other secondary ridges and small valleys. The area is made mainly of Judea group chalky rocks from the Cenomanian-Turonian epoch.

In order to illustrate the ridges and valleys and the extreme elevation differences, we present two elevation sections (one for each landscape unit):
- The elevation section of LU 34, from the 'Three Seas Lookout' eastward to Hamra: The lookout is located 1.5 km outside the Survey boundary, in the north-western part of the area, on one of the highest summits of Samaria, 860 m a.s.l. From it the section line turns eastwards on one of the steepest slopes of Samaria to Wadi et-Tal'ah, entering the northern area of the Survey territory, a descent of 460 m in a distance of 1.3 km. The escarpment is the border of the eastern Samaria Shoulder. From there the section line climbs east-north-east to 'Ein Sha'ab el-Bir, an ascent of 150 m in 1 km, continuing in the same direction, and descending 100 m in 1.5 km to the valley of Wadi Juni. From the wadi, the section line again climbs 150 m in 0.7 km to the ridge of Sheikh Kamel, and finally descends 650 m in 3 km down a steep escarpment in the direction of Hamra. The total descent is 910 m in 7.5 km. The section clearly demonstrates the topographical diversity and the elevation differences in the topography of LU 34, a terrain characterized by high terraces and long ridges crossed by deep wadis.
- The elevation section of LU 35, from Aqraba eastwards to Wadi Kamoneh: The Aqraba terrace is located on the western edge of the Survey. Its height is 700 m a.s.l. From the terrace the section line descends about 270 m in 3 km south-east to the terrace of E.P. 432. From there the descent continues an additional 70 m in 1 km to the level of the Gittit Valley. Within the valley, the section line continues eastward, descending about 260 m in 2 km to the lowest part of the section, the Sahel Afjeam Valley. The total descent amounts to 600 m through terraces along its 6 km route. This section also demonstrates the elevation variations of the unit and the nature of its landscape.

3. Climate, Water, Soil and Vegetation

A Mediterranean climate prevails in the eastern Samaria Shoulder. Steppe-like features gradually appear towards the east. The average annual precipitation is 300–400 mm, and the average annual evaporation rate is 1700 mm (Shachar 1995: 27-28). There are extreme variations in the rates of precipitation between the yearly seasons and between years (Halperin 1966: 51-61). The summer is long and hot. The average August temperature is 29°C. In the winter the average temperature is 13°C, and the weather is pleasant.

The main water sources are the following five springs (from north to south, Fig. 4):

1. 'Ein Sha'eb el-Bir (No. 187, coordinates 1872/1759). This spring is in the ridge of Rujm el-Ashar near Wadi Qard and Wadi Juni. Apparently, it watered the northernmost group of sites in LU 34, which are located in the area of the high ridge of E.P. 667 and Sheikh Kamel. There is a modern pump house at the site.
2. 'Ein el-Foqa (No. 173, coordinates 1881/1738). This is a spring in the high eastern part of Wadi el-'Ein, 1 km north-east of the Roman-Byzantine city at Khirbet Tana et-Tahta, apparently one of the two springs watering the city. There is a modern pump house at the site.
3. El-'Ein et-Tahta (No. 186, coordinates 1877/1737). This is a spring in the middle of Wadi el-'Ein, east of the Roman-Byzantine city at Khirbet Tana et-Tahta. There is a modern pump house at the site.
4. 'Ein Juheir (No. 189, coordinates 1851/1710). This is a spring in the upper northern part of Wadi Juheir, to the west of the slopes of the spur on which is located Khirbet Juraish, a Bronze and Iron Age city. There is a modern pool at the site measuring 5×5 m (Fig. 8) and an orchard. Nearby are remains of Iron Age II architecture and at least two pools or plastered installations, apparently the ancient spring house facility.

8. The modern pool at the spring of 'Ein Juheir (S. Bar).

5. Bir Mashkara (No. 190, coordinates 1855/1717). This is a spring in the middle part of Wadi Mashkara, east of the spur on which Khirbet Juraish is situated. There is a flourishing orchard with two modern pools (Fig. 9). In the modern maps the spring is marked mistakenly about 300 m west of its true location.

Other springs which might have served the region's inhabitants:
- 'Ein Mta'a (No. 188, coordinates 1867/1748) north of Wadi Qard. Now dry.
- 'Ein Hafireh and 'Ein Abu Daraj, west of the Sartaba ridge (No. 174, coordinates 1912/1679; and No. 177, coordinates 1909/1699).
- 'Ein el-Majdal, east of Majdal Bani Fadil (No. 185, coordinates 1849/1658).

The northern parts of LU 34 constitute a part of the southern drainage basin of Nahal Tirzah (Wadi Far'ah), and the southern parts of LU 34 together with LU 35 constitute a central part of the drainage basin of Wadi Ahmar and Nahal Fasael (Shachar 1995: 30).

There are three main types of soils in the eastern Samaria Shoulder: terra rossa, rendzina and thick alluvial soils – grumusols (this review is based on Dan 1977).
1. Terra rossa: the commonest type of soil over limestone and dolomite rocks in the moist and semi-moist zones of Samaria. The soil is clay, reddish-brown, and is readily permeable. The soil layer is shallow, and the rocks protrude

9. Aerial view to the west at Bir Mashkara (A. Solomon).

above the surface and among the soil patches. The cultivation depends on the soil depth and the amount of rocks.
2. Rendzina is found in two variants:
   - Dark rendzina is a fine-grained clayish shallow soil, accumulating in pockets among the hard caliche limestone rocks. It is not well suited to field crop cultivation because of the abundance of rocks, and therefore is usually used for tree plantations.
   - Colluvial-alluvial brown rendzina soils: these are deep soils containing variable quantities of stones and pebbles. They are found in valleys and wadis at the foot of the mountains where there are rendzina and terra rossa soils. These are fertile soils suitable for all crops.
3. Grumusols: these are deep, clayish, dark brown soils, covered by a grainy layer of topsoil. They are fertile, and are generally used for field crop cultivation.

The vegetation in the eastern Samaria Shoulder is composed of two phytogeographical provinces: the Mediterranean, which is the main one, and the Irano-Turanian. Most of the flora is *garrigue* and Mediterranean wasteland, vegetation dominated by shrub and sub-shrub coverage of 20–40%. Prominent are the shrubs of the hairy thorny broom (*Calicotome villosa*) and great burnet/poterium (*Sarcopoterium spinosum*) which grow on the slopes among the rocky outcrops, normally on the northern and western faces. Over the chalky outcrops and the slopes covered by a thin layer of soil are frequent germander plants (*Teucrium capitatum*) and varthemia (*Chiliadenus iphionoides*). Also very common are herbaceous plants, therophytes and perennials, mostly geophytes (Markus 1992: 50). The main geophytes are the maritime squill (*Urginea/Drimia maritima*) and branched asphodel (*Asphodelus ramosus*), and among the therophytes are oats, *elymus/chrithopsis* and wild emmer wheat. There are thinly spaced trees, mainly *Pistacia atlantica* and carob (*Ceratonia siliqua* L.).

4. Roads

No national or international arterial roads existed across the eastern Samaria Shoulder; only local ones (designated as category C in the MHCS). The width of most of the roads discovered does not exceed 2.5 m, supporting the assumption of their not being arterial roads. The ancient roads discovered in the Jordan Valley and Samaria, including eastern Samaria, have been dated to the Roman period, according to their place of departure, destination and the milestones found along them. In the eastern Samaria Shoulder, no sites appearing in the Madaba Map or the Peutinger Map nor milestones have been discovered.

Therefore, in order to link the roads to a certain period or culture we can rely only on remains and finds from the area. The sparse modern regional construction and agriculture confined only to the valleys contributed to the good preservation of the road system in the Survey area and aided the research.

Previous research into the ancient roads in the region comprises:
- The pioneering work of the British Survey participants is noteworthy in surveying the region and the roads before they underwent modern development (Conder and Kitchener 1882).
- Dorsey (1991) offered a description of the road system in the region, but based it only on the distribution of the central sites and the topography, without an actual field survey. Therefore, his proposals are only assumptions.
- Ilan and Damati (1975) surveyed most of the roads in the region in the framework of their research of the roads in the Samaria desert. Their work has great importance when added to the mapping of the roads by the British Survey.

Following is a description of the local roads in the eastern Samaria Shoulder (from south to north):
- Phasaelis–Neapolis (C41) (Conder and Kitchener 1882: 388; Thomsen 1917: 73; Ilan and Damati 1975: no. 1). A section of the main road from Jericho to Shechem/Neapolis, splitting into two principal branches at Phasaelis (near the modern village of Fasael); the present section and road C40 (no. 2 in Ilan and Damati) (see below). From the junction at Phasaelis, branch C41 of the road ascended over a spur south of Maale Ephraim and joined Rujm Abu Mukheir (Bar-Adon 1972: site 10; Zertal and Bar 2019: site 5). The remains of the road can still be seen. According to the members of the British Survey who mapped the entire length of the road, it continued a little further south along the spur to Khirbet Bani Fadil, where a branch ascended to Majdal Bani Fadil (see road C53). The road continued via the south-western part of the Gittit Valley to Khallet el-Hashbeh, and from there ascended to Aqraba and on to Shechem/Neapolis. Remains of sections of this road are still found at the edge of the valley west of E.P. 390 and south of E.P. 393. The continuation of the road has been damaged by the intensive cultivation of the area. Ilan and Damati (1975: 44–45) located two more parallel branches of the road in the Gittit Valley going north to Khirbet Bani Fadil and rejoining it at Khallet el-Hashbeh. We only managed to find its central route. It appears that the other branches have also been affected by agricultural activity. The road north of Khirbet Bani Fadil is about 5 m wide, with paving, kerbstones and support walls.

    Dorsey proposed (1991), based on known sites and topographical reasoning, that a road which existed in the Iron Age went north from the Gittit Valley, passed west of Wadi Zamor, reached the fort at Khirbet er-Risa (1), and continued north to the vicinity of Yanun. Such a road is not shown in the British Survey maps, and we did not find it during our Survey. In response to Dorsey's proposal, it should be remembered that archaeologically there is great difficulty in describing and proving the existence of unconstructed roads or paths. Nevertheless, it can be assumed that such roads and paths indeed linked Bronze and Iron Age hubs, prior to the construction of roads in the Roman period.

- Khirbet Bani Fadil–Majdal Bani Fadil (C53). This road branches off the Phasaelis-Neapolis road (C41) in the direction of Majdal Bani Fadil. The road appears in the British Survey map and Ilan and Damati (1975: no. 9). It passes close to the southern boundary of our Survey, but not within it. We did not investigate this road.
- Gittit Valley road (C58). During the survey, we found a road not marked in any previous documentation, passing through the Gittit Valley, and mostly visible in the eastern foot of the ridge of E.P. 432 and E.P. 419. This road linked all the agricultural sites around the edges of the valley. In the north it may have merged with the road along Wadi Ahmar (C50), and in the east perhaps it linked to the road ascending from Wadi Kamoneh (C54) to the Gittit Valley. This road is well preserved in Site 142, at the edge of the ridge of E.P. 419 which delimits the Gittit Valley. There it is nearly 2 m wide, and along it were remains of structures, identified perhaps as small strongholds or agricultural storage structures. The road's southern section disappears in the cultivated fields near Khirbet Mras ed-Din: however, it is probable that it joined the main Phasaelis-Neapolis road in the vicinity of Khallet el-Hashbeh (C41).
- Wadi Kamoneh road (C54). This road climbed from the southern part of Sahel Afjeam to the Gittit Valley via Wadi Kamoneh. The British Survey did not find it. It originates in Sahel Afjeam – it is not known if it was part of the Wadi Ahmar road (C50), or the branch bypassing Sahel Afjeam starting from road C40 and going through Sahel Afjeam itself (the branch appears in the British Survey as a main road). In a survey conducted in the vicinity of Gittit (Hadashot Arkheologiyot 45, 1973: 19) it is stated: "One of the roads joining at Wadi Afjeam is constructed on the slope and descends from the direction of Jebel Umm Halal. Further down it crosses Wadi Afjeam, passes by the stronghold and ascends in Wadi Kamoneh towards Khirbet et-Tawil and Aqraba. The road is nearly 2 m wide and is bounded by margin stones". Evidence supporting the first possibility is that the start of the road is in C50, which negates the second one that the road starts at the Sahel Afjeam bypass (a branch of C40). The road is clearly visible in the southern part of

Wadi Kamoneh valley and in sections in the narrow channel of the wadi in the direction of the Gittit Valley. Its continuation has been ruined by the intensive cultivation in the valley, but according to Ilan and Damati (1975: 47) it passed across the Gittit Valley and joined road C41 in the valley.

- Wadi Ahmar–Wadi Zamor road (C50). This road ran along the channels of Wadi Ahmar and Wadi Juheir. The British Survey did not locate it. It branched off (C40, see below) at Ras el-Hafireh, from where it descended to Sahel Afjeam, entering the deep riverbed of Wadi Ahmar. It is probable that the Wadi Kamoneh road (C54) and the Sahel Afjeam bypass (a branch of C40) branched off at its path in Sahel Afjeam, but exactly where is not known. Sections of the road appear along Wadi Ahmar, and support walls are prominent. The road does not exceed 2 m in width.

  In the western part of the wadi the road splits into two: A branch ascending north along Wadi el-Mashkara, the continuation of which is not clear. According to topographical analysis, it can be assumed that it linked with road C55 further up (see below: the road ascending from Wadi el-Kabi to the vicinity of Nebi Nun); and a branch of road descending south in Wadi Zamor. Many sections of this were visible high above the east bank of the wadi up to its exit to Khallet el-Hashbeh area. The end of the road was not found, but it is reasonable to assume that it joined the main road climbing to Aqraba (C41).

- Phasaelis–Neapolis road (C40) (Conder and Kitchener 1882: 388; Thomsen 1917: 73; Ilan and Damati 1975: no. 2). One of the branches of the main Jericho–Shechem/Neapolis road split at Phasaelis into two main roads: to C40 and C41 (see above). The road went up from Phasaelis north-north-west via the Wadi Ahmar valley, continuing to 'Ein Hafireh in the west of the Sartaba ridge. There it splits into two branches: the main branch (C50) descending to Sahel Afjeam, and the secondary one, the Sahel Afjeam bypass (see below), continuing via 'Ein Abu Daraj and Jebel el-Mahjarah.

- Sahel Afjeam bypass. This route appears in the British Survey map as the principal road from Phasaelis to Neapolis, descending from 'Ein Hafireh to the Sahel Afjeam valley, and further on joining the road along Wadi el-Kabi and continuing to Khirbet Tana et-Tahta. Nowadays the road scarcely exists because of the intensive agriculture in Sahel Afjeam. It is uncertain if the road started at 'Ein Hafireh as shown in the British Survey map, or a little further north at Ras el-Hafireh. It is also not clear if the southern part of the road is in fact road C50 which ascended Wadi Ahmar (not found in the British Survey), road C54 up Wadi Kamoneh (also not located by the British Survey), or that both of them started at the road through the centre of the valley.

  Currently two sections of the road remain: A small section attached to the ridge in the western side of the valley, the width of which is 3 m (in Site 86); and the northern end of the road north of Sahel Afjeam and E.P. 173, linking with junction 'Iraq ez-Zah. This junction was also reached from the east by road C40, the section coming from Jebel el-Mahjarah, and also road C55 from the west.

In light of the data in the British Survey and the scanty finds in the area, it may be assumed that an ancient road that did not survive ran along the western edge of the valley. There is no clear-cut answer to whether this is part of the main road to Neapolis (C40), as described in the British Survey map and Ilan and Damati, or is a secondary branch from it, according to the information now available from the field.

– Continuation of road C40 from Jebel el-Mahjarah. Road C40 continued north of the Jebel el-Mahjarah ridge, crossed the route of the modern Alon road, and connected to the 'Iraq ez-Zah junction. This is a junction of three roads: the present C40 road from the east, and ascending north along Wadi el-Kabi; road C55 extending west from the junction and ascending westward in the direction of Nebi Nun and road C40; and the Sahel Afjeam bypass coming from the south, the course of which is described above. From the 'Iraq ez-Zah junction the road continued along the narrow channel of Wadi

10. A section of the local road C40 which ascends via Wadi el-'Ein and 'Ein el-Foqa to Sheikh Kamel (S. Bar).

el-Kabi. Along it are seen many sections (see: Wadi Ahmar-Wadi Zamor road – C50, above), notably improvement work by means of support walls. At the outlet of the wadi, south-east of the city in Khirbet Tana et-Tahta, a fort was discovered beside the road (Site 55). The average width of the road in this section is 2.7 m, and at the exit to the plain it widens to 4 m. Road C57 (see below) branched off here. The road continued along a ravine east of the city, and a branch of it ascended to the city. It passed through Wadi el-'Ein and its two springs: El-'Ein et-Tahta and 'Ein el-Foqa, climbed over the spur between E.P. 394 and E.P. 557 (Site 49), and continued along the ridge to Sheikh Kamel. Here its width was just a little more than 2 m, typical of a secondary and not a main road (Fig. 10). Near E.P. 557 it was joined by road C56 from Khirbet Tana et-Tahta. The stretch of the road from Wadi el-'Ein to Sheikh Kamel (Site 11) is the best preserved, being continuously visible for 4 km. It is amazing that the entire section of the road passing the Roman-Byzantine city at Khirbet Tana et-Tahta and continuing along Wadi el-'Ein, does not appear at all in the British Survey map. It seems as if Khirbet Tana et-Tahta area was apparently omitted from the British Survey. Another road coming from the east (C51, see below) joined road C56 at Sheikh Kamel. After another 1 km an additional road from the north-east (C52, see below) joined it, and from here the road leads out of our Survey boundary, via Beit Dajan in the direction of Shechem-Neapolis.

The British Survey map shows a definite separation between the road ascending Wadi el-Kabi and continuing along Wadi et-Tal'ah (see below, road C57) via Beit Furiq to Neapolis, and the road going up from Nahal Tirzah through the Mekhora Valley on the ridge of Sheikh Kamel to the vicinity of E.P. 557, and continuing to Neapolis via Beit Dajan. From the British Survey viewpoint, these are two completely different roads. We failed to locate the road marked by them, ascending from Nahal Tirzah, and also the climb to the high ridge of E.P. 557, despite finding several sections of the road in the northern part of the Mekhora Valley climbing to 'Aqabet el-Butmeh, and another 6 m-wide section in Site 35. The British Survey researchers marked roads that we did not find, and on the other hand did not notice the clear routes of the two roads going up from Wadi el-Kabi and Khirbet Tana et-Tahta in the direction of E.P. 557 (C40 in the section Wadi el-'Ein and C56). Hence it is possible that the mapping of the roads in the area of Khirbet Tana et-Tahta was not accurate. Obvious evidence of this (as already mentioned) is their omission of the Roman-Byzantine city. Another possible explanation is that at the time of the British Survey the road up from Nahal Tirzah to Mekhora Valley and from there to the ridge of E.P. 557 was still visible, but did not survive due to the intensive cultivation in the valley.

- Wadi el-Kabi-Yanun (C55). This is a local road going westwards from 'Iraq ez-Zah junction on road C40, ascending in the wadis and over the spurs of Jaffa en-Nun in the general direction of Nebi Nun. The road has been preserved in two main sections: south of E.P. 259, and south of E.P. 474. Its width in these sections varies between 4 and 7 m (next to Site 65). A secondary branch of the road, about 5 m wide, branched from it south of E.P. 363 and descended along Wadi Sha'ab es-Saiyakh in the direction of Khirbet Tana et-Tahta and road C57. The road is not recorded in the British Survey. Ilan and Damati (1975: no. 8) identified 5 m-wide sections of the road.
- Khirbet Tana et-Tahta–Neapolis (C57) (Ilan and Damati 1975: 45). This is a road going south-east from road C40 from the Roman-Byzantine city at Khirbet Tana et-Tahta, near the fort in Site 55. According to the mapping of the British Survey team, this was the main road to Shechem-Neapolis. Their identification raises two problems:
  1. They did not identify the road system around the nearby city, and assumed that the road (C40 in our nomenclature) extended without secondary branches, not in Wadi el-'Ein, but in Wadi et-Tal'ah to Beit Furiq and on to Shechem.
  2. We failed to locate definite remains of a road in the route marked by the British Survey team. We are therefore obliged to assume that it was damaged by agricultural activity (which is not very widespread in the region) or the construction of modern unpaved roads in the narrow wadi. The issue remains unclear, awaiting future research when the area west of Khirbet Tana et-Tahta is surveyed.
- Khirbet Tana et-Tahta–Neapolis (C56). This is a local road going north from the Roman-Byzantine city at Khirbet Tana et-Tahta, ascending the ridges of E.P. 396 and E.P. 475, and linking to road C40 near E.P. 557. It is 5 m wide. This is one of the four roads to reach the central city of the region. The road was not discovered in previous researches.
- Nahal Tirzah-Neapolis (C51). This is a local road ascending from Nahal Tirzah, via the spurs of 'Iraq Labdeh and E.P. 271 up to Sheikh Kamel (Site 11), joining the Phasaelis–Neapolis road (C40). The section beside Site 15 is well preserved, and is about 3.5 m wide. The road was not identified in previous surveys.
- Nahal Tirzah-Neapolis (C52). This is another local road ascending from Nahal Tirzah, via the spurs of Aqbeth el-Qataf, and joining the Phasaelis–Neapolis road (C40) south-south-east of Beit Dajan. Sections of it are visible in the valley between E.P. 577 and E.P. 667. The road is within the northern boundary of the Survey, and was not discovered in previous surveys.

The multiplicity of roads in the region in which there are no large or important settlements, and with a sparse population, raises questions. Why were so many roads built in the eastern Samaria Shoulder, some of them close to each other? Two more pieces of information should be added to the query:
– The topography of the region allows linkage of the central mountain land with the Jordan Valley and the establishment of roads for the purpose.
– The abundance of roads is evidence of the concern of the governing regime in the region during the Roman and Byzantine periods.

Two aims could be suggested for the construction of the roads: a component of a military effort, or a part of the extensive agricultural layout developed in the region:
– Military reasons: the construction of roads which facilitates the movement of armies and the control of the land is known to us from the region; for example, the Roman military infrastructure which was established in the Jordan Valley, and perhaps in the fringes of Samaria as part of the effort to subdue the Bar Kochva rebellion (Zertal 2008: 64). Indeed here also are numerous forts and strongholds next to the roads. Historically, we know about the struggles between the Hasmoneans and the Romans, and about internecine struggles of the house of Herod connected to the Sartaba-Alexandrion fortress (see review in Zertal and Bar 2017: Site 173). Some of the roads may had already been built in the Early Roman period as a result of those struggles. Other conflicts were the Great Revolt against the Romans (in the Late Roman period) and the later Samaritan rebellions (Avi-Yonah 1956; Byzantine period). In spite of these valuable data, it is noteworthy that there is no direct and certain historical evidence mentioning such construction in a military context.
– Agricultural reasons: the archaeological finds show that in the Late Roman period unprecedented agricultural activity flourished in eastern Samaria and the Jordan Valley. A complex road network may have been built for utilizing the agricultural potential of the region, enabling access even by secondary and narrow roads to the fields, and transporting the produce to the large markets of the Central Hill Country and onward. We are not aware in the Land of Israel of any Roman period road system serving only agriculture, and therefore this proposition is also not certain.

Thus we are left without definite solutions to these queries.

26 CHAPTER ONE

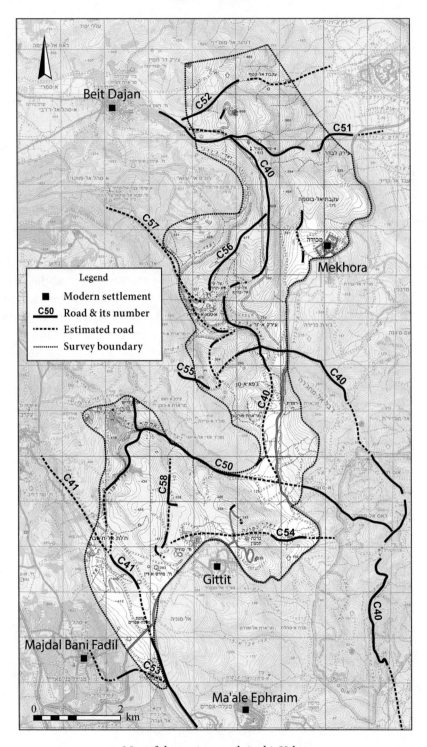

11. Map of the ancient roads in this Volume.

CHAPTER TWO

THE LANDSCAPE UNITS

A. LANDSCAPE UNIT 34 – SAMARIA MOUNTAINS SLOPE FROM NAHAL TIRZAH (WADI FAR'AH) TO WADI AHMAR

1. Landscape Unit 34: Topography and Boundaries

Landscape Unit 34 extends over an area of 21 sq. km, which includes two parallel ridges generally oriented from west to south-east, with narrow valleys between them, and two small fertile valleys in the south-eastern part.

The boundaries of the landscape are (Fig. 4):
– In the north: the boundary follows the slopes along the line Beit Dajan–Mekhora north-east of Nahal Tirzah. It passes between the eastern slopes of E.P. 708 north-west of E.P. 254, and from there south-east via E.P. 274 to 'Iraq Labdeh and the Alon road.
– In the east: the boundary runs along the Alon road from 'Iraq Labdeh in the north to et-Tzuna in the south. In the southern part of the Alon road, in the vicinity of Sahel Afjeam, we have broadened the area of LU 34 east of the road to include all the valley south-west of the Jebel el-Mahjarah ridge, between Mughur el-Ramdat and et-Tzuna. The broadening completes the Survey in a segment of territory west of the Sartaba Massif, not previously surveyed, belonging to Volume 4 (Zertal and Bar 2017).
– In the south: the boundary is Wadi Ahmar.
– In the west: from E.P. 708 the boundary descends south via E.P. 572, Wadi Juni and Wadi Qard. From the confluence of Wadi Qard and Wadi et-Tal'ah it continues south along the base of the steep eastern escarpment of E.P. 685. It then climbs south-west along Wadi Shaeb es-Saiyakh, and thence south to the spurs of Jaffa en-Nun, and further south to the deep Wadi Ahmar. The boundary continues west and up along the Wadi Ahmar channel to Kh. Juraish.

2. The Areas and their Settlement

1. Sheikh Kamel ridge and the slopes towards Nahal Tirzah and Wadi Juni

The ridge is narrow, not more than 1 km wide. It includes the following significant hillocks: E.P. 667, Sheikh Kamel, E.P. 557 and E.P. 394. The ridge's general orientation is from north-west to south, and it slopes down moderately to the south. Steep escarpments bound the ridge on two sides: in the west, the deep channel of Wadi Juni, and in the east, the slopes in the direction of Nahal Tirzah. East of E.P. 557 is a more moderate spur, 'Aqabet el-Butmeh.

The Roman Phasaelis–Neapolis road (C40) ran along the ridge, where other secondary roads joined it, ascending from Nahal Tirzah (C51 and C52) and Khirbet Tana et-Tahta (C56).

There are few settlements on the ridge and its slopes. Noteworthy are two large Middle Bronze Age II period sites, each of about 3 ha (30 dunams). In the eastern part of the ridge, above Wadi Juni, a vast site covering the hillock of E.P. 572 (Site 10) was discovered; and in the southern part, near Wadi el-'Ein and its springs, is another large settlement, Merah Arrar (2) (Site 51). Together with the settlement at 'Iraq ez-Zah (1) (see below) they are part of the group of developed rural Middle Bronze Age II period settlements in the Samaria desert fringes.

Remains from the Iron Age I were found in an extensive site of structures and an enclosure at Merah Arrar (Site 52).

From the Late Roman period, the main discoveries were mainly farmhouses, courtyards and enclosures, most of which continued to exist in the Byzantine period. A prominent concentration of such agricultural sites was found on the moderate spur of 'Aqbet el-Butmeh. A cemetery from these periods was found in Sheikh Kamel (Site 11): we suggest that it served as a regional cemetery.

2. Mekhora Valley

This is a small, fertile, cultivated valley south-east of the Sheikh Kamel ridge. Its area is about 5.5 sq. km. The valley is the last flat terrace suitable for cultivation before the steep eastern slopes descending to Nahal Tirzah.

Few sites have been discovered in the valley, apparently due to intensive agricultural activity. The most significant site is en-Najmeh (1) (Site 35), which was apparently a large farm, fort or inn during the Iron Age III, and was also inhabited during the Late Roman-Byzantine periods. The other sites at the edges of the valley, which are mostly enclosures and sherd scatters, have a clear linkage to agricultural activity. Terraces were found over large areas in the western slopes of the valley.

3. The spur of Khirbet Tana et-Tahta

This is a narrow elongated spur sloping moderately down from north to south. It is nearly 1 km wide, and its area is only 3.5 sq. km. The spur contains E.Ps. 475, 395 and 309 (Fig. 12), and is bordered by the deep Wadis Juni, Qard, et-Tal'ah and Khallet el-'Ein. In this part of LU 34 there are many archaeological sites connected to the Roman-Byzantine city at Khirbet Tana et-Tahta. The remains

12. The spur of Khirbet Tana et-Tahta, view to the north. In the foreground is the southern hillock of the Roman-Byzantine city, in the background is the Sheikh Kamel ridge (A. Solomon).

of the city are spread all over the summit of E.P. 309 and its slopes. Built-up areas have also been found on the saddle in the direction of E.P. 395 and on the spur north-east of the city centre. The necropolises of the city were discovered in the wadis and inner valleys surrounding the city to the east, north, and particularly to the north-west. West of the city, in Wadi Khallet el-'Ein, are two springs: 'Ein el-Foqa and 'Ein et-Tahta.

There are numerous agricultural sites over the central area and on the southern part of the spur of E.P. 395: farms, courtyards, enclosures and many sherd scatters. The deep wadis surrounding the spur are almost devoid of settlement remains, but many agricultural remains were identified in them. The agricultural remains in Wadi Khallet el-'Ein diminish towards the north of the wadi. Signs of agricultural activity were also found on the spur of E.P. 475.

A built Roman road (C56) goes up from the saddle north of the city, via E.P. 395 and E.P. 475, and joins the main road (C40) near E.P. 557. The Roman roads to Neapolis (C 40 and C57) passed along the channels of Wadi el-'Ein and Wadi et-Tal'ah.

This sub-region contains the densest concentration of sites of all the eastern Samaria shoulder areas. Almost all the sites are Roman-Byzantine.

4. The spurs of Jaffa en-Nun

The spurs slope down from east to west in the eastern part of the high eastern Samaria mountain country, east of the land block of Yanun-Nebi Nun and E.P. 777. In the east the spurs end in the Sahel Afjeam valley and Wadi el-Kabi. The area is mountainous and cut by narrow ravines. The western boundary of the Survey passes through its eastern slopes. Included in the area of the Survey are the spurs of E.P. 363 and E.P. 259 and the spurs south of them up to the channel south of Mughur Farqom (the spur of E.P. 420 is outside the Survey area).

There are two ancient sites of great interest in the area:
- The settlement at 'Iraq ez-Zah (1) (Site 60) is more than 12 ha (120 dunams) in area, and is one of the largest sites of the Middle Bronze Age II period in the desert fringes of Samaria. Other large sites are Sites 10 and 51.
- The fort at Jaffa en-Nun (1) (Site 66). This is a round Iron Age II-III fort, built as two concentric circles. The diameter of the outer circle is 50 m. According to the archaeological finds, a significant Iron Age settlement did not exist in the region. The presence of a fort and its period suggest the existence of an ancient road and/or the intension of the central government of the Kingdom of Israel or the Assyrian conqueror to control their borderlands. The fort is associated with two larger Iron Age III sites: the fort at Khirbet er-Risa (1) (Site 94) and the settlement at Mras ed-Din (Site 173). Apparently, there was also extensive activity in the region after the fall of the Kingdom of Israel.

Road C55 passed through this part of LU 34, and connected road C40 and Sahel Afjeam with the cluster of sites on the high mountain land in the vicinity of Yanun. A Roman-Byzantine fort was discovered near the road (Site 69).

There is much evidence of agricultural activity: farms, courtyards and enclosures from various periods, mostly Roman-Byzantine (e.g. Site 58).

5. Sahel Afjeam

This is a small fertile valley, 4.5 sq. km in area, penetrating into both LU 34 and LU 35. It is located north of the ridge of E.P. 337 and E.P. 338, west of the ridge of Jebel el-Mahjarah, and east of the ridges of Jaffa en-Nun and their spurs. In the very southern end of the valley, south of Wadi Ahmar which crosses its centre, is the small valley of Wadi Kamoneh. Sahel Afjeam is intensively cultivated nowadays, and archaeological remains were discovered only at the edges of the slopes of the ridges.

Large clusters of agricultural sites found in the sides of the valley, at the foot of the ridges surrounding it and the Kamoneh valley, were mostly from the Roman-Byzantine periods (Fig. 13). A Roman stronghold (Site 78) guarded the road (C40) at its northern exit from Sahel Afjeam. Another stronghold (Site 156) in the west of Wadi Kamoneh guarded the road (C54) ascending the wadi.

13. Kamoneh Valley in the southern part of Sahel Afjeam; at the centre is E.P. 162, and at the bottom of the photo is the courtyard of Site 175 (A. Solomon).

B. LANDSCAPE UNIT 35 – GITTIT VALLEY

1. Landscape Unit 35: Topography and Boundaries

Landscape Unit 35 spreads over an area of 21 sq. km, containing the Gittit Valley and the parallel ridges which divide the area in the general direction north-west–south-east.

The unit boundaries are (Fig. 4):
– In the north: Wadi Ahmar and Wadi Juheir.
– In the east and south: the Alon road up to Khirbet Bani Fadil.
–In the west: from the 'Ein Juheir-Khirbet er-Risa (1) line, via the western spurs above Wadi Zamor to Khallet el-Hashbeh. From there southwards in the eastern bottom part of the steep escarpment going down to the west from the ridges of the villages of Aqraba and Majdal Bani Fadil to Khirbet Bani Fadil.

2. The Areas and their Settlement

1. Wadi Ahmar

The channel of this deep narrow wadi, the width of which does not exceed 200 m, is the boundary between the two landscape units of the eastern Samaria Shoulder – LU 34 and LU 35 (Figs. 4, 14). Its eastern part penetrates into the

Sahel Afjeam valley and merges with Wadi el-Afjeam. It receives its water from the west from the three Wadis of el-Mashkara, Juheir and Zamor. On both its banks are ridges rising to 200 m above the riverbed. The wadi has served as a passage from the first half of the 5th millennium BCE. Along it were found sites representing almost continuous settlement which began at the end of the Neolithic period (Wadi Ahmar Terrace – Site 102), and continued from Wadi Raba Culture until the Chalcolithic – the sites of 'Ein Juraish, 'Ein Juheir (2) and Lower Juraish (Sites 80, 96 and 97), then to the Early Bronze Age I ('Ein Juraish – Site 80), and the Early Bronze Age II–III, particularly the fortified city at Khirbet Juraish – Site 64.

In relation to the sites in the wadi, attention is drawn to two issues:
- The group of Chalcolithic sites in Wadi Ahmar is one of the largest in eastern Samaria. During that period there was a tendency to settle in the Jordan Valley, and entry to the eastern Samaria Mountains was marginal (Bar 2014: 85–86). It has been suggested that the entry to previously unsettled areas resulted from economic factors, especially the cultivation of the olive, which dates from this period (Bar 2014: 86 and references therein). New research into the Chalcolithic period in northern Samaria shows relatively small settlements, which spread through the inner valleys and along the streams, and subsisted on olive cultivation and woodworking (Bar 2015a). Expansion to the mountainous region of the eastern Samaria Shoulder was observed only in Wadi Ahmar. However, in comparison to northern Samaria settlements, and to western Samaria sites (Zertal and Mirkam 2016: 34; Bar and Zertal 2020), the activity in the east was more intensive; a greater number of sites was discovered, and their average area was much larger.
- The fortified city at Khirbet Juraish (Site 64) is the only Bronze and Iron Age city discovered in the eastern Samaria Shoulder. The city layout, a fortified settlement at the edge of a spur, is a model repeated in eastern Samaria, and is typical of the period. The location of the city had many advantages: topographically it was positioned between two abundantly flowing springs ('Ein Juheir and Bir Mashkara), and it was high up, with a good lookout to the east and control of the route ascending the wadi. An economic advantage was that the climate and soil of the region were suitable for olive cultivation. Signs of continuity of habitation from the Chalcolithic period onwards were found in the city and its close vicinity.

In the Middle Bronze Age II, a flourishing habitation period in the eastern Samaria Shoulder, the importance of the wadi diminished. The settlement remains are poor, and are mostly found in Khirbet Juraish.

During Iron Age II the wadi again became the main route, and the city at Khirbet Juraish regained its importance. Two of the period's forts were discovered on the nearby summits dominating the vicinity: the unfinished fort at

14. Wadi Ahmar, the boundary between the LU 34 and LU 35, winter 2015 (S. Bar).

Kom Ali (Site 81) and the large fort at Khirbet er-Risa (1) (Site 94). At the end of the Iron Age, activity in Wadi Ahmar diminished again, and no sites of importance were found in it from the Persian and Hellenistic periods.

In the Roman period a local road (C50) ran through the wadi. Agricultural sites, farms and courtyards were established in the inner valleys of the wadi and by its banks. These continued in use until the Byzantine period. There are only a few remains from later periods.

2. Wadi Zamor

The deep narrow wadi is one of the tributaries of Wadi Ahmar. The wadi extends to the north from its beginning at Khallet el-Hashbeh, in the southwestern part of the Gittit Valley. The wadi channel is very narrow, and the sites are located on the slopes and mainly on the ridges above the wadi. Most of the sites represent Roman agricultural activities, e.g. the courtyard at Site 106, and multi-period sherd scatters.

The Roman road C50, a local road about 2 m wide, which connects Sahel Afjeam with Khirbet Juraish, runs through the eastern part of the wadi, and continues south to the Gittit Valley. There are support walls in many sections of the road.

On the spurs above the beginning of the wadi are three Medieval hamlets

(Sites 98, 112 and 125). Two of these existed until the Ottoman period. Cave sites, enclosures and courtyards of these periods were also found, probably satellite villages of the township of Aqraba and part of its agricultural hinterland.

3. The plateau of E.P. 432 and E.P. 419

This is a flat, moderate and rocky plateau in the top part of a broad spur, 2 sq. km in area. The spur borders the Gittit Valley, Wadi Ahmar and Wadi Zamor. Part of the plateau has undergone preparation for cultivation during recent decades. There are numerous sites on the plateau; the majority Roman-Byzantine and Medieval-Ottoman (The sites on the plateau slopes at the edges of the Gittit Valley are discussed below).

A few agricultural Middle Bronze Age II period sites, mostly courtyards and enclosures, are the most ancient signs of settlement in the plateau (Sites 134 and 135). Much reduced habitation continued in the Iron Age.

In the Roman period a change occurred. A fort was discovered (Site 137), alongside caves and agricultural sites – mostly courtyards, some of which continued in use into the Byzantine period (e.g. Site 131).

The Middle Ages are characterized by enclosures and caves, such as the sites in the valley north of E.P. 432 (Sites 105, 107, 110 and 111). Medieval sites are scattered over the plateau and its slopes (e.g. Site 126). Noteworthy are the well preserved farm at Site 109, and a Mamluk site, possibly a workshop, at Mugharet et-Tineh (Site 116). The Ottoman hamlet above Wadi Zamor (Site 112) was founded in the Middle Ages.

4. The ridge of E.P.s 335, 337 and 338

The high rocky ridge is on the east bordering the Gittit Valley. North of the ridge passes the deep channel of Wadi Ahmar, and in the centre, in the saddle between E.P. 338 and E.P. 337 is the channel of Wadi Kamoneh. Road C54 ascends parallel to Wadi Kamoneh from the Kamoneh Valley to the Gittit Valley.

The ridge is almost unsettled. There is only a single site with a Roman-Byzantine period sherd scatter and scanty remains of walls (Site 143). A small section of another road was discovered in the saddle between E.P. 338 and E.P. 337, which probably led from the Gittit Valley to the site. The agricultural sites on the eastern spurs descending from E.P. 337 in the direction of E.P. 162 are part of the Kamoneh Valley, which is the southern part of Sahel Afjeam (see above).

5. The Gittit Valley

This is an extensive fertile valley of about 10 sq. km, divided by low secondary ridges which run north-west to south-east. In the valleys between the wadis are plots of land suitable for cultivation. Currently field crops are cultivated in the valley (Fig. 15). In light of the archaeological finds and the descriptions of 19th century travellers (e.g. Van de Velde 1854, describing the beauty of the fields), it appears that the valley has been continuously cultivated since the Middle Bronze Age II period.

Before the Middle Bronze Age II period there was very sparse habitation in the valley, with very few sites, and scarce sherds (Site 165, and doubtfully Site 134). It is surprising that nearby, north of the valley in the Wadi Ahmar area, numerous signs of Chalcolithic and Early Bronze Age habitation were found, while no sherds of these periods were found in the sites in the Gittit Valley.

During Middle Bronze Age II, a settlement influx began in the valley, and villages and enclosures were built. The hub settlement, Sirt et-Turmus (1) (Site 144), was a very large village, 10 ha (100 dunams) in area. Many structures survived scattered over a moderate slope. The majority are rectangular, with courtyards attached to them. Courtyards unattached to structures were also found. In the valley are smaller villages of similar architectonic format (such as Sites 162 and 165). Noteworthy are the constructed courtyards. It is not certain if these served as dwellings, or only for agriculture (for example, Sites 169 and 178).

15. The cultivated fertile Gittit Valley, 2014. In the background on the hill is the Gittit water reservoir, and behind it is the rocky ridge of elevation points 335, 337 and 338 (S. Bar).

There is a single significant settlement in the valley from the Iron Age III: Khirbet Mras ed-Din (Site 173). It can be assumed that the site was a regional centre or a prosperous large fortified farm after the Assyrian conquest of the Kingdom of Israel. Small strongholds were discovered (Sites 142 and 165) north and west of Khirbet Mras ed-Din. It is interesting that the fortified Iron Age I site at Khirbet Isyar (Site 157) was no longer inhabited at this period.

As in other areas of the eastern Samaria Shoulder, here also the habitation dwindled during the Persian and Hellenistic periods, to be renewed in sites of agricultural nature during the Early Roman period.

In the Late Roman period habitation in the Gittit Valley reached its peak together with the rest of the eastern Samaria Shoulder. Numerous remains of agricultural sites were discovered in the valley, mainly courtyards serving for storage of crops. The forts dominating the roads in the valley are also prominent (C41, C54 and C58), as are the agricultural sites (Sites 133, 167 and 171). In Mras ed-Din (Sites 172 and 173) a tower from the Middle Roman period, part of a larger agricultural site, was excavated (see Appendix A).

During the Byzantine period there was a slight reduction in the number of sites, but the array of forts survived, as also did the extensive agricultural activity.

In the Early Moslem period the valley was abandoned.

During the Middle Ages, agricultural activity in the region was resumed. A typical pattern of that period was the resettlement, renovation and the reuse of the stones of sites remaining from the Late Roman and Byzantine periods.

In the Ottoman period the importance of the valley diminished again; no sites of this period were found, except for a small village, apparently a satellite village of Aqraba (Site 125).

Of interest is that during these periods both the residential and agricultural sites were located on the north-western faces of the spurs, while the other faces were thinly populated.

CHAPTER THREE

THE SETTLEMENT BY PERIODS

The eastern Samaria Shoulder is part of a borderland and a geographical bridge between the elevated areas of Samaria in the west, the Sartaba massif in the east, and Nahal Tirzah in the north. Like other regions in Samaria and in the Jordan Valley, which we had already surveyed, the eastern Samaria Shoulder had been surveyed in the past, but very superficially and not in detail. Only 15 of the 181 sites that we surveyed in the region and included in this book were found in previous surveys (mainly in the Samaria Survey B, by Porath, 1968, [unpublished]; and in the Southern Samaria Survey by Finkelstein et al. 1997). It is therefore obvious that the 166 sites that we discovered (over 90%), represent a completely new archaeological-historical picture of the region.

The nature of the habitation in the eastern Samaria Shoulder is almost totally agricultural. Apart from Khirbet Tana et-Tahta and Khirbet Juraish, no cities were established in the region, and most of the habitation was rural and/or nomadic.

The extent of habitation rose and fell continuously over the ages. From the 5th to the 3rd millennia BCE the habitation in the region was sparse. The first settlement drive occurred in the Middle Bronze Age II, and diminished during the Late Bronze Age. The number of sites increased in Iron Age I–II, and decreased again in the Persian and Hellenistic periods. In the Early Roman period another influx of activity began in the region, reaching its climax in the Late Roman period, and continuing through the Byzantine period, although not at the same rate. During the Early Moslem period the region was almost totally abandoned. In the Middle Ages habitation recovered, but in the Ottoman period there was a final severe depopulation, and the region was abandoned until modern settlement began in the second half of the 20th century.

1. PREHISTORY

In the eastern Samaria Shoulder, only 13 sites have been identified as prehistoric, representing 7.2% of the total number of sites included in this Volume. Not only is their number small, so also is their area.

There is little evidence of working Levallois cores in the most ancient site in the region, from the Middle Palaeolithic period (Site 99). Sparse finds, perhaps from the Upper Palaeolithic, were found in Sites 48 and 150. Three Epipalaeolithic sites were discovered (Sites 75, 76 and 150). Nine sites of the

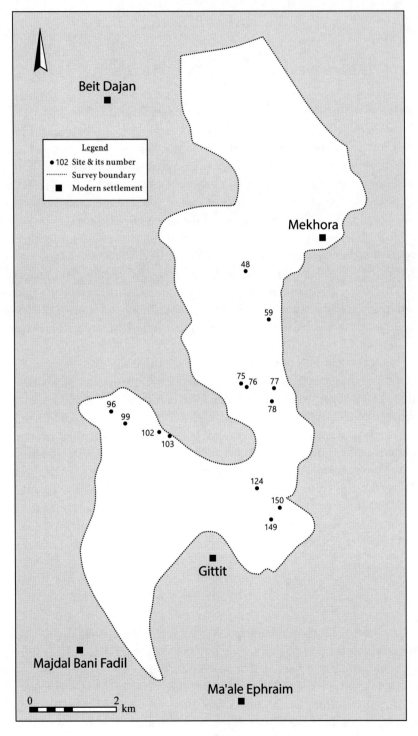

16. Map of prehistoric sites.

Neolithic period found were: two Pre-pottery Neolithic A sites (75 and 103), two Pre-pottery Neolithic B sites (78 and 149), one Pottery Neolithic site (103), and four Neolithic, not defined to sub-periods (59, 96, 102 and 124).

Comparison of the prehistoric settlement in the eastern Samaria Shoulder to two adjacent survey regions, LU 30 in the east (in Volume 4, the Sartaba ridge, situated next to the eastern Samaria Shoulder), and the south-eastern Samaria Shoulder to the south (Bar and Zertal 2019: 28) provides the following data:

- The number of early prehistoric periods (Middle and Upper Palaeolithic) is smaller than that in the eastern Samaria Shoulder.
- The number of Epipalaeolithic sites is almost the same in LU 30, but no sites from this period were found in the south-eastern Samaria Shoulder.
- The number of Neolithic sites in the surveyed territory included in this Volume is greater.

2. CHALCOLITHIC PERIOD (4800–3700 BCE)

Only 12 Chalcolithic period sites have been found in the eastern Samaria Shoulder, representing 6.6% of the total number of sites included in this Volume.

The distributions of sites in LU 34 and LU 35 are the same, but all the sites containing considerable finds of the period (over 40%), are located on the banks of Wadi Ahmar (the boundary between LU 34 and LU 35). The most prominent sites are the Wadi Ahmar Terrace (Site 102), which contained mainly finds of the Wadi Raba Culture, an Early Chalcolithic (or Late Neolithic) phase; and the sites around Khirbet Juraish and 'Ein Juheir spring, which belong to the Ghassulian phase of the period – the Late Chalcolithic (Sites 80, 96 and 97). This pattern of distribution of sites along some of the major streams on the eastern slopes of Samaria was noticed previously (Bar 2014: 86), and may be related to olive cultivation and a woodworking economy.

Comparison of the Chalcolithic period settlement in the eastern Samaria Shoulder with the settlement in the other regions of the Survey yields the following data:

- In Volume 4, which covers the narrow Jordan Valley and the Sartaba ridge, 29 sites have been related to the Chalcolithic period (14% of the total number of sites in that Volume), and in Volume 5, which covers the Middle Jordan Valley – 35 sites (22%). Hence, the relative number of the period's sites in the present survey area is much smaller. The Chalcolithic sites in the Jordan Valley are larger and richer than those in the eastern Samaria Shoulder.
- The south-eastern Samaria Shoulder is empty of Chalcolithic sites (Bar and Zertal 2019: 28) and Northern Samaria is sparsely populated (Bar 2015a).

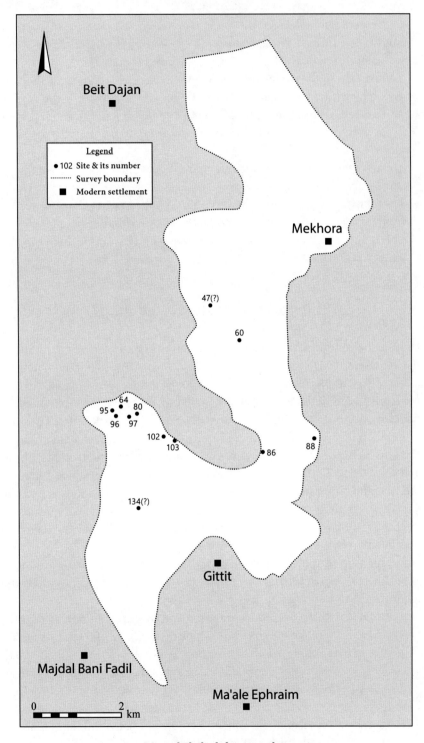

17. Map of Chalcolithic period sites.

- There are some similarities between the Chalcolithic sites in the present survey area and the Chalcolithic sites in the slopes of Samaria and the desert fringes, documented in Volume 2, and also with the Chalcolithic sites recorded in LU 30 in Volume 4 dealing with the Sartaba ridge, which is located close to the eastern Samaria Shoulder in the east. In all these regions the settlement was along streams: Bezeq and Tirzah in the survey areas described in Volumes 2 and 4, and along Wadi Ahmar in the current survey area. The number of sites is also similar, except in the Sartaba ridge itself (the south-western part reported in Volume 5), in which fewer Chalcolithic sites were found than in the eastern Samaria Shoulder.

It seems that the Chalcolithic sites in the eastern Samaria Shoulder were connected to the rich settlement activity at the Jordan Valley (Bar 2014), and not to the sparsely inhabited Samaria regions to the west. The impulse for this infiltration to previously poorly settled regions was probably economic, and influenced by the possibilities of better exploitation of olives in higher and wetter areas.

3. EARLY BRONZE AGE (3700–2500 BCE)

Eleven Early Bronze Age sites, which represent only 6% of the total number of sites included in this Volume, were discovered in the eastern Samaria Shoulder. There is no uniformity in the nature and distribution of the sites. Eight are in LU 34, and three in LU 35.

As in the Chalcolithic period, the EBA sites are concentrated around Khirbet Juraish (Site 64) – the fertile area around the springs of 'Ein Juheir and Bir Mashkara. In the village of 'Ein Juraish (Site 80), the activity lasted from the Late Chalcolithic period into the EBA I. The settlement later moved to the nearby city at Khirbet Juraish, which was founded at the end of the EBA I or the beginning of EBA II.

A considerable EBA II sherd scatter was collected in Khirbet er-Risa (2) (Site 100), which is also near Khirbet Juraish.

Another important EBA I site, which showed few traces of continuation into the EBA II, is the central settlement of 'Ein Mta'a (Site 24) north of Khirbet Juraish.

The following settlement picture can be drawn from the above data:

During the EBA I there were two central villages in the region, 'Ein Juraish and 'Ein Mta'a. The settlement at 'Ein Mta'a lost its importance in EBA II; and the village at 'Ein Juraish was moved to nearby Khirbet Juraish. A walled city was built during the EBA II at Khirbet Juraish, the sole Bronze Age city discovered in the region. The transition from villages to cities at the end of EBA I

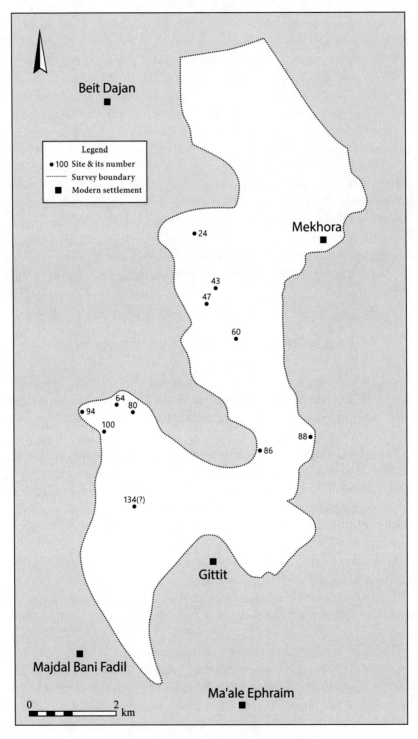

18. Map of Early Bronze Age period sites.

and the beginning of EBA II was noted in other areas of the eastern slopes of Samaria (Bar 2013). The other EBA sites were mostly insignificant sherd scatters.

It is interesting that no clues for this period's settlement were found, especially in the fertile Gittit Valley, in which there is considerable evidence of the Mediterranean agricultural economy in the form of grape and olive cultivation.

Comparison of the EBA settlement in the eastern Samaria Shoulder with the settlement in other regions surveyed by the MHCS presents a similar state of affairs:

- In Volume 4, 22 sites have been associated to the EBA (6% of the total number of sites), most in the Jordan Valley, and a few in the Sartaba area linking in the east to the current survey area. In Volume 5, 25 sites have been associated to the EBA (15% of the total).
- Analysis of the differences in the distribution of sites in the area according to periods shows that during the transition from the Chalcolithic to the EBA, the number of settlements in the Jordan Valley declined significantly, while increasing on the slopes of Samaria (Bar 2014: 124).
- In the fringes of Samaria, described in Volume 2, a similar picture appears: an increase in the number of settlements on the Samaria slopes during the EBA I, most of them unwalled, and an increase in the number of fortified settlements in the EBA II.
- In the south-eastern Samaria Shoulder 10 EBA sites were found with characteristics similar to those presented here (Bar and Zertal 2019: 29), probably representing the same cultural phenomenon.
- The main topographical characteristic of the sites in the various areas is the settlement near springs and sources of streams (such as Khirbet Juraish).
- Evidence for continuation of habitation from the Chalcolithic period into the EBA was found in more than half the sites in the various areas, yet there is almost no evidence of continuation from the EBA into the Intermediate Bronze Age.

4. INTERMEDIATE BRONZE AGE (2500–2000 BCE)

Only six Intermediate Bronze Age (also termed Middle Bronze I/Early Bronze IV) sites were found in the eastern Samaria Shoulder, representing only 3.3% of the total sites in Volume 6. In none of them did the number of sherds belonging to the period exceed 11%, indicating a very sparse settlement. All the sites are small sherd scatters, collected around later period structures (Sites 28, 44, 72 and 165), or settlement with few finds around earlier remains (Sites 24 and 100).

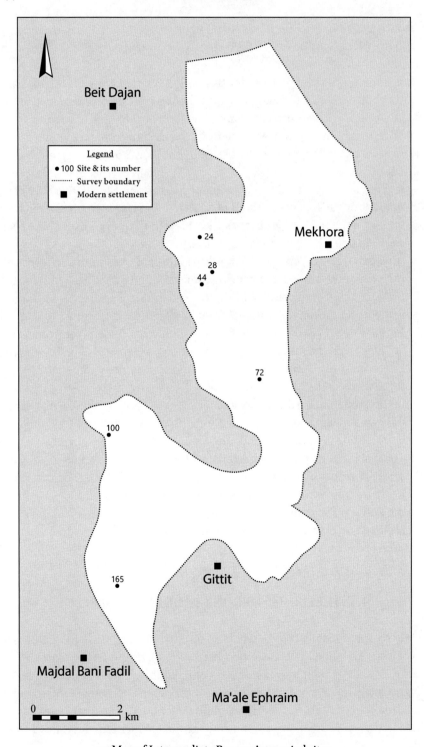

19. Map of Intermediate Bronze Age period sites.

Comparison of the IBA settlement in the eastern Samaria Shoulder with the settlement of the same period in other regions surveyed by the MHCS does not show a uniform situation.

In Volume 4, 14 sites have been associated to the IBA (7% of the total number of sites in that Volume), most of them in the Jordan Valley itself, and not in the Sartaba area, which is adjacent to the present survey area. In Volume 5, six sites were associated to the IBA (4% of the total). Also south of the Samaria Shoulder, in the south-eastern Samaria Shoulder, 7 IBA sites were found, mainly cemeteries concentrated in the vicinity of Ein Sammiyye spring (Bar and Zertal 2019: 31). This relatively small number is very surprising in light of the extensive settlement of the period (Bar et al. 2013; Bar 2015b; 2015c), discovered north of the current survey area in the eastern valleys and slopes of Samaria, particularly along the streams of Malha and Tirzah (in Volume 2, 39 sites were associated to the IBA, 14.5% of the total - Zertal 2008: 76).

5. MIDDLE BRONZE AGE II (2000–1550 BCE)

The first habitation boom occurred in the eastern Samaria Shoulder in the Middle Bronze Age II. Forty-two sites of the period were discovered, representing 23.2% of the total number of sites in Volume 6. Sixteen sites were found in LU 34 (17.2% of the number of sites in this LU). The settlement presence in LU 35 is much greater – 26 sites (29.5%). In half of the sites, more than 20% of the sherds were identified as being of this period, a significant revelation, enhancing the association of the architecture in the sites to the period, and supporting the understanding of the regional analysis of the settlement model.

The MBA II in the eastern Samaria Shoulder is disassociated from its former and later periods. Intermediate Bronze Age remains were found in only four of the sites of the period, showing that most of the sites were founded during the MBA II on virgin land, and not over previous settlements. There is doubtful evidence of continuation into the Late Bronze Age in only three sites. This is testimony to a major settlement influx into the region over a limited time.

The abundance of sites and the good preservation of the architecture enable us to typify the settlement models and to determine several types:
Permanent villages. These are classified according to their area into very large, possibly regional hubs; of area about 10 ha (100 dunams), and small, about 3 ha (30 dunams). In both LU 34 and LU 35 there is one large village and two small ones. The large villages are 'Iraq ez-Zah (1) in LU 34, and Sirt et-Turmus (1) in LU 35 (Sites 60 and 144). The small ones are E.P. 572 and Mrah Arrar (2) in LU 34, and E.P. 390 (2) and Khirbet Tawileh in LU 35 (Sites 10, 51, 162 and 165).

The villages, large and small alike, have similar characteristics:

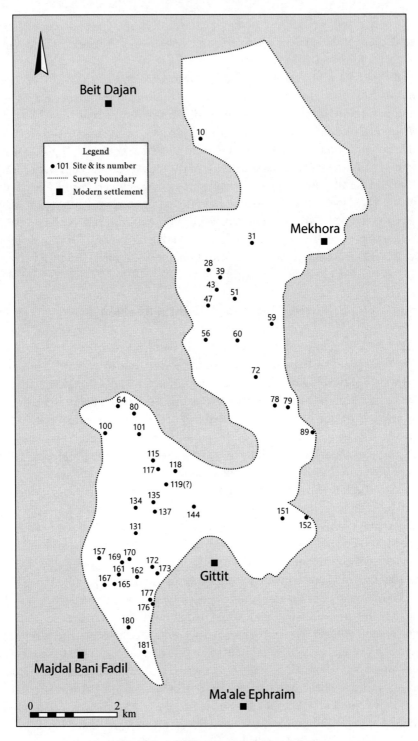

20. Map of the Middle Bronze Age II period sites.

- Preference of construction on slopes, occasionally rocky ones. The advantages of such a choice are: the availability of building material, and natural drainage of the slope, thus reserving the rock-free plots of land for cultivation.
- The use of support walls for levelling the surfaces on which the houses of the village were built.
- Some of the villages (e.g. Sites 10, 51 and 60) were encircled by a wall. According to the architecture, this was not a fortification or defensive wall; it was meant to mark and fence the boundary of the village, perhaps in order to prevent the escape of livestock.
- The main architectural pattern of the structures in the villages is a single rectangular room and a large square courtyard: in some of the courtyards there was a room or a set of rooms in the corner. Such structures appear in different combinations.
- Near the village there was generally a potentially arable area controlled and observed from the village.

Courtyards. There are two kinds of constructed courtyards: The elementary yard – a square or round structure (e.g. Sites 134, 170 and 176), and the composite courtyard – a square or rectangular courtyard to which are attached a room or set of rooms (e.g. Sites 117, 135 and 169). The composite courtyard was practically the basic unit, constructed singly in the area, and not as part of the village. Possibly this form served as a farm or independent family unit, physically detached from the village, but connected to it by trade, family relations, etc.

Sherd scatters. More than half the MBA II sites are sherd scatters. It can be assumed that some of the scatters are remains of unidentifiable covered sites. A scatter could also be evidence of local activities, such as pitching of tents and resting sites of shepherds away from their permanent domiciles, gatherings, markets, etc.

Comparison of the MBA II settlement in the eastern Samaria Shoulder with settlements of the same period in other regions surveyed by the MHCS does not show a uniform situation. In Volume 4, 16 sites have been related to the period (8% of the total), and in Volume 5, 27 sites (17% of the total).

However, the eastern valleys and slopes of Samaria enjoyed the same settlement influx as that of the desert fringes of Samaria to the north of the present area. In Volume 2 of the survey, dealing with this region (Zertal 2008: 78), 63 sites (23.8% of the total) have been related to the MBA II. In the south-eastern Samaria Shoulder 31 sites were found with characteristics similar to those presented here (Bar and Zertal 2019: 32). Part of this information was also presented in Haim Cohen's work (2013).

This impressive concentration of sites is one of the interesting cultural phenomena discovered during the Survey, but so far there are no historical sources which can shed light on the nature of the process. Because of the relatively sparse settlement emptiness which characterized the Jordan Valley at the time, it can be assumed that the main influence came from the Samaria Mountain settlements, mainly from the centre in Shechem, and possibly also from smaller cities, such as Tell Far'ah (North).

6. LATE BRONZE AGE (1550–1200 BCE)

Only four Late Bronze Age sites were found in the eastern Samaria Shoulder, constituting 2.2% of the total number of sites in this Volume; and the dating of two of these sites is uncertain.

LBA settlement in the eastern Samaria Shoulder is similar to settlement at the same period in other surveyed regions.

In Volume 2, nine sites have been associated to the period (3% of the total); in Volume 4 – apart from the Beit She'an Valley sites – two sites (less than 1%); in Volume 5, a single site (less than 1%); and in the south-eastern Samaria Shoulder six sites were found (Bar and Zertal 2019: 29). This shows that in the LBA there was almost no settlement in most of the MHCS Survey eastern areas. This is surprising, after the flourishing settlement in the preceding period. The change could be explained by the collapse of settlement in Canaan after the expulsion of the Hyksos from Egypt.

Only one site shows certain continuity from the previous period – Khirbet Juraish (Site 64), but the scarce pottery find (8%) is related jointly to the MBA II and LBA. It is noteworthy that in the Shechem syncline, west of the Survey area, a group of 18 sites of the period was discovered. These sites, which are described in Volume 1 of the Survey, belong to the periphery of the city of Shechem, a central city in Samaria, known from the El-Amarna letters. Apparently, the eastern Samaria Shoulder was not at all influenced by the settlement in the Shechem syncline.

7. IRON AGE I (1200–1000 BCE)

During Iron Age I a second settlement boom started in the eastern Samaria Shoulder, continuing until the end of the Iron Age.

Forty-four IA I sites were found in the region, 24.3% of the total number of sites in this Volume. Their distributions in the LUs are similar: 21 in LU 34 (22.5% of the unit sites) and 23 in LU 35 (26.1%). It must be noted that in half the sites only 10%, or even fewer of the sherds were identified as IA I; and in

THE SETTLEMENT BY PERIODS

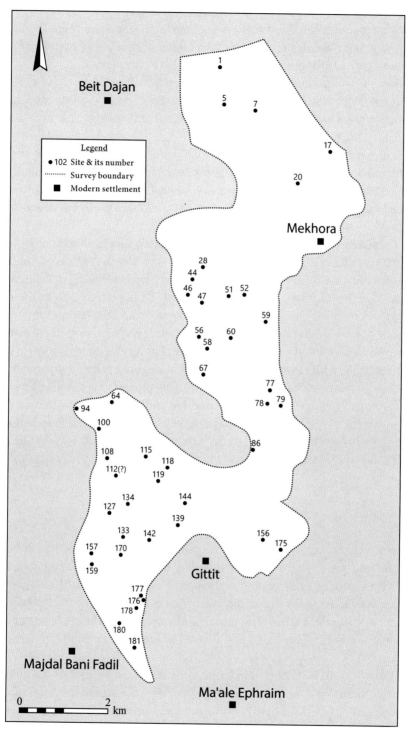

21. Map of Iron Age I period sites.

most of the sites the sherd scatters are poor, and in some of them the dating relies on body sherds only. Hence, the number of sites does not provide solid evidence of a representation of the period and its properties.

The enclosures and stone-circle sites (e.g. Sites 52 and 175), and the agricultural sites, which include mainly threshing floors and/or rock-hewn installations (e.g. Sites 5 and 86), are prominent among the sites which provided the majority of the IA I sherds.

Khirbet Isyar (Site 157) is outstanding for the settlement discovered in it, with remains of square-roomed structures scattered over an area of about 1 ha (10 dunams), and fortified by a 1.5–2 m wide wall. The settlement was probably a regional hub in IA I, and we presume that the arable IA activity around it was related to its inhabitants.

Comparison of the IA I settlement in the eastern Samaria Shoulder with the same period settlement in other regions surveyed by the MHCS presents an interesting situation: even more IA I sites were found in the Jordan Valley areas than here. In Volume 4, 60 sites were related to the period (29% of the total number of sites in the Volume), and in Volume 5, 66 sites (42% of the total), typified by various types of enclosures, including the 'foot-shaped enclosures' (Ben-Yosef 2007). But in all the surveyed regions a settlement transformation is noticeable, with a great increase in the number of IA I sites compared to the LBA, which left few traces in the region. This phenomenon is also found in other parts of eastern Samaria: for example, in Volume 2 of the Survey, dealing with the fringes of Samaria north of the present survey area, 47 IA I sites were identified versus the nine LBA sites; and in the south-eastern Samaria Shoulder 39 sites were found versus the six LBA sites (Bar and Zertal 2019: 29).

8. IRON AGE II–III (1000–586 BCE)

The second settlement boom in the eastern Samaria Shoulder, which began in the Iron Age I, reached its climax during the Iron Age II, when the number of sites identified as belonging to the period almost doubled. The settlement drive was linked to the economic and agricultural activity of the Kingdom of Israel in its border regions. The evidence also shows that the settlement in the region survived and was not badly affected by the Assyrian conquest (Iron Age III).

Eighty-two IA II–III sites were found, constituting 45.3% of the total number of sites in this Volume: 49 sites in LU 34 (52.7% of the sites in this unit), and 33 sites in LU 35 (37.5%). There is probably significance in the variance between the LUs, although its cause is not clear to us at the current stage of the research. IA II–III pottery was discovered in nearly half the sites in this survey area.

However a reservation should be made: in 44 of the 80 sites, not more than 10% of the sherds have been identified as belonging to these periods. This somewhat limits our understanding of the characteristics of these periods in the region.

The abundance of IA II–III sites in the region and the good preservation of the architecture in some of them enable us to typify the settlement patterns and to distinguish a number of types:

Fortified sites. This is a group divided into three sub-types: city, fortress and small fort or stronghold.

- A walled fortified city was discovered in Khirbet Juraish (Site 64), 1.5 ha (15 dunams) in area. Its foundations possibly originated in the EBA. In its upper part is an elevated acropolis, with a well-built central structure measuring 40×20 m, with walls more than 1 m thick.
- Three fortresses have been found: a circular fortress at Jaffa en-Nun (1) (Site 66), an unfinished fortress at Kom Ali (Site 81), and a square casemated fortress at Khirbet er-Risa (1) (Site 94). The fortresses show the existence of a governing power enforcing its control over the agricultural domain. Some of the fortresses existed in the days of the Kingdom of Israel; and Khirbet er-Risa (1) continued to exist in IA III; evidence of Assyrian rule in the territory of the Kingdom of Israel after the Assyrian conquest.
- Two pairs of strongholds were discovered at each of Sites 142 and 156. They are square or rectangular, and are built of very large stones. Their average measurements are 9×7 m. One pair of strongholds overlooked Wadi Kamoneh, and the other pair parts of the Gittit Valley. At least one of the sites (142) continued to be inhabited in IA III.

It should be noted that, apart from the fortress at Jaffa en-Nun (1), all the other seven fortified sites are found in or near the border of LU 35, although the number of IA II-III sites in LU 34 is higher.

Farms and agricultural structures. These are typified by round stone enclosures with dwellings and storage structures inside and nearby (e.g. Sites 5, 52, 163 and 175). In the vicinity of some enclosures are rock-hewn installations and threshing floors (e.g. Site 86).

Sherd scatters. The most common type of site from IA II–III (62 sites). It can be assumed that some of the scatters mark unidentifiable concealed built sites. The sherd scatters could also be evidence of local activities, such as tent encampments, gathering sites, markets, etc.

The site of Mras ed-Din (Site 173) was probably the centre of IA III activities in the Gittit Valley after the Assyrian conquest of the Kingdom of Israel.

Comparison of the IA II–III settlement in the eastern Samaria Shoulder with settlement in other regions surveyed by the MHCS shows a similar state of affairs – an increase in the number of settlements compared to the preceding

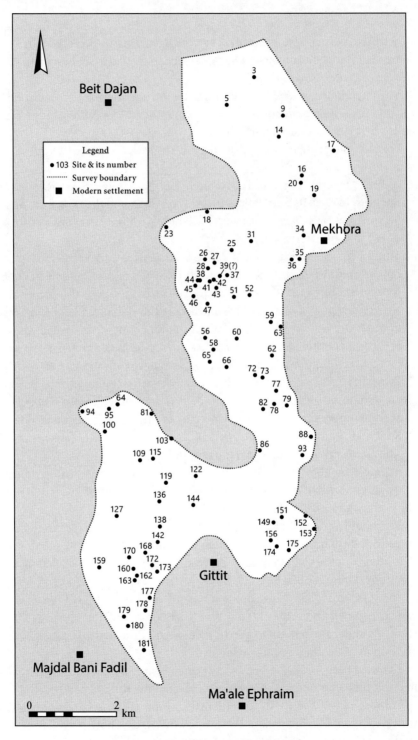

22. Map of Iron Age II–III period sites.

period, linked to the flourishing Kingdom of Israel.

In Volume 4, 93 sites have been associated to IA II–III (46% of the total number of sites in the Volume), and in Volume 5, 90 sites (57%). In the fringes of Samaria, north of this area, and within the Shechem syncline, the hub of the Kingdom of Israel, a similar picture appears – a settlement boom (Zertal 2004a: 54–55). In Volume 2, 86 sites were identified from IA II, as against 47 from IA I, and in the south-eastern Samaria Shoulder 70 sites were found (versus 39 from IA I).

The difference between the eastern Samaria Shoulder and the other areas of the Survey occurred after the Assyrian conquest in IA III. While in this survey area the settlements also continued to exist in IA III, in the Jordan Valley there was a marked decrease in the number of settlements, and the same applies to parts of the fringes of Samaria. The settlement in the eastern Samaria Shoulder during IA III could perhaps be linked to the expulsions and population exchanges carried out by the Assyrian regime, and the settling of Cutheans; or to the entry of Judeaite populations into the now empty and neglected areas in the traditional border regions between the Kingdoms of Israel and Judea (see Chapter 4).

9. BABYLONIAN AND PERSIAN PERIODS (586–332 BCE)

The Babylonian period in the region was short, and cannot yet be identified by an archaeological survey.

In the Persian period a drastic decline of habitation occurred in the eastern Samaria Shoulder. Only nine Persian period sites were found, representing 5% of the total number of sites in Volume 6: six in LU 34, and three in LU 35. These numbers are very surprising in light of the eastern Samaria Shoulder being part of the Persian Shamrayn (Samaria) province, and the dense settlement of the period, which was discovered in the Shechem Syncline, north-west of this area (Zertal 2004a: 56). It seems that the central government in Samaria did not give much consideration to the potential agricultural hinterland in the region, and abandoned it, leaving it to the negligible activity of shepherds, nomads and wayfarers (Tavger 2012). In eight of the nine sites the number of sherds identified with the Persian period did not exceed 10%. Also in Site 23, where the highest number of the period's sherds was collected (37%), there was only a sherd scatter, and the construction discovered there probably belongs to a later time. This indicates extremely sparse settlement.

Comparison of the Persian period settlement in the eastern Samaria Shoulder with settlement of this period in the other regions surveyed by the MHCS, shows a similar situation: in the Persian period there was a decline in the

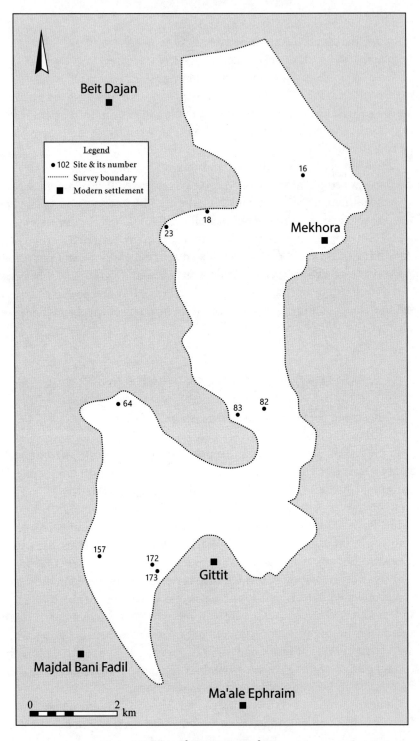

23. Map of Persian period sites.

number of settlements in the fringes of Samaria, north of Nahal Tirzah (Zertal 2008: 90-91), and also in the Jordan Valley. In Volume 4, only 16 sites have been associated to the period (7.8% of the total number of sites in the Volume), and in Volume 5, only 11 sites (7% of the total). In the south-eastern Samaria Shoulder 16 sites were found, also representing a noticeable decline from the IA prosperity (Bar and Zertal 2019: 41).

10. HELLENISTIC PERIOD (332–63 BCE)

Almost no change occurred during the Hellenistic period in the settlement of the eastern Samaria Shoulder, and the region was left largely desolate.

Only 11 Hellenistic sites were found, 6% of the total number of sites in Volume 6. Seven sites were found in LU 34, and four in LU 35. In all the sites the number of Hellenistic sherds did not exceed 18%, evidence of very sparse settlement. Part of the find was collected in courtyard sites. This leads to the hypothesis that the use of agricultural courtyards, very common later, especially in the Late Roman and Byzantine periods, had already occurred in the Hellenistic period. The rest of the pottery was collected from small sherd scatters, perhaps those left by shepherds, nomads or passers-by, additional evidence of the infrequent activity in the region.

The comparison of the Hellenistic settlement in the eastern Samaria Shoulder with the settlement in other regions surveyed by the MHCS does not show a uniform state of affairs. A settlement revival definitely occurred in some of the other regions. In Volume 4, 24 sites were associated to the period (12% of the total number of sites in the Volume). The abundance resulted from the construction of the fortress of Alexandrion on the Sartaba. In Volume 5, 25 sites were associated to the period (16% of the total). The increase came from the influence of the Hasmonean Kingdom, which encouraged the establishment of new cities in the Jordan Valley (Phasaelis and Archelais; Zertal and Bar 2019, sites 34 and 111).

Contrary to the above, in the fringes of Samaria, north of the present survey area, there was no change in the Hellenistic period, and the settlement continued scanty. In Volume 2, 24 sites were associated to the period, almost identically to the 23 sites from the previous Persian period, and in the south-eastern Samaria Shoulder 16 sites were found, identical to the previous period (Bar and Zertal 2019: 42).

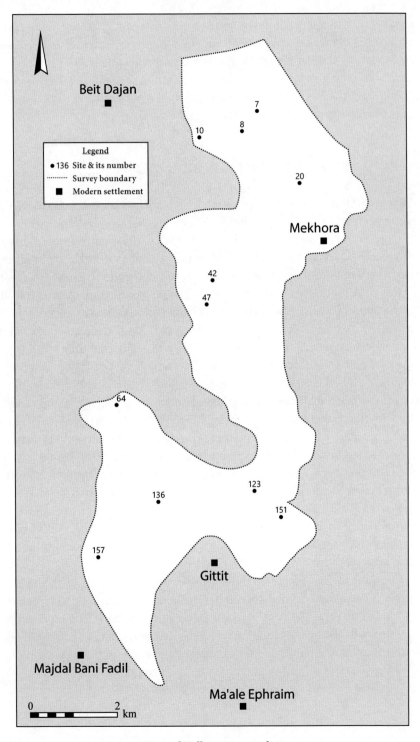

24. Map of Hellenistic period sites.

11. EARLY ROMAN PERIOD (63 BCE–73 CE)

The number of settlements in the eastern Samaria Shoulder increased during the Early Roman period. Thirty-eight ER sites were found in the region, 21% of the total number of sites in Volume 6. Their spread in both LUs is similar: 20 sites in Unit 34, and 18 in Unit 35. It is noteworthy that in 29 of the 38 sites (76.3%), the number of identified ER sherds exceeded 10%. The renewed interest in the region was possibly related to the construction of the Herodian fortress on the Sartaba, 5 km south-east of the eastern limit of this survey area and the road network leading to it.

Two prominent facts deserve attention:
- The city at Khirbet Tana et-Tahta (Site 47), which was founded in the ER period, became the focal city in the region later in the LR and Byzantine periods.
- The construction of square or rectangular courtyards built of large stones, utilized for agriculture purposes, which began in the Hellenistic period, was widespread during the ER period (e.g. Sites 106, 129 and 141. Regarding the nature of the Roman courtyard, see the description of the LR period below).

From the many agricultural sites: farms, courtyards, threshing floors and installations, it can be deduced that the region returned to become an agricultural hub for field crops, and served as the economic backbone for the settlements in Aqraba, the Sartaba fortress and Khirbet Tana et-Tahta.

A comparison of the ER settlement in the eastern Samaria Shoulder with the ER settlement in other regions surveyed by the MHCS does not show a uniform picture. In Volume 4, 19 sites were associated to the ER period (9.4% of the total number of sites in the Volume), slightly fewer than those from the Hellenistic period. In Volume 5, 34 sites were associated to the ER period (21.6% of the total), a little more than the Hellenistic period. As in the eastern Samaria Shoulder, in the fringes of Samaria north of the present survey area, there was also a clear increase in the number of sites during the Roman period. In Volume 2, 35 sites were associated to the ER period, versus 24 to the preceding Hellenistic, and in the south-eastern Samaria Shoulder 78 sites were found, compared with only 16 sites in the preceding period (Bar and Zertal 2019: 43).

12. LATE ROMAN PERIOD (73–313 CE)

During the Late Roman period, an unprecedented settlement boom occurred in the eastern Samaria Shoulder, unmatched in the research history of the MHCS in the other areas of Samaria and the Jordan Valley.

CHAPTER THREE

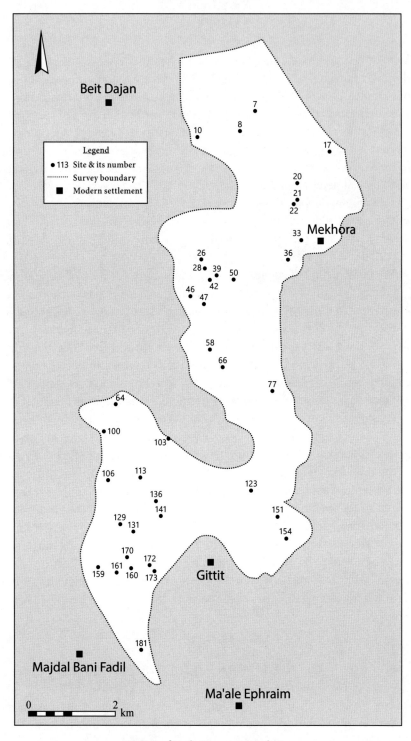

25. Map of Early Roman period sites.

THE SETTLEMENT BY PERIODS

One hundred and sixty-seven LR sites were found in the region, 92.2% of the total number of sites in Volume 6. Their frequencies are similar in both LUs. It is noteworthy that in 152 sites (81%) of the 167, the number of sherds identified with the subject period exceeded 10%, and LR pottery was found in all but 14 sites. These data enhance the certainty of the search and support the conclusions regarding the scale of activities.

The abundance of sites and the good state of preservation of the architecture in many of them enable us to typify the types of settlements and to distinguish a number of types:

Fortified Sites. These sites are divided into three sub-types:
- The city at Khirbet Tana et-Tahta (Site 47). Remains of structures begun in the ER period are spread over about 28 ha (280 dunams). These are built of large fieldstones, and are preserved to a height of 1–2 m. Many in situ jambs and lintels were noted. The majority of the houses are of the 'courtyard house with a cistern' type. The numerous cisterns are partially plastered, and stairs descend into them. There are many streets and alleyways. Apparently, the urban planning was only partial, and the houses in the city were set in blocks, *insulae*, without the street divisions typical of Roman city planning. In the western and southern parts of the city there are remains of a surrounding wall, perhaps a defence wall, about 2.5 m thick. It is likely that it served as urban demarcation.
- Four fortresses: A rectangular fortress, 36×28 m, near E.P. 474 (Site 69), dominates the area. The walls are built of fieldstones, and are 1.5 m thick. There are structures in the fortress, some of them built of ashlar stones. They include a tower 4×4 m, a reservoir, and rooms attached to the outer walls. The fortress is related to a road (C55) ascending and passing near it, from Wadi el-Kabi in the direction of Khirbet Yannun.

A trapezoidal fortress, 28×20×22×25 m, in the southern part of the Gittit Valley (Site 133). The outer wall is built of two rows of very large stones, reaching lengths of 1.5–2 m, weighing up to 500 kg. Some of the walls are preserved to a height of up to four courses (about 2 m). An opening 1.5 m wide was identified in the southern wall. The inner space of the fortress is empty. Along the north-western wall is a corridor-like set of rooms. Its total width, including the wall thickness, is 4–5 m. The corridor, 2.5 m wide inside, was roofed by large stone slabs, which were found together. A courtyard is attached to the fortress, but it is not clear if it is part of the original structure, or is a later extension.

A rectangular fortress near E.P. 432 (Site 137) overlooking the north part of the Gittit Valley and the road leading from it to Wadi Ahmar (C58). Part of the fortress was destroyed in modern times, and only the north-western wing and two watchtowers have been preserved. The fortress is well built of large partially worked stones. The north-western wall is 17 m long and nearly 1 m thick. The northern tower is apparently the principal fortification element. It measures 5×4 m, and is massively built, with walls 1.5 m thick. The south-eastern tower is smaller, about 4×3 m.

A rectangular fortress, 34×21 m, on a hillock dominating its vicinity in the east of the Gittit Valley (Site 171). The fortress controls the road network in the area, mainly the roads along the Gittit Valley (C41, C54 and C58). This fortress has been described by Porath (1968: site 166), and was totally ruined later. The construction is of cut stones and a few ashlar stones. Some of the corner stones have drafted margins. The interior is partitioned into rooms and courtyards. It should be noted that Porath found only Byzantine period sherds, but in the current survey most of the finds collected from the ruin heaps are LR.

There is similarity in architecture and dimensions in the fortresses, but great differences in their inner pattern. The four fortresses were built in the LR period, and according to the pottery continued to exist in the Byzantine period. Three were located in sites dominating the area, and two are next to a known ancient road. Only the fortress at Site 133 does not have such advantages, and its function is not clear.

- Three strongholds, similar in some of their characteristics:

An almost square stronghold, 9×7.5 m, in the exit of Wadi Qard south of Khirbet Tana et-Tahta (Site 55), part of Roman road C40. A number of courses of giant stones have been preserved, each weighing 2 tons and more. In the outer side of some of the stones is a protruding ledge with drafted margins. The structure is linked to the road from Khirbet Tana et-Tahta to the south-east.

A small stronghold, 6×6 m, in the north part of Sahel Afjeam (Site 78). It dominated the Sahel Afjeam valley and the road network passing through. The construction is of large stones.

A stronghold, about 10×10 m, which controlled the southern part of the Gittit Valley (Site 167). The walls are built of very large stones, and are about 1.5 m thick, preserved to a height of three courses.

The strongholds apparently guarded the roads and agricultural system, and together with the large fortresses complemented the defence of the area.

Agrarian Sites. This is the most common site of the LR settlement in the region. The sites are divided into a number of types:
- Farms. These are sites containing several architectural components, together, forming a farm:
- A central dwelling structure, normally a square structure in the centre of the site, surrounded by other structures.

- A courtyard or a cluster of courtyards, built of medium-sized and large stones, attached to the main residence structure or surrounding it. The area of the courtyards varies (similar to the range of dimensions given for isolated courtyards, below).
- Enclosures for livestock husbandry and/or threshing floors close to the farm.
- Rock-hewn installations of various functions around the farm: small ones such as basins and cup marks, and large ones such as winepresses and vats.

  Caves and/or cisterns were found in some of the farms.

  More than 15 LR sites were defined as farms. In some of them were found earlier sherd scatters without a clear connection to the farm main structure. Most of the farms were established in the LR, and continued to function in the Byzantine period. The farms were generally built on moderate slopes near valley ends, a location providing natural drainage, construction materials and a convenient approach to the fields in the nearby valleys. Examples of well-preserved farms are Sites 29, 104 and 123.
- Isolated courtyards: these are structures which are not a component of a farmhouse. Over 40 such courtyards have been found. They belong to a type of the commonest agricultural sites of the LR settlement in the region, additional evidence of the great agrarian activity in the eastern Samaria Shoulder at the time.

The courtyards have several common characteristics:

They are generally squarish: 45% are rectangular, 40% are square, and the rest have other shapes.

They can be classed into two groups according to the area: the small ones up to 200 sq. m, with typical dimensions of 15×10 m and 12×12 m; the large ones between 250 and 800 sq. m in area, typically measuring 30×18 m and 25×25 m. There are similar numbers of large and small courtyards.

Almost all the courtyards are empty. In some of them, the rock bed surface is exposed. An inner or outer square or rectangular small structure is attached to 20% of them, maybe serving for storage.

Most of the courtyards are surrounded by a wall built of one or two rows of medium-sized or large to very large boulders. The majority of the courtyard openings are up to 1 m threshold width between two monoliths.

Like the locations of LR farms, and apparently for the same reasons, these courtyards are also built over moderate slopes near valley limits, and close to arable land.

Judging by the narrow openings and the exposed rocky surfaces, it appears that the courtyards were not suitable for livestock husbandry (see another opinion at Spanier [1993] claiming that the yards served as livestock pens). Therefore it is reasonable to assume that they were generally used for

stockpiling produce from the nearby fields.
- Enclosures: this is generally a circular construction used for flock husbandry. Such construction was very common in the region, usually during periods preceding the LR period, especially in the IA. In spite of this, LR pottery was found in 10 of these enclosures. They are almost identical in diameter, 18 m on average, built of a single row of medium-sized and large rocks. No preferences have been noted in choosing the locations of the enclosures.
- Threshing floors: like the enclosures they are round, but their function, manner of construction and the topographical location differ. The threshing floors served as the accumulation and threshing place of the harvested cereals. The preferred place was an exposed rocky surface which served as floor, normally higher than the main farm building, and in places open to the winds. The threshing floors are encircled by small and medium-sized stones and are not built to any height. Small basalt stones, used in threshing sledges, were found in some of them. Other installations were found next to most of the threshing floors. More than 25 LR threshing floors were found in the eastern Samaria Shoulder, additional evidence of the intensive agricultural activity in the region.
- Isolated installations in the area: Structures of various types were discovered in the area, not related to a specific farm or other structure: winepresses, millstones, watchtowers (and see Appendix A for a report of an excavation of a Roman tower in Mras ed-Din), water pools, etc. They are reported below in the descriptions of the various sites, and in the indices of agricultural installations and other features at the end of this Volume. These installations also testify to the intensive agricultural activity in the region.

Other types:
- Caves: eight caves showing human activity have been discovered, all on moderate slopes by the edges of valleys and banks of wadis. No rock-cutting has been noted in the caves, and they seem to be in their natural state. Courtyards are attached to six of the caves dated to the LR (e.g. Sites 22, 70, 111 and 145). Some of the caves contain annexes or stone dividing walls. Without orderly excavation it is impossible to determine if caves were used for dwelling or agricultural usage, such as livestock husbandry or crop storage.
- Sherd scatters: we assume that some of the scatters prove the existence of unidentifiable concealed sites or another temporary use of the site: encampments, gatherings, markets, etc.
- Cemeteries: two LR cemeteries have been found: the cemetery of the city at Khirbet Tana et-Tahta (Site 40) and a cemetery without a settlement near

Sheikh Kamel (Site 11). The neighbourhood of the cemetery at Sheikh Kamel was not densely settled, and only a small farm was found; therefore it is to be considered differently from a cemetery next to a large settlement like the one at Khirbet Tana et-Tahta, and to treat it as a regional cemetery for the agrarian inhabitants of the area, or for nomads. In the site at Sheikh Kamel there is a tomb of a Middle Ages-Ottoman period holy man. The ancient cemetery is possible evidence of the holiness of the place since the LR period. Quite often, ancient cemeteries are discovered as a result of plundering in modern times. Obviously, many ancient cemeteries as yet undiscovered could teach us much about urban and rural burials in ancient times.

The sites, diverse in form and function, suggest that the eastern Samaria Shoulder during the LR period was an important agrarian centre, apparently greatly dependent on cereal cultivation in the Gittit and Sahel Afjeam valleys. The agricultural system was bolstered by a road network, fortresses and a great variety of agricultural facilities. It is noteworthy that despite the intensive agricultural activity, settlement was based almost solely on farms, and real villages were not established, except for two large centres: Khirbet Tana et-Tahta in LU 34, and Aqraba, adjacent in the north-west to LU 35, outside the limits of this survey. Apparently, the harvest exceeded the subsistence needs of the nearby regional habitants, and the surplus was marketed further away. Although there is no historical evidence of the markets for the produce of the eastern Samaria Shoulder, it can be assumed that the large and nearer cities in mountainous Samaria: Sebastia and Neapolis, among others, served as markets.

Comparison of the LR settlement in the eastern Samaria Shoulder with the LR settlement in other regions surveyed by the MHCS shows a similar situation. In Volume 2 an increase in the number of LR sites was noted, and 70 sites have been related to the LR period (26.2% of the total number of sites in the Volume). In Volume 4 an even greater increase is noted; 125 sites have been related to the period (61.8% of the total), and in Volume 5, 115 (73.2% of the total). This information is evidence of the great agricultural activity in the Jordan Valley and the fringes of Samaria during the LR period and a sharp increase in the number of settlements in comparison to the preceding period. However, the numbers in these regions do not reach the high percentage of sites recorded in the eastern Samaria Shoulder and in the nearby south-eastern Samaria Shoulder, where 135 sites (91.2% of the total) were found (Bar and Zertal 2019: 45).

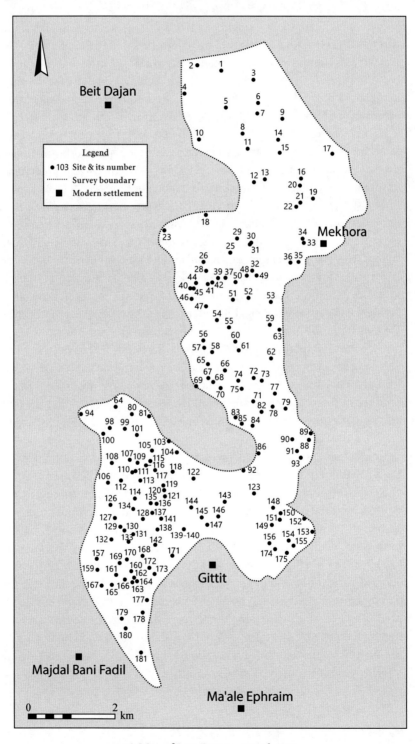

26. Map of Late Roman period sites.

13. BYZANTINE PERIOD (313–632 CE)

After the boom of the LR period the number of settlements in the eastern Samaria Shoulder declined, but it was still a very prominent settlement period.

One hundred and ten sites were found in the region, 61% of the total number of sites in Volume 6. They are equally frequent in both LUs. It should be noted that in 90 sites (81.8%) the number of LR sherds is over 10%. This fact adds to the credibility of the analysis, and supports the conclusions regarding the extent of activity in the region.

Another fact worthy of attention is that in all the sites except four (Sites 24, 27, 38 and 124), habitation continued from the LR to the Byzantine period. This information should be treated cautiously, due to the difficulty in distinguishing precisely between the sherds of these periods; especially in light of the fact that in some of these sites few sherds or only body fragments were collected. A well-known problem in surveys is to distinguish between pottery from the end of the Roman period and that from the beginning of the Byzantine, and indeed 30% of the sites have been defined as LR-Byzantine jointly.

Byzantine sites have several common characteristics:
- The region's LR trend continued in the Byzantine period, remaining a well-developed agrarian hub. Of the total number of sites, 43 (67%) were defined as agricultural. The sites are mostly farms and courtyards (see details in the LR, above).
- In the Byzantine period the city at Khirbet Tana et-Tahta continued to flourish; 28% of the hundreds of indicative sherds found in it belonging to the period. The city also expanded in the north-western quarter. The periphery of the city has many agricultural sites which were part of its economic hinterland. Most of the pottery collected in the plundered cemeteries around the city is also Byzantine.
- The use of strongholds for the protection of the roads and the agricultural areas continued in the Byzantine period. Sites 69, 133, 137, 167 and 171 continued their existence after the LR period.
- No evidence was found for the intensive Christian religious activity widespread in the southern Jordan Valley and in the valleys of the streams flowing eastwards from the mountainous slopes of Samaria and Judea to the River Jordan and the Dead Sea.

Comparison of the Byzantine settlement in the eastern Samaria Shoulder with settlement in other regions surveyed by the MHCS does not present a uniform situation. In many other regions there were fewer settlements than in the preceding period; but it was still a period of considerable habitation. In Volume 4, dealing with the Jordan Valley, 91 sites were related to the Byzantine period (44.6% of the total number of sites in the Volume), and in Volume 5, 67

66　　　　　　　　　　　　CHAPTER THREE

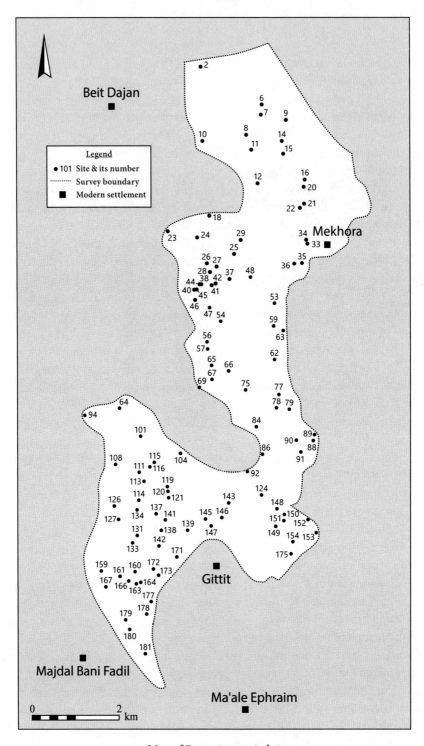

27. Map of Byzantine period sites.

sites (42.6%), despite the increase in Christian religious activity in the southern Jordan Valley and the Jericho area, south-east of the territory of this survey.

Unlike the situation in the Jordan Valley, in the desert fringes of Samaria north of the eastern Samaria shoulder there was an obvious increase in the number of settlements, and the rate of settlement doubled compared with the previous period. Thus in Volume 2, 144 sites were related to the Byzantine period versus 70 LR sites. A configuration of large townships containing sacred and public structures was discovered there, surrounded by smaller villages. Intensive agricultural activity all around the area was traced (Zertal 2008: 96). Prima facie it was expected that in the present research area close to the desert fringes of Samaria, a similar picture would be revealed, but the survey clearly showed a decrease, rather than an increase in the number of sites. The type of site is also different and, apart from Khirbet Tana et-Tahta, there is no evidence of towns and villages, but only small farms.

South of the eastern Samaria shoulder, in the adjacent south-eastern Samaria shoulder the picture is again somewhat different from the northern fringes. 84 sites (56.7% of the total) were found (Bar and Zertal 2019: 49), and the picture seems similar to the eastern Samaria shoulder, where the sites found have similar characteristics to those presented here.

14. EARLY MOSLEM PERIOD (632–1099 CE)

In the Early Moslem period a crisis befell the settlement of the eastern Samaria Shoulder. Only six EM sites were found, which is 3.3% of the total number of sites in Volume 6. These sites were not permanent settlements, and unlike the prosperity of the Roman-Byzantine periods, little agricultural activity existed. The highest number of EM sherds, 18%, was in Site 78. This number supports the assumption that the remains reflect limited temporary activity.

Comparison of the EM settlement in the eastern Samaria Shoulder with EM settlement in other regions surveyed by the MHCS shows a similar situation: there was a crisis in all the other regions as well, but with different ratios. In Volume 1, 70 sites have been related to the EM, versus 133 to the former Byzantine period; in Volume 2 there was a decline from 144 to 55; in Volume 4 from 91 to 23; and in Volume 5 from 67 to 22 sites. The sharpest decrease was noted in the current survey region in the eastern Samaria Shoulder, and also in the adjacent south-eastern Samaria Shoulder (from 84 sites to 11), showing continuity of the same cultural phenomenon.

The decrease in habitation probably started during the later phases of the Byzantine period after the failed Samaritan rebellions (mainly in the 6th Century CE; Avi-Yonah 1956). It appears that the Moslem conquest of 632 CE

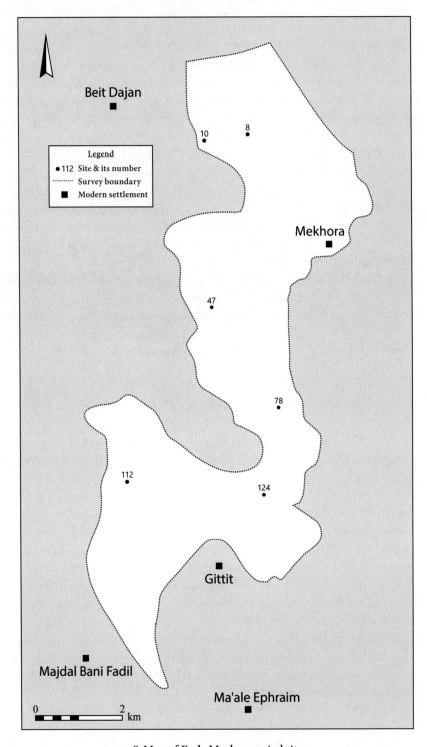

28. Map of Early Moslem period sites.

had a devastating effect on the remaining population, and the strong well-developed agricultural settlement system of the Byzantine period deteriorated rapidly. The decline of the country in Imperial and religious scales of importance, and the economic neglect by the state which characterized the Moslem dynasties (see discussion in Zertal 2008: 98), caused the complete destruction of settlement in eastern Samaria. In fact, in the EM period settlement in the region was almost non-existent.

15. MIDDLE AGES (1099–1510 CE)

In the Middle Ages, and particularly during the Mamluk period, there was an impressive recovery of the settlement in the eastern Samaria Shoulder.

Eighty-six sites of the period were found, representing 47.5% of the total number of sites in Volume 6; their frequency in both LUs is almost equal. However, it should be noted that of these, in 43 sites the number of sherds identified with the period did not exceed 10%.

Four aspects are especially prominent:
- The agricultural activity typical of the region during the Roman and Byzantine periods, almost extinct in the EM period, was revived in the MA. Most of the sites were renovated, restored and resettled agricultural sites of the Roman and Byzantine periods. Virtually no new agricultural sites established during the MA were found.
- In both LUs hamlets were found in the area of the villages of Majdal Bani Fadil, Aqraba and Beit Dajan (Sites 46, 98 and 112), apparently linked to the developed rural array in the mountainous land west of the present survey. Hence, although the number of sites in the eastern Samaria Shoulder is relatively high, the region was marginal during the MA.
- A significant utilization of caves and their vicinity is noted (Sites 105, 110 and 126). Of special interest is Site 116, Mugharet et-Tineh, which was perhaps a pottery workshop.
- The MA pottery is particularly coarse and poor. Very little typical painted Mamluk pottery was found, and hardly any glazed Crusader pottery.

Comparison between the MA settlement in the eastern Samaria Shoulder and the MA settlement in the other regions surveyed by the MHCS suggests a similar situation to all the other regions: there were more new settlements than in the previous period. In the adjacent region to the south, the southeastern Samaria Shoulder the increase was similar (from 11 sites to 64 sites), suggesting a possible geographical continuation of the same cultural entity to the south. In the Jordan Valley Volume 4, 64 sites have been related to the MA, and in Volume 5, 52 sites (more than double the number in the EM). In the

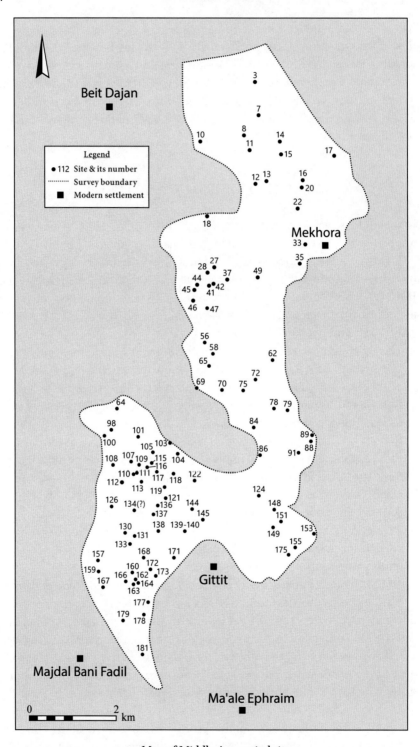

29. Map of Middle Age period sites.

fringes of Samaria, north of the present survey territory, there was an increase in the number of sites in the MA, although a more moderate one (69 sites versus 55). Hence, in the MA the eastern Samaria Shoulder region was richer in the number of sites than the Jordan Valley and the northern desert fringes of Samaria, apparently due to its proximity to the MA villages of the mountain country.

16. OTTOMAN PERIOD (1516–1918 CE)

After the recovery in the MA, a considerable decline occurred in the number of sites in the eastern Samaria Shoulder. Only 23 sites were found in the region, which is 12.7% of the total number of sites in Volume 6, their distribution in both LUs being almost equal. It is noteworthy that in 16 sites the number of sherds of the period did not exceed 20%, indicating a sparse settlement.

Most of the sites are agricultural, and like the MA settlement, the use of ancient Roman-Byzantine structures, mostly enclosures, courtyards and threshing floors, also continued in the Ottoman period. Among the period's sites two hamlets are prominent in LU 35 (Sites 118 and 139). Both overlooked the roads ascending from the Gittit Valley towards the large village of Aqraba, west of the survey zone, and both were apparently connected to it.

The comparison between the settlement in the eastern Samaria Shoulder during the Ottoman period and the settlement of the same period in the regions surveyed by the MHCS show a similar situation: in this period there was a sharp decline in the number of settlements throughout eastern Samaria and the Jordan Valley, and only a few temporary sites were discovered. In Volume 5, 20 sites were related to the Ottoman period (12.8% of the total number of sites in that Volume), in Volume 2, 26 sites (9.6% of the total), and in Volume 4, 16 sites (7.8% of the total). The information about the scanty settlement from the Ottoman period in the region fits the historical sources well (see below), confirming that the region had completely lost its importance, and was ruled by nomad Bedouin tribes.

This state of affairs lasted until modern times, until the settlement and development starting in 1967 changed the eastern Samaria Shoulder, turning vast areas of the region into a flourishing agricultural area.

CHAPTER THREE

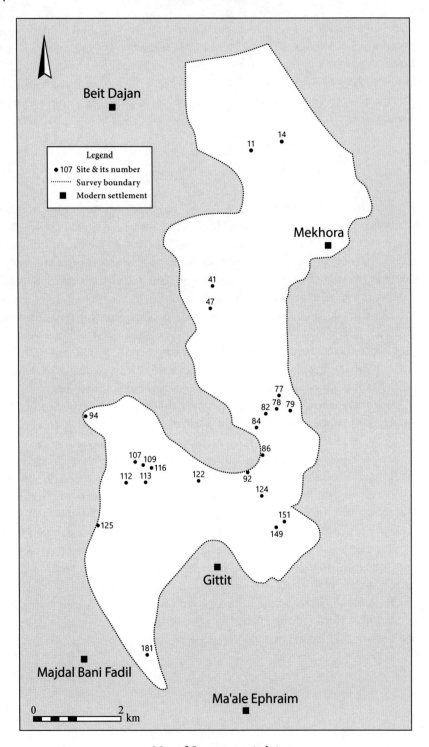

30. Map of Ottoman period sites.

CHAPTER FOUR

OUTLINE OF THE HISTORY OF THE REGION

When we come to describe the region's history, we face difficulties. Historians do not generally consider small areas such as the eastern Samaria Shoulder. In addition, there were almost no real cities in the region, and no sites identified as places mentioned in the Bible or in other historical sources.

The review below covers a broader territory than the present limited survey area in order to include nearby sites and events which influenced its inhabitants.

1. BRONZE AGES

From the Early Bronze Age to the Late Bronze Age (from the middle of the 4th to the last quarter of the 2nd millennium BCE) the settlement in the eastern Samaria Shoulder was exceedingly sparse. Only in the Middle Bronze Age II (the first half of the 2nd millennium BCE) was there a brief change, and a developed rural settlement existed in the region.

In the sources known to us from the Middle Bronze Age II, the Execration Texts and the Story of Sinuhe (ANET 328–329 and 18–22 respectively), there is no specific mention of the region or places within it. Zertal proposed (Zertal and Bar 2017: 61) that the *Kwsw* and *Swtw* tribes (tribe groups 50–53 in the Execration Texts) may have roamed the desert fringes of Samaria. He also suggested the possibility that the land of Yaa in the Story of Sinuhe was perhaps eastern Samaria, which climatically and ecologically suits the descriptions in the story. However, neither of these assumptions can be substantiated.

In the historical sources of the Late Bronze Age and the detailed descriptions in the El-Amarna Letters from the 14th century BCE, there is no particular reference to the eastern Samaria Shoulder, despite the numerous mentions of Shechem and its ruler Labaya/Labayu and the Habiru/Apiru tribes roaming the region. The eastern Samaria Shoulder is indeed not far from Shechem, the central city in north Samaria, which appears in the various sources, but almost no artefacts of the period have been found in the area, and the historical events apparently occurred in other regions of Samaria.

2. IRON AGES I–II

A single Iron Age I fortified settlement, Khirbet Isyar, was found in the eastern Samaria Shoulder. All the other finds are evidence of agricultural activity. There was a settlement drive in the Iron Age II, but except for Khirbet Juraish (which is not identified), no new cities were founded, and the main occupation continued to be agriculture. From this period survived the remnants of a number of forts, evidence of the interest of the central government in the region, and the possible transit routes passing through it from the Jordan Valley to the mountains and the centre of the Israelite monarchy.

The northern boundary of the eastern Samaria Shoulder, Nahal Tirzah, was the principal route between the Jordan Valley and the centre of Samaria and Shechem, and it is possibly the biblical 'way towards the sunset' (Deuteronomy, 11: 30) (Zertal 2018: 162). This route was probably used by the Aramean military expeditions against the Kingdom of Israel (Yadin 1964).

Jeroboam, son of Nebat, made the city of Tirzah (Tel el-Fara'a [north]), upstream of Nahal Tirzah, 20 km north-west of the eastern Samaria Shoulder, one of the capitals of the Kingdom of Israel; and 11 km west is Shechem, the central city in the mountain country. Hence, it is likely that the fertile region of the eastern Samaria Shoulder served as the agricultural hinterland to the main cities in northern Samaria.

Shoshenq I (925 BCE) during his campaign, descended on his way from the Samaria Mountains to the Jordan Valley, via the south-western corner of the eastern Samaria Shoulder. In the expedition list are Givon (no. 23), and then Migdal (no. 58), identified with Majdal Bani Fadil (Abel 1935: 272; Mazar 1986: note 11) or with the fort of Rujm Abu Mukheir (Zertal and Bar 2019: 77). Both identifications fit the ancient road descending from Shechem via Aqraba to Fasael Valley (marked by the Survey as C41), and indeed it is likely that an ancient road already existed there in the Iron Age.

The boundary between Manasseh and Ephraim passed through the eastern Samaria Shoulder: "And the border went out toward the sea by Michmethah on the north side; and the border turned about eastward unto Taanath-shiloh, and passed by it on the east to Janoah; And it went down from Janoah to Ataroth, and to Naarah, and came to Jericho, and came out at the Jordan." (Joshua, 16: 6-7).

Taanath-shiloh was identified in the past with Khirbet Tana el-Foqa, located 2 km north-west of Wadi Qard, at the northern boundary of the Survey (see Wallis 1961; Campbell 1991: 37–40; Finkelstein et al. 1997: 845–849), but it might have been located in Khirbet Tana et-Tahta, Site 47 (Zertal 2004b; Bar 2017). Janoah is apparently Khirbet Yanun or Nebi Nun: both are about 2 km west of the western Survey boundary. Zertal (Zertal and Bar 2019: 79–80), proposed identifying Ataroth with Khirbet 'Aujah el-Foqa in Nahal Yitav. Naarah appears to be Na'aran by the preservation of the name, although no Iron Age site was found near the Byzantine site of Na'aran; thus the identification remains unresolved, and Naarah might be identified in Khirbet 'Aujah el-Foqa. Hence, the Manasseh–Ephraim border passed from the Yanun/Nebi Nun vicinity to the area of Nahal Yitav. It seems that the boundary line followed the most prominent geographical feature in the region – the terrace of the mountainous Aqraba plateau. According to this idea, the boundary ran via Nebi Nun/Yanun to Aqraba, and on its route was constructed the large border fortress of Khirbet er-Risa (1), (Site 94). From here the boundary went south above and along the high ridge west of the Gittit Valley up to Majdal Bani Fadil (maybe Migdal, another fortress mentioned in the Shoshenq I campaign). From the topographical evaluation of this area of land, two alternatives can be suggested for the further extension of the boundary line: a) The boundary descended via the deep channel of Nahal Fasael, and then southward to Nahal Yitav; and b) The boundary went south from Majdal Bani Fadil through the Samaria desert to the deep channel of Nahal Yitav, the vicinity of the Iron Age city discovered at Khirbet Marjama, where the boundary descended eastward along the channel of the wadi to Khirbet 'Aujah el-Foqa. According to both these proposals, the eastern Samaria Shoulder was in the south of Manasseh's allotment, and later in the southern area of the Kingdom of Israel.

3. THE ASSYRIAN CONQUEST AND THE PERSIAN PERIOD

Unlike the situation in the Jordan Valley, the Sartaba area and the northern fringes of Samaria (Zertal 2008: 62-63; Zertal and Bar 2017: 67), great activity was identified in the eastern Samaria Shoulder in the period after the destruction of the Kingdom of Israel (Iron Age III), when Samaria was an Assyrian province. During the expulsions and population exchanges, Sargon II and his successors transferred exiles from across the Assyrian Empire to Samaria, settling them in place of the Israelite population. Some of the newcomers, among them Cutheans, were apparently settled in the triangular area of territory between the cities of Shechem, Samaria and Tirzah. The indicative artefact of the Cuthean settlement is the 'wedged impressed decorated bowl', also named 'cuneated bowl' (Zertal 1989; Itach 2015). If indeed, the remains of these bowls are evidence of the existence of Cuthean settlements or other ethnic groups, according to Zertal's belief, it can be concluded that the Cutheans settled in central and eastern Samaria, including a significant presence in the eastern Samaria Shoulder (Sites 35, 66, 94, 142, 151, 162, 168, 172-173, 178 and 181). Mras ed-Din (Site 173), was probably a centre for the inhabitants of the region, and at the site more than 20 fragments of wedged impressed decorated bowls were collected. Itach (2015: 86) summed up the subject: "...in the present state of evidence, it still seems to be fairly reasonable to link the cuneated impressed bowls with the exiles settled by the Assyrians in the Samaria province...at the end of the 8th century and during the 7th century BCE the concept of bowl impression was introduced by a group of exiles who perhaps came from the region of the cities Babylon and Cutha. The group was settled in the triangular area of Shechem-Samaria-Tirzah and the valleys nearby and produced the cuneated bowls. They are widespread in this area, where numerous farms were established in the second half of IA II...the impression and possibly the technical act of impression made it, whether wittingly or not, a symbol by which members of a certain population defined and distinguished themselves from their neighbours...".

In the excavation at Mras ed-Din a large proportion of the pottery assemblage from the Iron Age III destruction is typically Judeaite. What is the meaning of a Judeaite presence in the southern part of the conquered Kingdom of Israel at this time? Can it be a hint of an expansion of the Kingdom of Judea northwards into deserted areas in the southern parts of the now neglected Israelite territories? Or is it a new representation of the pottery assemblage of this region under the Assyrian oppressor? Was this carried out with the acceptance of, or coordination with, the Assyrian administration in the region? These are some of the key questions to be answered in the new excavation project at Mras ed-Din initiated in 2017.

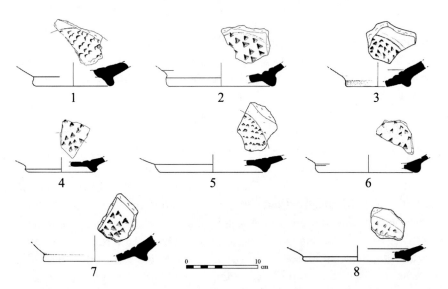

31. Cuneated bowls discovered by the MHCS in the eastern Samaria Shoulder: 1. Kh. Tawil (2); 2. en-Najmeh (1); 3, 7. Kh. er-Risa (1); 4-6. Mras ed-Din; 8. E.P. 390 (1).

OUTLINE OF THE HISTORY OF THE REGION

We are unable to identify the short Babylonian period archaeologically (586-539 BCE), and there are no historical traces of that period in eastern Samaria.

In the Persian period the eastern Samaria Shoulder was part of the Aqraba district (Avi-Yona 1962: 21–22). During this period a very sharp decline of habitation occurred, which can be observed across the entire Shamrayn province (Tavger 2012: 80). In light of the evidence from Dalia Cave in the Samaria desert, 12 km south-south-east of the eastern Samaria Shoulder (Lap 1993 and references therein), it seems that the region was a borderland, used by the Samaritan rebels as hiding places during the Macedonian conquest of 334 BCE. Safray (1980: 52) proposed that there were Edomite settlements in the Aqraba district, but no typical Edomite pottery was found in the survey.

The region is possibly mentioned in the Book of Judith (Grintz 1986), in which the plot tells of Holofernes, an Assyrian army general, who sent a mercenary army to block the routes of the reinforcements dispatched from Judea to the forces fortified in Bethulia and the neighbouring cities (apparently now the Dothan Valley area – Zertal 2009): "Then the children of Esau went up with the children of Ammon, and camped in the hill country over against Dothaim: and they sent some of them toward the south, and toward the east over against Ekrebel, which is near unto Chusi, that is upon the brook Mochmur;". Ekrebel (phonetically Aqrabim in Hebrew) is probably Aqraba (the settlement or the district), and the brook of Mochmur is apparently Wadi Ahmar, which is east of the settlement.

4. HELLENISTIC AND EARLY ROMAN PERIODS

In the Hellenistic Period there was no significant change in the settlement of the eastern Samaria Shoulder. It can be assumed that the construction of the fortress of Alexandrion by Alexander Jannaeus (War I, viii: 2) west of the eastern Samaria Shoulder led to the beginning of the revival of settlement in the region. Later, in the Early Roman period, Herod renovated the fortress (War I, xvi: 3), and a further increase in settlement in the region took place.

The borders of Judea and the Decapolis, particularly that of the Scythopolis district, ran along Nahal Tirzah, and the city of Corea in the floodplain of the stream (Qarawet et-Tahta – Zertal and Bar 2017: site 85) was "where you enter into the Country of Judea" (War I, vi: 5). Hence, the region of the eastern Samaria Shoulder was part of Judea (in the Aqraba district).

The settlement of Aqraba, which is close to the Survey boundary in the west, was a famous Jewish town from the beginning of the Second Temple times, and was the centre of the Jewish district of Aqrabtainu (Aqrabim, Acrabtenam). The settlement is mentioned in the Mishna: 'Aqraba in the north' (tractate

Maaser Sheni, 5: 2), apparently because it was one of the main border towns in the north of Judea. The Gittit Valley at the foot of Aqraba was apparently the agricultural hinterland of the town. Around it settled gentiles converted to Judaism, most of them Edomite (but no Edomite pottery was found in the region; for more about Aqraba see below in the discussion of the Late Roman-Byzantine periods).

At the outbreak of the Great Revolt, Johanan Ben Hananiah "was made the governor of the toparchies of Gophnitica and Acrabastene" (War II, xx: 4) which were settled by Jews (Avi-Yona 1962: 122). Shimon Bar Giora, one of the leaders of the revolt, was a native of the village of Geresh, identified with the village of Juraish, which is located south-west of Aqraba, 3 km west of the Survey area. Josephus Flavius wrote: "But for the Acrabbene toparchy, Simon, the son of Gioras, got a great number of those that were fond of innovations together, and betook himself to ravage the country" (War II, xxii: 2). Apparently Bar Giora took control of the area of Aqraba and its vicinity until he had to flee to Masada out of fear of the high priest Hanan and the leaders of the revolt in Jerusalem. Vespasian conquered the districts of Acrabtenam and Gophna about six months before the destruction of Jerusalem, and annexed them to the city of Flavia Neapolis-Shechem.

The Mishna is an additional source of information about the place. From the story of bringing Neta Revii (the fruit of a tree in the fourth year after its planting) to Jerusalem, we learn that grape-bearing vineyards were cultivated in the district of Aqraba (Borenstein 1993: 107). "[The fruit of] a vineyard in its fourth year was brought up to Jerusalem within a distance of one day's journey on each side. And what was the limit thereof? Elath on the south, Akrabah on the north" (tractate Maaser Sheni, 85: 42).

During this period the large city of Khirbet Tana et-Tahta flourished in the northern part of the eastern Samaria Shoulder. It is intriguing that the city is not mentioned in the sources of the period, although it was known to be a central settlement in the region.

5. LATE ROMAN AND BYZANTINE PERIODS

Settlement in the eastern Samaria Shoulder reached its peak in these periods. The northern part of the region served as the agricultural hinterland of the large settlement at Khirbet Tana et-Tahta, and the southern part continued to serve as the agricultural hinterland of Acrabtenam. Hadrian suppressed the Bar Kochba rebellion in 135 CE, annihilating the majority of the Jewish population of the region, and expelled the survivors. Samaritans settled in place of the Jews in the Acrabtenam district, and the province was transferred from Judea to Samaria (Safray 1980: 56). In our survey, no ethnic hallmarks or other remains of such a demographic upheaval have been found (but these are almost invisible from survey data).

Two Byzantine period maps are available – Madaba and Peutinger – and also the Onomasticon of Eusebius. However, there are no signs of the settlements in the maps at their supposed locations in the eastern Samaria Shoulder. The village of Thena is mentioned in the Onomasticon, located 10 miles east of Neapolis (site 493 by Eusebius, Nottley and Safrai 2005). According to Safray (1980: 52), the place intended is Khirbet Tana el-Foqa, because its distance from Shechem fits. Finkelstein et al. (1997: 845) agree to his proposal. On the contrary we think that the intention is Khirbet Tana et-Tahta (Site 47), where there are remains of a very large settlement, while the site of Tana el-Foqa is a much smaller settlement, which produced a very scanty Byzantine find (and see in detail in Bar 2017). Another suggested identification of Khirbet Tana et-Tahta with biblical Taanath-Shiloh is not certain (Conder and Kitchener 1882: 232; Wallis 1961; Campbell 1968: 31; Finkelstein et al. 1997: 845-849; Zertal 2004b). An additional identification is by Ptolemy (v: 16: 5; Nobbe 1845), of Tana et-Tahta as Thena, stating that this is a Samaritan city (Fig. 32 below).

Safray (1980: 52-53) proposed that the northern boundary of the Acrabtenam district passed south of the village of Taanath-Shiloh. If indeed so, the boundary passed within the boundary of LU 34. If the suggestion for this boundary line rests on the topography, then the deep channel of Wadi Ahmar up to the vicinity of Khirbet Juraish, and northwards and up to Khirbet Yanun, fits that boundary. Khirbet Yanun is identified with the village of Yanoah, mentioned in the Onomasticon as being related to the confines of Aqraba (Onomasticon no. 550; Avi-Yonah 1962: 122).

The struggle during the two major Samaritan revolts of 484 and 529 CE took place in the vicinity of Mount Gerizim and Shechem, apparently also influencing regions distant from the core of the revolts. Julianus Ben Sabar, the rebel leader, retreated in 529 CE to the mountains east of Shechem in order to conduct guerrilla warfare from there against the Byzantine regime. Julianus failed and was killed, and most of the rebels fled. The punitive Byzantine expeditions eliminated the sites of resistance in the mountains. Although there is no historical documentation stating in which mountains the rebels were hiding, the prominent ridges east of Shechem Jebel Kabir and the ridge of Nebi Nun in the western and north-western boundary of the Survey, not far from Khirbet Tana et-Tahta (Ptolemy's Samaritan Thena), are probable locations. The suppression of the rebellion in the mountains could have seriously affected the Byzantine settlements in the eastern Samaria Shoulder, and particularly Khirbet Tana et-Tahta. From the data of the Survey, it is impossible to decide precisely when the Byzantine settlement peaked, and when it started to decline to its final abandonment. The suppression of the Samaritan uprisings, especially that of 529 CE, was probably the initial crisis leading to the abandonment of the region in the Early Moslem period.

Throughout the Roman-Byzantine periods, the town of Acrabtenam was the hub of the region and the district capital (for bibliographical sources and

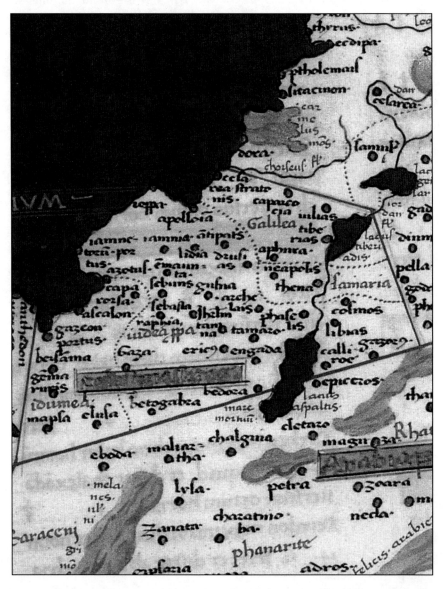

32. Map drawn by Domus Nicolaus Germanous after the fourth Asiatic Table by Ptolemy, Florence, 1474 (Nebenzahl 1986: Map 2). Note the location of Thena east of Shechem-Neapolis.

references concerning the town and the district see Tzafrir et al. 1994: 57). The town is mentioned in numerous sources: in the Madaba Map, where it appears under the caption "Acrabim is now Acrabtenam" (see Avi-Yona 1953: 143); in a marriage contract from 124 CE in the Wadi Murabba'at papyri (Benoit et al. 1961: document 115); as the eastern border of Judea placed 9 miles from Shechem (Eusebius, in Bagatti 1979: 45); and as a Samaritan centre in which resided Tzadok ben Tuvia the priest with twelve dignitaries of the community (Ben-Zvi 1976: 72). The attestations show that a Christian population also lived in the town (Bagatti 1979: 45). The town of Acrabtenam was indeed located a little outside the current Survey bounds, but its main agricultural land was spread through the fertile Gittit Valley, the sites of which are described extensively in LU 35.

6. EARLY MOSLEM, MIDDLE AGES AND OTTOMAN PERIODS

In the Early Moslem period the region belonged to Jund el-Urdun, the capital of which was Tiberias, and later on to Jund Filastin, with its capital, Ramla (Gil 1981: 77).

Despite the mentions of the city of Akrabah in the Samaritan sources, the eastern Samaria Shoulder was deserted.

The region does not appear in Bayer's research (1940) of Crusader settlement within the confines of Shechem, and the area is vacant in Crusader settlement maps (for example, Schein 1981: 314).

The documentation of the settlement recovery in the Middle Ages began in the days of the first Mamluk rulers in the 13th century CE: Baybars and Al-Mansur Qalawun, and particularly in the time of the later Sultan Malik Al-Nassir Muhammad ibn Qalawun (1310–1341 CE). Muhammad ibn Qalawun was known to be a great builder, who also developed the Samaria region and called eastern Samaria el-Mashreq (the East) (Yekutieli 1971: 209; Drori and Reiner 1981: 22, 38). The region was part of the El-Shams (Damascus) province, district (*amalya*) of Nablus (Shechem) (Drori and Reiner 1981: 33). This recovery was apparently reflected in the region of the eastern Samaria Shoulder, and indeed numerous sites of the period were found there.

In the Ottoman period, the region was part of *eyalet* (province) e-Sham and *sanjac* (district) Shechem. In the 16th century, the eastern Samaria Shoulder was in the *nahiya* (sub-district) of Jebel Qubal in *sanjac* Shechem (Nablus) (Cohen 1998). The region's population was divided into two major groups after the Mamluk period: Bani Kis and Bani Yemen. The division had no distinct geographical bounds, and affected all the population classes within the nomad Bedouin tribes, in the villages and even in the cities, and was prominent in the mountainous areas of the Shechem and Jerusalem districts.

In the census of 1596, published by Hutteroth and Abdulfattah (1977: 136), Tana, a small village with eight dwelling families is mentioned. They paid 33% tax from their crop, which was mainly wheat and olives. According to the documentation, the village was abandoned in the Ottoman period, and did not exist during the British Mandate. Other villages, located west of the Survey boundary or close to it, mentioned in the census are: Yanun and Majdal (18 families in each), and the large village of Aqraba (102 families).

Cohen (1998) shows that in the Ottoman period the village communities were divided into two main groups: the city/town/village itself (*albalda*) and the *mazra'ah*, the cultivated area in which the inhabitants of the village dwelt seasonally to work the land. Thus 'daughter villages' were started – settlements which were moved or newly founded by some of the inhabitants of an established settlement to exploit new land areas (Grossman 1977: 396). According to these observations, the whole area of the Gittit Valley can be defined as the *mazra'ah* of the large village of Aqraba, and maybe also that of the small village of Majdal Bani Fadil. Sites 118 and 139 can be defined as daughter villages of Aqraba, and Khirbet Bani Fadil (Site 181) as a daughter village of Majdal Bani Fadil.

Despite the reduction of settlement compared to that of the Middle Ages, agricultural activity still continued during the Ottoman period in the surrounding villages, as was also deduced from the impressions of Van de Velde who visited in the country in 1851–52, describing the fertile wheatfields in the Gittit Valley (Van de Velde 1854: 315).

CHAPTER FIVE

METHODOLOGICAL COMMENTS ON THE SURVEY

The Manasseh Hill Country Survey has been in progress for over 40 years. The experience gained during this time and the improving technical capabilities through the years have led to changes and updates in methodology and the performance and publication of the Survey. For the basic scientific principles of the Survey in detail, see Volume 1, Chapters 1 and 2 (Zertal 2004a).

Detailed below are the main changes which have been made in recent years in the execution and publishing of the Survey:

1. CHANGES IN THE METHOD OF EXECUTING THE SURVEY IN THE FIELD

The basic method of thorough survey on foot is still valid today. The spaces between the surveyors vary from 10 to 30 m according to the terrain. In densely built-up areas a complete survey on foot could not always be accomplished, and the same applies to cliffs which are difficult of approach, to fenced areas where entry is prohibited, or to minefields and deep caves.

A. From the beginning of the Survey until 2004, fixing the locations of the sites was based on the 1:50,000 topographic maps. Starting in 2004 the location has been determined by GPS and verified by a map. Elevations are still determined by a map, due to the problematic accuracy of GPS elevation measurement.

B. In 2010 scrutiny of satellite photographs was added to the foot survey. It is important to emphasize that this scrutiny is only a supplementary tool, and does not replace the complete foot survey in any way.

2. ADDITION OF MEASURED SITE PLANS TO THE TEXT AND THE USE OF AERIAL PHOTOGRAPHY

One of the significant features of the Survey is the emphasis over the past three decades on measuring and drawing the plans of sites and structures on the surface. A plan enables the researcher to show architectural details, which are not understandable or clear enough from the description or a photograph. The plan also assists in comparing various sites of the same type or the same chronological framework.

In the last few years, we have added the use of aerial photographs to our operation, helping to understand a site in relation to its surroundings, emphasizing its outstanding architectural features, and supplementing the details of the plan. An aerial photograph can replace a plan where taking measurements is impossible due to logistic difficulties, such as inaccessibility of a certain spot with the measuring equipment, e.g. the location of a site in a minefield (such as Khirbet ed-Dashe – Zertal and Bar 2019: site 38). In addition, aerial photographs help greatly in locating a site precisely in the area.

3. ALTERATIONS IN THE DETAILED PRESENTATION OF THE GEOGRAPHICAL AND ENVIRONMENTAL DATA OF EACH SITE AND THE ANALYSIS OF THE FINDS

A. Starting with the present Volume, the geographical location (the coordinates in the Israel Old Grid) appears as a ten-digit number instead of an eight-digit one. This is in order to be more accurate in locating sites, thus assisting the researcher and the traveller seeking the site.
B. Categories and sub-descriptions in the descriptive paragraphs: Name type, Site type, Topography and Soil type, have been added.
C. Site data: time of visits, number of collected sherds and number of surveyors, have been added.
D. As from Volume 4 the item 'visibility' has been omitted.
E. The dimensions of the site are based on the spread of finds in the area, and not solely by preserved architecture, except where a single structure or a defined architectural unit has been discovered.
F. The pottery gathering method has been altered as from Volume 2. The collecting is not done in sampling squares, but from the entire surface area of the site. Starting in the survey season of 2014, most of the finds were left in the individual sites after a primary documentation in the field. Only sherds required for further research and drawing were taken to the Survey laboratories.
G. Starting with the present Volume 6 all the indicative sherds collected in the Survey have been drawn (except duplicates of identical rims or a surplus of dateable finds which does not justify publishing several tables for a single site).
H. Starting with Volume 5 emphasis or notice of pottery identification based on body-sherds only has been added.

4. MISCELLANEOUS CHANGES

A. The descriptions of the Survey have been diversified over the years, and the following items have been added:
   - History of research and sources.
   - Detailed accounts of archaeological excavations conducted by members of the Survey (Shay Bar, Adam Zertal and Dror Ben-Yosef) within the boundaries of the surveyed tract of land, and summaries and extracts of publications by other researchers in the region.
   - Processing of the flint finds collected in the Survey sites by Haim Winter in Volumes 4 and 5, and by Sonia Pinsky in the present Volume 6.
B. Translating the Survey volumes into English included a complete scientific editing, which includes repeated visits to some sites, and supplements of newly published data photographed, measured or acquired since the initial survey. The survey was completed in areas which had not been fully surveyed previously. The outcome of the time gap between the primary publication in Hebrew and the later English one is that the Survey accounts in English are more up to date than those published earlier.

PART TWO

DESCRIPTION OF THE SITES

CHAPTER SIX

THE SAMARIA SLOPES FROM NAHAL TIRZAH TO WADI AHMAR - LANDSCAPE UNIT 34

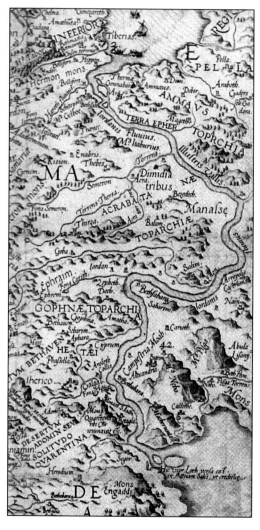

33. Map of the Holy Land, drawn by Laicksteen and Sgrooten, Antwerp, 1570 (in Nebenzahl 1986, map 29). Note the location of the ACRABATA toparchy north of the GOPHNAE toparchy.

Site 1: 18-17/78/1
ELEVATION POINT 577

Israel grid: 18776/17847
UTM grid: 7260/5653
Elevation: 577 m a.s.l., 300 m a.s.a.
Name: nearest place
Site type: sherd scatter, installations, structures and farm
Area: 4000 sq. m (4 dunams)
Topography: hillock
Rock type: Avdat Group

Soil: terra rossa, quality: 3
Cultivation: none
Cisterns: none
Water source: 'Ein ed-Dabbur (no. 111), 2.2 km distant
Road: Nahal Tirzah-Neapolis (C52), 300 m distant
Visit: June 2000; 5 surveyors; 72 sherds

Site on the moderately sloping hillock platform of E.P. 577 on Jebel Kabir, 3.3 km west of Hamra.

Site consists of three parts:
- Sherd scatter over a surface measuring about 100×100 m, close to E.P. 577. From the site there is a good view of Wadi Far'ah Valley.
- South of this surface are a farm and installations. In the eastern part of the farm are two small structures, possibly tombs.

  On the E.P. hillock itself there are no construction remains, only sherd scatter.
- About 200 m south-west of the farm are additional remains (see plan):
  - Two parallel rows of large stones orientated west-east. The northern row passes a rock with several hewn installations. The southern row is connected to a terrace that passes by through another rock with installations. The eastern end of the row surrounds gristmill stones in a semicircle. The millstones are 2 m in diameter, with square holes in the centre. Next to the millstones are a basin and other installations.
  - Wall oriented north-south, from west of the millstones crosses the saddle.
  - Circle of large stones, about 7 m in diameter.
  - In the south is a structure measuring 4×4 m.

The site appears to be a cluster of agricultural installations for processing agricultural produce: basins, craters and millstones.

It is not clear if the site also served for permanent dwelling.

Pottery: Iron I (body sherds) – 11%; Late Roman – 89%.
Other surveys: none.

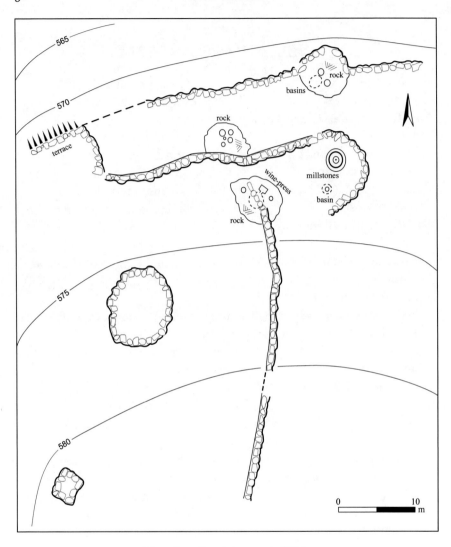

34. Plan of south-western part of E.P. 577.

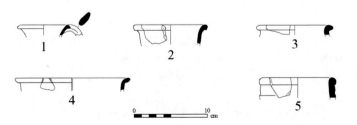

35. Pottery from E.P. 577 (all LR): 1-3. Jugs, lt brn; 4. Bowl, lt brn; 5. Jar, lt brn.

Site 2: 18-17/78/2

ZUHUR EL-MUSEIF

Israel grid: 18722/17859
UTM grid: 7255/5653
Elevation: 630 m a.s.l., 60 m b.s.a.
Name: nearest place
Site type: courtyard and farm
Area: 2000 sq. m (2 dunams)
Topography: slope
Rock: Judea Group
Soil: terra rossa, quality: 3

Cultivation: none
Cisterns: none
Water source: 'Ein ed-Dabbur (no. 111), 1.8 km distant
Road: Nahal Tirzah-Neapolis (C52), by the site
Visit: June 2000; 4 surveyors; 100 sherds

Site on an eastern slope of the ridge of Zuhur el-Museif, in an enclosed valley, 2 km east-north-east of Beit Dajan.

Courtyard, 25×25 m, built of one or two rows of large stones. In the north-western part is a room with an upright jamb. Two stone rollers or columns were found in the vicinity of the yard.

East of these is another small and irregular yard.

Numerous sherds are strewn about.

Pottery: Late Roman-Byzantine – 100%.
Other surveys: none.

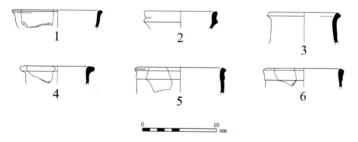

36. Pottery from **Zuhur el-Museif** (all LR-Byz) 1, 4. Bowls, org; 2, 5. Jugs, org; 3. Jug, lt brn; 6. Jar, org.

Site 3: 18-17/88/1
ELEVATION POINT 427

Israel grid: 18849/17823
UTM grid: 7268/5651
Elevation: 427 m a.s.l., 50 m a.s.a.
Name: nearest place
Site type: structure and threshing floors
Area: 1 ha (10 dunams)
Topography: hillock and a spur saddle
Rock: Judea Group

Soil: terra rossa, quality: 5
Cultivation: none
Cisterns: none
Water source: 'Ein ed-Dabbur (no. 111), 2.2 km distant
Road: Nahal Tirzah-Neapolis (C52), by the site
Visit: June 2000; 6 surveyors; 46 sherds

Site on a hillock and saddle on the northern slope of Jebel Kabir, 2.5 km west of Hamrah.

The site consists of two parts: on the hillock is a 7×7 m structure, built of large stones. Around it is a scanty scatter of sherds; and on the saddle are threshing floors and various walls.

A paved path leads from the saddle to the structure. Another path goes along on the eastern side of the hill.

Pottery: Iron II (body sherds) – 11%; Late Roman – 80%; Medieval (body sherds) – 9%.
Other surveys: none.

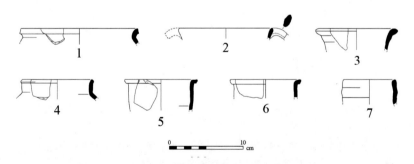

37. Pottery from E.P. 427 (all LR): 1-2. CPs, red; 3. Jug, lt brn; 4. Jug (?), lt brn; 5. Bowl, lt brn; 6. Bowl, red; 7. Jug, lt colour.

Site 4: 18-17/67/1
ELEVATION POINT 708 (SOUTH)

Israel grid: 18690/17796
UTM grid: 7252/5647
Elevation: 590 m a.s.l., 70 m a.s.a.
Name: nearest place
Site type: courtyard and installations
Area: 2000 sq. m (2 dunams)
Topography: slope
Rock: Judea Group
Soil: terra rossa, quality: 5
Cultivation: plantations by the site
Cisterns: none
Water source: 'Ein Sha'eb el-Bir
 (no. 187), 2 km distant
Road: Nahal Tirzah-Neapolis (C52),
 200 m distant
Visit: June 2000; 6 surveyors;
 25 sherds

Site on the slopes south of E.P. 708 at the edge of a cultivated saddle in the land-block of Zuhur el-Museif.

Large courtyard, 40×25 m, built of two rows of large and worked stones. In the north-western corner is a lime pit.

All around the site are many quarried places, basins and cup-marks.

Pottery: Late Roman – 100%.
Previous surveys: none.

Site 5: 18-17/77/1
ZUHUR ESH-SHAFA (2)

Israel grid: 18788/17763
UTM grid: 7262/5644
Elevation: 660 m a.s.l., 100 m a.s.a.
Name: nearest place
Site type: structure and installations
Area: 1 ha (10 dunams)
Topography: hillock
Rock: Judea Group
Soil: terra rossa, quality: 4
Cultivation: none
Cisterns: none
Water source: 'Ein Sha'eb el-Bir (no.
 187), 1.6 km distant
Road: Phasaelis-Neapolis (C40), 500
 m distant
Visit: June 1995; 4 surveyors; 53 sherds

Site near the hillock of E.P.667, north-west of the Mekhora-Beit Dajan road, 2.3 km east of Beit Dajan and 2.5 km north-west of Mekhora.

Several items:
- Small structure, 4×3 m, built of large field stones, some of which are megalithic. At the entrance is a threshold stone in situ.
- Small winepress, 5 m north of the structure.
- Around the structure are spread many installations and stone circles, the function of which is unknown.

The site was badly damaged during earthmoving operations.

Pottery: Iron I-II – 75%; Late Roman – 25%.
Flint: two non-indicative blades.
Other surveys: none.

Site 6: 18-17/87/1
ELEVATION POINT 667 (1)

Israel grid: 18860/17776
UTM grid: 7269/5645
Elevation: 510 m a.s.l., 30 m b.s.a.
Name: nearest place
Site type: courtyards
Area: 2000 sq. m (2 dunams)
Topography: saddle
Rock: Judea Group

Soil: terra rossa, quality: 5
Cultivation: none
Cisterns: none
Water source: 'Ein Sha'eb el-Bir
(no. 187), 2.1 km distant
Road: Nahal Tirzah-Neapolis (C52),
500 m distant
Visit: July 2000; 3 surveyors; 41 sherds

Site on a saddle over the slopes of Jebel Kabir, 2.7 km west of Hamrah and 800 m east of E.P. 667.

Three courtyards, built of medium sized and large stones. Some of the stones are scattered around.
- Large ancient enclosure, with a newly constructed threshing floor inside (no. 1 in plan).
- Large 19×14 m triangular courtyard whose eastern wing is slightly rounded (no. 2).
- Small triangular courtyard built of medium-sized stones (no. 3).

The courtyards served as a farm or seasonal site.

Pottery: Late Roman – 50%; Byzantine – 50%.
Other surveys: none.

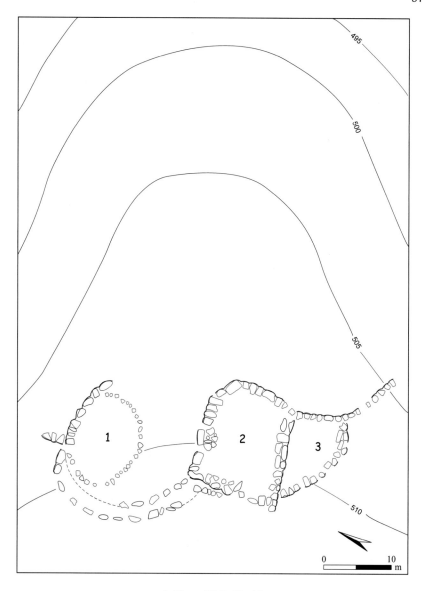

38. Plan of E.P. 667 (1).

39. Pottery from E.P. 667 (1): 1. Bowl, gr, Rom-Byz; 2. Bowl, lt brn, Rom-Byz.

Site 7: 18-17/87/2
ELEVATION POINT 667 (2)

Israel grid: 18854/17751
UTM grid: 7269/5643
Elevation: 530 m a.s.l., 30 m b.s.a.
Name: nearest place
Site type: courtyards and threshing floor
Area: 500 sq. m (0.5 dunam)
Topography: saddle
Rock: Judea Group

Soil: terra rossa, quality: 5
Cultivation: none
Cisterns: none
Water source: 'Ein Sha'eb el-Bir (no. 187), 2 km distant
Road: Nahal Tirzah-Neapolis (C52), 400 m distant
Visit: June 1995; 4 surveyors; 23 sherds

Site on the eastern slope of a saddle of E.P. 667, 3 km north-north-west of Mekhora.
Two small courtyards:
- Southern courtyard, 15×15 m, built of fieldstones. The surrounding wall thickness is 80 cm. Next to the yard is a small cupmark.
- Northern smaller courtyard, 10×10 m square, similarly built.

Semicircular threshing floor was noted 60 m north-east of the site. No sherds were found around it.

Pottery: Iron I – 9%; Hellenistic-Early Roman – 18%; Late Roman – 13%; Byzantine – 30%; Medieval – 30%.
Other surveys: none.

Site 8: 18-17/87/3
ZUHUR ESH-SHAFA (1)

Israel grid: 18821/17708 (winepress)
UTM grid: 7266/5638
Elevation: 610 m a.s.l., 50 m a.s.a.
Name: nearest place
Site type: farm, winepress and roads
Area: 2000 sq. m (2 dunams)
Topography: saddle
Rock: Judea Group
Soil: terra rossa, quality: 4

Cultivation: none
Cisterns: none
Water source: 'Ein Sha'eb el-Bir (no. 187), 1.5 km distant
Road: Nahal Tirzah-Neapolis (C51) and Phasaelis-Neapolis (C40), at the site
Visit: June 1995; 4 surveyors; 13 sherds

Site on Jebel Kabir, 300 m north of Sheikh Kamel tomb and 3 km north-west of Mekhora. A valley descends from the site towards the 'Aqabet el-Butmeh spur.

Farm with a double irregularly-shaped courtyard. The dimensions of the lower courtyard (the eastern) are 25×15 m, and the upper one (the western) are 15×10 m. The courtyards are built of large unworked stones. Apparently the yards were not built in one phase.

Small structure, 4×4 m, is attached in the west to the upper courtyard.

Quarried winepress located 20 m south of the farm, and 50 m further south a junction of two paved Roman roads, C40 and C51.

Pottery: Hellenistic – 15%; Roman – 15%; Byzantine – 15%; Early Moslem – 10%; Medieval – 35%; Modern (body sherds) – 10%.
Other surveys: none.

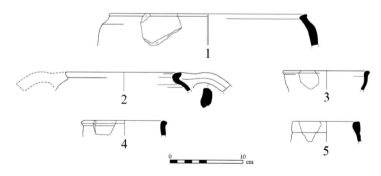

40. Pottery from **Zuhur esh-Shafa (1)**: 1. Bowl, lt brn, Med; 2. CP, drk brn, Byz-EM; 3. Bowl, org, Rom; 4. Bowl, yel, Rom; 5. Jar, lt brn, Rom.

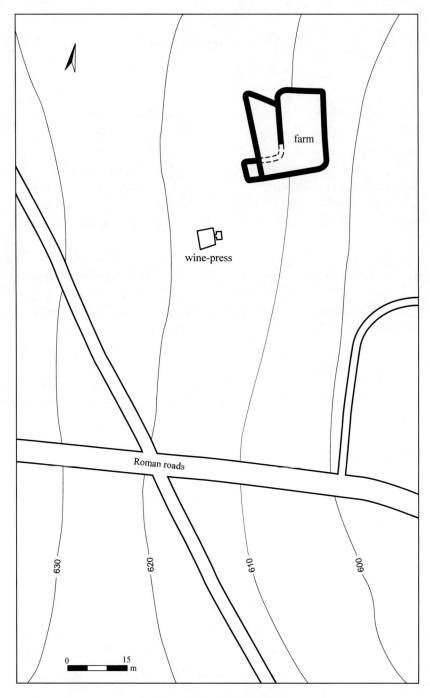

41. Plan of **Zuhur esh-Shafa (1)**.

Site 9: 18-17/97/1
WADI UMM EZ-ZRUB (1)

Israel grid: 18912/17740
UTM grid: 7275/5642
Elevation: 355 m a.s.l., 250 m a.s.a.
Name: nearest place
Site type: structures and terraces
Area: 2000 sq. m (2 dunams)
Topography: shoulder
Rock: Judea Group
Soil: terra rossa, quality: 6

Cultivation: none
Cisterns: none
Water source: 'Ein Sha'eb el-Bir (no. 187), 2.4 km distant
Road: Nahal Tirzah-Neapolis (C51), 500 m distant
Visit: November 2013; 3 surveyors; 50 sherds

Site on a shoulder above the northern bank of Wadi Umm ez-Zrub, 2.5 km west-south-west of Hamrah. There is a broad open view of Wadi Far'ah Valley, from Bab ed-Dayek in the south-east up to Tell esh-Shibli in the north-west.
Two structures:
- Rectangular structure, 13×5 m, built of medium sized and large stones. A wall nearly 1 m thick divides the structure into two at its centre.
- Structure built of small and medium-sized stones, about 30 m west of the rectangular structure, on a levelled surface supported by a semicircular terrace wall.

Considering the different construction styles, it can be concluded that the structures were built at different periods. The Iron Age sherds were collected in the first structure.

Over the shoulder, north-west of the structures, are numerous terrace walls, showing that the entire shoulder was cultivated.

Pottery: Iron II-III – 30%; Late Roman – 40%; Byzantine – 30%.
Other surveys: none.

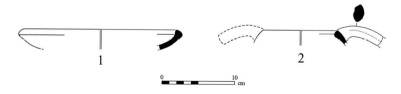

42. Pottery from **Umm ez-Zrub (1)**: 1. Bowl, drk brn, IA II; 2. Jar, lt brn, LR-Byz.

Site 10: 18-17/76/1
ELEVATION POINT 572

Israel grid: 18725/17695 (the centre of the site)
UTM grid: 7256/5637
Elevation: 540 m a.s.l., 30 m a.s.a.
Name: nearest place
Site type: large complex
Area: 3 ha (30 dunams)
Topography: slope
Rock: Judea Group

Soil: Mediterranean forest, quality: 3
Cultivation: none
Cisterns: 2
Water source: 'Ein Sha'eb el-Bir (no. 187), 1 km distant
Road: Phasaelis-Neapolis (C40), near the site
Visit: July 1999; October 1999, 7 surveyors; 90 sherds

Site extending over the hillock and the southern slope of E.P. 572, close to the Mekhora-Beit Dajan road, 1.7 km east-south-east of Beit Dajan. There is a good observation to Wadi Juni from the site.

In the site, is a complex encircled by a wall, except for its southern side. The wall thickness is about 1 m. It appears as if the southern wall was dismantled and its stones used for the construction of the Roman road to Neapolis. Alternatively, the ancient enclosure southern wall became the northern wall of the road.

The site consists of two main parts, northern and southern, plus other features:
- Northern part – an enclosure, 120×80 m, subdivided by a single-stone-thick wall. In the northernmost wing of the complex is a number of square installations, some of them which are integrated into the enclosure surrounding wall.
- Southern part – very steep and supported by an array of terraces. Apparently these are founded on ancient support walls. In the north wing is a later (Roman?) courtyard, for which stones from the original structures were used. This part was probably also sub-divided like the northern part.
- The Roman road from Phasaelis to Neapolis (C40) passing via the area of 'Iraq Rasifeh, is near the site. Apparently the builders of the road used stones from the site.
- South of Wadi Juni is a Hellenistic-Roman complex containing a structure with a winepress, a pit and a grave. Along the channel of Wadi Juni are dams.
- In and around the site are winepresses and other rock-cut installations.

The site belongs to the MBA II cluster of sites in the region, apart from the structures and installations from the Hellenistic and Roman periods.

LANDSCAPE UNIT 34

Pottery: Middle Bronze II – 78%; Hellenistic-Early Roman (body sherds) – 13%; Late Roman (body sherds) – 7%; Byzantine – 1%; Early Moslem – 1%.
Flint: 26 items: 3 cores, core waste, 10 flakes, 7 blades, 1 axe, 2 retouched blades, 1 non-indicative sickle blade and a geometric sickle blade. The geometric sickle blade can be related to the MBA II.
Other surveys: none.

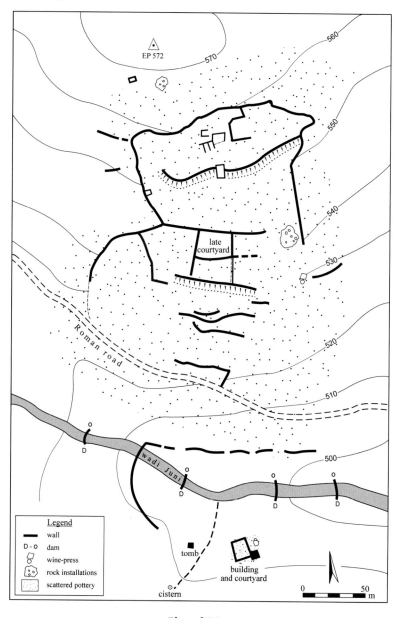

43. Plan of E.P. 572.

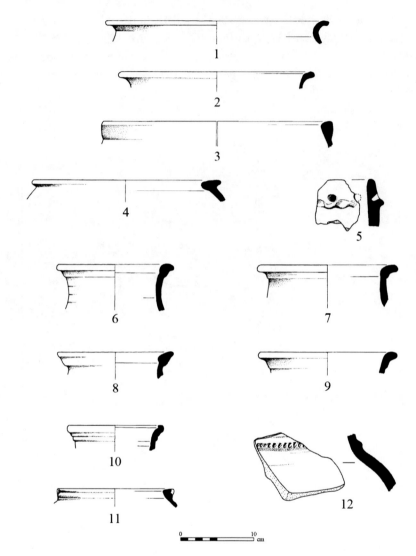

44. Pottery from **E.P. 572** (all MBA II except item no.11): 1-2. Krater, pink; 3. Krater (?), lt brn; 4. Krater, lt gr; 5. CP, lt brn, rope-orn; 6, 9. Jars, lt brn; 7, 10. Jars, pink; 8. Jar, gr; 11. CP, pink, Byz-EM; 12. Sherd, lt brn, rope-orn.

Site 11: 18-17/86/1
SHEIKH KAMEL

Israel grid: 18837/17675
UTM grid: 7267/5635
Elevation: 605 m a.s.l., 300 m a.s.a.
Name: ancient and on map
Site type: Sheikh's tomb, cemetery and installations
Area: 2000 sq. m (2 dunams)
Topography: spur
Rock: Judea Group

Soil: terra rossa, quality: 4
Cultivation: none
Cisterns: 1
Water source: 'Ein Sha'eb el-Bir (no. 187), 1.5 km distant
Road: Phasaelis-Neapolis (C40), near the site
Visit: June 1996; July 2015, 4 surveyors; 150 sherds

Site on a spur and shoulder on the ridge of Jebel Kabir, close to and east of the paved road from Mekhora to Elon Moreh, 3 km east-south-east of the village of Beit Dajan. There is a good lookout over the area of Mekhora and to the north of the Sartaba.

Deteriorating rectangular structure, 9×6 m. The entrance is in the north and has worked pilasters. The construction is of worked stones, nearly 1 m thick, and plastered inside. The western wall survives to a height of nearly 2 m. Only one or two courses of the eastern and southern walls survive.

Nearby are simple graves rock-cut in the limestone (not on plan). The entire cemetery has been plundered.

North of the ruined structure is a modern square structure, 6×6 m, with 1 m wide walls, with entrance in the northern wall.

A cistern is located about 100 m east of the modern structure.

Rock-cut installations in the rock surface about 40 m south of the modern structure.

The ruined structure should be identified as Sheik Kamel's tomb. It is not clear who destroyed it and when.

The site appears in the British Survey map (sheet XII, Sheikh Kamil) without description, but with the inscription: "Shejeret esh Sheikh Kamil" (the tree of Sheikh Kamil) (Palmer 1881: 207).

Pottery: Late Roman-Byzantine – 90%; Medieval (body sherds) – 5%; Ottoman – 5%.
Other surveys: none.

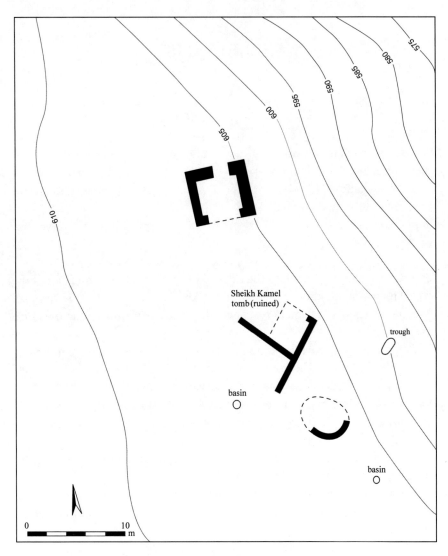

45. Plan of **Sheikh Kamel**.

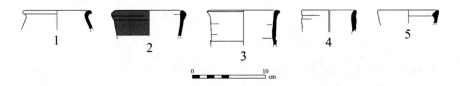

46. Pottery from **Sheikh Kamel** (all except no. 4 are LR-Byz): 1. Bowl, drk brn; 2. Jar, drk brn, blk slip; 3. Jar, lt brn; 4. Jar (?), lt colour, Ott (?); 5. Jug (?), blk.

Site 12: 18-17/86/2
WADI JUNI

Israel grid: 18850/17600
UTM grid: 7269/5628
Elevation: 530 m a.s.l., 40 m a.s.a.
Name: nearest place
Site type: farm
Area: 1000 sq. m (1 dunam)
Topography: moderate slope
Rock: Judea Group

Soil: terra rossa, quality: 4
Cultivation: none
Cisterns: none
Water source: 'Ein Sha'eb el-Bir (no. 187), 1.3 km distant
Road: Phasaelis-Neapolis (C40), near the site
Visit: April 1995; 4 surveyors; 61 sherds

Site on the Zuhur esh-Shafa ridge, west and nearby the Mekhora-Beit Dajan road, 500 m north-north-west of E.P. 557 and 2 km north-west of Mekhora.
Farm comprising:
- Small structure, about 5×5 m, built of very large stones. The inner plan is not clear because of collapses. The structure was apparently used for dwelling (no. 1 in plan).
- Large courtyard, 13×10 m, built of large stones. In the north-east side is a large stone pillar, possibly the place of the entrance (no. 2).
- Small courtyard, nearly 8×8 m, adjacent in the west to the large courtyard. The surrounding wall is built of two rows of large stones, and preserved to a height of two courses (no. 3).

Sherds, not in abundance, were collected all around the farm.

The site was probably used for temporary dwelling and storage of crops.

This site is possibly the ruin named Merah Arrar, mentioned in the British Survey (sheet XII) located east of 'Ein Sha'eb el-Bir and west of 'Aqabet el-Butmeh. No additional documentation is available about the site.

Pottery: Late Roman-Byzantine – 70%; Medieval (body sherds) – 5%; Modern – 25%.
Other surveys: none.

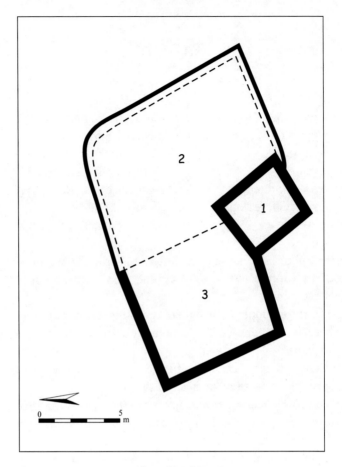

47. Plan of **Wadi Juni**.

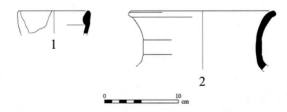

48. Pottery from **Wadi Juni**: 1. Jug, lt brn, Mod; 2. Jar, gr, Mod (?).

Site 13: 18-17/86/3
ELEVATION POINT 557

Israel grid: 18872/17606
UTM grid: 7271/5628
Elevation: 550 m a.s.l., 120 m a.s.a.
Name: nearest place
Site type: farm and road
Area: 500 sq. m (0.5 dunam)
Topography: saddle
Rock: Judea Group

Soil: terra rossa, quality: 6
Cultivation: none
Cisterns: none
Water source: 'Ein Sha'eb el-Bir (no. 187), 1.5 km distant
Road: Phasaelis-Neapolis (C40), near the site
Visit: July 2015; 5 surveyors; 10 sherds

Site on a saddle, 500 m north of E.P. 557 and 2 km north-west of Mekhora.

Farmhouse (?), 8×8 m, well-built of large stones, some showing chisel marks. The walls are double and 1.3 m thick. An entrance has been identified in the eastern wall.

Large quarried basin, 2 m in diameter, and several cup marks, near the structure.

An ancient road, 5 m wide, from the ridge in the west, ends at the site. This is apparently a secondary branch of the Phasaelis-Shechem (C40) road. Remains of at least 400 m of road are visible.

Very scanty ceramic find.

It seems that the site was founded in the Roman period, and was part of the large city in the Kh. Tana et-Tahta agricultural hinterland.

Pottery (body sherds): Late Roman – 80%; Medieval – 20%.
Other surveys: none.

Site 14: 18-17/96/1
WADI UMM EZ-ZRUB (2)

Israel grid: 18904/17695
UTM grid: 7274/5637
Elevation: 370 m a.s.l., 150 m a.s.a.
Name: nearest place
Site type: sherd scatter and enclosure
Area: 4000 sq. m (4 dunams)
Topography: spur
Rock: Judea Group
Soil: terra rossa, quality: 3

Cultivation: none
Cisterns: none
Water source: 'Ein Sha'eb el-Bir (no. 187), 2 km distant
Road: Nahal Tirzah-Neapolis (C51), 300 m distant
Visit: November 2013; 3 surveyors; 100 sherds

Site on a spur south of Wadi ez-Zrub, 2.7 km south-west of Hamrah centre.

In the centre of the spur is a large rounded support wall which forms a levelled platform of over 2000 sq. m free of rocks. There is also a large sherd scatter, mostly Medieval, collected from the levelled surface. No building stones were visible; perhaps tents were used.

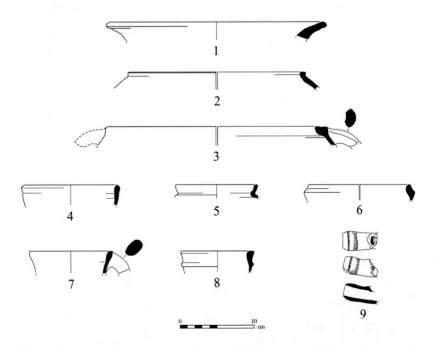

49. Pottery from **Wadi Umm ez-Zrub (2)**: 1. Krater/Jar, lt brn, Med; 2. Krater, lt brn, LR-Byz; 3. Krater, drk brn, Byz; 4. Bowl, drk brn, LR-Byz; 5. CP, lt brn, LR-Byz; 6. CP, drk brn, IA II; 7. Jug, lt brn, IA II; 8. Jug, reddish, LR-Byz; 9. Pipe, lt brn, Ott.

Enclosure, 10 m in diameter, built of small stones is located over the slope of the spur.

Further north along the spur are pottery concentrations, mainly from the Late Roman period.

Pottery: Iron II – 5%; Late Roman – 50%; Byzantine – 15%; Medieval – 25%; Ottoman – 5%.
Other surveys: none.

Site 15: 18-17/96/2

ELEVATION POINT 271 (WEST)

Israel grid: 18908/17667
UTM grid: 7274/5634
Elevation: 355 m a.s.l., 300 m a.s.a.
Name: nearest place
Site type: sherd scatter, road and enclosure
Area: 1000 sq. m (1 dunam)
Topography: spur
Rock: Judea Group
Soil: terra rossa, quality: 5

Cultivation: none
Cisterns: none
Water source: 'Ein Sha'eb el-Bir (no. 187), 2 km distant
Road: Nahal Tirza-Neapolis (C51), at the site
Visit: November 2013; 3 surveyors; 35 sherds in the scatter, 4 sherds in the structure

Site 500 m west of E.P. 271, 2.3 km north-north-west of Mekhora.
The three parts of the site are:
– Remains of a road (C51) 3-4 m wide, ascending from Wadi Far'ah Valley via E.P. 271 to the site, turning away from it south-easterly and vanishing. From the road set out walls, built of large boulders, apparently erected to mark agricultural plots.
– Sherd scatter on a spur above the road at the coordinates under which this site has been recorded.
– Rectangular enclosure or structure with one side rounded, 100 m down the spur, by the turn of the ancient road. The perimeter wall is built of one row of large and medium-sized stones. It is 16 m long, and one course high. In the corners of the structure are large monoliths.

Pottery: in the sherd scatter: Late Roman – 43%; Byzantine – 43%; unidentified – 14%. In the structure: Late Roman – 50%; Medieval (Mamluk) – 50%.
Other surveys: none.

Site 16: 18-17/96/3
BIR 'ABD EL-RAHMAN (1)

Israel grid: 18956/17609
UTM grid: 7279/5629
Elevation: 355 m a.s.l., 50 m b.s.a.
Name: ancient but not on map
Site type: farm and cistern
Area: 5000 sq. m (5 dunams)
Topography: mountainous plateau
Rock: Judea Group
Soil: terra rossa, quality: 6

Cultivation: none
Cisterns: 1
Water source: 'Ein Sha'eb el-Bir (no. 187), 2.2 km distant
Road: Nahal Tirzah-Neapolis (C51), 700 m distant
Visit: May 1995; November 2005; 4 surveyors; 125 sherds

Medium-sized site on the plateau of 'Aqabet el-Butmeh, near Bedouin tent encampments, 1.2 km north-west of Mekhora. An unpaved road from Mekhora passes nearby west of the site.

Well-built farmhouse 18×15 m. The surrounding wall is 1 m thick, built of a one row of large stones; next to it a row of smaller stones.

Wall of large stones, nearly 1.5 m thick, partially surviving about 50 m west

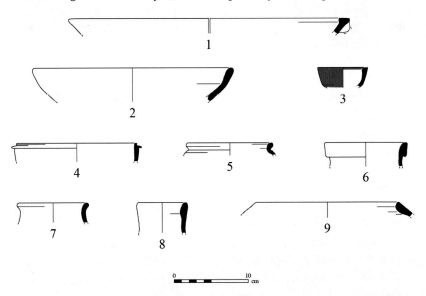

50. Pottery from **Bir 'Abd el-Rahman (1)**: 1-2. Bowls, lt brn, Med; 3. Bowl, lt brn, LR-Byz, dark slip on the rim inside; 4. Bowl, lt brn, LR-Byz; 5. CP, drk brn, LR-Byz; 6. Jar, lt brn, LR-Byz; 7. Jar, reddish, LR-Byz; 8. Jar, drk brn, LR-Byz; 9. Holemouth jar, lt brn, Med.

of the structure. Its relation to the farmhouse is not clear.

Courtyard containing a large bell-shaped rock-hewn cistern at the centre of the site. The diameter of the cistern opening is 70 cm. At the west and east of the courtyard are two 5 m-wide longitudinal rooms.

A small settlement, probably a farm linked to the cistern.

Pottery: Iron II (body sherds) – 10%; Persian (body sherds) – 5%; Late Roman – 40%; Byzantine – 25%; Medieval – 20%.
Other surveys: none.

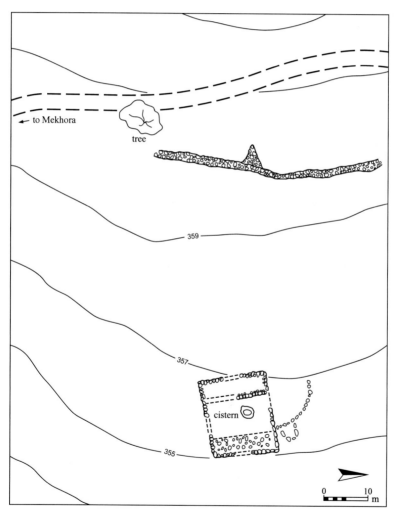

51. Plan of **Bir 'Abd el-Rahman (1)**.

Site 17: 19-17/06/1
'IRAQ LABADEH

Israel grid: 19028/17661
UTM grid: 7286/5634
Elevation: 140 m a.s.l., 150 m a.s.a.
 Name: nearest place
Site type: encampment, structure and installations
Area: 3000 sq. m (3 dunams)
Topography: edge of a spur
Rock: Judea Group

Soil: terra rossa, quality: 6
Cultivation: none
Cisterns: none
Water source: Nahal Tirzah (no. 104), 2.8 km distant
Road: Nahal Tirzah-Neapolis (C51), 400 m distant
Visit: May 1995; 4 surveyors; 20 sherds

Encampment site at the edge of a flat spur in the northern part of 'Aqabet el-Butmeh shoulder, 1.6 km north of Mekhora. From the site there is a good view of the eastern part of Nahal Tirzah.

Partially ruined structure, 3×4 m in the northern part of the site. 30-50 m from the structure are installations, mostly basins, hewn in the rocks.

At the edge of the spur is a sherd scatter.

Pottery (body sherds): Iron I – 15%; Iron II – 10%; Early Roman – 40%; Late Roman – 25%; Medieval – 10%.
Flint: 9 items: 3 flakes, 4 blades, 1 retouched blade and a scraper.
Other surveys: none.

Site 18: 18-17/75/1
WADI SHA'EB EL-BIR

Israel grid: 18740/17529
UTM grid: 7258/5620
Elevation: 435 m a.s.l., 80 m a.s.a.
Name: nearest place
Site type: sherd scatter
Area: 1000 sq. m (1 dunam)
Topography: spur
Rock: Judea Group
Soil: terra rossa, quality: 7

Cultivation: olives
Cisterns: none
Water source: 'Ein Sha'eb el-Bir
   (no. 187), 800 m distant
Road: Tana-Neapolis (C56), 600 m
   distant
Visit: June 2015; 7 surveyors;
   100 sherds

Large sherd scatter on a spur with view to the west towards the confluence of Wadi Qard, Wadi Juni and Wadi Sha'eb el-Bir, 2.5 km east of Mekhora and 1.5 km north of Tana et-Tahta.

Site completely ruined by extensive land preparation operations.

Pottery: Iron II (body sherds) – 10%; Persian (body sherds) – 3%; Late Roman – 57%; Byzantine (body sherds) – 10%; Medieval – 20%.
Other surveys: none.

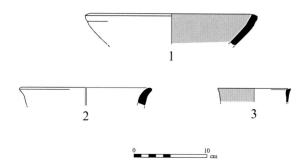

52. Pottery from **Wadi Sha'eb el-Bir:** 1. Bowl, lt brn, Med; 2. Jar (?), lt colour, Med; 3. Jug, lt colour, LR.

Site 19: 18-17/95/1
M'RAH ABU SUHEIL

Israel grid: 18982/17564
UTM grid: 7282/5624
Elevation: 300 m a.s.l., 0 m a.s.a.
Name: ancient but not in map
Site type: courtyard, threshing floor, caves and cistern
Area: 3000 sq. m (3 dunams)
Topography: mountainous plateau
Rock: Judea Group

Soil: terra rossa, quality: 4
Cultivation: none
Cisterns: 1
Water source: 'Ein el-Foqa (no. 173), 2.4 km distant
Road: Phasaelis-Neapolis (C40), 1.1 km distant
Visit: May 1995; 5 surveyors; 52 sherds

Site on the plateau of 'Aqabet el-Butmeh, 1 km north of Mekhora, below a large rocky shoulder.

Large square courtyard, 30×30 m, with wall 1.3 m thick, built from large stones. In the western side are two long narrow rooms, both 15×2 m. Other small rooms project from the corners of the western wall. The entrance to the courtyard has not been traced. No installations or other prominent finds were found.

Two caves with collapsed ceilings are on the northern and the southern sides of the courtyard, about 15 m distant from it.

A large threshing floor, nearly 16 m in diameter is about 45 m west of the courtyard. Next to the threshing floor is a quarried cistern.

Presumably a farm was established here in IA II, and in the Roman period the courtyard was built over it. Possibly part of the stones of the wall originate in the IA.

Pottery: IA II – 42%; Late Roman – 58%.
Other surveys: none.

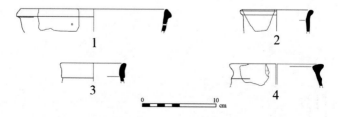

53. Pottery from **M'rah Abu Suheil**: 1. Bowl, lt brn, IA II; 2. Bowl, lt brn, LR; 3. Jar, lt brn, LR; 4. Jar, lt brn, IA II.

LANDSCAPE UNIT 34

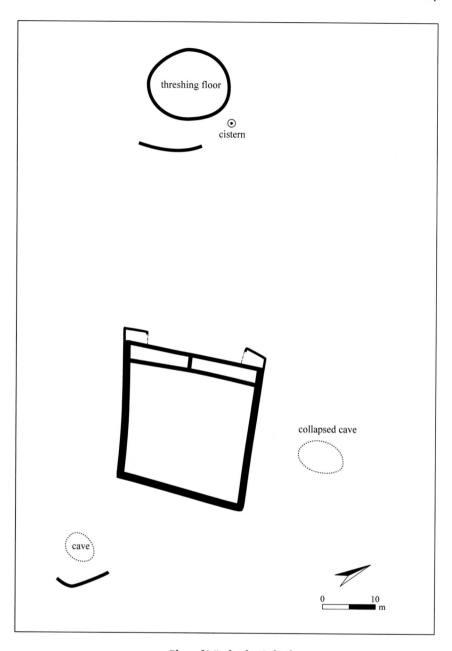

54. Plan of **M'rah Abu Suheil**.

Site 20: 18-17/95/2
BIR ʿABD EL-RAHMAN (2)

Israel grid: 18953/17593
UTM grid: 7279/5627
Elevation: 350 m a.s.l., 0 m a.s.a.
Name: nearest place
Site type: enclosures and installations
Area: 2000 sq. m (2 dunams)
Topography: a low hillock in edge of a valley
Rock: Judea Group
Soil: terra rossa, quality: 6
Cultivation: field crops by the site
Cisterns: none
Water source: ʿEin Shaʾeb el-Bir (no. 187), 2.4 km distant
Road: Phasaelis-Neapolis (C40), 600 m distant
Visit: November 2013; 4 surveyors; 70 sherds

Site on the plateau of ʿAqabet el-Butmeh, 1.2 km north-north-west of Mekhora. Remains of two enclosures and other structures:
- Southern enclosure open to the north, 15 m in diameter. Parts of its walls are reuse of sections of walls of ancient structures. In the south-western part are remains of a structure. A built cell projects out of the eastern side (no. 1 in plan). The date of this enclosure is uncertain.
- Northern enclosure open to the north, 30×20 m. The walls are irregular, apparently because they are built over ancient walls (no. 2).

South of enclosure no. 2 is a built *maqʿad* (Arabic: 'sitting place') with a concentration of building stones around it.

South of the enclosures are two rock-cut basins, 20-30 cm in diameter.

An abundant ceramic find and a number of threshing sledge basalt stones were collected.

The location of the site, 100 m south of Bir ʿAbd el-Rahman (1) farm (Site 16), hints that it probably served as a threshing floor and a place for processing cereals for the former site during the shared periods of occupation: IA II, Roman, Byzantine and Medieval periods.

Pottery: Iron I-II (body sherds) – 13%; Hellenistic (body sherds) – 7%; Early Roman – 7%; Late Roman – 43%; Byzantine – 15%; Medieval (Mamluk) (body sherds) – 15%.
Other finds: numerous threshing sledge stones.
Other surveys: none.

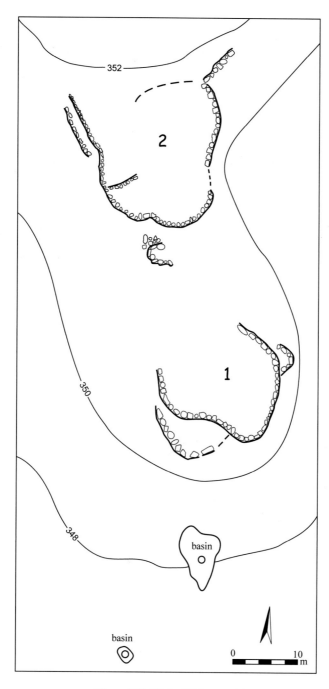

55. Plan of **Bir 'Abd el-Rahman (2)**.

56. Aerial view north-west of **Bir 'Abd el-Rahman (2)** (A. Solomon).

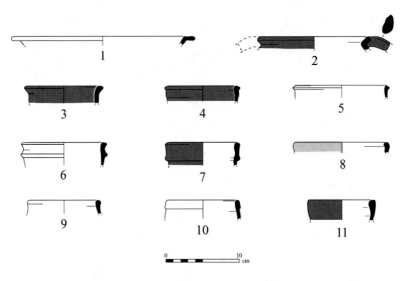

57. Pottery from **Bir 'Abd el-Rahman (2)**: 1. Bowl, red, Rom; 2. CP, drk brn, blk slip, Byz; 3. Jar, drk brn, drk brn slip, LR-Byz; 4. Jug, drk brn, drk brn slip, LR-Byz; 5. Jug, drk brn, LR-Byz; 6. Jug/jar, drk brn, LR-Byz; 7. Jar (?), drk brn, brn slip, Byz (?); 8. Jug (?), red slip, LR-Byz; 9-10. Jugs, lt brn, LR-Byz; 11. Jug, blk, blk slip, Byz (?).

Site 21: 18-17/95/3
'AQABET EL-BUTMEH (2)

Israel grid: 18955/17556
UTM grid: 7279/5623
Elevation: 320 m a.s.l., 50 m b.s.a.
Name: nearest place
Site type: enclosures and flint scatter
Area: 100 sq. m (0.1 dunam)
Topography: slope
Rock: Judea Group
Soil: terra rossa, quality: 8

Cultivation: none
Cisterns: none
Water source: 'Ein el-Foqa (no. 173), 2.1 km distant
Road: Phasaelis-Neapolis (C40), 900 m distant
Visit: November 2013; 3 surveyors; 146 sherds

Site over a moderate slope at the edge of a valley, 1 km north-west of Mekhora centre.

Site is a rectangular enclosure, 11×8 m, with rounded corners, built of medium to large stones. The inside of the enclosure is empty of remains. In the western part the bedrock is visible.

The site has abundant Roman and Byzantine pottery. South of the enclosure is a moderate flint scatter.

Pottery: Roman-Byzantine – 100%.
Flint: 16 items: one bladelet core, 12 flakes, 2 blades, and a borer.
Stone: 7 threshing sledge basalt stones.
Other surveys: none.

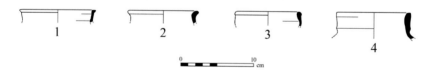

58. Pottery from 'Aqabet el-Butmeh (2) (all Rom-Byz): 1. Bowl (?), greyish; 2-3. Bowls, lt brn; 4. Jar, lt brn.

Site 22: 18-17/95/4
'AQABET EL-BUTMEH (1)

Israel grid: 18946/17546
UTM grid: 7278/5622
Elevation: 310 m a.s.l., 100 m b.s.a.
Name: nearest place
Site type: courtyard and cave
Area: 500 sq. m (0.5 dunam)
Topography: edge of valley
Rock: Judea Group
Soil: terra rossa, quality: 8

Cultivation: none
Cisterns: none
Water source: 'Ein el-Foqa (no. 173), 2 km distant
Road: Phasaelis-Neapolis (C40), 900 m distant
Visit: November 2013; 3 surveyors; 70 sherds

Site 1 km north-west of Mekhora centre, at the edge of a valley, on the unpaved road branching from road 508 to north-west.

Natural cave with two openings: east and west. Presently the cave is blocked by fallen rocks and impossible to learn its size and layout.

In the east is a 25×18 m courtyard, built of large stones, adjacent to the cave. The surrounding wall is partially built of two stone rows. In the north-eastern end of the courtyard the wall survived to a height of up to two courses. The western end of the north wall is attached to the eastern opening of the cave, and the southern wall is built south of that wall, adjacent to the route of the cliff.

The courtyard has been damaged in recent years by an unpaved road crossing it.

Beside the road, south of the courtyard, is a 50 m-long wall, built of medium-sized and large stones, perhaps remains of an ancient road.

The dating to the Roman-Byzantine periods is possible, but is only based on a large quantity of body sherds.

Pottery: Roman-Byzantine (body sherds) – 93%; Medieval – 7%.
Other surveys: none.

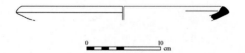

59. A sherd from **'Aqbet el-Butmeh (1)**: Bowl, lt brn, Med (?).

Site 23: 18-17/64/1
ELEVATION POINT 422

Israel grid: 18644/17496
UTM grid: 7248/5617
Elevation: 420 m a.s.l., 0 m a.s.a.
Name: nearest place
Site type: sherd scatter, structures and installations
Area: 2000 sq. m (2 dunams)
Topography: small valley
Rock: Judea Group
Soil: terra rossa, quality: 4
Cultivation: plantations
Cisterns: none
Water source: 'Ein Mta'a (no. 188), 300 m distant
Road: Tana et-Tahta-Neapolis (C57), 500 m distant
Visit: February 2000; 4 surveyors; 64 sherds

Site on the ridge of el-Ghashur in a small valley surrounded by low cliffs 3.5 km west of Mekhora and 5 km east of Beit Furiq. From the site is a steep descent to Wadi Qard. There is a flat saddle south of the site. The site was ruined during preparation of the area for planting an olive grove.

There are a few remains of structures and a massive wall. In the walls of the structures are embedded ashlar stones with drafted margins, identified as threshold stones.

Several cup marks and a mausoleum in the east side of the site.

A medium number of sherds were collected, mainly in the olive grove in the saddle in the south.

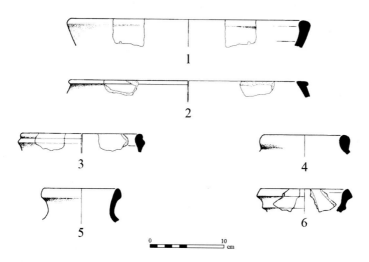

60. Pottery from E.P. 422: 1. Bowl, drk brn, IA II; 2. Krater, drk brn, IA II; 3. CP, drk brn, IA II; 4-5. Jars, lt brn, Pers; 6. Jar, drk brn, IA II.

Pottery: IA II – 28%; Persian – 37%; Late Roman-Byzantine (body sherds) – 35%.
Flint: 19 items: 1 flake core, 9 flakes, 6 blades, 1 burin, 1 retouched flake and 1 retouched blade.
Other surveys: none.

Site 24: 18-17/74/1
'EIN MTA'A

Israel grid: 18711/17480
UTM grid: 7255/5615
Elevation: 410 m a.s.l., 80 m a.s.a.
Name: nearest place
Site type: large settlement
Area: 5 ha (50 dunams)
Topography: moderate slope
Rock: Judea Group
Soil: terra rossa, quality: 5

Cultivation: none
Cisterns: 1
Water source: 'Ein Mta'a (no. 188), 500 m distant
Road: Tana -Neapolis (C56; C57), 800 m distant
Visit: December 1999; 4 surveyors; 230 sherds

Site over a moderate slope which descends to the escarpment of Wadi Qard, in the eastern part of the ridge of el-Ghashur, in the spurs area of Wadi Qard, in the triangle Beit Dajan, Beit Furiq and Khirbet Tana et-Tahta. South of the site and nearby is a large valley surrounded by a low cliff.

There are remains of a large EBA settlement in the area; part of which spread over two terraces below the cliff.

Terrace walls divide the settlement into areas. The walls may have been erected on top of earlier walls. A long wall dividing the settlement from north to south was apparently the eastern enclosure wall.

In the southern part of the site, next to the cliff, are two large stone heaps, 10-20 m in diameter, about 6 m high. The heaps (plus others) may conceal structures. North of the heaps were identified numerous remains of walls. The settlement was apparently densely built.

Rock-cut installations and plastered cistern were also found.

According to evidence of the local inhabitants a spring named 'Ein Mta'a once flowed 500 m west of the site. Until about 50 years ago, water was still drawn from it, but nowadays it is dry. Apparently the settlement depended on two springs: this one and 'Ein Sha'eb el-Bir.

Many sherds were found, mostly in the area between the southern wall and the cliffs further south. Much EBA Ib 'Um Hammad Ware' pottery type was found (Bar 2010).

The bulk of the pottery is from the EBA I, and continuation to EBA II is evident. Apparently, in the EBA I the settlement was the important one in the region; and at the transition to EBA II it lost its importance, possibly because it was not protected by a wall, unlike other period sites in the region, such as Kh. Juraish (Site 64) for example.

The site has been partially ruined by land preparation for modern agriculture.

Pottery: Early Bronze I – 87%; Early Bronze II – 7%; Intermediate Bronze – 1%; Byzantine – 5%.
Flint: 98 items: 2 flake cores, 1 blade core, 2 bladelet cores, 4 core wastes, 34 flakes, 16 blades, 2 retouched flakes, 5 retouched blades, 4 Canaanean blades, 2 Canaanean retouched blades, 5 Canaanean sickle blades, 17 scrapers, 3 borers and a burin. The Canaanean blades are indicative of the EBA.
Stone: 3 basalt bowls, a basalt chalice base and a basalt pierced handle. Also 20 fragments of basalt and limestone grinding tools.
Other surveys: none.
Additional bibliography: Bar 2014, site 54.

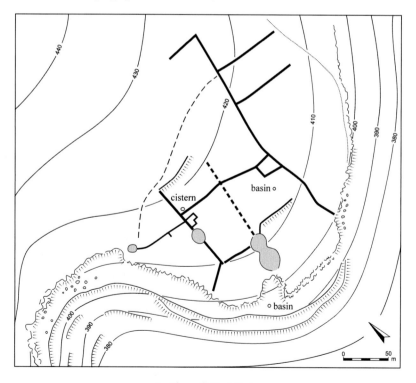

61. Plan of 'Ein Mta'a.

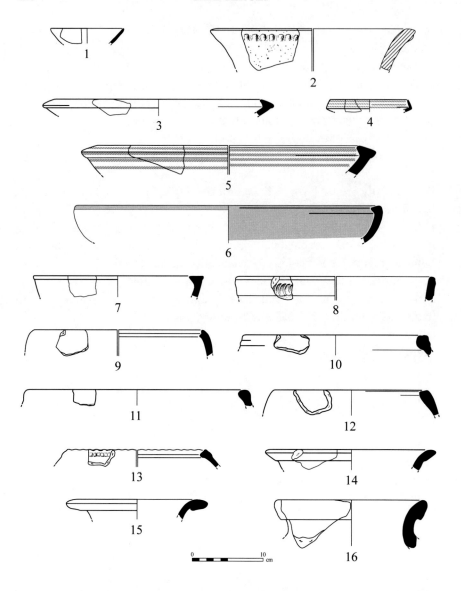

62. Finds from **'Ein Mta'a**, part 1 (all EBA I-II): 1. Bowl drk brn; 2. Basalt bowl, protruding orn below the rim; 3. Platter, lt brn; 4. Platter, lt brn, lt brn burnish inside and outside; 5. Large bowl, drk brn, red burnish inside and out; 6. Bowl, brn, red burnish inside and out over the rim; 7. Bowl, drk gr; 8. Bowl (?), drk brn, thumbed dec outside; 9. Holemouth jar, drk brn; 10-12. Holemouth jars, lt brn; 13. Jar, drk brn, protruding dec over wavy rim; 14. Jar, drk gr; 15-16. Jars, drk brn.

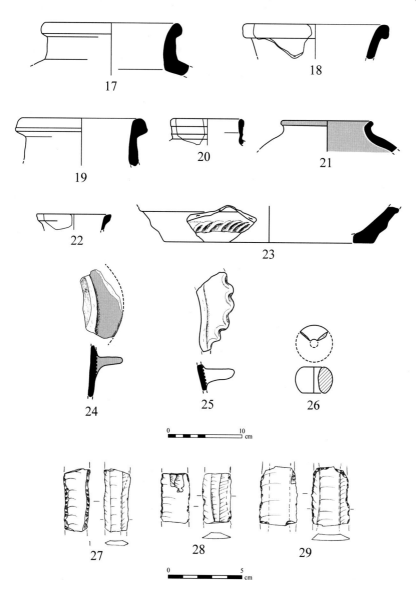

63. Finds from **'Ein Mta'a**, part 2: 17-19. Jars, drk brn, EBA I-II; 20. Jar, lt brn, Byz; 21. Jar, brn, red paint inside and out over rim, EBA I; 22. Jug, drk gr, Byz; 23. Flat base, rope dec, EBA I; 24. Ledge handle, brn, red paint, EBA; 25. Ledge handle, brn, EBA; 26. Basalt mace head, EBA; 27-29. Retouched sickle blades, EBA I-II.

Site 25: 18-17/74/2
ELEVATION POINT 395 (2)

Israel grid: 18796/17442
UTM grid: 7263/5611
Elevation: 388 m a.s.l., 30 m a.s.a.
Name: nearest place
Site type: enclosure
Area: 100 sq. m (0.1 dunam)
Topography: slope
Rock: Avdat Group

Soil: rendzina, quality: 5
Cultivation: none
Cisterns: none
Water source: 'Ein et-Tahta (no. 186), 700 m distant
Road: Tana -Neapolis (C56), by the site
Visit: June 2015; 3 surveyors; 40 sherds

Site on a moderate slope in a small valley descending south to El-'Ein et-Tahta, 1.2 km north-east of Kh. Tana et-Tahta and 2 km west of Mekhora.

A circular enclosure, 15 m in diameter with surrounding wall built of one row of medium-sized and large boulders. In the northern part the rock is exposed.

There are numerous terraces nearby the enclosure.

Apparently, the site is linked to the agricultural hinterland of the large city at Kh. Tana et-Tahta.

Pottery (body sherds): IA II – 25%; Late Roman – 25%; Byzantine – 50%.
Other surveys: none.

Site 26: 18-17/74/3
ELEVATION POINT 395 (7)

Israel grid: 18732/17421
UTM grid: 7258/5610
Elevation: 385 m a.s.l., 80 m a.s.a.
Name: nearest place
Site type: sherd scatter and structure
Area: 1500 sq. m (1.5 dunams)
Topography: shoulder
Rock: Avdat Group
Soil: terra rossa, quality: 7

Cultivation: none
Cisterns: none
Water source: 'Ein et-Tahta (no. 186),
 800 m distant
Road: Tana -Neapolis (C56),
 300 m distant
Visit: June 2015; 3 surveyors;
 165 sherds

Small site on a shoulder in the north-western slope of E.P. 395, south and above Wadi Qard, 2.5 km west of Mekhora.

There is a 3×3 m structure, built of very large boulders, for stockpiling agricultural produce.

North of the structure, in a small field, over the slope descending towards Wadi Qard, is an ample sherd scatter.

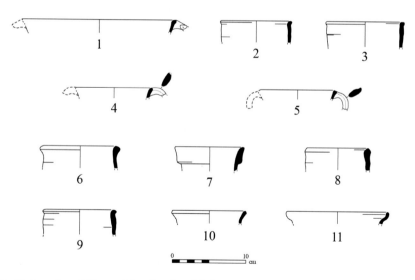

64. Pottery from E.P. 395 (7): 1. Bowl, reddish, Rom; 2. Bowl, lt colour, Rom; 3. Bowl (?), reddish, Rom; 4. CP (?), drk brn, Rom; 5. CP (?), reddish, Rom; 6. Jar, lt brn, Rom-Byz; 7. Jar, lt colour, Rom; 8. Jar, lt colour, Rom-Byz; 9. Jar, drk brn, Rom Byz; 10-11. Jugs, reddish, Rom.

The site is probably part of the agricultural hinterland of the Roman-Byzantine city at Kh. Tana et-Tahta, and belongs to a group of agricultural period sites on the ridge of E.P. 395.

Pottery: Iron II (body sherds) – 3%; Early Roman – 61%; Late Roman – 30%; Byzantine – 6%.
Other surveys: none.

Site 27: 18-17/74/4
ELEVATION POINT 395 (1)

Israel grid: 18759/17414
UTM grid: 7260/5611
Elevation: 390 m a.s.l., 100 m a.s.a.
Name: nearest place
Site type: caves, terraces and road
Area: 1 ha (10 dunams)
Topography: slope
Rock: Avdat Group

Soil: terra rossa, quality: 6
Cultivation: none
Cisterns: none
Water source: 'Ein et-Tahta (no. 186), 600 m distant
Road: Tana -Neapolis (C56), by the site
Visit: June 2015; 3 surveyors; 50 sherds

Site on a steep slope next to the hillock of E.P. 395, 1 km north of Kh. Tana et-Tahta and 2.3 km west of Mekhora.

Along the cliff line, which is more than 300 m long, are numerous caves, small alcoves and rock shelters, settled presently by shepherds and local inhabitants.

The caves share similar characteristics: many charred soot stains on the ceilings and walls, evidence of human usage for many years; quarried shelves and small cells and levelling of the rock surfaces, fitting the caves for human use and dwelling.

Nowadays the caves are used for the same purposes: livestock husbandry and residence.

The find in the caves is rather uniform and contains:
1. Pottery, mostly Byzantine, the beginning of the intensive use of the caves, which were apparently a component of the agricultural hinterland of the nearby city at Kh. Tana et-Tahta.
2. Medieval ceramic evidence of continuation of the usage of the caves also during the decline of the city of Kh. Tana et-Tahta.

3. Modern ceramics, evidence of intensive activity of local shepherds in the caves, also taking place at present.

Description of the caves:

	Waypoint	Entrance width (m)	Depth (m)	Maximum height (m)	Remarks
A	18770/17431	18	6	3.5	Constructed wall remains outside the cave
B	18766/17425	7, 5	4, 3	2.5, 2	Two attached caves. Modern yard in between. The height of the surrounding wall is 3 m
C	18762/17420	15, 5	8, 3	2.5, 2	Two nearby caves. A round modern enclosure attached to the bigger cave. The height of the surrounding wall is 2.5 m
D	18758/17412	12	-	-	There is a new concrete construction in the cave, preventing investigation inside. Outside is a modern coral. No finds
E	18755/17403	20	8	3	A cave with collapsed ceiling. Walls remains at the entrance and outside. In the south more blocked openings with modern concrete
F	18756/17397	-	-	-	A cave with collapsed ceiling. Modern construction preventing investigation inside
G	18749/17394	7, 9	4, 6	2.5, 2	Two nearby caves. Rock hewing remains

Remains of a branch of the Tana-Neapolis road (C56) were found below the caves not far from their entrances, passing over the slope, mostly north of the site in the ascent towards E.P. 475.

There is a concentration of numerous terraces over the slope, evidence of intensive agricultural activity.

Pottery: Iron II (body sherds) – 10%; Byzantine – 60%; Medieval (body sherds) – 10%; Modern – 20%.
Other surveys: none.

Site 28: 18-17/74/5
ELEVATION POINT 395 (6)

Israel grid: 18740/17403
UTM grid: 7258/5608
Elevation: 385 m a.s.l., 0 m a.s.a.
Name: nearest place
Site type: sherd scatter
Area: 1 ha (10 dunams)
Topography: spur
Rock: Avdat Group
Soil: terra rossa, quality: 6

Cultivation: none
Cisterns: none
Water source: 'Ein et-Tahta (no. 186), 400 m distant
Road: Tana -Neapolis (C56), 100 m distant
Visit: June 2015; 3 surveyors; 140 sherds

Site on a moderate spur of E.P. 395, 500 m north of the northern hill of Kh. Tana et-Tahta and 2.5 km west-south-west of Mekhora.

Abundant sherd scatter over expanded area of rocky surfaces and pockets of soil in the small flat inner valley in the site. A few wall remains also found, not showing a plan.

The site was probably used for erecting tents or other temporary constructions, mainly during the Byzantine period, and was linked to the nearby city at Kh. Tana et-Tahta.

Pottery: Intermediate Bronze (body sherds) – 11%; Middle Bronze II (body sherds) – 3%; Iron I – 7%; Iron II – 3%; Early Roman – 11%; Late Roman – 22%; Byzantine – 29%; Medieval – 14%.
Other surveys: none.

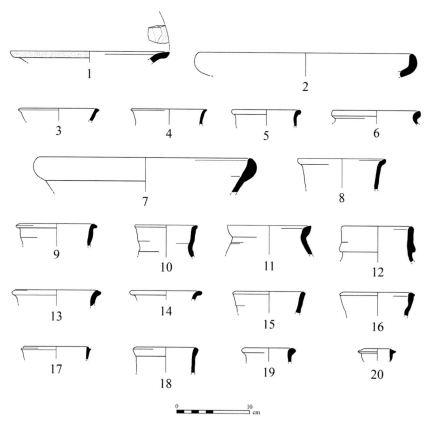

65. Pottery from **E.P. 395 (6)**: 1. Bowl, lt brn, yel glaze, Med; 2. Bowl, drk brn, IA I; 3. Bowl, lt brn, LR; 4. Bowl (?), lt brn, LR; 5. Bowl, lt brn, LR-Byz; 6. CP (?), lt brn, LR; 7. Pithos (?), lt brn, IA I-II; 8. Jar, lt brn, Rom; 9-10. Jars, lt brn, LR; 11-12. Jars, lt brn, LR-Byz; 13. Jug (?), lt brn, Rom; 14-15, 20. Jugs, lt brn, Rom-Byz; 16. Jug, lt brn, LR; 17, 19. Jugs, lt brn, Rom; 18. Jug, drk brn, LR-Byz.

Site 29: 18-17/84/1
ELEVATION POINT 475

Israel grid: 18810/17476
UTM grid: 7265/5615
Elevation: 475 m a.s.l., 30 m b.s.a
Site type: structure, courtyard, threshing floor and installations
Area: 500 sq. m (0.5 dunam)
Topography: edge of spur by valley margins
Rock: Judea Group

Soil: terra rossa, quality: 6
Cultivation: none
Cisterns: none
Water source: 'Ein el-Foqa (no. 173), 1 km distant
Road: Tana -Neapolis (C56), 300 m distant
Visit: April 1995; 5 surveyors; 60 sherds

Site at the western edge of an inner valley, over the spur descending southwesterly towards Kh. Tana et-Tahta.

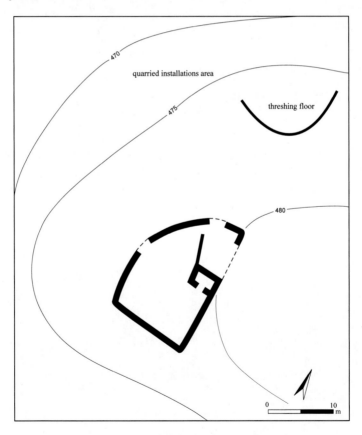

66. Plan of **E.P. 475**.

Rectangular structure, 7×5 m, built of a double row of partially worked fieldstones. The wall thickness is 1.5 m. An entrance was identified in the southern wall, in which there is threshold stone with a door locking recess.

Courtyard, 15×10 m and rounded on the north-eastern side, abuts the south-eastern corner of the structure. The entrance is in the east. In the eastern part of the courtyard are two structures (not in plan): the courtyard stones were used for their construction.

Semicircular threshing floor, 250 m north of the structure, 10 m in diameter. Installations area about 30 m north-west of the structure.

Pottery: Late Roman – 60%; Byzantine – 40%.
Other surveys: none.

67. Pottery from E.P. 475: 1. Bowl, red, LR-Byz; 2. Jar, drk brn, LR-Byz.

♦ ♦ ♦

Site 30: 18-17/84/2

KHALLET EL-LOZ (1)

Israel grid: 18842/17463
UTM grid: 7268/5614
Elevation: 455 m a.s.l., 0 m a.s.a.
Name: nearest place
Site type: structure, courtyard, threshing floor and installations
Area: 400 sq. m (0.4 dunam)
Topography: saddle
Rock: Judea Group

Soil: terra rossa, quality: 5
Cultivation: none
Cisterns: none
Water source: 'Ein el-Foqa (no. 173), 900 m distant
Road: Phasaelis-Neapolis (C40), 300 m distant
Visit: April 1994; 3 surveyors; 17 sherds

Site on a spur descending southwards to wadi Khallet el-'Ein.

There is a small 3×3 m structure, built of partially worked fieldstones.

South of it is a triangular courtyard. In the courtyard north wall an entrance with threshold, jamb and lintel by their side.

About 20 m north of the structure are rock-cut installations and a semicircular threshing floor, about 15 m in diameter.

Over the entire spur are remains of agricultural activity: terraces and a few sherds.

Pottery: Late Roman (body sherds) – 100%.
Other surveys: none.

Site 31: 18-17/84/3
KHALLET EL-LOZ (2)

Israel grid: 18840/17462
UTM grid: 7268/5614
Elevation: 455 m a.s.l., 0 m a.s.a.
Name: nearest place
Site type: enclosure
Area: 100 sq. m (0.1 dunam)
Topography: saddle
Rock: Judea Group
Soil: terra rossa, quality: 5

Cultivation: none
Cisterns: none
Water source: 'Ein el-Foqa (no. 173), 700 m distant
Road: Phasaelis-Neapolis (C40), 300 m distant
Visit: March 2015; 5 surveyors; 35 sherds

Site on a rocky spur north and above Wadi Khallet el-'Ein, 1.5 km west of Mekhora and 1.5 km north-east of Kh. Tana et-Tahta.

Round enclosure, 20 m in diameter, with surrounding wall built of large and medium-sized boulders.

Apparently the site belonged to the agricultural area around the focal settlement at Kh. Tana et-Tahta.

Pottery: Middle Bronze II (body sherds) – 14%; Iron II – 6%; Late Roman – 80%.
Other surveys: none.

68. Pottery from **Khallet el-Loz (2)**: 1. Bowl, lt brn, LR; 2. Krater/jar, lt brn, IA II; 3. Jug, lt brn, LR.

Site 32: 18-17/84/4
WADI KHALLET EL-'EIN (2)

Israel grid: 18844/17405
UTM grid: 7269/5608
Elevation: 380 m a.s.l., 0 m a.s.a.
Name: nearest place
Site type: enclosure and structures
Area: 500 sq. m (0.5 dunam)
Topography: edge of valley
Rock: Judea Group
Soil: terra rossa, quality: 7

Cultivation: cereals and legumes
Cisterns: none
Water source: 'Ein el-Foqa (no. 173), 400 m distant
Road: Phasaelis-Neapolis (C40), 200 m distant
Visit: March 2015; 5 surveyors; 15 sherds

Site on the western bank of Wadi Khallet el-'Ein, 400 m north-east of the spring of 'Ein el-Foqa.

Rectangular enclosure, 20×8 m, built of large and medium-sized stones, partially survives. In the north-western corner is a circular room, 2.5 m in diameter. Another round structure with similar dimensions is just outside the south-eastern corner. Apparently, these round structures are later than the enclosure itself.

Tower, 4×4 m, built of large stones, 30 m south-west of the enclosure.

Long terrace walls extend over a great area around the tower and over the slope above the enclosure.

Pottery (body sherds from around the tower): Late Roman – 100%.
Other surveys: none.

Site 33: 18-17/94/1
ELEVATION POINT 293

Israel grid: 18962/17468
UTM grid: 7280/5615
Elevation: 240 m a.s.l., 50 m b.s.a.
Name: nearest place
Site type: enclosure, structure and sherd and flint scatters
Area: 1000 sq. m (1 dunam)
Topography: spur
Rock: Judea Group
Soil: terra rossa, quality: 8

Cultivation: none
Cisterns: none
Water source: 'Ein el-Foqa (no. 173), 1.7 km distant
Road: Phasaelis-Neapolis (C40), 1 km distant
Visit: November 2013; 3 surveyors; sherds: enclosure 100, north structure 17, field scatter 41.

Site on a low spur at the edge of a valley, 300 m west of Mekhora and close to the north of the site of Mekhora pool (Site 34).

Circular enclosure, 20 m in diameter, with surrounding wall built of medium sized-large stones. Its southern side at the edge of the spur serves as a support wall to the entire site.

An inner area of the enclosure is vacant, apart from the remains of a wall at the eastern side. The rock surfaces are high; hence it was probably used as a threshing floor.

There are many terraces over the slopes near the enclosure and the fields around.

In the field, 50 m east of the enclosure are sherd and flint scatters.

About 40 m north of the enclosure are remains of a structure, seemingly another circular enclosure.

Pottery: in the enclosure: Roman-Byzantine – 95%; unidentified – 5%. In the northern structure: Roman-Byzantine – 89%; unidentified – 11%. In the field: Roman-Byzantine – 90%; Medieval (?) – 3% (a single sherd); unidentified – 7%.
Flint: 57 items: 45 flakes, 6 blades, 1 bladelet, 3 retouched blades, and a truncation.
Other surveys: none.

LANDSCAPE UNIT 34

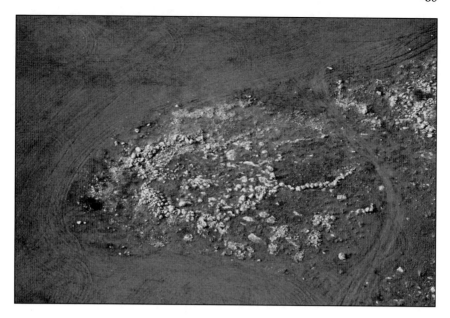

69. Aerial photo looking west of **E.P. 293** (A. Solomon).

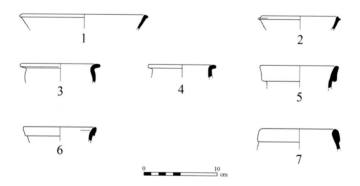

70. Pottery from **E.P. 293**: 1-4. Bowls, lt brn, Rom-Byz; 5-6. Jugs, lt brn, Rom-Byz; 7. Jar, drk brn, Rom-Byz.

Site 34: 18-17/94/2
MEKHORA POOL

Israel grid: 18960/17473
UTM grid: 7280/5615
Elevation: 245 m a.s.l., 0 m a.s.a.
Name: given by the Survey
Site type: structures
Area: 3000 sq. m (3 dunams)
Topography: moderate slope
Rock: Judea Group
Soil: terra rossa, quality: 8

Cultivation: field crops by the site
Cisterns: none
Water source: 'Ein el-Foqa (no. 173), 1.8 km distant
Road: Phasaelis–Neapolis (C40), 1.1 km distant
Visit: December 2013; 4 surveyors; 60 sherds

Site at the edge of en-Najmeh Valley, over the slope descending south from Mekhora reservoir, 300 m west of Mekhora, north of and close to site E.P. 293 (Site 33).

Along a cultivated field are scattered structures built of very large stones:
- In the west are remains of a square tower covered by large cleared stones. An enclosing wall ascends from the tower over the slope northwards (no. 1 in plan).
- Large oval structure, 17×12 m, built of very large stones in the header mode. Parts of the support wall have two rows of stones. The southern third of the structure is paved with very large stones (no. 2).
- In the east is a structure similar to no. 2, but badly damaged by stone-clearing works (no. 3). Between structure no. 2 and 3 are walls built of large stones.

In the north is agricultural terraced land.

Apparently the site was built as an agricultural facility, but the great number of sherds indicates the likelihood of a settlement at the site.

Pottery: Iron II (body sherds) – 8%; Late Roman – 67%; Byzantine – 25%.
Flint: 3 items: flake, blade and bladelet.
Other surveys: none.

LANDSCAPE UNIT 34

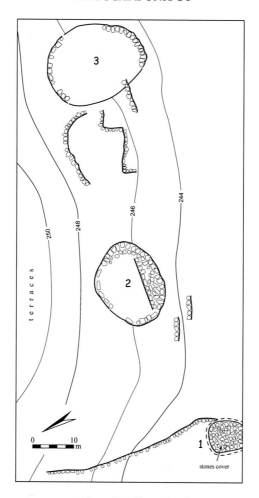

71. Plan of **Mekhora Pool**.

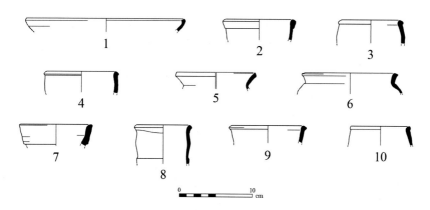

72. Pottery from **Mekhora Pool**: 1. Bowl, reddish, LR; 2. Bowl, lt brn, LR-Byz; 3-4. Bowls, reddish, LR-Byz; 5-6. CPs, reddish, LR; 7. Jar (?), lt colour, LR-Byz; 8-10. Jars, drk brn, LR.

Site 35: 18-17/94/3
EN-NAJMEH (1)

Israel grid: 18950/17422
UTM grid: 7280/5611
Elevation: 238 m a.s.l., 15 m a.s.a.
Name: nearest place
Site type: farm, threshing floors, road and road station
Area: 2.5 ha (25 dunams)
Topography: moderate hillock
Rock: Judea Group

Soil: brown forest, quality: 5
Cultivation: none
Cisterns: none
Water source: 'Ein el-Foqa (no. 173), 1.4 km distant
Road: Phasaelis-Neapolis (C40), 1 km distant
Visit: April 1999; 5 surveyors; 308 sherds

Extensive site on a rocky broad shoulder between two valleys: Jureth Kreira in the east and en-Najmeh Valley in the west, in the western part of the longitudinal valley between Mekhora and Gittit, 400 m south-west of Mekhora. The Alon road passes nearby on the eastern side of the site.

The site has three parts:
- In the centre is a large complex, containing two square conjoined courtyards. The surrounding walls are well built of large stones. The structures inside the courtyards were built in various periods. The dimensions of the northern courtyard are 30×30 m. Two towers or rooms project from the corners of the northern wall. Along the inner side of the eastern wall are attached five rooms identical in area, about 5×4 m each. A long structure is attached to the northern wall in the north-western corner. The southern courtyard is 25×15 m, containing various structures and walls.
- Another courtyard, 25×25 m, built with the same masonry as the large complex, 100 m south-east of it. A small structure is attached to the south-eastern corner of this courtyard, and an irregular courtyard projects southwards from it.
- Between the large complex and the southern courtyard, about 35 m from both of them and a little eastward, are three threshing floors in a semicircle; each one about 15 m in diameter.
- A 6 m wide Roman road crosses the site from north to south, bordered by two rows of large stones and between them were identified remains of paving, the middle of which is missing. The northern section of the road, about 150 m long, ascends the northern slope. A winding wall starts westward from its southern end, ending in a small courtyard, 10×10 m. The southern section of the road, about 100 m long, is also curved, and reaches the southern courtyard. A stone circle about 10 m in diameter is adjacent to the southern end.

- Another winding wall about 30 m west of the large complex, perhaps for agricultural purposes.

West of the site are recent stone clearing heaps. Obviously the site has undergone recent disturbance and construction.

It can be assumed that the site was a large farm and roadhouse. This assumption rests on the dominant location over the neighbourhood, the Roman road and the row of rooms in the large complex.

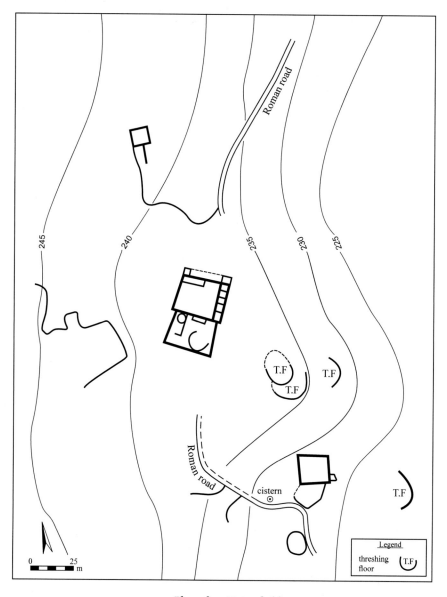

73. Plan of **en-Najmeh (1)**.

74. Aerial view north at the farm at **en-Najmeh (1)** (A. Solomon).

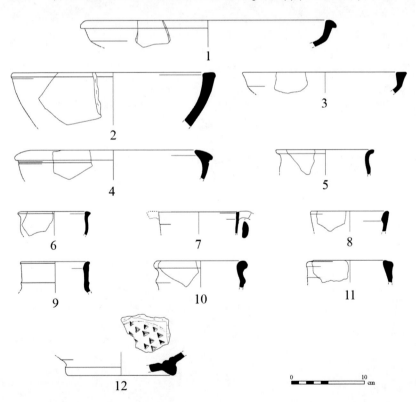

75. Pottery from **en-Najmeh (1)**: 1, 3-4. Bowls, lt brn, IA II-III; 2. Bowl, lt gr, Med; 5. Bowl, lt brn, LR-Byz; 6. Bowl, drk brn, LR-Byz; 7. Bowl (?), drk brn, LR; 8. Jar, lt brn, Mod (?); 9. Jar, lt brn, Rom; 10-11. Jars, drk brn, IA II-III; 12. Bowl, cuneated dec inside, lt gr, IA III.

Pottery: Iron II-III – 50%; Late Roman-Byzantine – 38%; Medieval – 10%; Modern – 2%.
Flint: 11 items: 5 flakes, 4 blades and 2 scrapers.
Stone: a limestone bowl and fragments of basalt grinding tools.
Other surveys: none.

Site 36: 18-17/94/4
EN-NAJMEH (2)

Israel grid: 18931/17421
UTM grid: 7277/5610
Elevation: 250 m a.s.l., 0 m a.s.a.
Name: nearest place
Site type: sherd scatter
Area: 2000 sq. m (2 dunams)
Topography: plain
Rock: Judea Group
Soil: Mediterranean brown forest,
quality: 8
Cultivation: field crops near the site
Cisterns: none
Water source: 'Ein el-Foqa (no. 173), 1.2 km distant
Road: Phasaelis-Neapolis (C40), 600 m distant
Visit: November 2013; 3 surveyors; 120 sherds

Sherd scatter in a flat valley, 800 m south-west of Mekhora.

The western part of the valley is rich in agricultural terraces and sherd scatters, mostly from the Roman period. A few building stones are scattered around.

The northern part of the site has been disturbed by modern agriculture.

Apparently, several constructions or tents, mainly dating to the Roman-Byzantine periods, stood here. The place was probably connected to en-Najmeh (1) (Site 35), the central settlement in the area, which is 200 m east of the site.

Pottery: Iron II (body sherds) – 8%; Early Roman – 13%; Late Roman – 50%; Byzantine – 25%; Modern – 4%.
Other surveys: none.

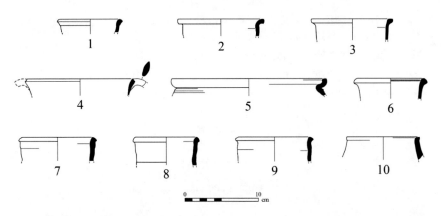

76. Pottery from **en-Najmeh (2)**: 1-3. Bowls, lt brn, Rom; 4. CP, lt brn, Rom; 5. CP, lt brn, Rom-Byz; 6. Jug/jar, drk brn, Rom; 7. Jar, drk brn, Rom-Byz; 8. Jar, lt brn, Rom; 9. Jar/jug, lt brn, Rom; 10. Jar (?), lt brn, Mod (?).

◆ ◆ ◆

Site 37: 18-17/73/1
WADI KHALLET EL-'EIN (3)

Israel grid: 18786/17389 (centre of the site)
UTM grid: 7263/5606
Elevation: 290 m a.s.l., 70 m b.s.a.
Name: nearest place
Site type: courtyards complex
Area: 3 ha (30 dunams)
Topography: slope
Rock: Avdat Group

Soil: Mediterranean brown, quality: 4
Cultivation: none
Cisterns: none
Water source: 'Ein et-Tahta (no. 186), 300 m distant
Road: Phasaelis-Neapolis (C40), by the site
Visit: June 2015; 4 surveyors; 110 sherds

Site at the bottom of E.P. 394 slope, between the springs of 'Ein el-Foqa and 'Ein el-Tahta, above the channel of Wadi Khallet el-'Ein, 1 km north-east of the city at Kh. Tana et-Tahta. About 400 m from the site and south of it is the Roman water pool bearing the Arabic name Birket Wadi el-'Ein (Site 50).

Site is a complex of eight courtyards, seven of which are arranged in a semi-circle, open to the wadi.

The southern wing contains three courtyards:
– Square courtyard, 10×10 m, and a track from it to the north.
– Two rounded courtyards, 20 m and 15 m diameter. A two-room structure is

attached on the north to the outside of the smaller courtyard, and a single room structure is attached to the west inner side of the larger courtyard.

The northern wing contains four courtyards:
– Two attached rectangular courtyards. The easternmost is the smaller of the two. In its north corner is a room.
– A round courtyard, 14 m in diameter, with a cell inside, and walls 1 m thick. The cell abuts the east side of the larger rectangular courtyard of the northern wing (above).
– Further north-west is an elliptical courtyard. An elongated cell is adjacent to the outside of the north-western wall of the yard.

By the wadi, west of the north wing, is another elliptical courtyard, 30×17 m.

The courtyards form a complex which was apparently used for agricultural use, such as livestock husbandry and storage of crops. This site adds up to a

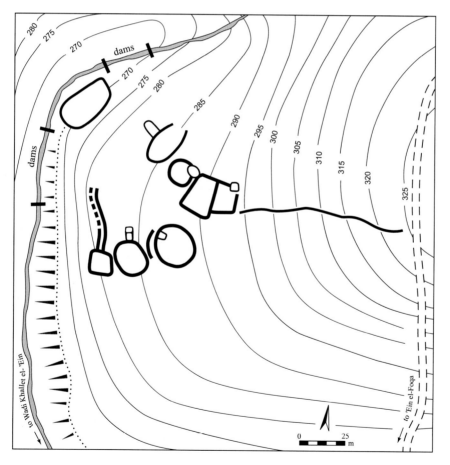

77. Plan of **Wadi Khallet el-'Ein (3)**.

78. Pottery from **Wadi Khallet el-'Ein (3)**: 1. CP, lt brn, LR; 2. Jug, drk brn, LR; 3. Jug, lt brn, LR-Byz.

large group of sites in the agricultural hinterland of Kh. Tana et-Tahta.

Note: the majority of the sherds were collected in the upper part of the slope, while a relatively small portion was collected from the courtyards.

Pottery: Iron II (body sherds) – 5%; Late Roman – 68%; Byzantine – 18%; Medieval (body sherds) – 9%.
Other surveys: none.

◆ ◆ ◆

Site 38: 18-17/73/2

TANA ET-TAHTA CEMETERY (1)

Israel grid: 18721/17378 (centre of the site)
UTM grid: 7256/5605
Elevation: 320 m a.s.l., 0 m a.s.a.
Name: given by the Survey
Site type: burial caves
Area 5000 sq. m: (5 dunams)
Topography: edge of valley
Rock: Avdat Group

Soil: terra rossa, quality: 6
Cultivation: none
Cisterns: none
Water source: 'Ein et-Tahta (no. 186), 500 m distant
Road: Tana-Neapolis (C56), 200 m distant
Visit: June 2015; 3 surveyors; 55 sherds

Site at the edge of an inner valley, north-north-east of Kh. Tana et-Tahta, 2.8 km west-south-west of Mekhora.

Several dozen burial caves, all of which have been plundered. The burials were discovered along a 350 m stretch at the foot of a low cliff in the eastern part of the valley. The caves are full of silt, and it is very difficult to trace their openings. Heaps of earth dug out of them mark their locations. Byzantine sherds were collected from the heaps. Above some of the caves are rock-cuttings. Along the edge of the cliff is a thin wall, perhaps used to divert water and silt.

An empty stone sarcophagus was found in one of the caves, the ceiling of which had partially collapsed (coordinates 187266/173747).

Below is a list of coordinates of the main cave openings discovered in the area: 187315/173828; 187265/173924; 187077/173895; 187111/173888; 187145/173873; 187163/173841 (three caves); 187229/173799 (three caves); 187362/173917; 187331/173861.

Apparently the site is the main exposed section of the cemeteries of the Roman-Byzantine city at Kh. Tana et-Tahta (see also Site 40). It is intriguing that almost all the finds from this cemetery were dated to the Byzantine period, while those from the Roman period, the time of the greatest prosperity of the city, have not yet been found.

Pottery: Iron II (body sherds) – 4%; Byzantine – 96%.
Other surveys: none.

79. A sherd from **Tana et-Tahta Cemetery (1)**:
jug, lt brn, Byz.

♦ ♦ ♦

Site 39: 18-17/73/3
ELEVATION POINT 395 (3)

Israel grid: 18769/17389 (centre of the site)
UTM grid: 7260/5606
Elevation: 320 m a.s.l., 70 m b.s.a.
Name: nearest place
Site type: sherd scatter, structure and installations
Area: 3000 sq. m (3 dunams)
Topography: spur and its slope
Rock: Avdat Group

Soil: terra rossa, quality: 4
Cultivation: none
Cisterns: none
Water source: 'Ein et-Tahta (no. 186), 200 m distant
Road: Phasaelis-Neapolis (C40), 300 m distant
Visit: June 2015; 3 surveyors; 200 sherds

Site on a south-eastern spur of E.P. 395 ridge, west and above Wadi Khallet el-'Ein, 500 m north-east of Kh. Tana et-Tahta and 2.4 km south-west of Mekhora.

In the upper part of the site, on the spur, is a terrace (?) wall built of large stones.

In the north part of the site is a square cell, 2×2 m. Hewing in the rock was identified on the slope below the cell, possibly the blocked entrance of a burial

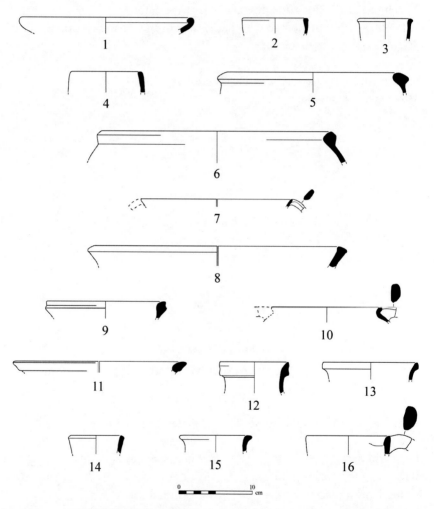

80. Pottery from E.P. 395 (3): 1. Bowl, lt brn, MB II; 2-3. Bowls, lt brn, Rom; 4. Bowl, drk brn, Rom; 5. Krater, lt brn, IA II; 6. Krater, greyish, MB II; 7. CP, lt brn, Rom; 8. CP (?), drk brn, MB II; 9. CP, lt brn, IA II; 10. CP (?), lt brn, Rom; 11. Jar, lt brn, MB II; 12. Jar, lt brn, Rom; 13. Jug, lt brn, IA II (?); 14-15. Jugs, lt brn, Rom; 16. Jug, lt brn, MB II.

cave. A broken limestone cistern opening was found next to it. Nearby was a rock-cut cupmark.

An abundant sherd scatter, mainly dated to the MBA IIb, was collected from the entire area of the spur and the slope descending towards Wadi Khallet el-'Ein.

Pottery: Middle Bronze IIb – 80%; Iron II – 7%; Roman – 13%.
Flint: 17 items: 13 flakes, 1 blade, 2 scrapers and a borer.
Stone: two basalt grinding stones.
Other surveys: none.

◆ ◆ ◆

Site 40: 18-17/73/4
TANA ET-TAHTA CEMETERY (2)

Israel grid: 18704/17365 (centre of the site)
UTM grid: 7255/5604
Elevation: 325 m a.s.l., 30 m a.s.a.
Name: given by the Survey
Site type: burial caves and quarry
Area: 1 ha (10 dunams)
Topography: spur
Rock: Avdat Group

Soil: terra rossa, quality: 6
Cultivation: none
Cisterns: many
Water source: 'Ein et-Tahta (no. 186), 700 m distant
Road: Tana-Neapolis (C56; C57), 400 m distant
Visit: June 2015; 3 surveyors; 60 sherds

Site at the edge of a small fertile valley over a spur of E.P. 395, east and above Wadi Qard, 300 m north-west of Kh. Tana et-Tahta.

There is a large ancient quarry with numerous openings of rock-hewn and plundered burial caves. In some of the caves in the south of the spur can be seen modern activity: dwelling, storage and livestock corrals.

Apparently, this site was a western wing of the cemetery of the nearby city in Kh. Tana et-Tahta. The main part, the cemetery of Tana et-Tahta (1) (Site 38), is located in the eastern side of the valley, about 250 m east of this burial cave cluster.

Pottery: Late Roman – 25%; Byzantine – 50%; Modern – 25%.
Other surveys: none.

Site 41: 18-17/73/5
ELEVATION POINT 395 (5)

Israel grid: 18744/17375
UTM grid: 7258/5605
Elevation: 354 m a.s.l., 20 m a.s.a.
Name: nearest place
Site type: structure, burial cave and oil press
Area: 1000 sq. m (1 dunam)
Topography: spur

Rock: Avdat Group
Soil: terra rossa, quality: 6
Cultivation: none
Cisterns: none
Water source: 'Ein et-Tahta (no. 186), 300 m distant
Road: Tana-Neapolis (C56), at the site
Visit: June 2015; 3 surveyors; 55 sherds

Site at the north edge of Kh. Tana et-Tahta, on a slope of E.P. 395, 2.8 km south-south-west of Mekhora.

There are remains of a burial cave with a collapsed ceiling and a crypt inside it. Above it is much hewing in the rock. By the cave, opposite the entrance, are remains of a wall built of medium-sized stones. The wall curves to enclose a small courtyard.

Attached to the cave in the east are remains of a square structure, 7×7 m, built partially of worked ashlars and divided into two equal cells.

An oil press is located 30 m south of the cave containing a rock hewn laver with two basins next to it.

The site appears to be part of a farm.

The cave was apparently used for burial, being a part of the cemetery which spreads over the spurs and valleys north of the city at Kh. Tana et-Tahta (see above Sites 38 and 40).

Pottery: Iron II (body sherds) – 9%; Late Roman – 30%; Byzantine – 43%; Medieval – 9%; Ottoman – 9%.
Other surveys: none.

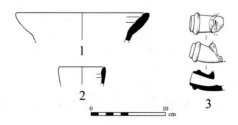

81. Pottery from **E.P. 395 (5)**: 1. Bowl, lt brn, Med; 2. Bowl (?), lt brn, Rom-Byz; 3. Pipe, drk brn, Ott.

Site 42: 18-17/73/6
ELEVATION POINT 395 (4)

Israel grid: 18752/17379
UTM grid: 7259/5605
Elevation: 365 m a.s.l., 50 m a.s.a.
Name: nearest place
Site type: courtyards, threshing floors, and oil press
Area: 5000 sq. m (5 dunams)
Topography: upper slope
Rock: Avdat Group

Soil: terra rossa, quality: 2
Cultivation: none
Cisterns: none
Water source: 'Ein et-Tahta (no. 186), 500 m distant
Road: Tana-Neapolis (C56), by the site
Visit: June 2015; 8 surveyors; sherds: 258 (the farm); 50 (plunder waste).

Site on the upper slope of E.P. 395, 600 m north of Tana et-Tahta. North of the site is a series of dwelling caves [see Site E.P. 395 (1), Site 27]. From the site is a view to the springs at Tana area.

Series of enclosures cut into the natural rock surface of the cliffs for threshing floors and other uses. On top of these are courtyards, oil presses, a rock-cut staircase etc.

The site has two wings with two separate plans:

1. Lower eastern wing:
– Upper elliptical courtyard, 15×9 m, built of medium-sized stones. The walls, maximum 1 m high and 80 cm thick, are founded on a rock-hewn levelled cliff. The entrance, 1 m wide, is at the east, framed by two tall jamb stones. The construction appears to be relatively new (no. 1 in plan; Fig. 82).
– Oil press containing a round and finely hewn stone laver/basin, 2 m in diameter, with a socket for the centre axis, at a lower level of the eastern wing, 50 m north-east of the first courtyard. Around it is a 1 m wide hewn path for the beast of burden. The laver stone was cracked in antiquity, with a southward extension of the crack in the rock surface (no. 2). There could have been a linkage between the oil press and the wing of the central part of the site (see below).
– Set of three rock-cut stairs in the upper part of the wing, north of the first courtyard and attached to it, connecting the two wings of the site. The bottom step is 7 m wide and the tread depth is 1.5 m; the second step is 2.5 m wide with 80 cm tread depth. The third step is part of the upper surface (no. 3).
– Hewing and a cell, 8×7 m, built of medium-sized stones 35 m from the first courtyard, at the north-western edge of the complex (no. 4).
– Large surfaces of natural rock bounded by walls between the highest cliff

154　　　　　　　　　　　　　　　CHAPTER SIX

(the steps cliff) and the oil press. The surfaces were cleared, levelled, and used for installation of threshing floors or other utilities. The low cliffs which border the rock surfaces have been improved by hewing. In places where there are no cliffs, bounding walls were erected (no. 5).

2. Upper western wing, located 30 m west of the lower wing with two courtyards and a constructed road.
– Courtyard, 17×10 m, built of large stones around a rock surface. In the southern part are two small cells, apparently for storing produce (no. 1 in plan, Fig. 83).

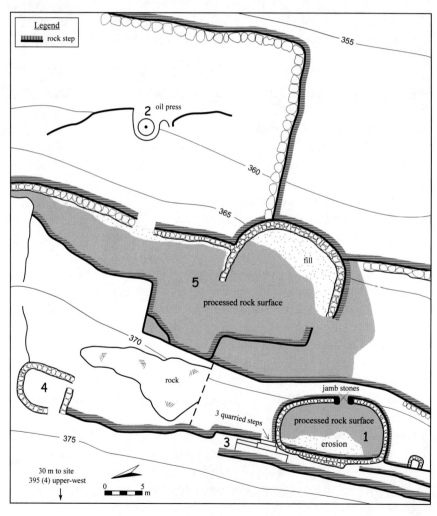

82. Plan of lower eastern wing of **E.P. 395 (4)**.

- Trapezoidal courtyard, 10 m north of the first courtyard in this wing. Maximum length 24 m, and width 9 m. Also built of medium-sized stones around processed rock surfaces (no. 2).
- Constructed road adjacent to both courtyards (C56) ascends north-eastwards from Tana et-Tahta. Remains of the road were discovered further up ascending towards E.P. 475.

It appears as if the site did not serve for dwelling, but was used for agricultural purposes such as threshing floors and oil production. The sophisticated utilization of the combination of cliffs and rock surfaces found in this site is a unique phenomenon in our survey so far.

In the northern part of the site was revealed a plunder pit (out of limits of the plans). A large number of sherds, mostly from the LR period, was collected from the earth taken out of the pit. Probably a burial cave belonging to the nearby large city at Kh. Tana et-Tahta was plundered here.

Pottery: In the agricultural structures: Iron II – 22%; Hellenistic (body sherds) – 2%; Early Roman – 3%; Late Roman – 40%; Byzantine – 31%; Medieval – 2%. In the plundered pit: Hellenistic (body sherds) – 2%; Late Roman – 96%; Byzantine (body sherds) – 2%.
Other surveys: none.

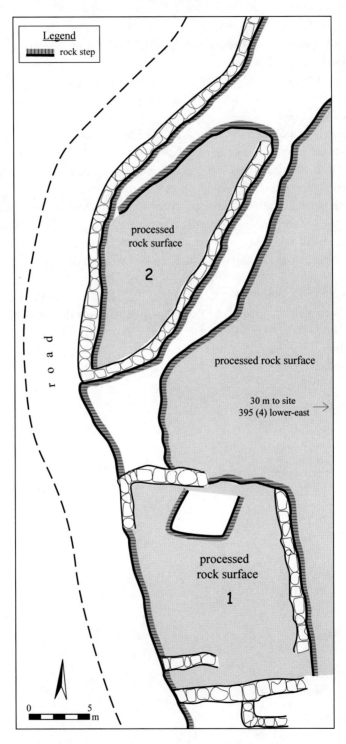

83. Plan of upper western wing of E.P. 395 (4).

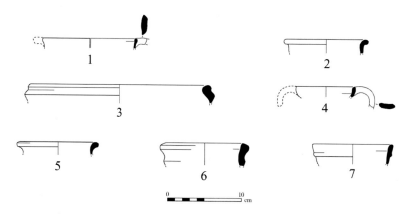

84. Pottery from **E.P. 395 (4), farm:** 1. Bowl (?), lt brn, Rom; 2. Bowl, lt brn, Rom; 3. CP, drk brn, IA II; 4. CP, red, ER; 5. Jug, lt brn, Rom; 6. Jar/jug, lt brn, IA II; 7. Jug, drk brn, Rom.

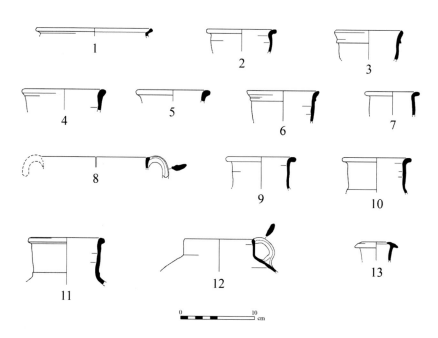

85. Pottery from **E.P. 395 (4), plunder pit:** 1, 3-7. Bowls, lt brn, LR; 2. Bowl, gr, LR; 8. Bowl (?), lt brn, LR; 9. Jar, drk brn, LR; 10-11. Jars, lt brn, LR; 12. Jug (?), lt brn, LR; 13. Jug, lt brn, LR.

Site 43: 18-17/73/7
TANA CAVE

Israel grid: 18760/17360
UTM grid: 7261/5604
Elevation: 280 m a.s.l., 20 m a.s.a.
Name: given by the Survey
Site type: burial cave
Area: 100 sq. m (0.1 dunam)
Topography: slope
Rock: Avdat Group
Soil: terra rossa, quality: 6

Cultivation: none
Cisterns: none
Water source: 'Ein et-Tahta (no. 186),
    100 m distant
Road: Phasaelis-Neapolis (C40),
    100 m distant
Visit: November 1982; 4 surveyors;
    46 sherds

EBA I burial cave surveyed by the Southern Samaria Survey (Finkelstein et al. 1997: 848), described as follows: "A burial cave. Pottery collected from a pile of earth removed by looters. The Iron II sherd certainly originated from the nearby site".

The cave was not located by us.

Pottery: Early Bronze I – 96%; Middle Bronze II – 2%; Iron II – 2%.
Additional bibliography: Bar 2014, site 59.

Site 44: 18-17/73/8
ELEVATION POINT 395 (8)

Israel grid: 18719/17378
UTM grid: 7256/5605
Elevation: 328 m a.s.l., 0 m a.s.a.
Name: nearest place
Site type: enclosure and walls
Area: 500 sq. m (0.5 dunam)
Topography: edge of valley
Rock: Avdat Group

Soil: terra rossa, quality: 6
Cultivation: none
Cisterns: none
Water source: 'Ein et-Tahta (no. 186),
    500 m distant
Road: Tana-Neapolis (C56),
    100 m distant
Visit: July 2015; 4 surveyors; 150 sherds

Site at the edge of a small inner valley adjacent to Tana et-Tahta cemetery (1) (Site 38), 300 m north-west of the northern hillock of Kh. Tana et-Tahta and 2.9 km south-south-west of Mekhora.

There are several parts to the site:
- Elliptical enclosure at the centre, 25×18 m, built of boulders and large stones. The southern wall remained up to a maximum four courses high (2 m). Abutting the enclosure in the west are two rectangular cells built of medium-sized stones. Two openings of plundered burial caves were discovered near the enclosure.
- 5 m east and above the enclosure is a terrace wall extending hundreds of metres, enclosing the inner valley and the channel from the east. The centre of Tana et-Tahta cemetery (1) (Site 38) is attached to the wall in the east.
- Between the southern part of the enclosure and the terrace wall are two other walls enclosing two built spaces, creating a triangle-like built form. The sides are the terrace walls, the elliptical enclosure wall and another wall. The built triangle is divided into two secondary spaces by another wall extending north-south. Most of the pottery was collected in this area.

This composite site can be affiliated to the agricultural hinterland of the multi-period settlement at Kh. Tana et-Tahta.

Pottery: Intermediate Bronze (body sherds) – 3%; Iron I-II (body sherds) – 13%; Late Roman – 34%; Byzantine – 40%; Medieval (body sherds) – 10%.
Flint: 4 items: 2 flakes, 1 blade and a bladelet.
Other surveys: none.

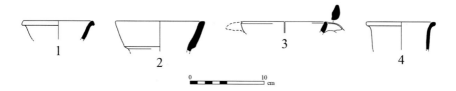

86. Pottery from E.P. 395 (8): 1. Bowl, reddish, LR-Byz; 2. Jar, reddish, LR-Byz; 3. Jug, reddish, LR-Byz; 4. Jug (?), reddish, LR.

Site 45: 18-17/73/9
ELEVATION POINT 395 (9)

Israel grid: 18711/17366
UTM grid: 7255/5604
Elevation: 320 m a.s.l., 0 m a.s.a.
Name: nearest place
Site type: enclosures
Area: 300 sq. m (0.3 dunam)
Topography: edge of valley
Rock: Avdat Group

Soil: terra rossa, quality: 7
Cultivation: none
Cisterns: none
Water source: 'Ein et-Tahta (no. 186), 600 m distant
Road: Tana-Neapolis (C56; C57), 300 m distant
Visit: July 2015; 4 surveyors; 50 sherds

Site at the edge of a small inner valley, 400 m north-north-west of Kh. Tana et-Tahta and 3 km south-south-west of Mekhora.

Two enclosures, 20 m apart:
- Southern enclosure is circular, 16 m in diameter. The surrounding wall is built of medium-sized stones, and preserved up to two courses high. The western part of the enclosure is exposed rock. The majority of the collected pottery is from this enclosure.
- Northern enclosure is rectangular, 17×10 m. Despite its considerable destruction, it is possible to trace the various construction stages. The base of the surrounding wall is built of medium-sized stones and is 80 cm thick. At a

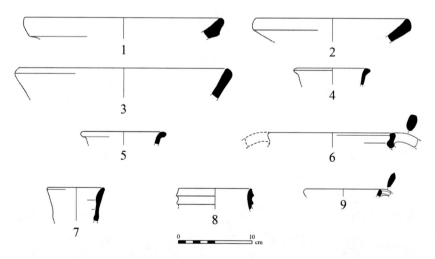

87. Pottery from E.P. 395 (9): 1-3. Bowls, lt brn, Med; 4. Bowl, lt brn, LR-Byz; 5. Bowl (?), drk brn, LR-Byz; 6. CP, lt brn, LR-Byz; 7. Jar (?), lt brn, Mod (?); 8. Jug, lt brn, LR-Byz; 9. Jug, lt brn, LR-Byz.

later stage other walls and courses built of smaller stones were added. In the western part which is not built, a rocky step about 2 m high was put to use. Remains of later construction, were found in the southern part of the enclosure.

Above and near the site were discovered large areas of one of the Tana et-Tahta cemeteries, Tana et-Tahta Cemetery (2) (Site 40).

This site is included in the large group of sites forming the agricultural hinterland close to Kh. Tana et-Tahta.

Pottery: Iron II (body sherds) – 4%; Late Roman – 16%; Byzantine – 10%; Medieval – 60%; Modern – 10%.
Other surveys: none.

◆ ◆ ◆

Site 46: 18-17/73/10
KHIRBET TANA ET-TAHTA (WESTERN QUARTER)

Israel grid: 18709/17342 (centre of the site)
UTM grid: 7255/5602
Elevation: 312 m a.s.l., 0 m a.s.a.
Name: given by the Survey
Site type: a settlement next to a city
Area: 5 ha (50 dunams)
Topography: moderate slope and spur
Rock: Judea Group

Soil: terra rossa and Mediterranean brown, quality: 3
Cultivation: none
Cisterns: 1
Water source: 'Ein et-Tahta (no. 186), 800 m distant
Road: Tana-Neapolis (C56; C57), by the site
Visit: July 2015; 5 surveyors; 180 sherds

Site on the western spur on which are found the remains of the city of Kh. Tana et-Tahta. The site is 700 m distant from the city centre, separated by a deep and wide ravine. The remains of the city at Kh. Tana et-Tahta consist of at least three parts: the city on the hillock, the northern quarter and the western quarter.

The settlement comprises complexes, courtyards and structures.

South of the unpaved road that crosses the site are two complexes:
Complex no. 1: Two combined courtyards, 20×20 m. Next to them are two round rooms 6 m in diameter. The construction is shoddy (no. 1 in plan).
Complex no. 2: A large courtyard, 20×20 m. In the north are two adjacent round rooms. Close to the rooms in the north is a cistern, and around it a wall.

East of the courtyard on the eastern side of the spur is a cave, 6 m long with an entrance 2 m wide (no. 2 and 3).

North of the unpaved road are three complexes of courtyards and round structures.

Western complex: A courtyard measuring 20×15 m, and next to it two semicircular structures.

Eastern complex: Two large incomplete courtyards, and north of them four round structures and sections of a courtyard.

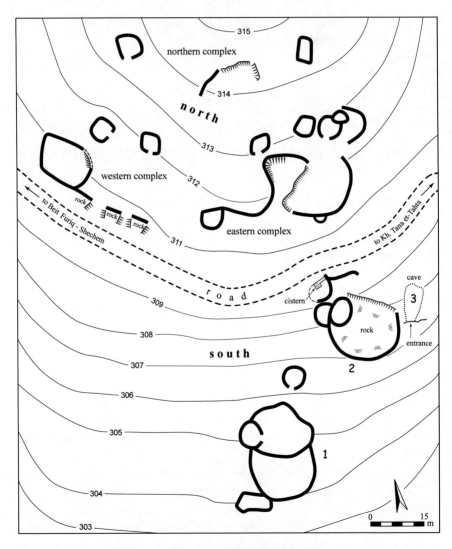

88. Plan of **Kh. Tana et-Tahta (Western Quarter)**.

Northern complex: Unfinished courtyard and two rounded structures.

It is doubtful whether these remains were part of the Roman-Byzantine city of Tana et-Tahta proper, or were a separate settlement. It should be taken into account that the construction is elementary and shoddy, and in the Roman-Byzantine city there are no designs such as small round structures. Possibly these finds are a later expansion (Medieval?) of the original Roman settlement.

The ceramic find is similar to that found in other parts of the city.

Pottery: Iron I-II – 12%; Early Roman – 8%; Late Roman – 39%; Byzantine – 17%; Medieval (body sherds) – 14%; unidentified – 10%.
Other surveys: none.

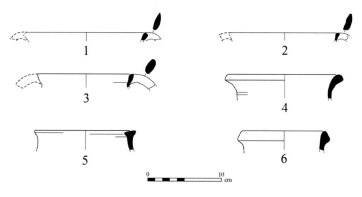

89. Pottery from **Kh. Tana et-Tahta (Western Quarter):** 1-3. CPs, lt brn, Rom; 4. Jar, lt brn, LR-Byz; 5. Jar (?), drk brn, LR-Byz; 6. Jug, lt brn, IA I-II.

Site 47: 18-17/73/11
KHIRBET TANA ET-TAHTA

Israel grid: 18740/17326 (centre of the site)
UTM grid: 7259/5600
Elevation: 300 m a.s.l., 100 m a.s.a.
Name: ancient and on map
Site type: tell and city
Area: 28 ha (280 dunams)
Topography: hillock, saddle and slopes
Rock: Judea Group
Soil: terra rossa, quality: 7
Cultivation: none
Cisterns: numerous
Water source: 'Ein et-Tahta (no. 186), 400 m distant
Road: Tana-Neapolis (C56; C57), and Phasaelis-Neapolis (C40) at the site
Visit: April 1999 and many more; 8 surveyors; 450 sherds

Large site, possibly a city, in the Tana valley, 2.7 km west-south-west of Mekhora. Near the city are two springs. Roman roads connected it to the Jordan Valley and Shechem/Neapolis.

There are several parts to the site:
- **City centre on the southern hillock** (no. 4 in plan): These are dense remains of structures over an area of about 15 ha (150 dunams). The construction is of large fieldstones and most of the walls survived to a height of 1 to 2 m. Many jambs and lintels *in situ*. The majority of the houses belong to the 'house with a cistern' type. Some of the numerous cisterns are still plastered, with steps descending into them.

  Many streets and alleyways can be seen; however, the destruction makes certain identification difficult. Apparently, this was the ancient nucleus of the settlement. The entire southern part is undergoing an ongoing process of destruction and plunder.

  In the western and southern parts of the tell are remains of a massive wall about 2.5 m thick, which bordered the city.

  On the north-eastern slope of the hillock is a sheikh's tomb which has been converted to a mosque (no. 3 in plan).
- **North quarter** (no. 5 in plan): The quarter stretches over a moderate slope, north of the saddle in the centre of the city. The quarter is rectangular, 200-250 m. The construction is similar to that in the southern hillock.
- **el 'Ein el-Foqa – the upper spring** (no. 1 in plan): The spring is at coordinates 1881/1738, 900 m north-east of the centre of the city. The spring flows from a rocky layer in the northern bank of Wadi Khallet el-'Ein. Next to the spring is a built aqueduct covered by stone slabs. The duct is 25 m long, 1.7 m inner height and 1 m wide. The duct is designed to carry water south-westerly

into a constructed pool, 8×3 m. The construction appears to be new, but the foundations are ancient. Nowadays the discharge of the spring is low.

About 300 m south-west, on the southern slope of Wadi Khallet el-'Ein, is another pool, 12×6 m, well-built of ashlars with many layers of plaster (no. 8 in plan). The pool's date is not clear, but it seems that its foundations are from the Roman period (see Site 50).

- **'Ein et-Tahta – the lower spring** (no. 2 in plan): The spring is at coordinates 1877/1737, at the bottom of Wadi Khallet el-'Ein. The spring's flow is not abundant. Next to it is a constructed pool. The place is described in the Ephraim Survey: 'A spring whose water runs along a channel into a plastered reservoir. An earlier reservoir, south of the modern one. Pottery collected near the spring and on the slope above it' (Finkelstein et al. 1997: 849).
- **Dwelling and burial caves:** Many caves were found, most were used for dwelling or storage, and a few for burials. Most of the dwelling caves have an adjoining courtyard. The locations of the main concentrations of caves (some are out of the area of the plan) are: Wadi Khallet el-'Ein, close to 'Ein et-Tahta; on the eastern slope of the spur of E.P. 395; near the northern 'quarter' of Tana et-Tahta; and in a small valley west of the site.
- **Roads:** A paved Roman road (C 40) leads to the city from the south-east, ascending over the north-eastern slope of the city centre. The road extends in the direction of Neapolis along three routes: east of the city via Wadi Khallet el-'Ein (C 40), in the north via E.P. 475 (C 56) and in the north-west via Wadi Tal'ah (C 57) (see detailed description in the introduction chapters).
- **Courtyards:** At the edges of the hillock, and along the slopes around the city are built courtyards and corrals from various periods, some of which were apparently built after the abandonment of the Byzantine city. The original stones were in secondary use in later construction. The main concentration of courtyards is at coordinates 1881/1740.
- **Millstones:** At least three were located in the outskirts of the city at coordinates 1878/1738, 1881/1740 and at 1881/1733.

The Survey of South Samaria visited the site in 2016 and noted a public structure close to the mosque. Walls built of ashlars and a forum paved with stone slabs were identified. A drainage channel passed beneath the paving. In the centre of the saddle between the hills, an underground complex of at least ten storage pits, interconnected by narrow passages, was discovered. The original openings of the pits were blocked by stone slabs (information from Dvir Raviv, Aharon Tavger, Beni Har-Even and Yevgeny Aharonovitz).

Wallis (1961) started the attempts to identify the city, proposing that this was Taanath-Shiloh, a biblical settlement existing between the allotments of the Tribe of Ephraim and the tribe of Manasseh. The settlement is mentioned in the Book of Joshua (16: 6-7), under the description of the Tribe of Ephraim's allotment:

> 'Then the border went westward at Michmethath on the north, and the border turned about eastward to Taanath-shiloh and continued beyond it to the east of Janoah. It went down from Janoah to Ataroth and to Naarah, then reached Jericho and came out at the Jordan...'

This is a probable identification. Another candidate for Taanath-Shiloh is Kh. Tana el-Foqa, 3.5 km north-east of the city (Campbell 1991, site 18). In both sites IA pottery was found, and both bear the name Tana which resembles the name Taanath.

In Eusebius' Onomasticon (Notley and Safrai 2005, site 493) the village of Taanah appears to be near Aqraba, south-east of Shechem.

Unlike other opinions, identifying the village of Taanah from the Onomasticon with Kh. Tana el-Foqa (Finkelstein et al. 1997: 845 and references therein), our view is that the Roman-Byzantine identification fits Kh. Tana et-Tahta better (see detailed account in Chapter 4 above). In the South Samaria Survey it is proposed to identify the place with Ptolemais' Taana (V:16: 5; Nobbe 1845); and it seems that this identification indeed fits (Bar 2017).

According to Grossman (1986: 355) a small village existed in the Ottoman period, and eight tax-paying families lived there at the time. The village was deserted during the period.

Pottery: Chalcolithic (?)/Early Bronze I – 2%; Middle Bronze II – 2%; Iron I – 4%; Iron II – 8%; Hellenistic – 2%; Early Roman – 11%; Late Roman – 25%; Byzantine – 28%; Early Moslem – 2%; Medieval – 7%; Ottoman – 9%.
Flint: 5 items: 1 flake, 1 blade, 2 retouched blades and a scraper.
Other surveys: Campbell 1991: 37-40; Finkelstein et al. 1997: 845-849.
Additional bibliography: Bar 2014, site 58.

LANDSCAPE UNIT 34

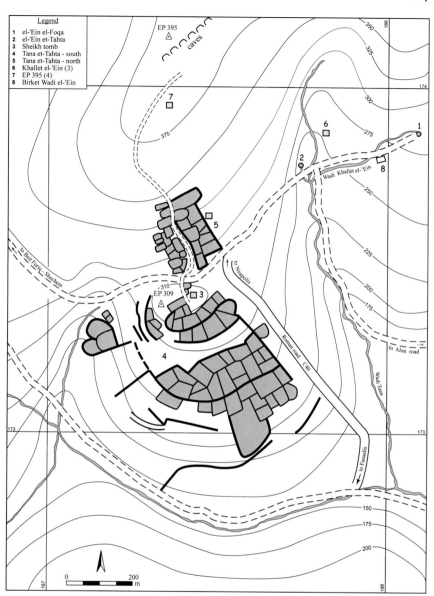

90. Plan of **Kh. Tana et-Tahta**.

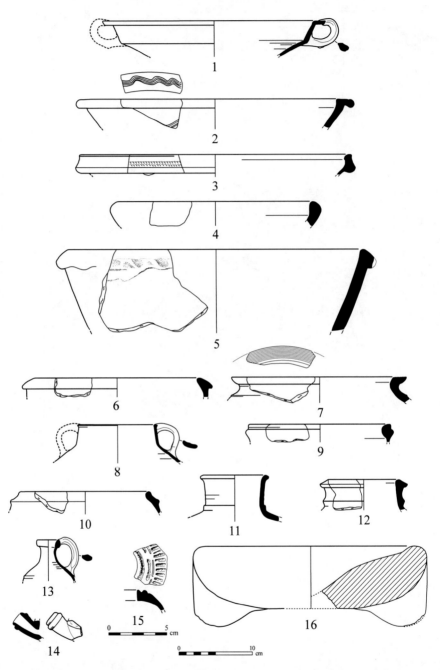

91. Finds from **Kh. Tana et-Tahta**: 1. Bowl, lt brn, LR-Byz; 2. Krater, red, incised dec on rim, Byz-EM; 3. Bowl, red, roulette dec, Byz; 4. Bowl, lt brn, IA I; 5. Krater, gr, rope dec on rim, Med; 6. Bowl, lt brn, IA II; 7. Krater, lt brn, incised dec on rim, Byz; 8. CP, red, ER; 9. CP, lt brn, IA II; 10. CP, lt brn, IA I-II; 11. Jar, blk, LR; 12. Jar, gr, IA II; 13. Juglet, gr, ER; 14. Pipe, gr, Ott; 15. Lamp, red, Byz; 16. Bowl, white limestone.

92. Aerial view north of **Kh. Tana et-Tahta** (A. Solomon).

93. Aerial view west at the southern hillock of **Kh. Tana et-Tahta** (A. Solomon).

Site 48: 18-17/83/1

'EIN EL-FOQA

Israel grid: 18832/17392
UTM grid: 7267/5607
Elevation: 367 m a.s.l., 40 m a.s.a.
Name: nearest place
Site type: farm, cave, oil press and flint scatter
Area: 2,500 sq m (2.5 dunams)
Topography: slope
Rock: Judea Group

Soil: terra rossa, quality: 7
Cultivation: none
Cisterns: 1
Water source: 'Ein el-Foqa (no. 173), 200 m distant
Road: Phasaelis-Neapolis (C40), 100 m distant
Visit: March 2015; 5 surveyors; 20 sherds

Site above and north of the spring of 'Ein el-Foqa.

Structure, 20×10 m, built of large stones and divided in the centre by a partition wall. The southern wall of the structure is founded on rock and is built of large boulders. It is one boulder thick and is preserved to four courses high (about 2 m). In the north-eastern corner is a 2×2 m room, the walls of which are preserved up to 1.5 m high.

On the slope between the structure and the spring and east of the structure are numerous terrace walls.

Remains of a plastered cave about 50 m down the slope; next to it is a stone well head. Wall remains about 100 m east of the structure (Israel grid 1884/1739), which do not form a clear plan, and an oil press basin quarried in the bedrock were also noted.

On a rocky strip by the spring, 200 m south-east from the site, Hovers and Bar-Yosef (1987: 79) found a flint scatter, apparently Upper Palaeolithic.

Apparently this is a small LR period farmhouse in the rural periphery of the hub settlement at Kh. Tana et-Tahta.

Pottery: Late Roman – 75%; Byzantine – 25%.
Other surveys: Hovers and Bar-Yosef 1987.

94. Pottery from 'Ein el-Foqa (all LR-Byz): 1. Bowl, reddish; 2. Jug, lt colour; 3. Jug (?), gr; 4. Jug, reddish.

Site 49: 18-17/83/2
WADI KHALLET EL-'EIN (1)

Israel grid: 18854/17393
UTM grid: 7270/5607
Elevation: 385 m a.s.l., 0 m a.s.a.
Name: nearest place
Site type: road and courtyard
Area: 2 ha (20 dunams)
Topography: edge of valley
Rock: Judea Group
Soil: terra rossa, quality: 7

Cultivation: field crops by the site
Cisterns: none
Water source: 'Ein el-Foqa (no. 173), 400 m distant
Road: Phasaelis-Neapolis (C40) at the site
Visit: March 2015; 4 surveyors; 30 sherds

Site with a Roman road, a courtyard and various agricultural remains northwest of Kh. Tana et-Tahta and 0.4 km east of 'Ein el-Foqa spring.

A 300 m section of the Roman road Phasaelis–Neapolis (C 40) was found in this site. This is one of the main local roads in the road network of the eastern

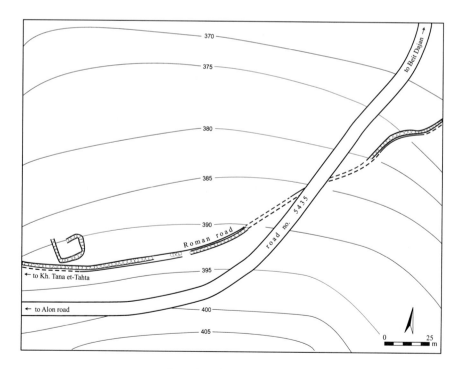

95. Plan of **Wadi Khallet el-Ein (1)**.

Samaria Shoulder. This section starts from Tana et-Tahta, passes the main spring ('Ein el-Foqa), and continues north-east to Beit-Dajan and Shechem/Neapolis.

The width of the road proves that the section is a branch of the principal road. The walls of the road are only intermittently preserved. They are built of one or two rows of stones, 2 courses high (about 1 m), a height meant to prevent beasts of burden deviating from it. There are a number of openings in the walls for entry and exit, but the road proper is a complete intact unit.

Close to the road is a 12×10 m courtyard open to the south-west. Apparently the courtyard was part of the road layout, serving for storage of crops and goods.

West of the road is a valley about 500 m long and 250 m wide. Next to it are various remains of agriculture and residences. Coordinates along the road section and of the main agricultural features are:

Israel grid	Elevation	Remarks
188643/173952	394 m	Obvious road section setoff (crossed by road 5345)
188620/173939	384 m	Road width 2.2 m
188589/173926	378 m	Road width 2.0 m
188560/173916	376 m	Road width 2.0 m. Site of the courtyard
188449/173902	364 m	Road width 2.1 m. Above this spot are terraces on the slope towards the modern roadway to Tana et-Tahta
188464/173904	361 m	Supporting walls from the western wall of the road and perpendicular to it, to the preserved section in the direction of Tana et-Tahta; probably serving also as dams or agricultural terraces along the channel
188438/173901		Dam no. 1
188434/173900		Dam no. 2
188398/173887		Dam no. 3. At this point the wall has been preserved up to 5 courses high (about 2 m). The construction is of large stones
188378/173880		Dam no. 4

Pottery (in and surrounding the courtyard): Late Roman – 83%; Medieval (body sherds) – 17%.
Other surveys: none.

Site 50: 18-17/83/3
BIRKET WADI EL-'EIN

Israel grid: 18807/17379
UTM grid: 7265/5605
Elevation: 295 m a.s.l., 60 m b.s.a.
Name: local
Site type: water pool
Area: 1000 sq. m (1 dunam)
Topography: slope
Rock: Judea Group
Soil: terra rossa, quality: 4

Cultivation: none
Cisterns: none
Water source: 'Ein el-Foqa (no. 173), 300 m distant
Road: Phasaelis-Neapolis (C40) by the site
Visit: January 2015; 4 surveyors; 22 sherds

Site in Wadi el-'Ein at the bottom of a steep slope between the springs of 'Ein et-Tahta and 'Ein el-Foqa (the springs that watered the settlement at Kh. Tana et-Tahta).

Well-built pool, 16.5×6.5 m. The surrounding 1 m thick wall is built of one row of slightly worked large stones. Inside the wall are two layers of small stones under a thick layer of plaster. The total thickness of the walls including the coating is 1.1 to 1.3 m. One third of the south-eastern wall is built and the rest is cut into the bedrock.

At the time of the visit (2015), the pool was partially full with water, proof of its hydraulic qualities. The bottom was covered by a thick layer of silt, making it impossible to estimate the original depth. The area is about 100 sq. m. Assuming a depth of 3 m, the pool could contain about 300 cubic m of water.

It is not absolutely clear how the pool was filled; however, it can be assumed that some sort of aqueduct carried water from the upper spring – 'Ein el-Foqa to the pool. The pool served for watering the fertile valley of the wadi below it and was part of the region's water network.

There is a certain similarity in the manner of construction of the pool to the pool of Tel Sheikh Diyab in the Jordan Valley (Zertal and Bar 2019, site 23).

Pottery: Roman (body sherds) – 100%.
Other surveys: none.

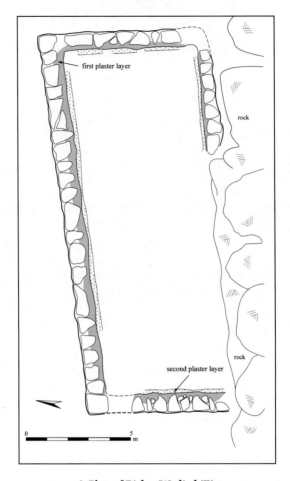

96. Plan of **Birket Wadi el-'Ein**.

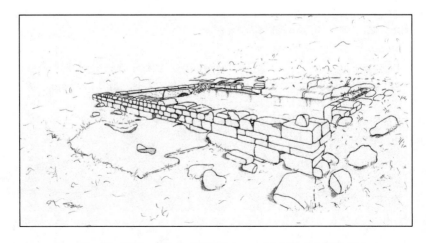

97. Sketch of **Birket Wadi el-'Ein** (view south) (O. Avizel Gadir).

98. Aerial photo of **Birket Wadi el-'Ein** (view north) (A. Solomon).

Site 51: 18-17/83/4
MERAH ARRAR (2)

Israel grid: 18800/17340
UTM grid: 7264/5602
Elevation: 325 m a.s.l., 50 m a.s.a.
Name: nearest place
Site type: large complex of courtyards and structures
Area: 3.5 ha (35 dunams)
Topography: slope
Rock type: Judea Group

Soil: brown forest, quality: 2
Cultivation: none
Cisterns: none
Water source: 'Ein et-Tahta (no. 186), 400 m distant
Road: Phasaelis-Neapolis (C40), 400 m distant
Visit: June 1999; May 2015; 6 surveyors; 230 sherds

Broad site on the shoulder of Merah Arrar ridge, west and next to the unpaved Mekhora-Jebel Kabir road, 700 m east of Kh. Tana et-Tahta.

The site consist of three main parts:
– Built-up nucleus about 80×80 m (6,400 sq m – 6.4 dunams). The structures are encircled by a 2 m thick enclosure wall built of large fieldstones. At the bottom north-western corner is a four-roomed structure with a round courtyard. In the centre of the area are three groups of structures and rooms of

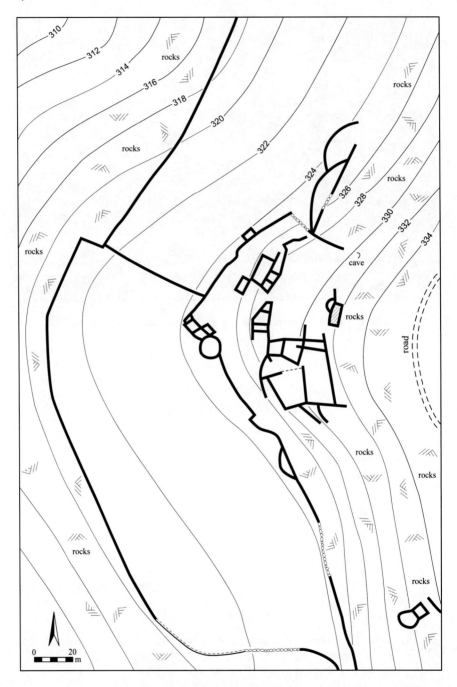

99. Plan of **Merah Arrar (2)**.

various dimensions, mostly about 5×5 m. The construction is good, resembling the construction of other MBA II sites in the region.
- Sherds were collected from a scatter on a shoulder stretching 60 m westwards from the centre of the site, hinting that perhaps once structures stood here. At the edge of the slope is a 700 m long enclosing wall, the function of which is not clear.
- On the rocky slope in the southern part are isolated structures with courtyards, which were possibly part of the site (outside the plan).

The site was built and functioned during the MBA II, and is one of a very large group of other period sites in the desert fringes of Samaria.

A ruin named Merah Arrar is included in the British Survey map (sheet XII) east of 'Ein Sha'ab el-Bir, west of Aqbet el-Butmeh and 2.5 km north of the subject site; but with no documentation.

Pottery: Middle Bronze II – 80%; Iron I-II – 5%; Late Roman (body sherds) – 15%.
Flint: 20 items: 10 flakes, 2 blades, 1 sickle blade, 4 scrapers, 2 retouched flakes and a retouched blade. The find is probably from the Middle Bronze II.
Other surveys: none.

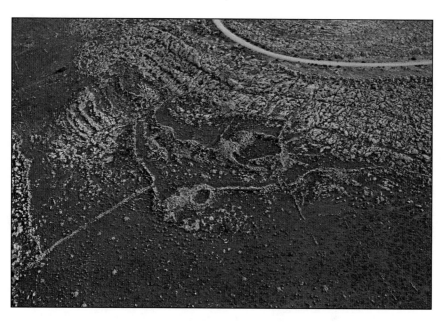

100. Aerial view to the north-east of **Merah Arrar (2)** (A. Solomon).

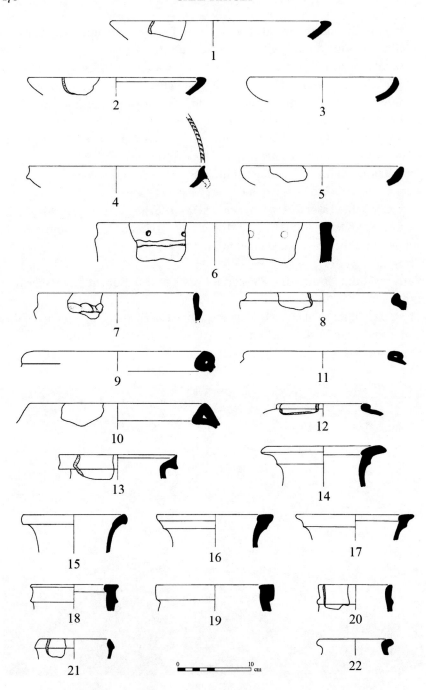

101. Pottery from **Merah Arrar (2)** (all except no. 3, 5, 8 and 21 are from MB II):
1-2. Bowls, buff; 3. Bowl, gr, IA I; 4. Bowl, pink, rope orn; 5. Bowl, brn, IA I;
6, 7, 9, 10. CPs, lt brn; 8. CP, brn, IA II; 11, 12. Holemouth, brn; 13, 14, 17. Jars, buff;
15, 16, 18, 19. Jars, brn; 20. Jug, brn; 21. Jug, brn, IA I; 22. Jug, pink.

Site 52: 18-17/83/5
MERAH ARRAR (1)

Israel grid: 18837/17345
UTM grid: 7268/5602
Elevation: 365 m a.s.l., 50 m a.s.a.
Name: Ancient, but not on map
Site type: enclosure
Area: 3,000 sq. m (3 dunams)
Topography: rocky hillock
Rock type: Judea Group
Soil: brown forest, quality: 3

Cultivation: none
Cisterns: none
Water source: 'Ein el-Foqa (no. 173),
　500 m distant
Road: Phasaelis-Neapolis (C40),
　500 m distant
Visit: April 1995; May 2015;
　4 surveyors; 60 sherds

Site on a low rocky hillock in the southern part of Zuhur esh-Shafa ridge, 2 km south-west of Mekhora.

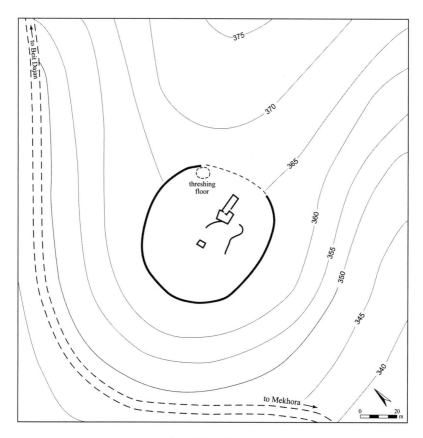

102. Plan of **Merah Arrar (1)**.

Round enclosure, 60 m diameter, centred at the summit of the hill. The 1 m thick surrounding wall is built of one row of very large stones. Most of the wall is intact, apart from its eastern section.

In the top part of the enclosure is a 6×5 m structure, built of large stones, preserved up to 2 courses high. North of the enclosure are remains of a round threshing floor. Inside the enclosure are other structures, some with attached courtyards.

This is an Iron Age enclosure typical of the agricultural activities from this period in eastern Samaria and the Jordan Valley.

Pottery: Iron I – 30%; Iron II – 60%; Late Roman (body sherds) – 10%.
Other surveys: none.

Site 53: 18-17/83/6

WADI MANZAL (1)

Israel grid: 18887/17335
UTM grid: 7273/5601
Elevation: 275 m a.s.l., 60 m a.s.a.
Name: nearest place
Site type: structure, cave and cistern
Area: 4,000 sq. m (4 dunams)
Topography: slope
Rock type: Judea Group
Soil: terra rossa, quality: 3

Cultivation: none
Cisterns: 1
Water source: 'Ein el-Foqa (no. 173), 900 m distant
Road: Phasaelis-Neapolis (C40), 900 m distant
Visit: December 1999; 3 surveyors; 17 sherds

Site on the southern side of a terraced and cultivated saddle, on the steep south-eastern slope of E.P. 394, above Wadi Manzal, 1.5 km south-south-west of Mekhora.

Ruined structure built of large stones, and possibly a courtyard.

Large cave with collapsed ceiling, a crushing basin *in situ*, and a currently operative cistern.

This is probably a LR-Byz farm, part of the agricultural hinterland of Kh. Tana et-Tahta.

Pottery: Late Roman-Byzantine – 100%.
Other surveys: none.

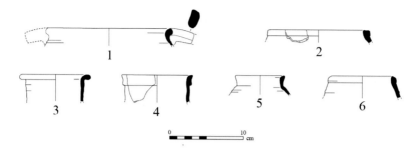

103. Pottery from **Wadi Manzal (1)** (all are LR-Byz): 1. CP, lt brn; 2. Bowl, lt brn; 3. Jug, drk brn; 4. Jug, drk brn; 5. CP, org; 6. Jug (?), drk brn.

◆ ◆ ◆

Site 54: 18-17/72/1

TANA ET-TAHTA (SOUTH-WEST)

Israel grid: 18766/17296
UTM grid: 7261/5597
Elevation: 235 m a.s.l., 60 m a.s.a.
Name: given by the survey
Site type: courtyard, structure, caves and sherd scatter
Area: 2,000 sq. m (2 dunams)
Topography: spur
Rock type: Judea Group

Soil: terra rossa, quality: 6
Cultivation: none
Cisterns: none
Water source: 'Ein et-Tahta (no. 186), 700 m distant
Road: Phasaelis-Neapolis (C40), 100 m distant
Visit: July 2015; 4 surveyors; 50 sherds (enclosure); 30 sherds (burial cave)

Site at the edge of a spur descending eastwards from Kh. Tana et-Tahta to Wadi al-Kabi, 400 m south-east of the southern side of Kh. Tana et-Tahta and 3 km south-west of Mekhora. From the site there is a broad view to the channel of Wadi el-Kabi and to the ridges of 'Iraq ez-Zah and Jebel em-Mahjarah.

There are three elements:
- Square courtyard, 24×24 m, built of gigantic boulders. In the north-east corner is a plundered cave.
- At the bottom of the cliff, below the square courtyard in the south, is another plundered cave. There is an abundant Byzantine Period sherd scatter.
- At the bottom of the spur, 50 m south of the square courtyard and close to the valley plain of Wadi el-Kabi, are remains of a large well-built structure (perhaps enclosure?); the walls of which appear to be support walls on the slope; sections of which survived to a height of more than 2 m.

This site is one of a large group of agricultural sites and caves, apparently used mainly for agriculture and burial, surrounding the large Rom-Byz settlement at Kh. Tana et-Tahta.

Pottery: in the courtyard: Late Roman – 40%; Byzantine – 60%. In the burial cave: Byzantine – 100%.
Other surveys: none.

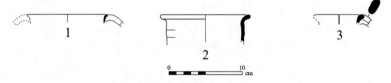

104. Pottery from **Tana et-Tahta (South-West)**, enclosure: 1. CP (?), lt brn, LR; 2. Jug, drk brn, LR – Byz; 3. Jug, lt brn, LR – Byz.

105. Pottery from **Tana et-Tahta (South-West)**, plundered cave: 1-2. Jars, lt colour, Byz.

Site 55: 18-17/72/2

'IRAQ EZ-ZAH (3)

Israel grid: 18791/17280
UTM grid: 7263/5596
Elevation: 200 m a.s.l., 100 m b.s.a.
Name: given by the survey
Site type: fort, structures, and road
Area: 500 sq. m (0.5 dunam)
Topography: bottom of a slope
Rock type: Judea Group
Soil: terra rossa, quality: 4

Cultivation: none
Cisterns: none
Water source: 'Ein el-Foqa (no. 173), 1 km distant
Road: Phasaelis-Neapolis (C40), at the site
Visit: January 2015; 5 surveyors; 25 sherds

Site at the edge of a slope at the entrance to the narrow crevice of Wadi el-Kabi, 400 m north of 'Iraq ez-Zah and 800 m south-east of the outskirts of Kh. Tana et-Tahta.

Well-built fort, 9×7.5 m, a component of the Roman road (C40) layout. From the southern corner a wall sets out towards the road in the wadi. This wall section is 2.5 m long and 2.5 m thick. The fort has been almost completely destroyed. The north-eastern wall, which is built of huge stones, has been mainly preserved. Each stone weighs about 2 tons, and some have projections and drafted margins. Architectural analysis shows that probably only the filling level below the floor survived: the floor itself and the superstructure did not.

Based on the remains of the wall from the fort toward the wadi, it seems that the structure was intended to block and guard the wadi and the road within. However, remains of an extension of the wall could not be found opposite the

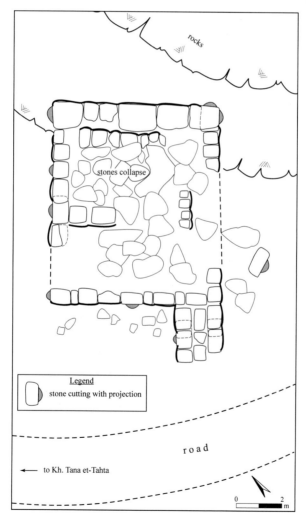

106. Plan of 'Iraq ez-Zah (3).

projecting wall on the other side of the road; thus this suggestion is only hypothetical. The margin drafting might indicate an official construction together with the construction of the road, or later.

South of the fort are two structures, used perhaps as watchtowers (outside the plan). One (1879/1728) is round, 18 m diameter and built of large stones. The second (1880/1730) is also built of large stones, but is completely ruined, so its original plan is unknown. Possibly these structures relate to another parallel road located above them.

Several coordinate readings were taken along the upper parallel road:
- At coordinates 18793/17290 the road is built of two rows of large stones, preserved up to 2 courses high and 2.6 m wide.
- At coordinates 18799/17295 part of the road, built of two rows of large stones and 2.2 m wide, is segmented; however most of it is visible.
- At coordinates 18804/17299 the road has been affected by the flank of an unpaved path and is 2.8 m wide.

Pottery (from the fort): Late Roman – 100%.
Other surveys: Ilan and Damati 1975: 45.

107. 'Iraq ez-Zah (3): reconstruction proposal, view north-east (O. Avizel Gadir).

108. 'Iraq ez-Zah (3), view south (I. Bejerano).

109. Pottery from 'Iraq ez-Zah (3): 1. Bowl, lt brn, LR; 2. Jug, lt brn, LR.

Site 56: 18-17/72/3
SHA'AB ES-SAIYAKH (2)

Israel grid: 18734/17250
UTM grid: 7258/5592
Elevation: 280 m a.s.l., 0 m a.s.a.
Name: nearest place
Site type: courtyards and structures
Area: 2,500 sq. m (2.5 dunams)
Topography: edge of valley
Rock type: Judea Group

Soil: terra rossa, quality: 8
Cultivation: none
Cisterns: none
Water source: 'Ein et-Tahta (no. 186), 1.3 km distant
Road: Tana-Neapolis (C57), 300 m distant
Visit: July 2015; 4 surveyors; 30 sherds

Site at the edge of a valley above the eastern bank of Wadi Sha'ab es-Saiyakh, 700 m south of Kh. Tana et-Tahta and 3.2 km south-west of Mekhora. There is a lookout to the ravines of Wadi el-Kabi and the ridges surrounding Kh. Tana et-Tahta.

There are several components:
- In the eastern part is a rectangular courtyard built of boulders and large stones. Only the northern and western parts have been preserved. Threshing sledge stones collected in the centre of the courtyard on an exposed rock, are evidence that the courtyard was used as a threshing floor.
- Above and south of the courtyard are two 4×4 m built cells, possibly used for storage of produce.
- West of the courtyard is another courtyard, 18×12 m, well-built with two rows of large stones with a filling of medium-sized and smaller stones. The walls are 1 m thick on average, preserved to a height of 4 courses (about 1.5 m). A similar construction has also been observed in the nearby site of Sha'ab es-Saiyakh (1) (Site 57).
- In the western part of the site is a structure, 5×5 m, built of medium-sized and large stones.
- Other walls which do not form a clear plan and agricultural terraces are scattered over the entire site area.

It seems that the site was part of the agricultural hinterland of the large settlement at Kh. Tana et-Tahta.

Pottery: Middle Bronze II (body sherds) – 7%; Iron I (body sherds) – 10%; Late Roman-Byzantine – 33%; Medieval (body sherds) – 50%.
Other surveys: none.

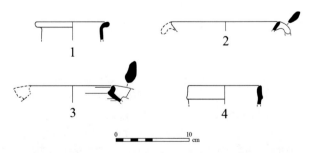

110. Pottery from **Sha'ab es-Saiyakh (2)** (all LR-Byz): 1. Bowl (?), lt brn; 2. CP (?), lt brn; 3. CP, lt brn, 4. Jug/jar, lt brn.

Site 57: 18-17/72/4
SHA'AB ES-SAIYAKH (1)

Israel grid: 18736/17235	Soil: terra rossa, quality: 8
UTM grid: 7258/5591	Cultivation: none
Elevation: 305 m a.s.l., 120 m a.s.a.	Cisterns: none
Name: nearest place	Water source: 'Ein et-Tahta (no. 186), 1.3 km distant
Site type: courtyard	
Area: 100 sq. m (0.1 dunam)	Road: Tana-Neapolis (C57), 500 m distant
Topography: slope	
Rock type: Judea Group	Visit: July 2015; 4 surveyors; 10 sherds

Site on the north-western slope of E.P. 363, south of Kh. Tana et-Tahta, 3.5 km south-west of Mekhora. There is a lookout from the site to the vast landscape of Wadi el-Kabi, Kh. Tana et-Tahta and to the ridges east of Beit-Dajan.

Courtyard, 15×9 m, well-built of two rows of boulders infilled with medium-sized and small stones. The walls are 1.2 m thick, preserved up to 5 courses (about 2 m).

The site was probably part of the hinterland of the large settlement at Kh. Tana et-Tahta. The construction of the walls resembles the fortress of es-Sireh (1) (Site 133), but the dimensions of this courtyard are much smaller.

Pottery (body sherds): Late Roman – 50%; Byzantine – 50%.
Other surveys: none.

Site 58: 18-17/72/5
ELEVATION POINT 363

Israel grid: 18752/17224
UTM grid: 7260/5590
Elevation: 363 m a.s.l., 0 m a.s.a.
Name: nearest place
Site type: farm, courtyard, cave and
    threshing floor
Area: 5000 sq. m (5 dunams)
Topography: summit
 Rock type: Judea Group

Soil: Mediterranean-brown, quality: 4
Cultivation: none
Cisterns: none
Water source: 'Ein et-Tahta (no. 186),
    1.5 km distant
Road: Wadi el-Kabi-Yanun (C55),
    300 m distant
Visit: April 1999; May 2015; 4
    surveyors; 200 sherds

Site located in a bleak hilly area of E.P. 363 ridge, 1.2 km south of Kh. Tana et-Tahta and 3.5 km south-west of Mekhora.

Site has three distinct parts:
- Farm containing a structure, 6×5 m, courtyard and installations (no. 1 in plan). The structure is ruined, and according to the number of stones was two storeys high.

    Large courtyard, about 30×25 m, borders the structure in the east. The courtyard is encircled by two types of walls: a large fieldstone wall, and a wall of medium-sized well cut stones. Two walls which are another part of the farm start from the courtyard, going north and east.

    Two large basins, 55 cm in diameter and about 45 cm deep, are cut in the rocky surface inside the courtyard.

    This is a typical LR farm situated in the hinterland of Kh. Tana et-Tahta.
- Winepress (no. 2) with a threshing surface 3.5×3.5 m, nearly 40 m east of the farm. A rock-carved conduit leads from it to the juice collecting vat about 1×1×1 m.
- A well-built courtyard 120 sq. m in area and a cave (no. 3), about 80 m east of the farm structure. The surrounding wall is irregular, of average thickness 1 m and maximum preserved height 1.5 m, with an entrance in the south. The construction appears to be rather new, i.e this courtyard is a later addition to the farm structure. A large cave was discovered beneath the western wall of the courtyard.

A cupmark was found about 80 m east of the farm.

Pottery: Iron I-II – 10%; Early Roman – 15%; Late Roman – 45%; Medieval – 10%; Modern – 20%.
Other surveys: none.

LANDSCAPE UNIT 34

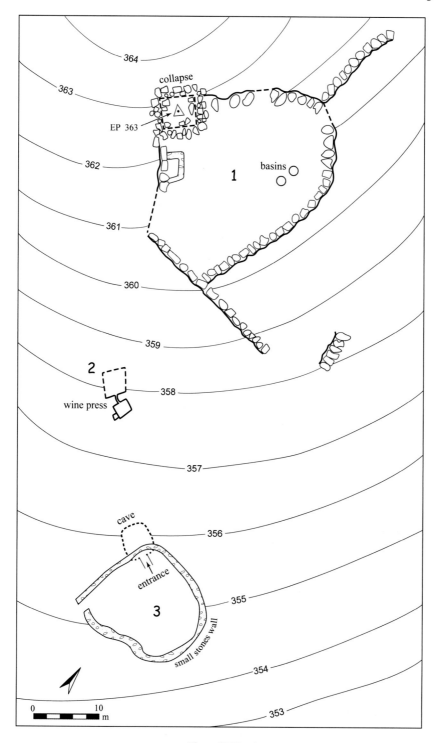

111. Plan of E.P. 363.

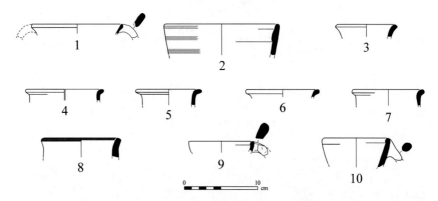

112. Pottery from E.P. 363: 1. CP, reddish, LR; 2. Jar, lt brn, LR; 3-4, 6-7. Jugs, lt brn, LR; 5. Jug, drk brn, IA II (?); 8. Jug, lt brn, blk orn on rim inside and outside, Med; 9. Jug, lt brn, IA II (?); 10. Jug, lt brn, Med.

Site 59: 18-17/82/1

ELEVATION POINT 394 (SOUTH)

Israel grid: 18883/17285
UTM grid: 7272/5596
Elevation: 255 m. a.s.l., 6 m. b.s.a.
Name: nearest place
Site type: courtyard, walls and sherd and flint scatters
Area: 1 ha (10 dunams)
Topography: small valley
Rock type: Judea Group

Soil: terra rossa, quality: 7
Cultivation: field crops by the site
Cisterns: none
Water source: 'Ein el-Foqa (no. 173), 1.2 km distant
Road: Phasaelis-Neapolis (C40), 400 m distant
Visit: December 1999; 3 surveyors; 40 sherds

Site at the edge of a small cultivated valley on the descending slope west of the Alon road, 2 km south-west of Mekhora.
    Site has two parts:
- The south-western part is a series of tall parallel walls, built of large stones. The walls appear to have been terraces. Here only were collected numerous flint items.
    South-east and close to the walls is an irregular courtyard, about 20×14 m, and an IA and Roman-Byzantine pottery scatter.
- The northern part comprises a number of walls and built sections.

This is a scattered settlement subsisting on the fertile soil that existed in the area, part of the hinterland of Kh. Tana et-Tahta. An earlier Neolithic site was also located here.

Pottery: Middle Bronze II – 5%; Iron I-II – 25%; Late Roman-Byzantine – 70%.
Flint: 430 items: 4 flake cores, 6 blade cores, 7 bladelet cores, 2 ridged blades, 15 core wastes, a hammerstone, 203 flakes, 120 blades, 38 bladelets, 2 retouched flakes, 6 retouched blades, 2 retouched bladelets, 2 blades with notch, 5 scrapers, 1 truncation, 3 burin wastes, 2 burins, 1 borer and 11 scrapers.
The flint finds are evidence of local flaking/knapping, which, although not fully indicative, suggests that some of it is from the Neolithic Period.
Other surveys: none.

113. Plan of **E.P. 394 (South)**.

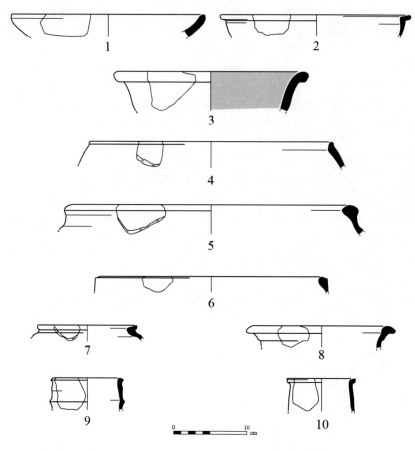

114. Pottery from E.P. 394 (South): 1. Bowl, org, IA I; 2. Bowl, org, LR-Byz; 3. Bowl, lt brn, red slip inside, IA I-II (?); 4. Krater, org, IA II (?); 5. Krater, drk brn, IA I-II; 6. CP, drk brn, IA II; 7. CP, org, LR-Byz; 8. Jar, gr, MB II; 9. Jar, org, LR; 10. Jug, gr, LR-Byz.

Site 60: 18-17/82/2
'IRAQ EZ-ZAH (1)

Israel grid: 18806/17249 (at the site centre)
UTM grid: 7265/5592
Elevation: 230 m a.s.l., 40 m a.s.a.
Name: nearest place
Site type: complex of structures and courtyards
Area: 12 ha (120 dunams)
Topography: saddle and slope
Rock type: Judea Group

Soil: Mediterranean brown, quality: 5
Cultivation: none
Cisterns: none
Water source: 'Ein et-Tahta (no. 186), 1.3 km distant
Road: Phasaelis-Neapolis (C40), 400 m distant
Visit: April 1999; 6 surveyors; 200 sherds

Broad and scattered site on a saddle and slopes south-west of E.P. 259 and the spur descending from E.P. 363 in a north-easterly direction, 1 km south-east from Kh. Tana et-Tahta and 2.6 km south-west of Mekhora. The site also extends eastwards towards the ravine through which ascends an unpaved road from the Mekhora-Gittit road to Jaffa en-Noon.

The site is triangular: the vertex is at the north of the saddle between E.P. 259 and the spur whose summit is E.P. 363. From this vertex the site broadens southward towards the ravine, extending and crossing it and then reaching its southern side.

Structures are spread over most of the site and the area is densely built over. The walls are built of large stones and are 1–1.5 m thick. The preservation is good, although it seems that the site underwent changes in the Roman period. The houses were transformed into terraces and various structures. However, the original walls are still traceable.

The site has six parts:
- Enclosure wall (no.1 in plan): the site is surrounded by an enclosure wall which is preserved mainly in the east and south; other sections possibly remained in the western slope. In the eastern part, over the low side of the hill of E.P. 259, the wall is doubled and the space between the two walls is 3-4 m. The wall extends southward as a single row of large stones, reaching and crossing the ravine, disappearing until it reappears further south over the spur of the hill descending north from Jaffa en-Noon.
- The centre of the site (no. 2) is an open space, 60×10 m, at the centre of the saddle. To the north of this space are courtyards, structures and walls. In the centre the space is enclosed by a double wall which is part of the

enclosure wall. In the south of the space is a very thick wall rising to a height of 5 m, with a structure or tower at its centre. Around the space are various structures and a later courtyard, 15×15 m.
- Structures on the western slope (no. 3): west of the space – the entire rocky slope up to elevation line 250 m is covered by dwelling structures built of large fieldstones. The structures rest on support walls. During the Roman Period the support walls were transformed into agricultural terraces, and some of the structures were converted to courtyards.

The abundance of sherds is evidence of a dense settlement.
- The area south of the ravine (no. 4): contained an enclosure wall and a number of structures, which also became agricultural courtyards and structures in the Roman period.
- The ravine and the dams (no. 5): At the bottom of the ravine are at least two built dams, but it is difficult to determine their date.
- E.P. 259 hillock (outside the plan): On the hillock are remains of a ruined structure, perhaps a fort, and a Middle Bronze II and Roman period sherd scatter.

The site was a central settlement during the MBA II, and part of a very large group of other period sites in the desert fringes of Samaria. Sherds of other periods attest to agricultural works at the site during the LR period and scant activity at other periods.

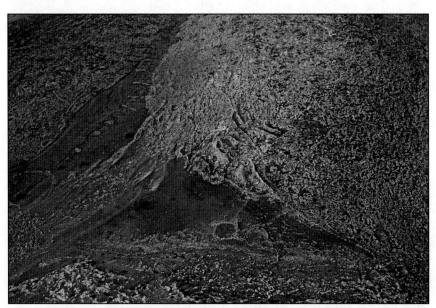

115. Aerial view south-west of 'Iraq ez-Zah (1) (A. Solomon).

Pottery: Chalcolithic/Early Bronze I – 1%; Middle Bronze II – 84%; Iron I (body sherds) – 1%; Iron II – 4%; Late Roman (body sherds) – 10%.
Other surveys: none.
Bibliography: Bar 2014, site 60.

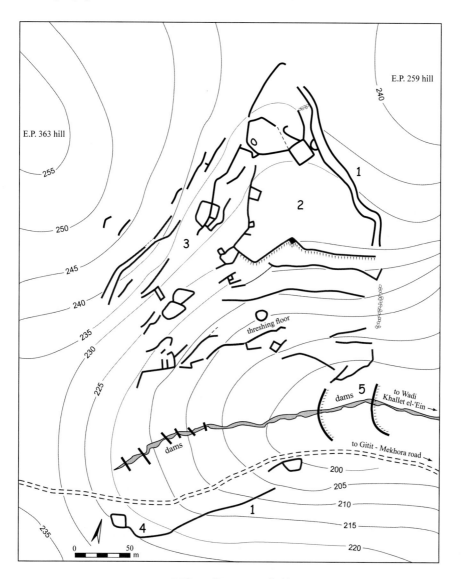

116. Plan of 'Iraq ez-Zah (1).

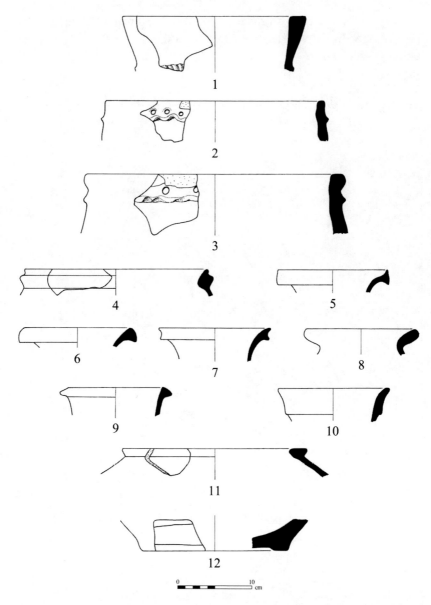

117. Pottery from 'Iraq ez-Zah (1) (all except 1, 4 are MB II): 1. Bowl, drk brn, rope orn, Chal/EB I (?); 2-3. CPs, drk brn; 4. CP, brn, IA II; 5-7, 9. Jars, buff; 8. Jar, drk brn; 10. Jar, pink; 11-12. Kraters, gr.

Site 61: 18-17/82/3
'IRAQ EZ-ZAH (2)

Israel grid: 18812/17229
UTM grid: 7266/5590
Elevation: 210 m a.s.l., 50 m b.s.a.
Name: nearest place
Site type: courtyard, structure and road
Area: 100 sq. m (0.1 dunam)
Topography: slope
Rock type: Judea Group

Soil: terra rossa, quality: 5
Cultivation: none
Cisterns: none
Water source: 'Ein et-Tahta (no. 186), 1.3 km distant
Road: Wadi el-Kabi-Yanun (C55), by the site
Visit: May 2015; 5 surveyors; 30 sherds

Site on a moderate slope south of E.P. 259, 1.3 km south-east of Kh. Tana et-Tahta and 3 km south-west of Mekhora.

Well-built rectangular courtyard, 15×8 m. The foundations of the walls contain boulders, with medium-sized and small stones above them. The walls are 1 m thick and have been preserved to a maximum height of 1 m. The entrance is in the northern wall.

Another structure, rounded and full of silt, abuts the courtyard in the west. It is difficult to understand its precise form.

South and west of the courtyard are large concentrations of terraces and an ancient road (C55).

Pottery: Late Roman (body sherds) – 100%.
Other surveys: none.

Site 62: 18-17/82/4
WADI EL-KABI

Israel grid: 18886/17210
UTM grid: 7273/5589
Elevation: 200 m a.s.l., 60 m a.s.a.
Name: nearest place
Site type: farm, tower and
  installations
Area: 1500 sq. m (1.5 dunams)
Topography: flat hillock
Rock type: Judea Group

Soil: Mediterranean brown, quality: 4
Cultivation: none
Cisterns: none
Water source: 'Ein el-Foqa (no. 173),
  1.9 km distant
Road: Phasaelis-Neapolis (C40),
  200 m distant
Visit: April 1999; 4 surveyors; 45 sherds

Site on a flat hillock, 300 m west of the Alon road and 2.9 km south-south-west from Mekhora. The deep Wadi el-Kabi surrounds the hillock in the south and west.

There are three parts to the site:
- Rectangular courtyard, 15×13 m, with a surrounding wall 1 m thick built from two rows of fieldstones. In the southern wall is an opening. A rectangular room adjoins inside the south-western corner of the courtyard.
- Rectangular structure, about 6×4 m, built of large stones, 25 m south-west from the courtyard. It probably served as a tower, or for agricultural storage.
- There are three clusters of mortars and basins, twelve in all. Two, about 70 cm in diameter and about 30 cm deep, were found close to the tower. In both other clusters they are about 20 cm in diameter and 10 cm deep.

A small farmhouse existed here, mainly during the LR-Byzantine periods. Some sort of activity occurred in Medieval (Mamluk) times. There is no certain chronological relation between the farm, the tower and the installations in the vicinity.

The site probably existed during IA II, based on the numerous body sherds of the period.

Pottery: Iron II (body sherds) – 25%; Late Roman – 30%; Byzantine – 25%; Medieval (Mamluk) (body sherds) – 20%.
Other surveys: none.

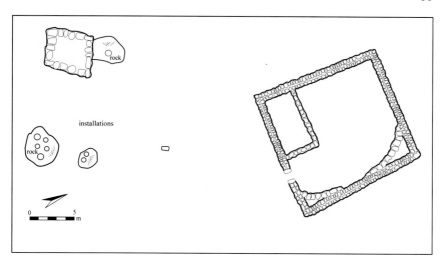

118. Plan of **Wadi el-Kabi**.

Site 63: 18-17/92/1

WADI MANZAL (2)

Israel grid: 18907/17276
UTM grid: 7275/5597
Elevation: 220 m a.s.l., 0 m a.s.a.
Name: nearest place
Site type: farm and courtyard
Area: 3000 sq. m (3 dunams)
Topography: slope
Rock type: Judea Group
Soil: terra rossa, quality: 6

Cultivation: none
Cisterns: none
Water source: 'Ein el-Foqa (no. 173), 1.4 km distant
Road: Phasaelis-Neapolis (C40), 400 m distant
Visit: March 2015; 4 surveyors; 70 sherds

Site at the edge of a cultivated shoulder west and above the road which ascends from the Alon road in the direction of Elon Moreh, 2 km south-south-west from Mekhora.

Farm made of two parts:
– In the eastern part of the site is a complex of very well-built structures and courtyards. At the bottom of the steep eastern slope are at least two rooms, built of very large stones and ashlars. For the construction much use has been made of sections of the natural cliffs. Three courtyards abut both

rooms, the walls of which are simple and one stone thick. Apparently, the complex was built in the LR period.

There is no construction further east due to the steepness of the slope.
– Another courtyard with rounded corners, 16×16 m, is located about 70 m west of the complex. The surrounding wall is built of one row of large stones.

Pottery: Iron II – 15%; Late Roman – 70%; Byzantine – 15%.
Other surveys: none.

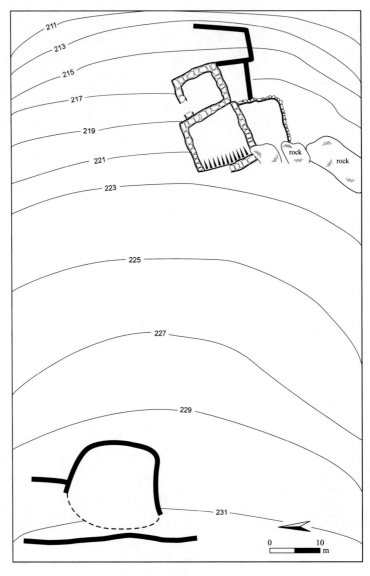

119. Plan of **Wadi Manzal (2)**.

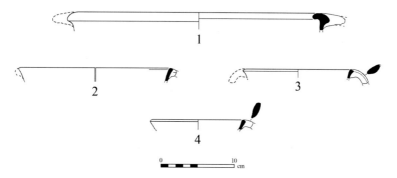

120. Pottery from **Wadi Manzal (2)**: 1. Krater, lt brn, IA II; 2. Bowl (?), reddish, LR-Byz; 3. CP, reddish, LR-Byz; 4. Jug, reddish, LR-Byz.

Site 64: 18-17/51/1

KHIRBET JURAISH

Israel grid: 18536/17104 (centre of the site)
UTM grid: 7238/5577
Elevation: 420 m a.s.l., 100 m a.s.a.
Name: ancient and on map
Site type: fortified tell
Area: 1.5 ha (15 dunams)
Topography: high hillock over spur
Rock type: Judea Group

Soil: brown forest, quality: 4
Cultivation: none
Cisterns: 2
Water source: 'Ein Juheir (no. 189), 200 m distant
Road: 'Ein Hafireh-Wadi Zamor (C50), 200 m distant
Visit: January 1999; 2014 and more; 6 surveyors; 174 sherds

Fortified tell at the top of a high hillock surrounded by steep ravines. The hillock is located on the slope of a spur descending south-east. East of the site is Wadi Mashqara, in which are a flowing spring, a water pool and a garden. Wadi Juheir, in which is 'Ein Juheir, surrounds the tell east and south. Along the course eastwards Wadi Juheir becomes the large Wadi Ahmar, along which and east of the site an ancient road (C50) passes.

The 'acropolis' is a structure, 40×20 m, at the top of the hillock. It is built of large stones and the surrounding wall is 1-1.5 m thick.

East of it is a broad room, 5 m wide. This structure is apparently later than the large upper structure. During a repeated visit at the site in 2014 the structure was found to be badly damaged by plundering.

A fortification wall starts from the 'acropolis', and descends over the slope in a direct line eastwards. At the middle of the slope the wall turns at a right angle southwards, and encircles the entire eastern part of the site. In the western slope only sections of the wall remain. The wall is built of very large stones and is 4 m thick. Apparently it was built in the EBA, based on its resemblance to the walls of the period in el-Makhruq (Eisenberg et al. 1993; Zertal 2008, site 269) and in Kh. Rahiyeh (Bar and Zertal 2019, site 7).

There is a sharp conspicuous corner, 50 m further along the wall on the eastern slope, maybe a tower or a gate, where fairly large structures abut the wall.

Inside the site are several large courtyards, the walls of which are modern, but erected on ancient foundations.

In the lower part of the site is a corral built in the same manner.

Chalcolithic pottery was found in the southern lowermost part of the site close to the north bank of the wadi. Chalcolithic presence here is also represented by three adjacent sites from this period near 'Ein Juheir spring (Sites 80, 96 and 97) and constitute one of the finest examples of the penetration of the Chalcolithic society into the higher Samaria region with the favourable Mediterranean climate, necessary to the cultivation of olives.

Porath (1968, site 142) found: "a ruin at the edge of a spur...its area about 5 dunams. Stones cleared and cultivated... Pottery: Early Bronze, Iron I-II". Our dates and description are much more detailed.

Pottery: Chalcolithic – 11%; Chalcolithic-Early Bronze – 17%; Early Bronze II-III – 11%; Middle Bronze II-Late Bronze – 8%; Iron I – 4%; Iron II – 35%; Persian-Hellenistic – 2%; Roman-Byzantine – 3%; Medieval – 9%.
Flint: 33 items: 4 flake cores, 2 bladelet cores, 11 flakes, 6 blades, 4 scrapers, 1 sickle blade and 5 Canaanean blades. The finds are highly probable from the Chalcolithic and EBA.
Stone: 3 V-shaped basalt bowl fragments, 2 fragments of a basalt fenestrated stand, a basalt mace head; 2 granite grinding stones. Some of the finds are highly probably Chalcolithic.
Other surveys: Porath 1968, site 142; Finkelstein 1986: 132; Finkelstein et al. 1997, 832-834.
Additional bibliography: Bar 2014, site 64.

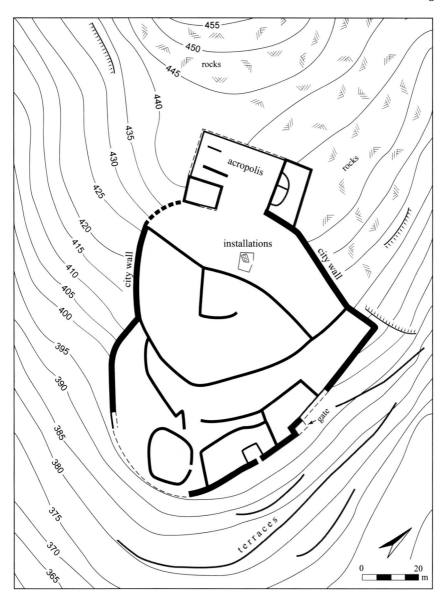

121. Plan of **Kh. Juraish**.

122. Aerial photo of the hillock of **Kh. Juraish**, view north-west (A. Solomon).

123. Aerial photo of **Kh. Juraish**, view north-west. Note the wadis of el-Mashqara and Juhair (A. Solomon).

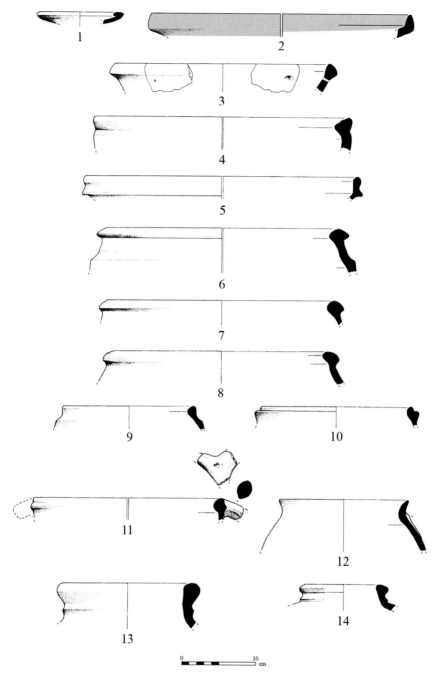

124. Pottery from **Kh. Juraish**: 1. Bowl, lt colour, EB II-III; 2. Platter, lt colour, red slip in and out, EB II-III. 3. Bowl, lt brn, IA II; 4. Krater, lt brn, IA II; 5, 10-11. CPs, lt brn, IA II; 6-8. Kraters, drk brn, IA II; 9. Krater, lt colour, Rom (?); 12. CP, lt brn, EB; 13. Pithos, drk brn, IA I; 14. Jar, lt colour, IA II.

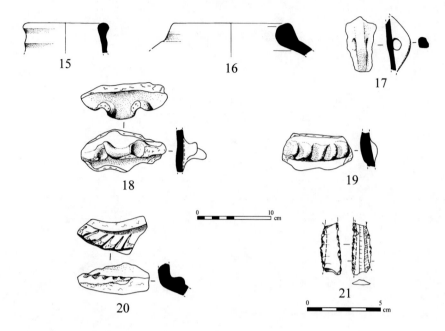

125. Finds from **Kh. Juraish**: 15. Jar, lt brn, IA II; 16. Holemouth pithos, lt brn, IA I-II; 17. Lug handle, lt colour, Chal; 18. Ledge handle, lt brn, EB I-II; 19. Body sherd, lt brn, rope orn, Chal; 20. Jar shoulder, lt brn, rope orn, EB; 21. Retouched sickle blade, EB.

Site 65: 18-17/71/1

JAFFA EN-NOON (3)

Israel grid: 18743/17199
UTM grid: 7259/5587
Elevation: 363 m a.s.l., 0 m a.s.a.
Name: nearest place
Site type: structures and road
Area: 3000 sq. m (3 dunams)
Topography: moderate slope
Rock type: Judea Group
Soil: terra rossa, quality: 8

Cultivation: field crops by the site
Cisterns: none
Water source: 'Ein et-Tahta (no. 186), 1.8 km distant
Road: Wadi el-Kabi–Yanun (C55), at the site
Visit: December 2014; 4 surveyors; 200 sherds

Site at the north flank of Jaffa en-Noon valley, 1.4 km south of Kh. Tana et-Tahta and 3.8 km south-west from Mekhora. Near the site passes an unpaved road ascending to the Alon road.

The site consists of two main parts whose connection is not certain.
- At the centre of the site are a number of structures, well-built of medium-sized stones. The site went through destruction and many changes, and therefore the nature of the structures is not clear. Perhaps the structures had an agricultural function as farm buildings.
- Road C55 passes through the site. It is nearly 7 m wide, coming from Tana et-Tahta, descending at the edge of the field of Jaffa en-Noon, to the region of Yanun. The road is flanked by two rows of large stones and in the spacing between them are paving and steps.

Abundant sherd scatter, indicating a settlement.
It is very reasonable that the main activity occurred in the LR-Byzantine periods when the road and the settlement functioned together.

Pottery: Iron II – 3% (body sherds); Late Roman – 75%; Byzantine – 15%; Medieval – 2%; unidentified – 5%.
Flint: 3 items: 1 flake, 1 scraper and a non-indicative sickle blade.
Other surveys: none.

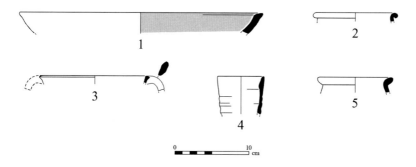

126. Pottery from **Jaffa en-Noon (3):** 1. Bowl, lt colour, red slip inside, Med; 2. Bowl, lt brn, LR; 3. CP, lt brn, LR; 4. Jar, lt brn, LR-Byz (?); 5. Jug (?), lt brn, LR-Byz.

Site 66: 18-17/71/2
JAFFA EN-NOON (1)

Israel grid: 18781/17187
UTM grid: 7263/5586
Elevation: 320 m a.s.l., 30 m a.s.a.
Name: ancient but not on map
Site type: fortress, courtyards and cave
Area: 1000 sq. m (1 dunam)
Topography: hillock
Rock type: Judea Group
Soil: terra rossa, quality: 5

Cultivation: none
Cisterns: none
Water source: 'Ein et-Tahta (no. 186), 1.9 km distant
Road: Wadi el-Kabi-Yanun (C55), 100 m distant
Visit: April 1999 and more; 4 surveyors; 120 sherds

Site on a low hillock at the edge of the high saddle of Jaffa en-Noon, 1.4 km south of Kh. Tana et-Tahta and 3.6 km south-west of Mekhora. There is a good lookout from the site to Kh. Tana et-Tahta area and to the Wadi Afjam plain.

On the hillock is a round fortress, built of two concentric circles. The outer circle is incomplete, about 50 m in diameter. The inner circle is 25 m in diameter and is partially irregular. The walls are built of medium-sized fieldstones and are 1.5 m thick.

In the southern side of the inner circle is a built opening with two jambs, apparently the entry into the inner circle. In this location the space between the circles is 7–10 m.

A wall from the northern part of the inner circle connects the circles.

The outer wall continues 50 m further west, apparently leading towards the entrance to the fortress.

About 50 m west of the fortress is a small irregular courtyard, 10 m in diameter. The opening of the courtyard is in the east and next to it is a smaller inner circular structure.

There is a cave in the western side of the courtyard.

A long east-west terrace wall, in the centre of which are two small round courtyards, connects the courtyard and the fortress.

The site is probably an IA fortress or a structure with no known parallels. It rises above its surroundings, appearing as a small mound, and served as a lookout for the nearby area.

Pottery: Iron II-III – 60%; Early Roman – 10%; Late Roman – 20%; Byzantine – 10%.
Other surveys: none.

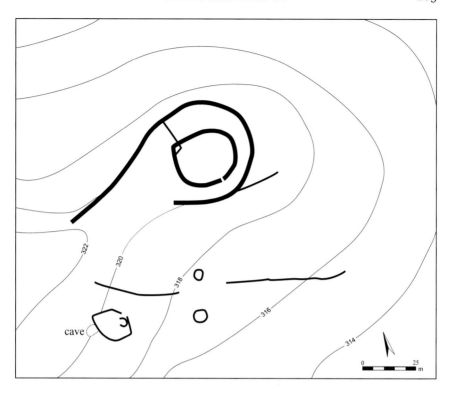

127. Plan of **Jaffa en-Noon (1)**.

128. Aerial photo of **Jaffa en-Noon (1)**, looking north-west (A. Solomon).

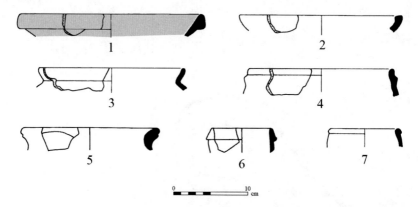

129. Pottery from **Jaffa en-Noon (1)**: 1. Bowl, drk brn, red slip inside and outside, IA II; 2. Bowl, brn, IA II-III; 3. Bowl, pink, ER; 4. CP, lt brn, IA II; 5. Jar, brn, Rom; 6. Jar, blk, Byz; 7. Jar, pink, LR.

◆ ◆ ◆

Site 67: 18-17/71/3

JAFFA EN-NOON (5)

Israel grid: 18744/17169
UTM grid: 7259/5584
Elevation: 370 m a.s.l., 10 m a.s.a.
Name: nearest place
Site type: courtyards, enclosure and cisterns
Area: 2000 sq. m (2 dunams)
Topography: edge of valley
Rock type: Judea Group

Soil: terra rossa, quality: 6
Cultivation: none
Cisterns: 2
Water source: 'Ein et-Tahta (no. 186), 2.1 km distant
Road: Wadi el-Kabi-Yanun (C55), by the site
Visit: July 2015; 5 surveyors; 25 sherds

Site at the bottom of the steep eastern slope of E.P. 474, at the centre of the Jaffa en-Noon ridge, 1.5 km south of Kh. Tana et-Tahta and 4 km north of Gittit. The site has several components:
– Large irregular courtyard in the northern part of the site. The enclosing 76 m long wall is built of large and medium-sized stones and is preserved to a height of up to 4 courses (1.5 m). The wall is semi-ellipse, and does not extend into the western part of the courtyard. It is probable that at this side the rocky slope served as an enclosing wall. An inner wall built of medium-sized stones, about 5–10 m from and parallel to the outer wall, creating a 50 cm step above the courtyard level.

- Southern courtyard attached in the south to the northern one and built in almost identical form, an irregular semi-elliptical structure, using the rocky cliffs of the slope as an enclosing wall. The outer 50 m long wall is built of large and medium-sized stones, and is preserved up to 5 courses (about 1.5 m). Here is a parallel inner wall, averaging 5m from the outer wall, and an elevated step, almost 1 m higher than the courtyard surface level.
- Round enclosure, 10 m in diameter, built of large and medium-sized stones, about 10 m east of the large two courtyards. The north-eastern part of the enclosure is supported by a double support wall built of large stones.
- East of the southern courtyard are remains of walls and rock-cuttings which failed to yield a clear scheme.
- Cistern, 50 m east from the southern courtyard. Next to it is an ancient quarried pit.

The site consists of an advanced LR period layout of courtyards located at the hinterland of the large settlement at Kh. Tana et-Tahta.

The parallel wall design of the large courtyards is unique to this region, and its purpose is not obvious.

Pottery: Iron I – 4%; Late Roman – 88%; Byzantine – 4%; Modern – 4%.
Other surveys: none.

130. Pottery from **Jaffa en-Noon** (5): 1. Bowl, lt brn, Rom-Byz (?); 2. Pithos, lt brn, IA I.

Site 68: 18-17/71/4
MUGHUR ET-TIREH

Israel grid: 18756/17160
UTM grid: 7260/5583
Elevation: 360 m a.s.l., 10 m a.s.a.
Name: nearest place
Site type: courtyards
Area: 1000 sq. m (1 dunam)
Topography: plateau
Rock type: Judea Group

Soil: terra rossa, quality: 7
Cultivation: none
Cisterns: none
Water source: 'Ein et-Tahta (no. 186), 2.1 km distant
Road: Wadi el-Kabi-Yanun (C55), at the site
Visit: May 2015; 4 surveyors; 17 sherds

Small site on a plateau at the centre of the Jaffa en-Noon ridge, at the bottom of the steep eastern slope of E.P. 474, 1.6 km south of Kh. Tana et-Tahta and 3.9 km north of Gittit. The ancient road ascending from Wadi el-Kabi to Yanun (C55) is adjacent to the site.

There are two courtyards:
– Small upper courtyard, 15×15 m, built of two rows of fieldstones with

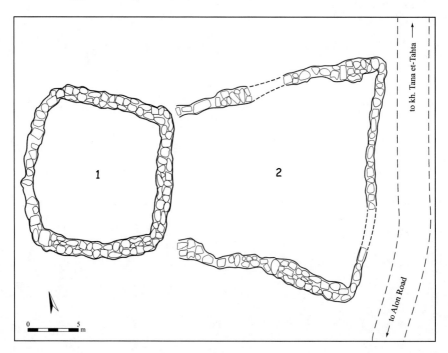

131. Plan of **Mughur et-Tireh**.

in-filling. The surrounding wall is 1 m thick and the construction is very crude (no. 1 in plan).
- Large irregular courtyard, also crudely built. The enclosure wall is built mostly of one row of fieldstones (no. 2).

The courtyards were utilized for storage of crops as was customary in the Roman and Byzantine periods. It was part of the hinterland of the large settlement at Kh. Tana et-Tahta during the LR period.

There were very few sherds.

Pottery: Late Roman (body sherds) – 100%.
Other surveys: none.

Site 69: 18-17/71/5

ELEVATION POINT 474

Israel grid: 18717/17150
UTM grid: 7256/5582
Elevation: 450 m a.s.l., 100 m a.s.a.
Name: nearest place
Site type: fortress and pool
Area: 1000 sq. m (1 dunam)
Topography: slope
Rock type: Judea Group
Soil: terra rossa, quality: 3

Cultivation: none
Cisterns: quarried pool
Water source: 'Ein Juheir (no. 189), 2 km distant
Road: Wadi el-Kabi-Yanun (C55), by the site
Visit: February 2000; 4 surveyors; 40 sherds

Site on a moderate slope within a high mountainous area, close to and south of E.P. 474, 1.7 km south of Kh. Tana et-Tahta and 4.2 km south-west of Mekhora.

Well-built fortress. The dimensions of the central structure are: north and south wings: 28 m long, east and west wings: 36 m long. The perimeter wall is about 1.5 m thick, well-built of two rows of medium-sized fieldstones.

The inside space is divided: The eastern part contains an inner structure, 25×20 m. In the west are two long narrow spaces ending in a small room in the north-western corner of the structure. In the southern part are two rooms; the wall of one ruined. Abutting both rooms from the north, in the centre of the inside space of the fort, is a small cell, 4×4 m, with thick walls.

All the inner walls are well built of stones, some of which are ashlars. The walls are one stone thick.

In the north-eastern side of the fortress is a cave opening.

Outside the fortress nearby the north-eastern corner is a nicely quarried pool, 8×5 m; presently the depth is 1 m. The pool was probably the water source of the site.

The dominating location, the good construction and the ancient road next to it show that the site served as a fortress for observation and road maintenance during the LR and Byzantine periods.

Pottery: Late Roman – 50%; Byzantine – 40%; Medieval – 10%.
Other surveys: none.

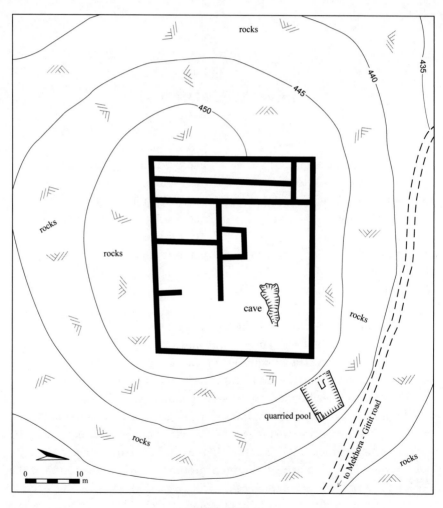

132. Plan of **E.P. 474**.

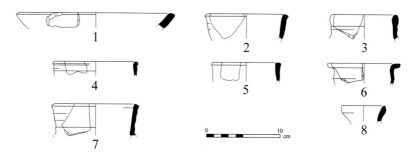

133. Pottery from **E.P. 474**: 1. Bowl, org, Med; 2. Bowl, buff, Rom (?); 3, 7. Jars, drk brn, LR; 4. Jug (?), org, LR-Byz; 5. Jar, drk brn, LR-Byz; 6. Bowl, org, LR; 8. Juglet, org, LR-Byz.

◆ ◆ ◆

Site 70: 18-17/71/6

JAFFA EN-NOON (6)

Israel grid: 18772/17145
UTM grid: 7262/5582
Elevation: 300 m a.s.l., 30 m a.s.a.
Name: nearest place
Site type: cave, enclosure, structure and cisterns
Area: 3000 sq. m (3 dunams)
Topography: slope and edge of valley
Rock type: Judea Group

Soil: terra rossa, quality: 7
Cultivation: none
Cisterns: 3
Water source: 'Ein et-Tahta (no. 186), 2.3 km distant
Road: Wadi el-Kabi-Yanun (C55), 300 m distant
Visit: July 2015; 5 surveyors; 10 sherds

Site on the eastern slope of E.P. 474, in the ridge of Jaffa en-Noon, 3.5 km north of Gittit.
   There are two parts, not related to each other:
− Dwelling cave, 20 m long and 4 m high. The entrance is 1 m wide. The ceiling is charred. At the entrance and inside the cave are remains of walls, evidently prepared for dwelling. In front of the cave is a round courtyard, 15 m diameter, whose surrounding wall is built of large and medium-sized stones, and has been preserved up to a height of 6 courses (2 m). On the slope below the courtyard and the cave are supporting walls.
− Irregular enclosure, 18×15 m, about 35 m south of the dwelling cave. The enclosing wall is built of two rows of medium-sized stones with infill of small stones. In the southern side is a 2 m wide built entrance between two monoliths. Most of the inner surface of the enclosure is bare rock. Another 6×6 m square structure adjoins the enclosure in the south-east.

In the slope above the cave and the enclosure are three openings of cisterns. There is a very scanty sherd scatter.

Pottery (body sherds): Late Roman – 40%; Medieval – 10%; Modern – 50%.
Other surveys: none.

Site 71: 18-17/81/1

MUGHARET ET-TIREH

Israel grid: 18848/17116
UTM grid: 7269/5584
Elevation: 180 m a.s.l., 20 m b.s.a.
Name: nearest place
Site type: courtyard, cave and cistern
Area: 1500 sq. m (1.5 dunams)
Topography: edge of valley
Rock type: Judea Group

Soil: brown forest, quality: 6
Cultivation: none
Cisterns: 1
Water source: 'Ein et-Tahta (no. 186), 2.3 km distant
Road: Phasaelis-Neapolis (C40) 'Wadi Afjam bypass', 200 m distant
Visit: May 2008; 4 surveyors; 20 sherds

Site in the spur country west of Alon road, on the slope ascending north to a small valley originating in the spur sloping east from Mughur et-Tireh, 4 km north of Gittit.

Courtyard, 23.5×21 m. The south and west wings have been preserved only in part. The encircling wall is built of one row of large stones, of maximum height three courses (1 m), but mostly only one course surviving.

At the top south-western corner of the courtyard is a cave, about 10×10 m, with a collapsed roof. Only the entrances in the north and south sides remain. The fallen boulders of the ceiling can still be recognized.

An operating cistern, about 40 m south-west of the courtyard in the spur above, apparently served as the water source for the courtyard.

Pottery: Late Roman (body sherds) – 100%.
Other surveys: none.

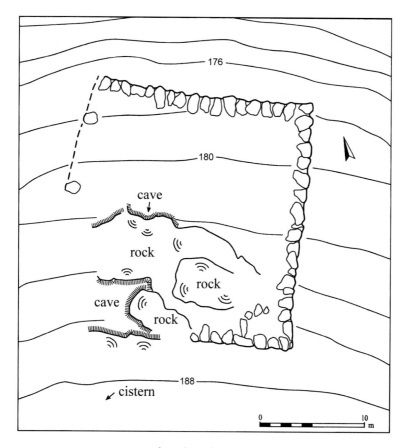

134. Plan of **Mugharet et-Tireh**.

Site 72: 18-17/81/2
JAFFA EN-NOON (2)

Israel grid: 18849/17169
UTM grid: 7270/5585
Elevation: 170 m a.s.l., 30 m b.s.a.
Name: nearest place
Site type: courtyards
Area: 3000 sq. m (3 dunams)
Topography: slope and edge of valley
Rock type: Judea Group
Soil: terra rossa, quality: 6

Cultivation: none
Cisterns: none
Water source: 'Ein et-Tahta (no. 186), 1.2 km distant
Road: Phasaelis-Neapolis (C40) 'Wadi Afjam bypass', by the site
Visit: January 2006; 6 surveyors; 65 sherds

Site at the northern edge of a small channel descending eastwards to Wadi el-Kabi, at the bottom of a rocky slope by a field, 500 m west of Alon road.

There are two courtyards, where most areas are rock outcrops, built on natural steps in the slope.
– The lower eastern courtyard, an irregular rhombus, about 25×25 m, is the larger of the two. The southern wall fits the contours of the slope (no. 1 in plan).
– Smaller elliptical courtyard, 15×8 m, about 50 m west of the eastern courtyard. Another small courtyard abuts it in the east (no. 2).

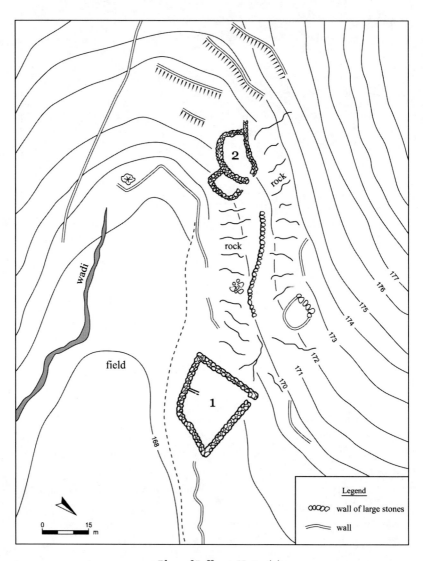

135. Plan of **Jaffa en-Noon (2)**.

There are two stages of construction in both courtyards. The 1 m thick surrounding wall was built of two rows of very large stones with a filling between them in the first stage. A construction of small stones was added on top in the second stage, apparently in the Medieval period.

Covering the entire slope are terraces built of large and medium-sized stones, taking advantage of the rocky steps for support. The slopes around the ravine are well terraced.

The area has many courtyards, terraces and steps, obvious signs of highly developed agriculture, mainly of the LR period.

Pottery: Intermediate Bronze (body sherds) – 3%; Middle Bronze II (body sherds) – 6%; Iron II (body sherds) – 8%; Late Roman – 66%; Medieval – 17%. **Other surveys:** none.

136. Pottery from **Jaffa en-Noon (2)**: 1. Jug, drk brn, LR; 2. Jug, lt brn, LR; 3. Jar, gr, LR; 4. Bowl base (?), lt brn, Med.

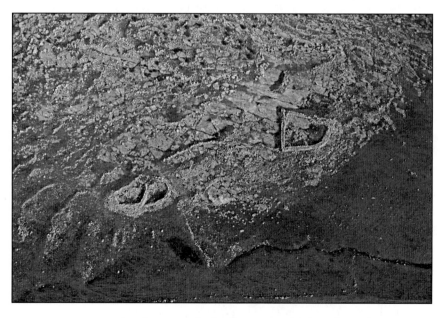

137. Aerial view north of **Jaffa en-Noon (2)** (A. Solomon).

Site 73: 18-17/81/3
JAFFA EN-NOON (7)

Israel grid: 18866/17161 (centre of site)
UTM grid: 7271/5584
Elevation: 155 m a.s.l., 60 m b.s.a.
Name: nearest place
Site type: courtyards
Area: 3000 sq. m (3 dunams)
Topography: edge of valley and slope
Rock type: Judea Group
Soil: terra rossa, quality: 6
Cultivation: none
Cisterns: none
Water source: 'Ein et-Tahta (no. 186), 2.5 km distant
Road: Phasaelis-Neapolis (C40) 'Wadi Afjam bypass', by the site
Visit: March 2006; April 2014; 4 surveyors; 15 sherds

Site consists of two courtyards on both sides of the old Gittit-Mekhora road, close to the site of Jaffa en-Noon (2). The courtyards are about 120 m apart.

The southern structure is a small, irregular, carelessly built, courtyard, 15×12 m, in the lower part of the slope descending northwards to the valley of the wadi. Many sections of its walls are two stones (about 1 m) thick. The southern wall is built of one row of large stones laid on a low rocky cliff. North of the courtyard are traces of a funnel-shaped entrance. A room or cell is attached to the inside of the western wall whose construction is secondary and later (no. 1 in plan).

A wall projects westwards from the courtyard, forming another courtyard. This wall is also carelessly built.

The northern courtyard, is about 12×12 m, 20 m north of the old asphalted road. Unlike the southern courtyard, this one is meticulously built. The enclosing wall is 1.5–2 m thick, built of two rows of medium-sized and large stones with an infill. The northern part of the wall has been demolished, and only its foundations remain. In the north-western wall is an opening with a jamb stone. In the north-east corner of the courtyard is a round cell. Another similar cell adjoins the outer side of the south-eastern wall (no. 2 in plan).

A wall about 3 m thick and about 40 m long starts from the southern corner of the northern courtyard, built as a terrace wall along the slope.

The courtyards apparently functioned together with the nearby multi-period site, Jaffa en-Noon (2) (Site 72), although in both courtyards the bulk of the find is from a single period, LR.

Pottery: Iron II (body sherds) – 10%; Late Roman – 90%.
Other surveys: none.

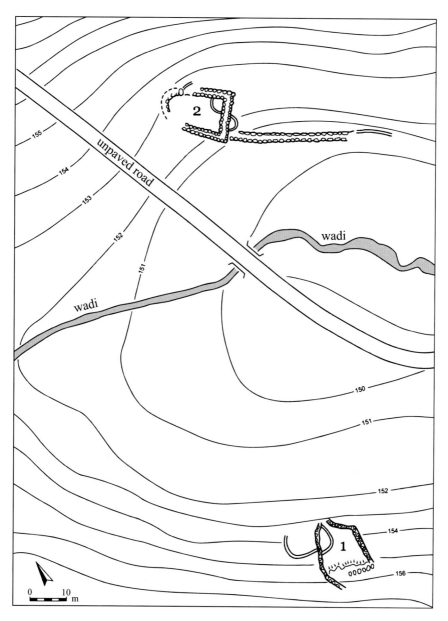

138. Plan of **Jaffa en-Noon** (7).

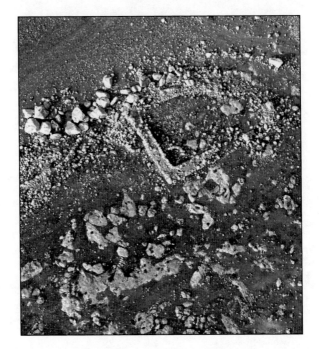

139. Aerial view of the northern courtyard at **Jaffa en-Noon** (7) (A. Solomon).

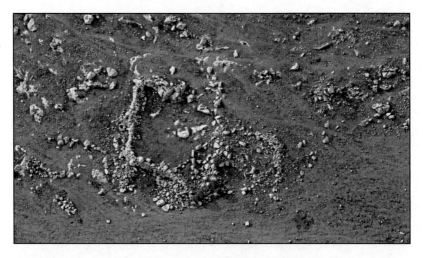

140. Aerial view of the southern courtyard at **Jaffa en-Noon** (7) (A. Solomon).

141. Sherd from **Jaffa en-Noon** (7): jug, drk brn, LR.

Site 74: 18-17/81/4
JAFFA EN-NOON (8)

Israel grid: 18811/17162
UTM grid: 7266/5584
Elevation: 246 m a.s.l., 50 m b.s.a.
Name: nearest place
Site type: courtyard and cistern
Area: 5000 sq. m (5 dunams)
Topography: small valley
Rock type: Judea Group

Soil: Mediterranean brown, quality: 5
Cultivation: none
Cisterns: 1
Water source: 'Ein et-Tahta (no. 186), 2.2 km distant
Road: Wadi el-Kabi-Yanun (C55) 500 m distant
Visit: June 2015; 8 surveyors; 70 sherds

Site in a small valley on the ridge of Jaffa en-Noon, 3.6 km south-west of Mekhora.

Several features indicate intensive agricultural activity in the Roman period:
– Rectangular courtyard, 25×18 m, built on a rocky surface on a slope. Sections of the enclosing wall are built of two rows of small stones or one row of large stones. The entrance is in the north-west. An outside cell abuts the wall by the entrance. The courtyard is levelled by supporting walls, some of which reach a height of up to 2 m. There are no signs of dwellings, and apparently the courtyard was used for storage of agricultural produce (no. 1 in plan).
– Constructed cistern with an embankment around it (no. 2), 50 m north of the courtyard. A trough for watering livestock abuts the cistern. At least two modern water collecting channels lead to the cistern (no. 3).
The entire area of the site was supported by terrace walls forming cultivated fields.

It is apparent that this site is one of a large group of agricultural sites in the region, constituting part of the agrarian hinterland of the large settlement at Kh. Tana et-Tahta during the Roman period.

Pottery: Late Roman (2nd-3rd centuries CE) – 100%.
Other surveys: none.

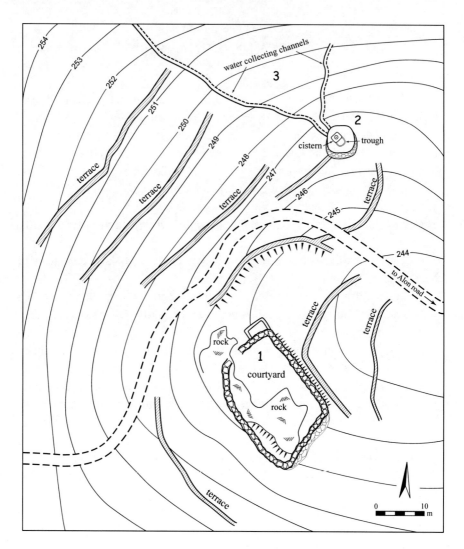

142. Plan of **Jaffa en-Noon (8)**.

143. Pottery from **Jaffa en-Noon (8)**: 1-2. Bowls, lt brn, LR; 3-4. Jugs, lt brn, LR.

Site 75: 18-17/81/5
JAFFA EN-NOON (9)

Israel grid: 18820/17144
UTM grid: 7267/5582
Elevation: 240 m a.s.l., 0 a.s.a.
Name: nearest place
Site type: threshing floors, installations and prehistoric
Area: 7000 sq. m (7 dunams)
Topography: plateau
Rock type: Judea Group
Soil: Mediterranean brown, quality: 3
Cultivation: none
Cisterns: none
Water source: 'Ein et-Tahta (no. 186), 2.4 km distant
Road: Wadi el-Kabi-Yanun (C55) 600 m distant
Visit: June 2015; 8 surveyors; 130 sherds

Site on the flat plateau on the ridge of Jaffa en-Noon, 3.8 km south-west of Mekhora. A rocky axis used for agricultural purposes extends along it.
The site has three features:
- Two threshing floors, with collapsed walls, originally about 10 m in diameter, on the rock surfaces in the plateau. They relate to a later phase of the site.
- Two small structures, about 5.5×4 m, built of small stones, possibly used for grain storage. The structures appear to be modern.
- At least five basins cut in the rock surface in the north of the site.

Traces of three recesses which were put into use and/or partially improved.

The site was used as a hub of threshing floors and other agricultural installations, and was part of the agrarian hinterland of the large settlement at Kh. Tana et-Tahta, mainly during the LR and Byzantine periods. The agricultural installations were also used in the Medieval period.

Abundant flint finds close to the site are evidence of prehistoric presence (see below).

Pottery: Late Roman – 46%; Byzantine – 15%; Medieval – 23%; unidentified – 16%.
Flint: 186 items: 1 flake core, 3 bladelet cores, 1 ridged blade, 112 flakes, 18 blades, 39 bladelets, 1 Canaanean blade, 3 scrapers, 7 retouched bladelets and a backed sickle blade. The backed sickle blade and the bladelets are dated to the latest phases of the Epipalaeolithic or the beginning of the Pre Pottery Neolithic A. The Canaanean blade suggests an EB presence at the site.
Stone: 40 basalt threshing sledge stones.
Other surveys: none.

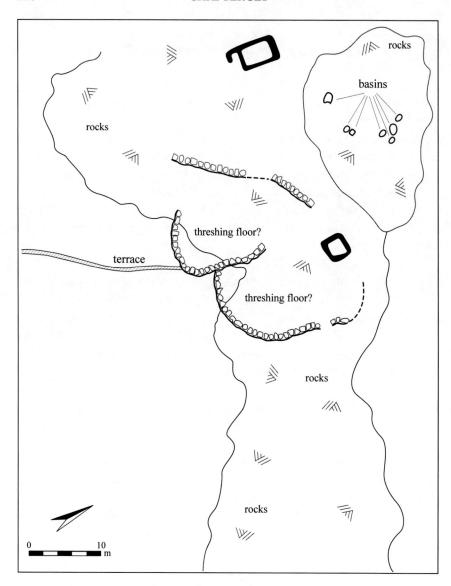

144. Plan of **Jaffa en-Noon (9)**.

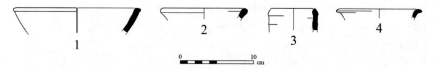

145. Pottery from **Jaffa en-Noon (9)**: 1. Bowl, drk brn, Med; 2. Bowl, drk brn, LR-Byz; 3. Jar, drk brn, LR-Byz; 4. Jug, drk brn, LR-Byz.

Site 76: 18-17/81/6
JAFFA EN-NOON (4)

Israel grid: 18832/17138
UTM grid: 7268/5581
Elevation: 225 m a.s.l., 80 a.s.a.
Name: nearest place
Site type: flint scatter
Area: 500 sq. m (0.5 dunam)
Topography: slope of a spur
Rock type: Judea Group

Soil: terra rossa, quality: 5
Cultivation: none
Cisterns: none
Water source: 'Ein et-Tahta (no. 186), 2.4 km distant
Road: Phasaelis-Neapolis (C40) 'Wadi Afjam bypass', 400 m distant
Visit: June 2015; 3 surveyors

Site at the edge of a spur on the ridge of Jaffa en-Noon, 3.5 km north-north-east of Gittit.

Flint scatter on the rocky surface. Artefacts were collected among the rocks and in soil pockets, although items were scattered all over the spur area. There may be linkage between this site and the prehistoric find at the site of Jaffa en-Noon (9) (Site 75 above).

Flint: 159 items: 1 flake core, 6 bladelet cores, 5 core wastes, 98 flakes, 13 blades, 16 bladelets, 2 microburin wastes, 2 retouched bladelets, 7 side scrapers, 2 scrapers, and 7 retouched blades. The microburin waste and the bladelets show highly reasonably that at least some of the finds belong to the Epipalaeolithic period.
Stone: a basalt pestle fragment.
Other surveys: none.

Site 77: 18-17/81/7
FARQOM CAVE (2)

Israel grid: 18896/17132
UTM grid: 7274/5581
Elevation: 135 m a.s.l., 20 a.s.a.
Name: nearest place
Site type: sherd and flint scatters and agricultural structures
Area: 1 ha (10 dunams)
Topography: hillock
Rock type: Mount Scopus Group
Soil: terra rossa, quality: 6
Cultivation: none
Cisterns: 2
Water source: 'Ein Abu Daraj (no. 177), 2.5 km distant
Road: Phasaelis-Neapolis (C40) 'Wadi Afjam bypass', 200 m distant
Visit: December 1994; 4 surveyors; 64 sherds

Site on a flat summit close to the west of the Alon road, 4 km east-north-east of the centre of Gittit.

At the west of the site is a small structure surrounded by threshing floors.

In the east is a cave, about 20 conical basins cut in the rocky surface and a cistern.

In the south-east is a cluster of caves, threshing floors and other installations.

In the south is a new cistern.

This is a multi-period agricultural working area. There is a moderate sherd scatter in various areas and a very numerous flint collection.

Pottery: Iron (body sherds) – 6%; Roman-Byzantine – 31%; Ottoman – 63%.
Flint: 133 items: 2 flake cores, 4 blade cores, 3 bladelet cores, 2 core wastes, 46 flakes, 32 blades, 28 bladelets, 6 retouched blades, 2 retouched bladelets, 2 borers, 1 burin, 1 scraper, and 5 side scrapers. The find is proof of flint industry, but is not indicative for determination of the period.
Other surveys: none.

LANDSCAPE UNIT 34

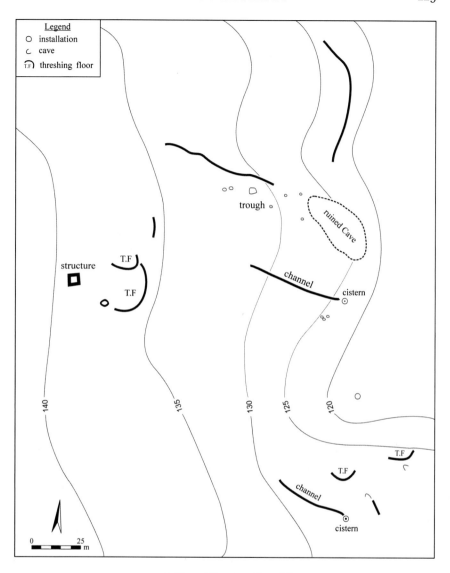

146. Plan of **Farqom Cave (2)**.

Site 78: 18-17/81/8
MUGHUR EL-RAMDAT (1)

Israel grid: 18890/17106 (centre of the site)
UTM grid: 7273/5578
Elevation: 130 m a.s.l., 20 a.s.a.
Name: nearest place
Site type: sherd and flint scatters and structures
Area: 2 ha (20 dunams)
Topography: flat hillock
Rock type: Judea Group

Soil: terra rossa, quality: 3
Cultivation: none
Cisterns: 2
Water source: 'Ein Abu Daraj (no. 177), 2.5 km distant
Road: Phasaelis-Neapolis (C40) 'Wadi Afjam bypass', by the site
Visit: January 2014; January 2016; 5 surveyors; 400 sherds

Agricultural site spread over a broad hillock near and above the site where the old Alon road sets out from the new one, 3.8 km south-south-west of Mekhora.
Features:
- Small tower, built of large stones, possibly a fort, in the centre of which is a later stone circle 3 m in diameter. Next to the fort is another similar modern stone circle. There is a good lookout from the tower to the valley of Wadi Ahmar.
- Four threshing floors: two east of the tower and two at the southern lower part of the hill. They are of identical construction: a semicircle filled and levelled to create a platform for a threshing floor, encircled by stones. More threshing floors south of the old Alon road, 200 m south of the centre of the site.
- Built channels for collecting and draining runoff water to two cisterns.
- East-west wall, about 150 m long, built of large stones, in the north part of the hill. The eastern end of the wall turns north, descends on the slope and disappears. This wall may be for separating agricultural plots.
- Large artificial crater, approximately 30 m long, 10 m wide and 3 m deep, dug opposite a small cliff.
- Several caves with collapsed ceilings in the cliff (not on plan). At the bottom of the hill southern slope are two caves, diameters 4-5 m. Stone walls adjoin the entrances.

Cup marks of various dimensions are scattered around the site.
The site has many Pre-Pottery Neolithic B flint artefacts.

Pottery: Middle Bronze II (body sherds) – 10%; Iron I-II (body sherds) – 6%; Late Roman – 45%; Byzantine-Early Moslem – 18%; Medieval – 19%; Ottoman – 2%.

Flint: 441 items: 4 flake cores, 4 blade cores, 6 bladelet cores, 2 naviform cores, 13 core wastes, 192 flakes, 82 blades, 72 bladelets, 26 side scrapers, 9 retouched flakes, 15 retouched blades, 2 retouched bladelets, 2 backed blades, 1 denticulate blade, 2 backed bladelets, 6 borers, 1 scraper and 2 burins. The naviform cores are evidence of the Pre-Pottery Neolithic B period.
Stone: 20 basalt stones of threshing sledge.
Other surveys: none.

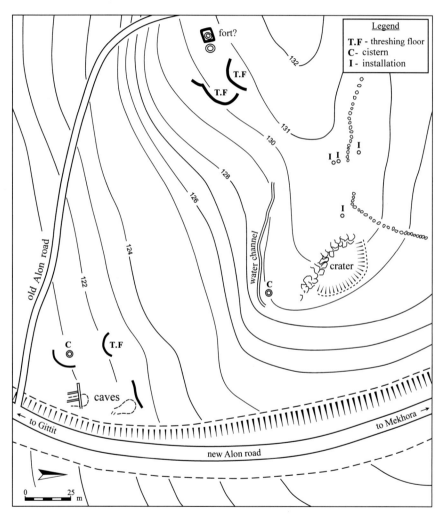

147. Plan of **Mughur el-Ramdat (1)**.

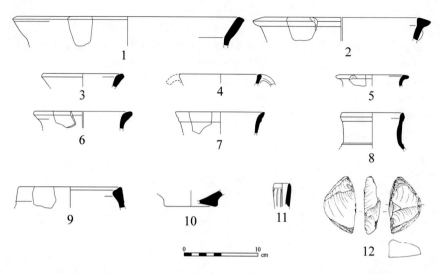

148. Finds from **Mughur el-Ramdat (1)**: 1. Krater (?), lt brn, Med; 2. Krater, drk brn, EM; 3. Jug, drk brn, LR-Byz; 4. CP, red, LR; 5. Jug, red, LR-Byz. 6. Jar, lt gr, LR-Byz; 7. Jug, blk, LR; 8. Jar, lt brn, LR; 9. Jar, lt brn, Byz-EM; 10. Bowl base (?), lt brn, Med (?); 11. Pipe, lt brn, Ott; 12. Bladelets core, PPNB.

♦ ♦ ♦

Site 79: 18-17/91/1

MUGHUR EL-RAMDAT (2)

Israel grid: 18920/17100
UTM grid: 7277/5578
Elevation: 130 m a.s.l., 70 b.s.a.
Name: nearest place
Site type: structures and caves
Area: 8,000 sq. m (8 dunams)
Topography: edge of valley
Rock type: Judea Group
Soil: terra rossa, quality: 4

Cultivation: none
Cisterns: none
Water source: 'Ein Abu Daraj (no. 177), 2 km distant
Road: Phasaelis-Neapolis (C40) 'Wadi Afjam bypass', 300 m distant
Visit: January 2014; 4 surveyors; 100 sherds

Site on a spur close to the confluence of Wadi el-Afjam with a short ravine west of Jebel Mahajrah, 200 m east of the Alon road and 2 km south from Mekhora. Several structures:
– Wall about 50 m long ascending from west to east in the western part of the site. The construction is of two rows of large stones, some very large. The function of the wall is not clear.

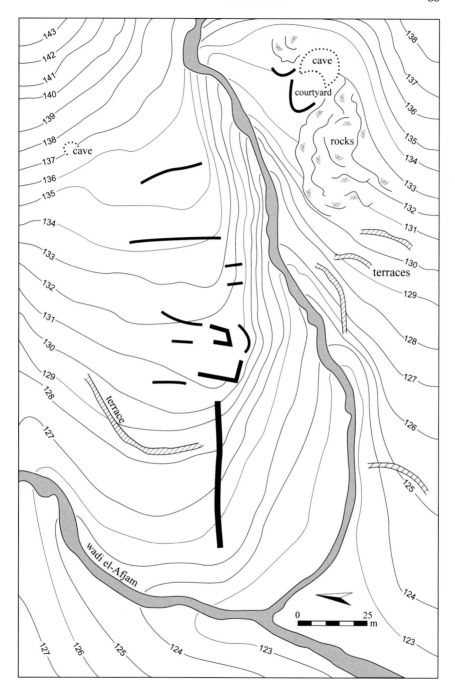

149. Plan of **Mughur el-Ramdat (2)**.

- Several structures near the assumed extension of the wall eastwards.
- Large cave (appearing in the map as Mughar Ramdat) about 70 m from the eastern end of the wall, on the south bank of the Jebel Mahajreh tributary. In front of it is a small courtyard, 15×7 m, built of large stones. In the northern slope above the site is the small opening of another cave.

On both sides of the tributary are terrace remains.

Pottery: Middle Bronze II (body sherds) – 8%; Iron I-II (body sherds) – 10%; Late Roman – 50%; Byzantine – 10%; Medieval (Crusader and Mamluk) – 10%; Ottoman and Modern – 12%.
Flint: 10 items: 5 flakes, 4 blades and a side scraper.
Other surveys: none.

Site 80: 18-17/50/1

'EIN JURAISH

Israel grid: 18572/17089
UTM grid: 7242/5576
Elevation: 315 m a.s.l., 30 m b.s.a.
Name: given by the Survey
Site type: walls, road and sherd and flint scatters
Area: 1.5 ha (15 dunams)
Topography: small valley and area by ravine
Rock type: Judea Group

Soil: brown forest, quality: 4
Cultivation: none
Cisterns: none
Water source: Bir Mashkara (no. 190), 400 m distant
Road: 'Ein Hafireh-Wadi Zamor (C50), at the site
Visit: January 1999; 7 surveyors; 200 sherds

Extended site east and below Kh. Juraish (Site 64), in the channel of Wadi Mashkara, which descends from the north and meets the wide riverbed of Wadi Ahmar.

The site covers an area 250 m long and 60-70 m wide.

East above the channel is a wall of large stones supporting a constructed road. This is apparently the ancient road which descends from the north-west along Wadi Ahmar (branch of road C50). There are remains of a built path 100 m up the slope, parallel to the ancient road.

A low cliff extends about 150 m, parallel to the ancient road. Above the cliff is a line of structures and scattered walls. Some of the wall remains do not form definite structures; they were probably destroyed by cultivation.

Several support walls at the bottom of the slope east of the lines of structures. Small dam in a small ravine descending to Wadi Mashkara.

Sherd and flint scatters along the entire structure stretch.

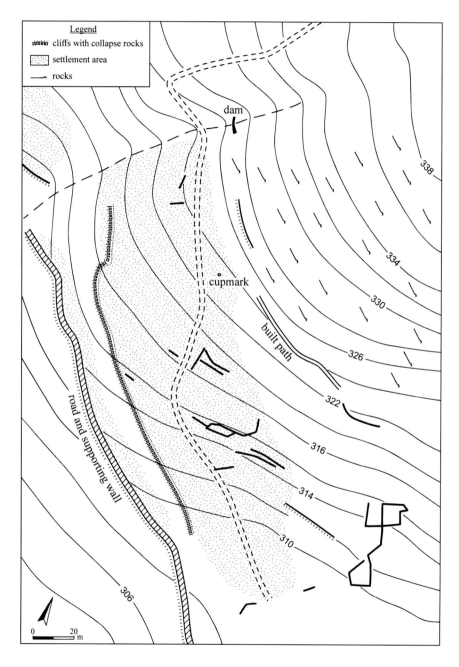

150. Plan of 'Ein Juraish.

The Chalcolithic cluster here is represented by three adjacent sites from this period in the vicinity of 'Ein Juheir spring (Sites 64, 96 and 97), and constitutes one of the finest examples of the penetration of the Chalcolithic society into the higher Samaria region with a favourable Mediterranean climate, necessary for the cultivation of olives. In 'Ein Juraish a habitation continues to the EB I, unlike Sites 96 and 97, which are single-period.

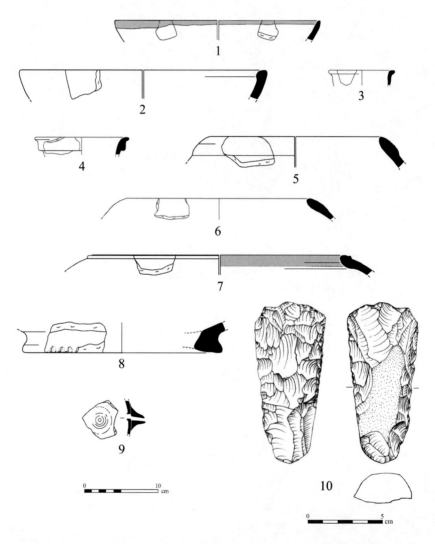

151. Finds from 'Ein Juraish: 1. Bowl, brn, red slip in and out on rim, EB I; 2. Bowl, brn, EB I; 3. Bowl, org, LR; 4. Jar, gr, MB II; 5. Holemouth jar, brn, EB I; 6. Holemouth jar, lt brn, Chal; 7. Holemouth jar, brn, red slip inside, EB I; 8. Base, rope orn, EB I; 9. Spout, brn, EB I; 10. Adze, Chal.

Pottery: Chalcolithic – 40%; Early Bronze I – 54%, Middle Bronze II – 2%; Late Roman – 4%.

Flint: 124 items: 1 flake core, 1 blade core, 2 bladelet cores, 2 core wastes, 47 flakes, 17 blades, 4 Canaanean blades, 6 retouched flakes, 11 retouched blades, 17 side scrapers, 8 borers, 1 fan scraper, 1 backed sickle blade, 1 non-indicative sickle blade and an adze. The adze is evidence of the Chalcolithic period, and the Canaanean blades of the EBA.

Other surveys: none.

Bibliography: Bar 2014, site 65.

◆ ◆ ◆

Site 81: 18-17/60/2

KOM ALI

Israel grid: 18611/17083
UTM grid: 7246/5575
Elevation: 350 m a.s.l., 90 m a.s.a.
Name: ancient but not on map
Site type: unfinished fort
Area: 4,000 sq. m (4 dunams)
Topography: hillock
Rock type: Judea Group
Soil: terra rossa, quality: 5

Cultivation: none
Cisterns: none
Water source: Bir Mashkara (no. 190), 800 m distant
Road: 'Ein Hafireh-Wadi Zamor (C50), 300 m distant
Visit: November 1998; 4 surveyors; 40 sherds

Site on a broad summit north of Wadi Ahmar, 3.5 km north-north-west of Gittit. North of the site is a small cultivated valley and to the west is Kh. Juraish.

Unfinished fort.

A stone wall surrounds the summit of the hill on the north and west. The effort invested in its construction is most impressive. The wall is about 4 m thick, built with two rows of large stones with infill of smaller stones. The length of the preserved section is about 90 m.

The wall turns in a bend towards the summit. The southern section of the northern longer arm was built over the steep slope descending to Wadi Ahmar, and only traces remain, the rest having been washed away. There are steps as in the south-western part of the site.

There are no other structures in the summit area, only sherd scatters.

The remains appear to be an IA fort guarding the ancient road descending via Wadi Ahmar. Apparently the fort was abandoned after its construction began.

It is very probable that the fort was linked to the nearby IA fortified sites at Kh. Juraish (Site 64) and Kh. er-Risa (1) (Site 94).

Pottery: Iron II – 85%; Late Roman (body sherds) – 15%.
Other surveys: none.

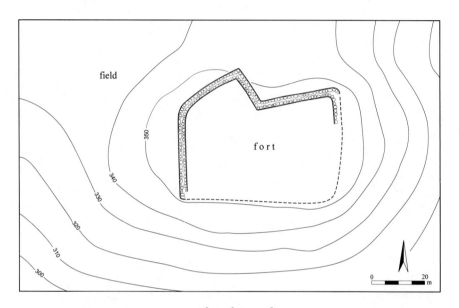

152. Plan of **Kom Ali**.

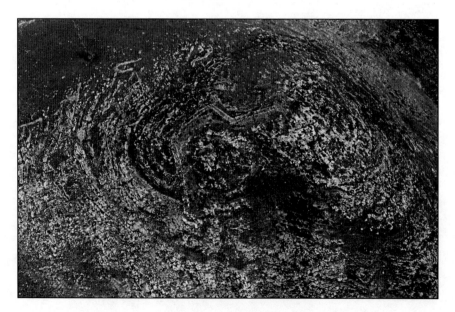

153. Aerial view north of **Kom Ali** (A. Solomon).

Site 82: 18-17/80/1
FARQOM CAVE (1)

Israel grid: 18867/17098
UTM grid: 7271/5578
Elevation: 130 m a.s.l., 10 m a.s.a.
Name: nearest place
Site type: threshing floors, structures and cistern
Area: 1 ha (10 dunams)
Topography: spur and valley edge
Rock type: Mount Scopus Group

Soil: brown lithosol, quality: 8
Cultivation: none
Cisterns: none
Water source: 'Ein Abu Daraj (no. 177), 2.5 km distant
Road: Phasaelis-Neapolis (C40) 'Wadi Afjam bypass', 300 m distant
Visit: December 1994; 4 surveyors; 63 sherds

Site at the edge of Jaffa en-Noon spur, west of the Alon road, in the north of the Sahal Afjam valley, 3.5 km north-north-east of Gittit. The site is marked in the map as Farqom Cave.

There are several well-built round threshing floors of medium-sized fieldstones. The foundations of the threshing floors are built of large stones. There are remains of walls by the threshing floors.

About 130 m west of the threshing floors are remains of a structure 12×8 m.

West of this structure is a quarried cistern; with a collecting channel leading to it.

Pottery: Iron II – 15%; Persian – 20%; Late Roman – 40%; Ottoman (body sherds) – 25%.
Other surveys: none.

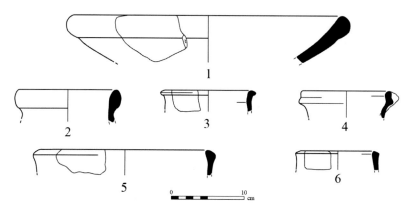

154. Pottery from **Farqom Cave (1)**: 1. Mortarium, lt brn, Pers; 2. Jar, lt brn, Pers; 3. Jug, lt brn, LR; 4. Jug, lt brn, IA II; 5. Jug, lt brn, IA II; 6. Jug, drk brn, LR.

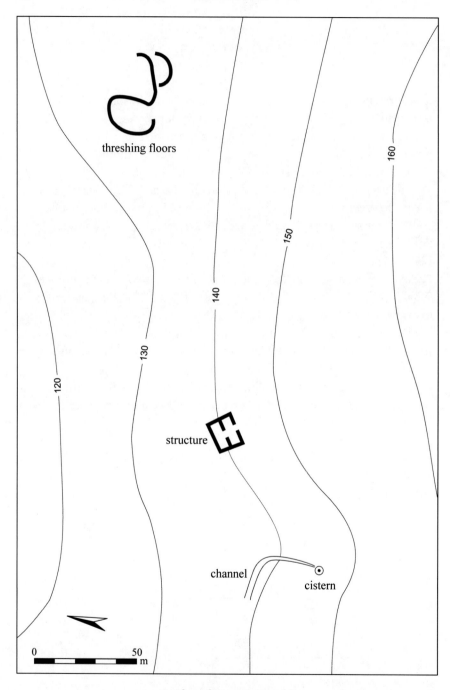

155. Plan of **Farqom Cave (1)**.

Site 83: 18-17/80/2
WADI FARQOM (1)

Israel grid: 18807/17080
UTM grid: 7266/5576
Elevation: 135 m a.s.l., 50 m b.s.a.
Name: nearest place
Site type: structure
Area: 2,000 sq. m (2 dunams)
Topography: slope
Rock type: Judea Group
Soil: terra rossa, quality: 6

Cultivation: none
Cisterns: none
Water source: Bir Mashkara (no. 190), 2.8 km distant
Road: Phasaelis-Neapolis (C40) 'Wadi Afjam bypass', 400 m distant
Visit: December 2005; 2014; 4 surveyors; 15 sherds

Site on a steep slope descending of the north into the narrow channel of Wadi Farqom, 800 m west from the Alon road and 3 km north of Gittit.

Structure built of very large stones on rocky steps parallel to the channel. The construction is massive and very impressive. The structure rests on a foundation wall 1-2 m thick and three courses high, built of very large stones, preserved for 25 m. In the south end the wall turns east, forming a narrow 5 m wide structure. Walls supporting the main structure built of medium-sized stones descend from it to the channel.

The structure, probably dated to the LR period, was the main component of the site, but its exact nature is unclear.

Pottery: Persian – 10%; Late Roman – 90%.
Other surveys: none.

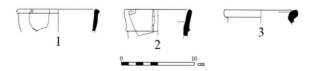

156. Pottery from **Wadi Farqom (1)**: 1. Bowl, org, LR; 2 jar, lt brn, LR; 3. Jar, drk brn, Pers.

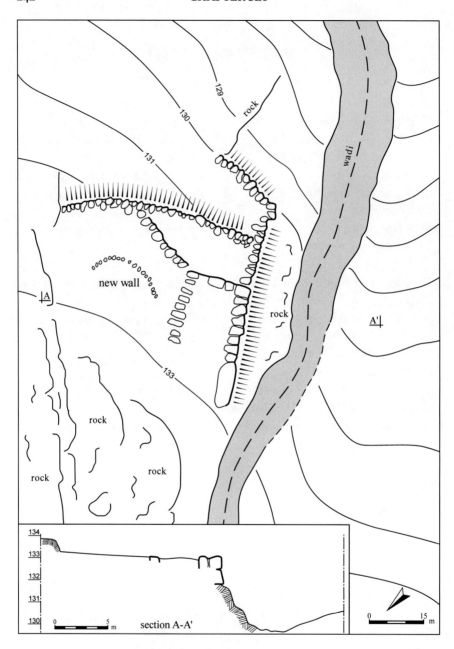

157. Plan of **Wadi Farqom (1)**.

Site 84: 18-17/80/3
WADI FARQOM (2)

Israel grid: 18842/17063
UTM grid: 7269/5574
Elevation: 134 m a.s.l., 50 m b.s.a.
Name: nearest place
Site type: farm, cave and cistern
Area: 2,000 sq. m (2 dunams)
Topography: bottom of slope
Rock type: Avdat Group
Soil: terra rossa, quality: 8

Cultivation: field crops by the site
Cisterns: 1
Water source: 'Ein Abu Daraj (no. 177), 2.6 km distant
Road: Phasaelis-Neapolis (C40) 'Wadi Afjam bypass', 200 m distant
Visit: December 1994; December 2013; 4 surveyors; 200 sherds

Small site on the south bank of Wadi Farqom, 700 m west of the Alon road and 3.2 km north-north-east of Gittit. East and north of the site extend extensive cultivated fields.

Large courtyard, about 30×15 m, built of two rows of large stones. The courtyard is divided to two unequal parts. Five courses of the northern support wall survive.

North and below the eastern wall is a long narrow courtyard, about 30×5 m, built of medium-sized stones. The courtyard borders a cultivated field; and another small courtyard adjoins it in the south-east.

The construction quality of both lower courtyards is by far inferior to that of the larger upper one, which is apparently the earlier courtyard; and both the lower ones are later annexes.

It can be assumed that the site functioned as a farm.

Above the farm is a large cave, 25×10 m, of average height of 2.5 m, collapsed in several places. The cave is in use at present.

West of the farm is a cistern; around its opening is a new water collecting structure, apparently receiving water drained from the rocky slope. The cistern was empty at the time of the survey.

The farm is typical of sites spread along the Gittit and Sahel Afjam Valleys. Habitation continuity is prominent.

Pottery: Late Roman – 50%; Byzantine – 20%; Medieval – 25%; Ottoman (body sherds) – 3%; Modern – 2%.
Stone: basalt bowl.
Other surveys: none.

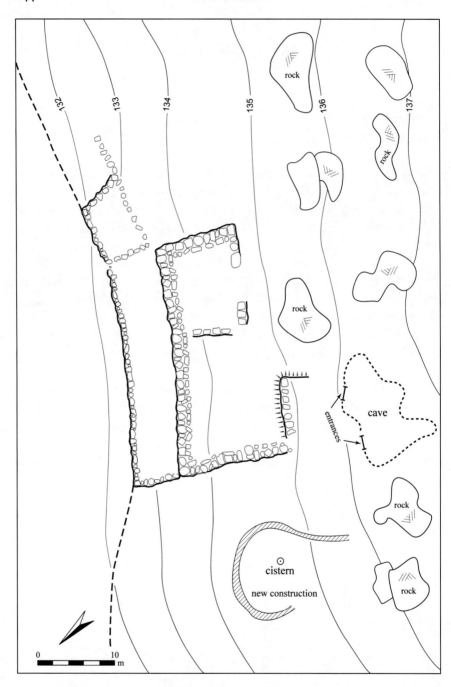

158. Plan of **Wadi Farqom (2)**.

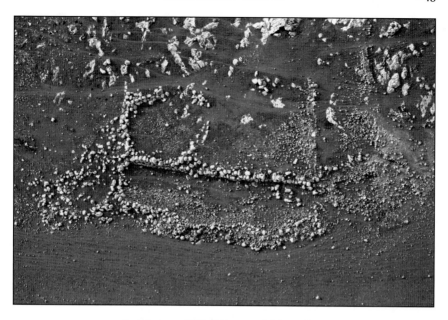

159. Aerial view of **Wadi Farqom (2)** (A. Solomon).

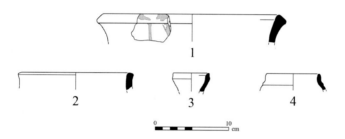

160. Pottery from **Wadi Farqom (2)**: 1. Krater (?), lt colour, red paint outside, Med; 2. Jar (?), gr, Med; 3. Jug, gr, LR-Byz; 4. Jug (?), lt brn, LR-Byz.

Site 85: 18-17/80/4
WADI FARQOM (3)

Israel grid: 18820/17068
UTM grid: 7267/5574
Elevation: 150 m a.s.l., 70 m b.s.a.
Name: nearest place
Site type: large courtyard and cisterns
Area: 2,500 sq. m (2.5 dunams)
Topography: slope
Rock type: Judea Group
Soil: terra rossa, quality: 6
Cultivation: field crops by the site
Cisterns: 3
Water source: 'Ein Abu Daraj (no. 177), 2.7 km distant
Road: Phasaelis-Neapolis (C40) 'Wadi Afjam bypass', 400 m distant
Visit: December 2013; 4 surveyors; 8 sherds

Site on a steep slope descending to Wadi Farqom in the south where the wadi narrows, 800 m west of the Alon road and 3.2 km north-north-east of Gittit.

Large well-built courtyard, about 30×30 m. The perimeter wall is built with one row of large stones. In the lower northern part is a 28 m long support wall. Inside the courtyard are several support walls and exposed rocks.

Wall built of large stones, about 40 m north of the courtyard centre, enclosing the lower part between the courtyard and the field.

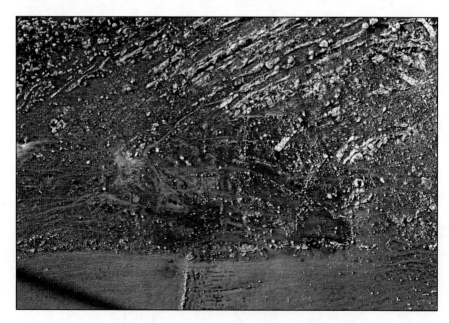

161. Aerial view south at **Wadi Farqom (3)** (A. Solomon).

New *maq'ad* about 20 m west of the courtyard.

Three cisterns 60 m east of the courtyard (out of plan).

Bedouin corrals and modern tent encampments surround the courtyard on three sides.

Very few sherds, but dating is certain.

This courtyard is one of the many Roman-Byzantine square courtyards in eastern Samaria which were used for livestock husbandry and crop storage.

Pottery: Late Roman (body sherds) – 100%.
Other surveys: none.

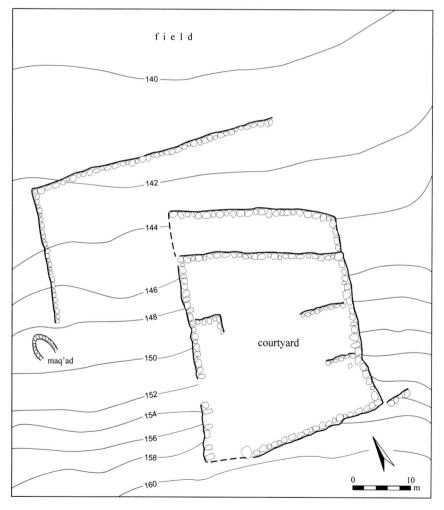

162. Plan of **Wadi Farqom (3)**.

Site 86: 18-17/80/5
WADI ZAMOR (4)

Israel grid: 18859/17002
UTM grid: 7271/5568
Elevation: 100 m a.s.l., 10 m a.s.a.
Name: nearest place
Site type: settlement and road
Area: 2.3 ha (23 dunams)
Topography: edge of valley
Rock type: Judea Group
Soil: terra rossa, quality: 6

Cultivation: none
Cisterns: 2
Water source: 'Ein Abu Daraj (no. 177), 2.4 km distant
Road: Phasaelis-Neapolis (C40) 'Wadi Afjam bypass', at the site
Visit: December 1994; 2005; 2014; 9 surveyors; 96 sherds

Site at the end of a spur descending to the edge of the Wadi Zamor valley, north of the streambed, at the bottom of a slope on the border of Sahel Afjam, 400 m west of the Alon road.

The site consists of two parts:
1. Southern part is a farm, containing a courtyard, a structure and a cistern. The courtyard is irregular, 40×25 m. The construction of the surrounding wall shows two phases: the lower courses are built of large stones and the upper ones of small stones. The entrance is in the west side. A new drainage channel has been bulldozed along the site destroying a 25 m long section of the wall in the eastern side facing the wadi. Further north the wall reappears, but only the bottom course remains in this section.

Inside the north-eastern part of the courtyard is a dwelling structure, 8×4 m, with walls 80 cm thick and an entrance in the east. The structure has windows and roofing concrete beams, proof of a modern construction or modern renovation. In the courtyard are a cistern and three heaps of medium-sized stones.

About 15 m north of the courtyard is a 35×20 m built platform and support walls. In the northern part of the platform is a concrete floor. The platform was apparently meant for additional structures, possibly for a dwelling.

South of the farm are remains of a constructed ancient road (C40), built with two rows of kerbstones. The road is about 3 m wide and is oriented southward along the edge of the slope. The road also served as an erosion prevention terrace, forming a large field south-west of the farm complex.

Disorder in the site results from land preparation works, cultivation and modern constructions.

2. Northern part (outside the plan) is 120 m long and 50-60 m wide. Up the slope are several structures, built of large flat stones.

At the southern part of the northern area is a structure, 7×4 m. North of the structure is an irregular room built of large stones, with several walls abutting it. West of the room is a long terrace wall and a cistern.

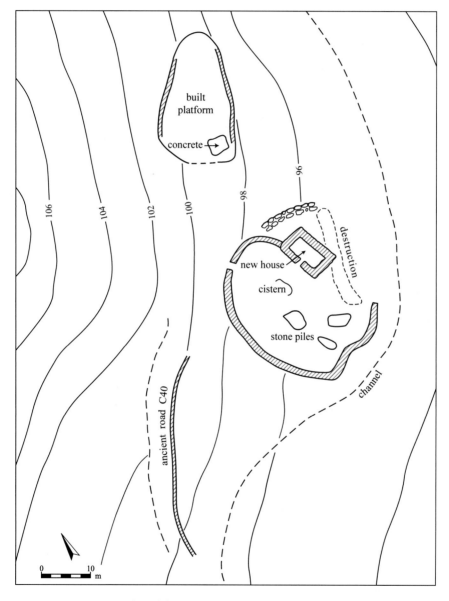

163. Plan of the southern part of **Wadi Zamor (4)**.

164. Aerial view to the north-west at the southern part of **Wadi Zamor (4)** (A. Solomon).

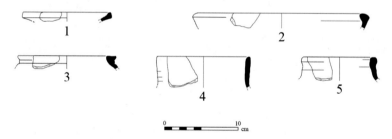

165. Pottery from **Wadi Zamor (4)** (northern part): 1. Bowl, red, IA I-II (?); 2. Bowl, red, IA I-II; 3. CP, lt brn, LR; 4. Jar, blk, LR-Byz, 5. Jar, blk, IA I-II.

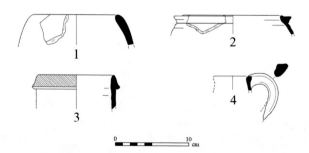

166. Pottery from **Wadi Zamor (4)** (southern part): 1. Holemouth jar, lt brn, Chal/EB; 2. CP, gr, LR; 3. Jar, gr, Ott; 4. Jug, lt brn, LR-Byz.

Among the structures are several sections of rounded walls, which apparently were components of threshing floors.

The number of sherds is quite large considering the architectural finds; suggesting the existence of a settlement.

Flint artefacts were also collected.

Pottery: In the southern part: Chalcolithic/Early Bronze – 5%; Late Roman-Byzantine – 60%; Medieval – 10%; Ottoman – 25%. In the northern part: Iron I-II – 70%; Late Roman-Byzantine – 30%.
Flint: 24 items: 1 flake core, 15 flakes, 6 blades, and 2 side scrapers.
Other surveys: none.

◆ ◆ ◆

Site 87: 18-17/90/1
JEBEL EL-MAHJARAH (10)

Israel grid: 18922/17059
UTM grid: 7277/5573
Elevation: 130 m a.s.l., 20 m a.s.a.
Name: nearest place
Site type: caves and cistern
Area: 2,000 sq. m (2 dunams)
Topography: slope
Rock type: Judea Group
Soil: terra rossa, quality: 8

Cultivation: none
Cisterns: 1
Water source: 'Ein Abu Daraj (no. 177), 1.8 km distant
Road: Phasaelis-Neapolis (C40) 'Wadi Afjam bypass', 600 m distant
Visit: January 2014; 4 surveyors; 3 sherds

Agrarian site over a moderate slope descending from the east of the Gittit Valley (the Wadi Ahmar valley), 4 km south of Mekhora.

There are two features:

1. Cave with a courtyard in front. The mouth of the cave is about 10×7 m, and nearly 5 m deep. Seemingly the courtyard served as a corral.

    About 20 m above the courtyard and about 50 m north-east of the cave is another courtyard appearing to be modern (outside the plan).

2. About 100 m south-south-east of the cave is a complex of another cave and a cistern. The cave is 15 m deep and 7 m wide. It has charred ceiling. The entrance to the cave is supported by a wall, which also supports a high earth rampart piled around the cistern.

The cistern has a modern cover and still contains water (January 2014). Two channels drain the rain water from the slope to the cistern.

Pottery: 3 unidentified body sherds.
Other surveys: none.

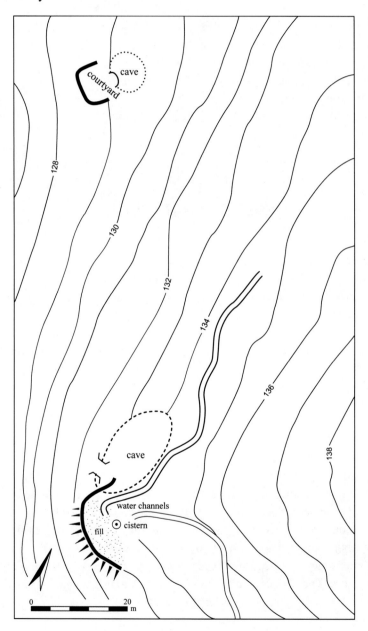

167. Plan of **Jebel el-Mahjarah (10)**.

Site 88: 18-17/90/2
JEBEL EL-MAHJARAH (9)

Israel grid: 18974/17032
UTM grid: 7282/5571
Elevation: 170 m a.s.l., 50 m a.s.a.
Name: nearest place
Site type: walls, sherd and flint scatters
Area: 3,000 sq. m (3 dunams)
Topography: slope
Rock type: Judea Group

Soil: terra rossa, quality: 3
Cultivation: none
Cisterns: none
Water source: 'Ein Abu Daraj (no. 177), 1.2 km distant
Road: Phasaelis-Neapolis (C40), 800 m distant
Visit: December 2013; 5 surveyors; 350 sherds

Site on a moderate slope in the south-western part of Jebel el-Mahjarah, south of the ravine which empties into Wadi el-Afjam.

Abundant sherd and flint scatters over a considerable area, remains of ancient walls, which do not yield a plan, and remains of a modern tent encampment and numerous terrace walls.

Pottery: Chalcolithic/Early Bronze I (body sherds) – 5%; Iron II (body sherds) – 3%; Late Roman – 57%; Byzantine – 23%; Medieval (body sherds) – 12%.
Flint: 95 items: 1 flake core, 2 bladelet cores, 64 flakes, 14 blades, 1 bladelet, 9 side scrapers, 2 borers, 1 retouched blade, and a retouched bladelet. The find is evidence of flint working, but is not indicative. Some of the pottery finds support a possible Chalcolithic/EBA presence at the site; and the flint, although not indicative, might belong to assemblages from these periods.
Stone: limestone bowl.
Other surveys: none.

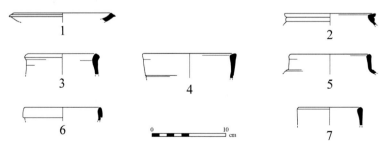

168. Pottery from Jebel el-Mahjarah (9): 1. Bowl, lt brn, LR; 2. Bowl, drk brn, LR-Byz; 3. Jar, drk brn, LR-Byz; 4. Jar (?), lt brn, LR; 5. Jug, lt brn, LR; 6. Jug, lt brn, LR; 7. Jug, drk brn, LR-Byz.

Site 89: 18-17/90/3
JEBEL EL-MAHJARAH (6)

Israel grid: 18977/17047
UTM grid: 7283/5572
Elevation: 180 m a.s.l., 20 m a.s.a.
Name: nearest place
Site type: cave
Area: 100 sq. m (0.1 dunam)
Topography: slope
Rock type: Judea Group
Soil: terra rossa, quality: 3

Cultivation: none
Cisterns: none
Water source: 'Ein Abu Daraj (no. 177), 1.2 km distant
Road: Phasaelis-Neapolis (C40), 800 m distant
Visit: December 2013; 5 surveyors; 90 sherds

Site on a steep slope of Jebel el-Mahjarah, above the channel of a Wadi el-Afjam tributary and close to the site of Jebel el-Mahjarah (9) (Site 88).

Rectangular cave about 15 m deep and maximum 4 m high. The ceiling is sooty. In the eastern part of the cave is a square cell, 4×4 m and maximum 3 m high.

Most of the sherds were collected on the steep slope between the cave entrance and the wadi channel.

Pottery: Middle Bronze II (body sherds) – 3%; Late Roman – 50%; Byzantine – 39%; Medieval – 8%.
Other surveys: none.

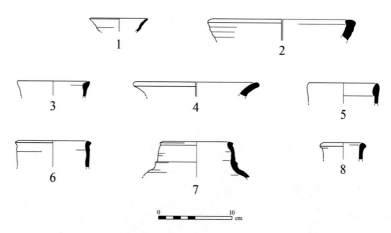

169. Pottery from **Jebel el-Mahjarah (6):** 1. Bowlet, drk brn, LR-Byz; 2. Bowl, lt brn, LR-Byz; 3. Bowl, drk brn, LR-Byz; 4. Jar, lt brn, Med; 5-7. Jars, drk brn, LR-Byz; 8. Jug, drk brn, LR-Byz.

Site 90: 18-17/90/4
JEBEL EL-MAHJARAH (8)

Israel grid: 18938/17034
UTM grid: 7279/5571
Elevation: 125 m a.s.l., 20 m a.s.a.
Name: nearest place
Site type: enclosure
Area: 300 sq. m (0.3 dunams)
Topography: spur
Rock type: Judea Group
Soil: terra rossa, quality: 5

Cultivation: none
Cisterns: none
Water source: 'Ein Abu Daraj (no. 177), 1.5 km distant
Road: 'Ein Hafireh-Wadi Zamor (C50), 800 m distant
Visit: December 2013; 3 surveyors; 70 sherds

Site on a moderate spur west of the valley of Wadi el-Afjam.

Round enclosure, 20 m in diameter, built of large and medium-sized stones. It was in use during the LR and Byzantine periods.

Large sherd scatter.

Pottery: Late Roman – 34%; Byzantine – 66%.
Other surveys: none.

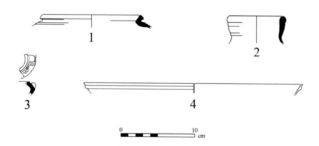

170. Finds from **Jebel el-Mahjarah (8)**: 1. CP, blk, LR-Byz; 2. Jar, lt brn, LR-Byz; 3. Lamp, lt brn, Byz; 4. Bowl (?), green glass, LR-Byz.

Site 91: 18-17/90/5
JEBEL EL-MAHJARAH (11)

Israel grid: 18946/17009
UTM grid: 7279/5569
Elevation: 120 m a.s.l., 10 m a.s.a.
Name: nearest place
Site type: enclosure
Area: 1,000 sq. m (1 dunam)
Topography: moderate slope
Rock type: Judea Group
Soil: terra rossa, quality: 8

Cultivation: none
Cisterns: none
Water source: 'Ein Abu Daraj (no. 177), 1.5 km distant
Road: 'Ein Hafireh-Wadi Zamor (C50), 700 m distant
Visit: January 2014; 5 surveyors; 70 sherds

Site on a very low hillock east of Sahel Afjam, 500 m from the Alon road and 4.5 km south of Mekhora.

Remains of a large round enclosure, 16 m diameter. The encircling wall is built of one row of large and medium-sized stones. The northern wall virtually did not survive due to cultivation in the vicinity.

The enclosure served as a corral.

According to the pottery, the enclosure existed over many periods.

Pottery; Late Roman – 21%; Byzantine – 44%; Medieval – 28%; Modern – 7%.
Other surveys: none.

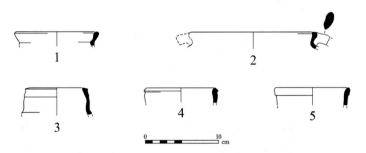

171. Pottery from **Jebel el-Mahjarah (11)**: 1. CP, lt brn, LR; 2. CP, lt brn, Med (?); 3. Jar, lt brn, LR-Byz; 4. Jar, gr, LR-Byz; 5. Jug, lt brn, LR-Byz.

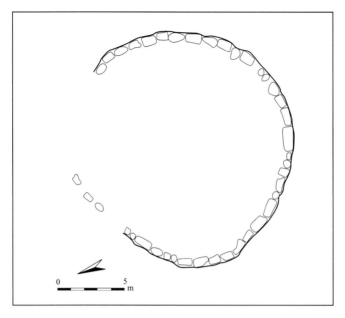

172. Plan of **Jebel el-Mahjarah** (11).

Site 92: 18-16/89/1
WADI ZAMOR (5)

Israel grid: 18823/16967
UTM grid: 7267/5564
Elevation: 110 m a.s.l., 15 m a.s.a.
Name: nearest place
Site type: courtyard, structure and threshing floors
Area: 2,500 sq. m (2.5 dunams)
Topography: edge of valley
 Rock type: Judea Group

Soil: terra rossa, quality: 6
Cultivation: none
Cisterns: 1
Water source: 'Ein Abu Daraj (no. 177), 2.7 km distant
Road: 'Ein Hafireh-Wadi Zamor (C50), 100 m distant
Visit: December 1994; 4 surveyors; 55 sherds

Site north of Wadi Zamor (Ahmar), near at its entrance to the valley, 700 m west of Alon road and 2 km north-north-east of Gittit.

An irregular rectangular courtyard, 38×20 m, built of large stones, with an entrance in the north-eastern side. Inside, at the western corner of the courtyard is a small structure with two cells. Another structure is attached outside at the eastern corner. A round threshing floor, about 17 m diameter, abuts the outer southern corner.

About 40 m west of the courtyard, over the slope, are two pairs of threshing floors.

Small structure with two cells, perhaps grain silage, attached to the eastern pair of threshing floors.

The chronological connection between the courtyard and the threshing floors is not clear.

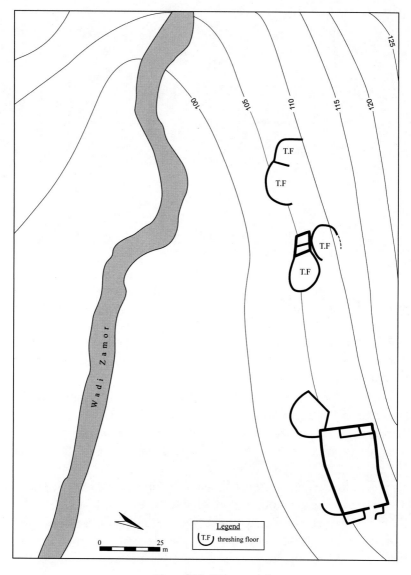

173. Plan of **Wadi Zamor (5)**.

Pottery: Late Roman-Byzantine – 55%; Ottoman – 45%.
Flint: 6 items: 1 flake core, 1 bladelet core, 3 flakes, and a blade.
Other surveys: none.

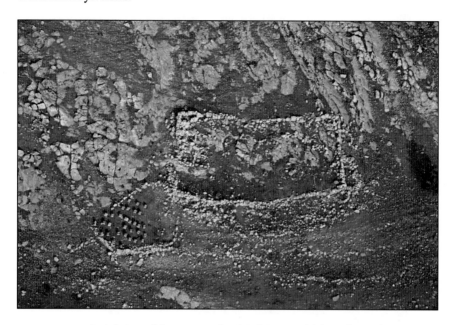

174. Aerial view of the courtyard at **Wadi Zamor (5)** (A. Solomon).

175. Pottery from **Wadi Zamor (5)** (all LR-Byz): 1. Jug, lt brn; 2. Bowl, lt brn; 3. Jug, drk brn; 4. Bowl (?), drk brn.

Site 93: 18-16/99/1
JEBEL EL-MAHJARAH (7)

Israel grid: 18954/16991
UTM grid: 7280/5567
Elevation: 130 m a.s.l., 30 m a.s.a.
Name: nearest place
Site type: structures
Area: 500 sq. m (0.5 dunam)
Topography: slope
Rock type: Judea Group
Soil: terra rossa, quality: 8

Cultivation: none
Cisterns: none
Water source: 'Ein Abu Daraj (no. 177), 1.4 km distant
Road: 'Ein Hafireh-Wadi Zamor (C50), 700 m distant
Visit: December 2013; 5 surveyors; 20 sherds

Site on a moderate slope down from a hill east of Sahel Afjam, 500 m from Alon road and 4.7 km south of Mekhora. Deep wadis isolate the hill on both sides and merge with Wadi el-Afjam.

Two rectangular structures, built of large stones and without inner division, about 30 m apart.

The south-eastern structure is about 12×5 m. It seems as if the western support wall was double. A stone with recesses was found near the structure.

The north-eastern structure is 8×5 m.

It is probable that both structures served as guard towers.

Pottery: Iron II (body sherds) – 40%; Late Roman – 60%.
Other surveys: none.

LANDSCAPE UNIT 34

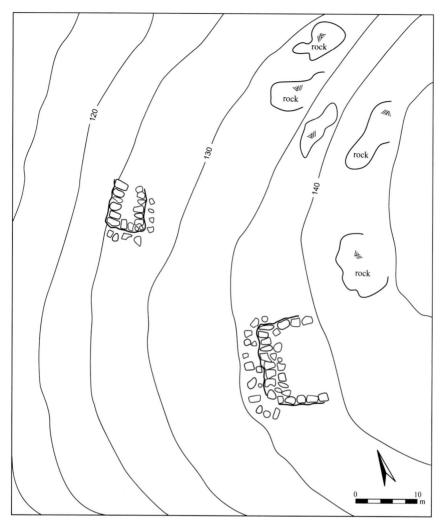

176. Plan of **Jebel el-Mahjarah (7)**.

CHAPTER SEVEN

THE VALLEY OF GITTIT - LANDSCAPE UNIT 35

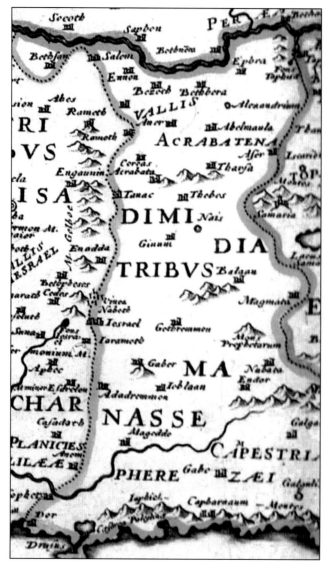

177. Enlargement of the Manasseh allotment from a map of Palestine by Briet, Paris, 1641 (in Nebenzahl 1986, map no. 45). Note the location of the Aqrabtana toparchy.

Site 94: 18-17/40/1
KHIRBET ER-RISA (1)

Israel grid: 18456/17089
UTM grid: 7230/5576
Elevation: 515 m a.s.l., 100 m a.s.a.
Name: ancient and on map
Site type: large fortress, structures and installations
Area: 4 ha (40 dunams)
Topography: high hillock
Rock type: Judea Group

Soil: brown forest, quality: 4
Cultivation: none
Cisterns: about 20
Water source: 'Ein Juheir (no. 189), 500 m distant
Road: 'Ein Hafireh-Wadi Zamor (C50), 1 km distant
Visit: May 1998 and more; 6 surveyors; 150 sherds

Site on a very prominent hillock, 1.5 km east of Aqraba. The hill is bordered by deep wadis: Wadi el-Majdar to the north, Wadi Zamor to the east, and a deep nameless ravine to the west. The site completely dominates its vicinity visually.

Large fortress, 65×55 m, well-built of large and medium fieldstones. In the western side are three rows of 6 to 7 m wide casements completely preserved. The fortress has four corner towers flush with the walls. Inside the courtyard are other structures which are difficult to define due to entangled vegetation coverage at the time of the survey mapping of the site.

Close to the north-eastern corner of the fortress is a fortified entrance gate which includes an approach road passing along the outer side of the eastern wall and ascending to the entrance; an opening between four standing monoliths with bolt holes; and a right-angled entrance of the road into the fortress courtyard.

Additional structures are outside the fortress, to the east and mainly south of it on a broad saddle.

An outer wall built of large stones surrounds the hillock to the south and west. At the south-western end the wall turns east. The wall apparently surrounded the entire hillock; probably serving as an extra outer fortifying element. Near the south-western corner of the wall is another two-room structure.

Around the fortress are rock-cut winepresses, plundered burial caves and numerous installations.

There are abundant sherds.

This was an important fortress, probably an official one, guarding the approach from the Mediterranean high region of Samaria to the desert fringes in the east and the Jordan Valley.

Porath (1968, site 149) describes: "An Iron Age II fortress at the top of a hillock... guards the paths from the Jordan Valley (Tell Sheikh Abu Diyab) to Aqraba and Shechem... The fortress is built in the format of Iron Age II fortresses with a surrounding casemate wall, towers in the corners, and small projections and recesses... The walls have been preserved relatively better in the west and south; They are built with two faces of fieldstones with earth and gravel infilling. In the western and eastern sections of the wall gutters were cut in a large stone...quarried cisterns...The pottery find is from the Israelite II, (Byzantine), (Ottoman) periods".

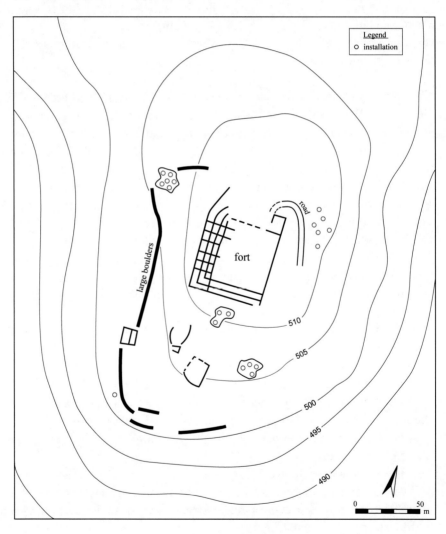

178. Plan of **Khirbet er-Risa (1)**.

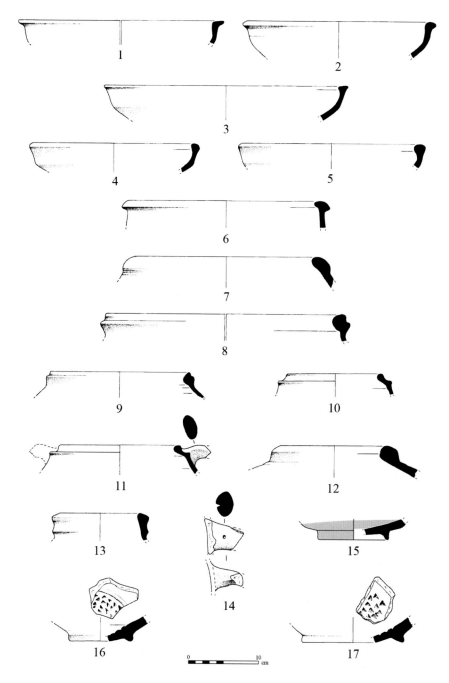

179. Pottery from **Khirbet er-Risa (1)** (all except nos. 12, 14, 16-17 are from IA II-III): 1-5. Bowls; 6-7. Kraters; 8-11. CPs; 12. Holemouth pithos, IA I-II; 13. Jar; 14. Indented handle, IA I-II; 15. Bowl base, red slip in and out; 16-17. Bowl bases, cuneated dec (IA III).

Pottery: Early Bronze (body sherds) – 2%; Iron I – 4%; Iron II-III – 82%; Late Roman-Byzantine (body sherds) – 8%; Ottoman (body sherds) – 4%.
Other surveys: Porath 1968, site 149; Finkelstein et al. 1997: 826-827.
Additional bibliography: Conder and Kitchener 1882: 391 (Khurbet Abu Risah); GL: 116.

◆ ◆ ◆

Site 95: 18-17/50/1
'EIN JUHEIR (1)

Israel grid: 18517/17096
UTM grid: 7237/5577
Elevation: 370 m a.s.l., 60 m b.s.a.
Name: nearest place
Site type: structure, cistern and installations
Area: 250 sq. m (0.25 dunam)
Topography: slope
Rock type: Judea Group
Soil: terra rossa, quality: 6
Cultivation: modern garden
Cisterns: none
Water source: 'Ein Juheir (no. 189), at the site
Road: 'Ein Hafireh-Wadi Zamor (C50), 600 m distant
Visit: November 2014 and more; 5 surveyors; 40 sherds

Site 20 m west of 'Ein Juheir spring, one of the two springs of the nearby fortified site in Khirbet Juraish.

Remains of a large structure, exposed due to plundering. The walls are built of large boulders. Together with the structure is a plastered cistern, 2 m in diameter and 1.5 m deep.

Modern water reservoir near the structure, serving the garden. Near the garden are the drainage channel and a rock-cut tunnel carrying water from the spring to a reservoir and an ancient structure nearby.

Traces of cup marks on the cliff north of the IA structure and remains of numerous terraces on the slope above.

It is possible that the structure served as the spring-house during the IA.

Pottery: Chalcolithic – 5%; Iron II – 95%.
Flint: 4 items: 2 flakes and 2 blades.
Other surveys: none.

180. The modern water reservoir at ʿEin Juheir (1) (I. Bejerano).

181. The plastered cistern at ʿEin Juheir (1) (I. Bejerano).

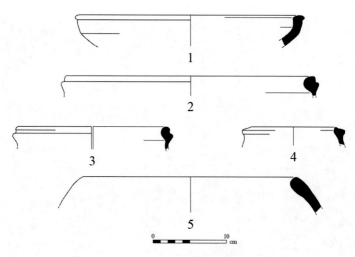

182. Pottery from 'Ein Juheir (1): 1. Bowl, gr, IA II; 2-3. CPs, lt brn, IA II; 4. Jar, gr, IA II; 5. Holemouth jar, lt colour, Chal.

Site 96: 18-17/50/2

'EIN JUHEIR (2)

Israel grid: 18523/17082
UTM grid: 7237/5575
Elevation: 300 m a.s.l., 90 m b.s.a.
Name: nearest place
Site type: sherd and flint scatters
Area: 1000 sq. m (1 dunam)
Topography: slope
Rock type: Judea Group
Soil: terra rossa, quality: 5

Cultivation: plantation
Cisterns: none
Water source: 'Ein Juheir (no. 189), 200 m distant
Road: 'Ein Hafireh-Wadi Zamor (C50), 400 m distant
Visit: November 2014; 4 surveyors; 60 sherds

Site on the south bank of Wadi Ahmar, 200 m east of 'Ein Juheir and 400 m west of the confluence of Wadi Zamor and Wadi Ahmar. The ridge of Khirbet Juraish rises above and north of the site.

Many flint items and sherds were collected from a small surface on the southern slope of the wadi. It is likely that a structure or cluster of structures, destroyed during land cultivation, once existed. Currently, olive and other fruit trees are planted here.

The site is probably linked to the Chalcolithic site at Lower Juraish (Site 97) located 300 m to the west. The Chalcolithic cluster in Wadi Ahmar is represented by three adjacent sites from this period in the vicinity of 'Ein Juheir spring (Sites 64, 80 and 97), and constitutes one of the finest examples of the penetration of the Chalcolithic society into the higher Samaria region, benefiting from a favourable Mediterranean climate necessary for the cultivation of olives.

Pottery: Chalcolithic – 100%.
Flint: 153 items: 2 flake cores, 107 flakes, 10 blades, 9 bladelets, 6 side scrapers, 3 borers, 2 retouched flakes, 1 reaping knife, 4 adzes, and 3 axes. Most of the assemblage is dated to the Chalcolithic period. The axes might indicate an earlier Neolithic presence at the site.
Stone: four basalt grinding fragments.
Other surveys: none.

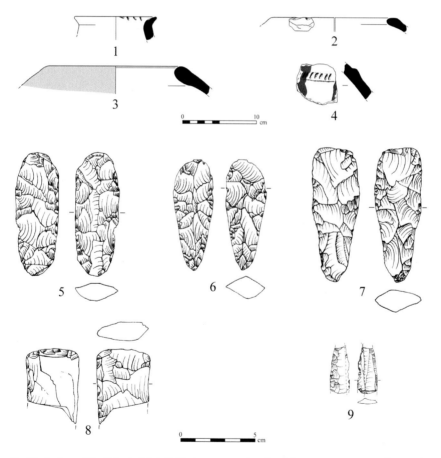

183. Finds from 'Ein Juheir (2) (all Chal except 5-7): 1. Jar, lt brn, rope orn; 2. Holemouth jar, rope orn; 3. Holemouth jar, lt brn, red slip outside; 4. Body sherd, lt brn, rope orn; 5-7. Axes, Neolithic/Chal; 8. Bifacial; 9. Retouched Sickle blade.

Site 97: 18-17/50/3
JURAISH (LOWER)

Israel grid: 18553/17081
UTM grid: 7240/5575
Elevation: 290 m a.s.l., 20 m a.s.a.
Name: given by the Survey
Site type: sherd scatter
Area: 2000 sq. m (2 dunams)
Topography: moderate slope
Rock type: Judea Group
Soil: brown forest, quality: 3

Cultivation: none
Cisterns: none
Water source: 'Ein Juheir (no. 189), 400 m distant
Road: 'Ein Hafireh-Wadi Zamor (C50), 400 m distant
Visit: December 2007; 2014; 5 surveyors; 80 sherds

Site located on a slope dropping south-eastward from Khirbet Juraish (Site 64) to Wadi Ahmar.

There is a sherd scatter over a small area between terraces and cultivated fields.

No remains of structures are visible.

This site is one of a group of sites from the Chalcolithic period in Wadi Ahmar. The Chalcolithic cluster is represented here by three adjacent sites from this period in the vicinity of 'Ein Juheir spring (Sites 64, 80 and 96) and constitute one of the finest examples of the penetration of the Chalcolithic society into the higher Samaria region with the favourable Mediterranean climate, necessary in the cultivation of olives.

Pottery: Chalcolithic – 100%.
Flint: 7 items were collected, an axe among them.
Stone: a basalt bowl with triangle incisions, a basalt V-shaped bowl fragment, and a basalt incense burner fragment. All the stone finds are dated to the Chalcolithic period.
Other surveys: none.
Bibliography: Bar 2014, site 66.

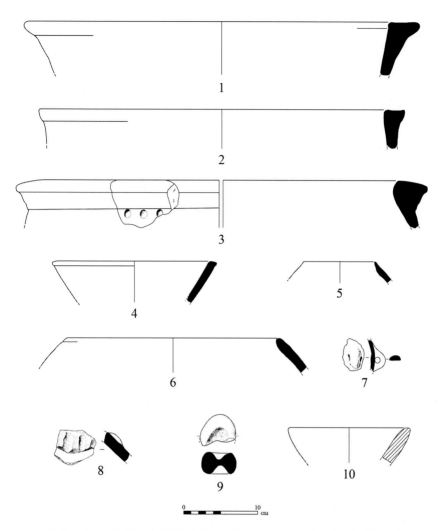

184. Finds from **Juraish (Lower)** (all Chal): 1-2. Basins/ Kraters, lt colour; 3. Basin/ Krater, lt colour, thumb-indented rim outside; 4. Bowl, lt colour; 5-6. Holemouth jars, lt brn; 7. Lug handle, lt colour; 8. Body sherd, rope orn, lt brn; 9. Bi-conical bowlet, limestone; 10. Bowl, basalt.

Site 98: 18-17/50/4
ES-SILEM

Israel grid: 18521/17059
UTM grid: 7237/5573
Elevation: 370 m a.s.l., 90 m a.s.a.
Name: local
Site type: village and installations
Area: 2000 sq. m (2 dunams)
Topography: slope
Rock type: Judea Group
Soil: terra rossa, quality: 3

Cultivation: plantations
Cisterns: none
Water source: 'Ein Juheir (no. 189), 500 m distant
Road: 'Ein Hafireh-Wadi Zamor (C50), 500 m distant
Visit: February 2015; 5 surveyors; 100 sherds

Site on a moderate slope south and opposite Kh. Juraish, 1.7 km south-east of Nebi Noon and 2 km east of Aqraba. The land is now planted with olives and almonds.

This is a small Medieval hamlet of three units:
- Eastern residence that consists of a round room, 6 m in diameter, with two entrances. The north-western part is a corridor leading to a partially blocked cave. The cave is part of the dwelling complex (no. 1 in plan).
- Western dwelling unit consisting of two attached rounded units with a single entrance. The walls, 1 m maximum thick, are built of small stones laid haphazardly (no. 2).
- Winepress, with a 1.5 m in diameter laver in the centre, many parts of which are broken, quarried in the rock bed. Around the laver stone is a 90 cm wide incised pathway for the donkey rolling the crushing stone (no. 3).

Cup marks have been found.

The site is adjacent to a terrace wall of large stones.

Pottery: Late Roman – 30%; Medieval (Mamluk) – 70%.
Other surveys: none.

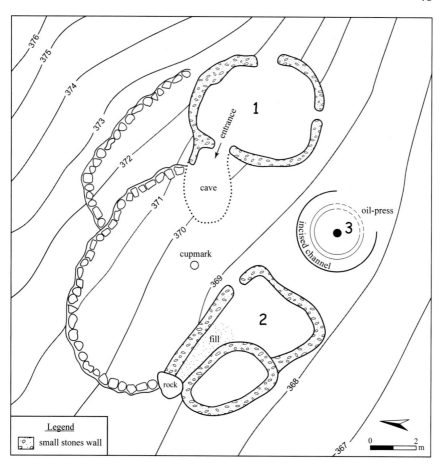

185. Plan of **es-Silem**.

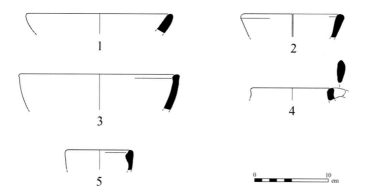

186. Pottery from **es-Silem**: 1, 3. Bowls, lt brn, Med; 2. Bowl, dk brn, LR; 4. Jug, lt brn, Med; 5. Jug, dk brn, LR.

187. The winepress at **es-Silem** (I. Bejerano).

Site 99: 18-17/50/5
WADI ZAMOR (10)

Israel grid: 18557/17058
UTM grid: 7240/5573
Elevation: 230 m a.s.l., 150 m b.s.a.
Name: nearest place
Site type: enclosure
Area: 2000 sq. m (2 dunams)
Topography: confluence of wadis
Rock type: Judea Group
Soil: terra rossa, quality: 6

Cultivation: none
Cisterns: none
Water source: 'Ein Juheir (no. 189), 600 m distant
Road: 'Ein Hafireh-Wadi Zamor (C50), by the site
Visit: March 2014; 4 surveyors; 10 sherds

Site at the confluence of Wadi Juheir and Wadi Zamor, 2 km east of Aqraba and 400 m south of Kh. Juraish.

Elongated triangular enclosure with a small sherd and flint scatter.

Pottery (body sherds): Late Roman – 80%; Modern – 20%.

Flint: 15 items: 1 flake core, 1 blade core, 3 Levallois cores, 3 flakes, 3 blades, and 3 side scrapers. The Levallois cores are evidence of the Middle Palaeolithic period.

Other surveys: none.

Site 100: 18-17/50/6

KHIRBET ER-RISA (2)

Israel grid: 18506/17045
UTM grid: 7235/5572
Elevation: 400 m a.s.l., 120 m a.s.a.
Name: nearest place
Site type: sherd scatter, installations and a cistern
Area: 3.5 ha (35 dunams)
Topography: slope
Rock type: Judea Group

Soil: terra rossa, quality: 7
Cultivation: none
Cisterns: 1
Water source: 'Ein Juheir (no. 189), 600 m distant
Road: 'Ein Hafireh-Wadi Zamor (C50), 400 m distant
Visit: November 2014; 6 surveyors; 380 sherds

Site on a slope of a spur above the confluence of Wadi Ahmar and Wadi Zamor, 600 m south-east of Kh. er-Risa (1) (Site 94) and 2 km east of Aqraba. A modern unpaved road crosses the site from north to south.

Sherd scatter over a very broad area.

The slope is partially terraced: however, no ancient construction remains could be found.

Cistern at the upper part of the slope (coordinates 1849/1703), with a modern iron lid and encircled by a cemented surface. Several rock-cut cup marks at the same coordinates.

Pottery: Early bronze I – 40%; Intermediate Bronze (body sherds) – 3%; Middle Bronze II – 26%; Iron I-II – 13%; Roman – 8%; Medieval – 2%; Unidentified – 8%.

Flint: 22 items: 2 flake cores, 12 flakes, 4 blades, 1 bladelet, 1 retouched flake, 1 non-indicative sickle blade and a Canaanean blade. The Canaanean blade testifies that at least part of the find belongs to the Bronze Age.

Other surveys: none.

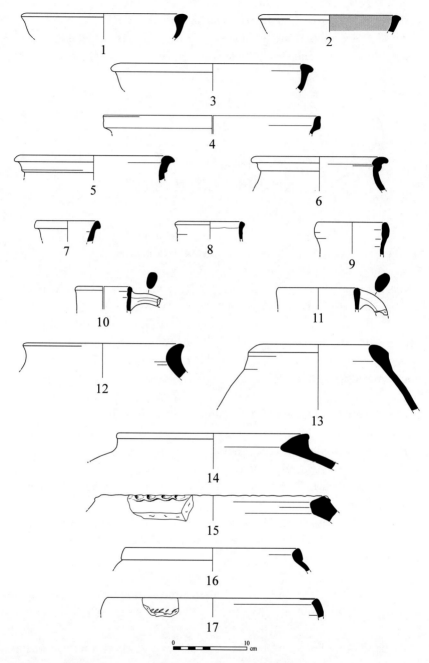

188. Pottery from **Khirbet er-Risa (2)**: 1, 3. Bowls, lt brn, IA II; 2. Bowl, lt brn, red slip, IA II; 4. CP, dk brn, IA I; 5. Jar, lt brn, MB II; 6. Jar, lt gr, MB II; 7. Jug, dk brn, Rom; 8. Jug, lt brn, Rom; 9, 11. Jugs, lt brn, IA I-II; 12. Jar, lt brn, EB I; 13. Jar, lt brn, Med; 14. Holemouth jar, lt brn, EB I; 15. Basin (?), lt brn, thumbed rope orn, EB I; 16. CP, lt brn, MB II; 17. Holemouth jar, lt brn, rope orn, EB I.

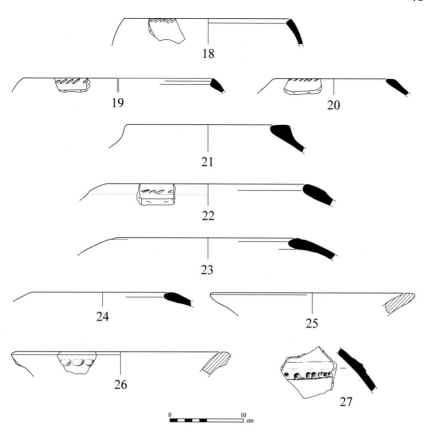

189. Finds from **Khirbet er-Risa (2)**: 18. Holemouth jar, dk brn, rope orn, EB I; 19-20, 22, 24. Holemouth jars, lt brn, rope orn, EB I; 21, 23. Holemouth jars, lt brn, EB I; 25. Bowl, basalt, EB I; 26. Bowl, basalt, rope orn, EB I; 27. Body sherd, lt brn, net pattern stamp orn, Med.

Site 101: 18-17/50/7
WADI ZAMOR (9)

Israel grid: 18584/17042
UTM grid: 7244/5571
Elevation: 280 m a.s.l., 80 m a.s.a.
Name: nearest place
Site type: enclosure
Area: 2,000 sq. m (2 dunams)
Topography: shoulder on a slope
Rock type: Judea Group
Soil: terra rossa, quality: 8

Cultivation: none
Cisterns: none
Water source: 'Ein Juheir (no. 189), 1 km distant
Road: 'Ein Hafireh-Wadi Zamor (C50), 100 m distant
Visit: March 2014; 5 surveyors; 50 sherds

Site located on the shoulder of a steep slope, on the south bank of Wadi Ahmar and above the confluence of Wadi Ahmar with Wadi Zamor, 2.5 km east of Aqraba. On the shoulder, south of the site and close to it, is a cultivable plain.

There is an irregular enclosure.

Pottery: Middle Bronze II – 10%; Late Roman – 30%; Byzantine – 40%; Medieval – 20%.
Flint: 4 items: 2 flakes and 2 retouched blades.
Other surveys: none.

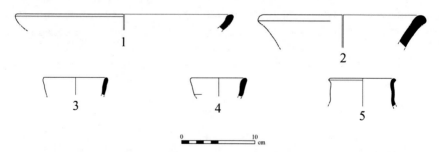

190. Pottery from **Wadi Zamor (9)**: 1. Bowl, lt brn, MB II; 2. Jar (?), lt brn, Med; 3. Jug, dk brn, LR-Byz; 4. Jar, lt brn, LR-Byz; 5. Jar, lt brn, LR.

Site 102: 18-17/60/1
WADI AHMAR TERRACE

Israel grid: 18632/17039
UTM grid: 7248/5571
Elevation: 190 m a.s.l., 150 m b.s.a.
Name: given by the Survey
Site type: sherd and flint scatter
Area: 2,000 sq. m (2 dunams)
Topography: shoulder above wadi
Rock type: Judea Group
Soil: brown forest, quality: 5

Cultivation: none
Cisterns: none
Water source: 'Ein Juheir (no. 189), 1.5 km distant
Road: 'Ein Hafireh-Wadi Zamor (C50), by the site
Visit: February 2014 and more; 7 surveyors; 120 sherds

Site on a shoulder south of Wadi Ahmar riverbed and above it.

Many Late Neolithic and Chalcolithic sherds and flint items (from Wadi Raba Culture to Ghassulian Chalcolithic).

There are no architectonic remains.

Pottery: Late Neolithic-Chalcolithic – 100%.
Flint: 249 items: 5 flake cores, 3 blade cores, 2 bladelet cores, 1 core waste, 1 ridged blade, 174 flakes, 18 blades, 13 bladelets, 8 retouched blades, 5 borers, 4 burins, 1 fan scraper, 2 scrapers, 4 backed and truncated sickle blades, 4 sickle blades, 1 chisel, 2 adzes, and 1 unidentified bifacial. The find is from the Wadi Raba culture throughout the Ghassulian Chalcolithic.
Stone: 12 items, all Neolithic/Chalcolithic, among them a fenestrated stand, a grooved item and a pestle.
Other surveys: Finkelstein et al. 1997: 842.
Additional bibliography: Bar 2014, site 67.

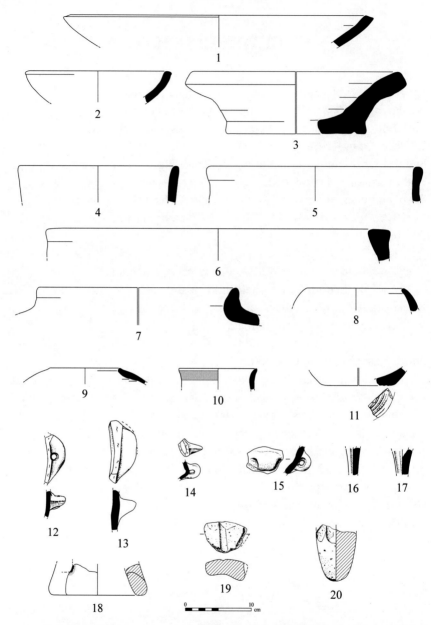

191. Finds from **Wadi Ahmar Terrace** (all Neolithic-Chalcolithic): 1. Bowl, lt brn; 2. Bowl, reddish; 3. Industrial utensil, greyish; 4. Jar (?), brn-reddish; 5. Krater (?), lt colour; 6. Krater (?), lt colour; 7. Pithos, brn-reddish; 8. Holemouth jar, lt brn; 9. Holemouth jar, greyish; 10. Jar (?), lt brn, red orn on rim outside; 11. Base, mat impression outside, lt colour; 12. Lug handle, lt colour; 13. Ledge handle, greyish; 14. Churn handle, lt colour; 15. Lug handle, lt colour; 16-17. Cornets, lt colour; 18. Fenestrated stand, black, basalt; 19-20. Grooved items, black, basalt.

Site 103: 18-17/60/2
WADI AHMAR VALLEY

Israel grid: 18658/17029 (centre of the site)
UTM grid: 7251/5570
Elevation: 190 m a.s.l., 130 m b.s.a.
Name: given by the Survey
Site type: broad site with numerous finds
Area: 10 ha (100 dunams)
Topography: wadi valley
Rock type: Judea Group

Soil: brown forest, quality: 5
Cultivation: field crops by the site
Cisterns: 3
Water source: 'Ein Juheir (no. 189), 1.5 km distant
Road: 'Ein Hafireh-Wadi Zamor (C50), at the site
Visit: February 2014 and more; 8 surveyors; 600 sherds

Large cluster of sites in an inner valley where Wadi Ahmar widens, 1.5 km south-east of Kh. Juraish and 2.8 km north-north-west of Gittit. The site is surrounded by cliffs and steep slopes making accessibility difficult.

For the sake of easier description the site has been divided to nine sections and each part is described separately, including the finds found in it:

1. North-western section (Israel grid: 18646/17041). On the slope descending to the wadi are terrace walls and a built threshing floor. The threshing floor rests on the rocky cliff. Apparently this is an extension of the Wadi Ahmar terrace, the nearby site in the north-west (Site 102), (no. 1 in plan).
   Pottery (70 sherds): Late Pottery Neolithic-Chalcolithic – 80%; Late Roman – 20%.
   Flint: 28 items: 4 flake cores, 1 blade core, 15 flakes, 4 blades, 1 scraper, 1 retouched flake, 1 unidentified bifacial and Amuq-type arrowhead. The finds support the pottery dates of Late Neolithic and Chalcolithic periods.

2. Area enclosed by walls on a slope east of section no. 1, between the two river-beds descending from the north to Wadi Ahmar (Israel grid: 18651/17040).
   Close to it, on a low hill, is a modern well-built structure (Ottoman?), with arches and a courtyard.
   In the high northern part of the area is a rock shelter, in front of which are built terraces or support walls (Israel grid: 18652/17043). By the rock shelter are four rock-cut cup marks (no. 2 in plan).
   Pottery (150 sherds): Chalcolithic – 26%; Roman – 34%; Medieval – 20%; Modern – 20%.
   Flint: 52 items: 1 flake core, 40 flakes, 4 blades, 3 bladelets, and 4 scrapers.
   Stone: a limestone bowl and a limestone bowlet.

3. On the north bank of the wadi are two well-built courtyards or enclosures (Israel grid: 18655/17033), (no. 3 in plan).
   Pottery: (8 body sherds): Chalcolithic – 25%; Roman – 75%.
4. This section contains several structures (no. 4 in plan).
   Round structure (Israel grid: 18663/17035), 20 m in diameter, built on top of earlier remains.
   East of the round structure is a small modern structure with two large courtyards. The structure has entrances with monoliths.
   North-east of the modern structure is a cave.
   Pottery (80 sherds): Chalcolithic – 80%; Roman – 6%; Medieval – 6%; Unidentified – 8%.
   Flint (12 items): 1 blade core, 6 flakes, 3 blades, 1 retouched blade and a Byblos type arrowhead. The arrowhead indicates a Pottery Neolithic A date.
5. In the area descending to a tributary of Wadi Ahmar east of no. 4 – no archaeological finds (no. 5 in plan).
6. A cave, a cistern, a cupmark and walls (no. 6 in plan) on a spur south of Wadi Ahmar.
   Pottery (45 body sherds): Chalcolithic – 33%; Roman – 67%.
7. A small courtyard at the mouth of a tributary from the south and emptying into Wadi Ahmar (no. 7 in plan).
   Pottery (3 body sherds): Roman – 100%.
8. In the south-east of this part of the site are courtyards and installations.
   A constructed road (C50) crosses the site and the ravine which empties to Wadi Ahmar (no. 8 in plan).
   Pottery (30 body sherds): Iron II – 16%; Roman – 84%.
9. In a rocky area in the west of the site in this section (Israel grid: 18644/17027) are several structures and installations (no. 9 in plan): several courtyards, threshing floors, a cupmark, and a winepress crushing stone. About 10 m west of the crushing stone was traced a quarrying of another, unfinished crushing stone.
   Pottery (80 body sherds): Roman – 50%; Medieval – 50%.

Other surveys: none.

192. Plan of **Wadi Ahmar Valley**.

193. Aerial photo of the **Wadi Ahmar Valley**, looking south-west. Sections 1-5 and 7 are well seen. In the top right hand corner is the Wadi Ahmar terrace site (Site 102) (A. Solomon).

194. **Wadi Ahmar Valley**, section 4, view to north (S. Bar).

195. **Wadi Ahmar Valley**, sections 2-3, view to north (S. Bar).

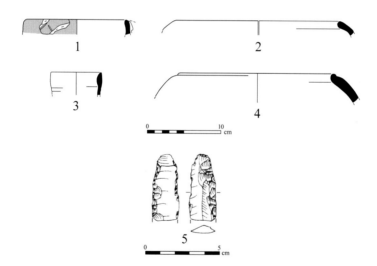

196. Finds from **Wadi Ahmar Valley** (section 1): 1. Bowl (?), dk brn, red slip outside, LR; 2. Bowl, (?), lt brn, LR; 3. Jar/jug, lt brn, LR; 4. Holemouth jar, lt colour, Chal; 5. Amuq arrowhead, Pottery Neolithic A.

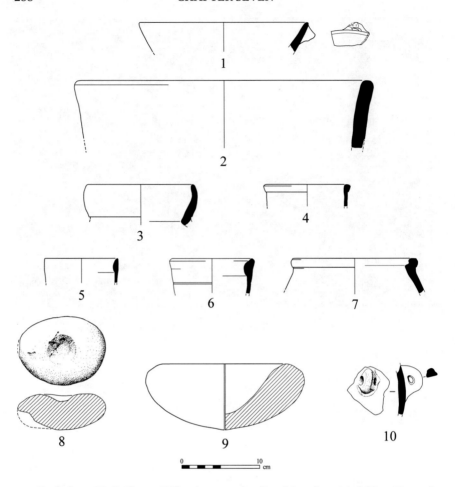

197. Finds from **Wadi Ahmar Valley** (section 2): 1. Bowl, lt colour, Med (?); 2. Krater, lt colour, Med; 3. Jar, lt brn, Chal; 4. Jug (?), lt brn, Rom; 5-6. Jugs, dk brn, Rom (?); 7. Jar, blk, Mod; 8. Bowlet, limestone; 9. Bowl, limestone; 10. Lug handle, lt colour, Chal.

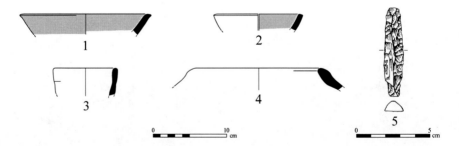

198. Finds from **Wadi Ahmar Valley** (section 4): 1. Bowl, lt brn, painted lt brn in and out, Chal; 2. Bowl, lt brn, residual red painting inside, Chal; 3. Jar, lt brn, Rom; 4. Jar, lt brn, Med; 5. Byblos type arrowhead, Pottery Neolithic A.

Site 104: 18-17/60/3
WADI ZAMOR (8)

Israel grid: 18674/17004
UTM grid: 7252/5568
Elevation: 190 m a.s.l., 40 m b.s.a.
Name: nearest place
Site type: farm and enclosures
Area: 2,000 sq. m (2 dunams)
Topography: valley edge
Rock type: Judea Group
Soil: terra rossa, quality: 8

Cultivation: field crops by the site
Cisterns: none
Water source: 'Ein Juheir (no. 189), 1.9 km distant
Road: 'Ein Hafireh-Wadi Zamor (C50), by the site
Visit: March 2014; 3 surveyors; 250 sherds

Site on a rocky slope descending to a field spread over several dunams on the southern bank of Wadi Ahmar, above the channel of the wadi and about 120 m from it, 2.5 km north-north-west of Gittit. The Sartaba summit and parts of Sahl Afjam are visible from the site.

Well preserved farm containing a residence structure with courtyards attached to it on the north and south.
– The residence structure is 12×10 m. The nucleus of the structure is built of large worked stones. Its construction differs from that of the courtyards

199. **Wadi Zamor (8)**, view south (I. Bejerano).

(below). Inside it are two subdivided elongated spaces. Two additional rooms and an irregular space abut the north-eastern corner of the structure (no. 1. in plan).
- Southern courtyard. Above and south of the residence structure a 16×16 m large courtyard is attached, built of one row of medium-sized stones (no. 2).
- Low northern courtyard, 16×12 m, attached at the north to the residence structure. A shoddily built terrace separates the lower side of the courtyard from a cultivated field (no. 3).
- About 35 m east of the farm is a poorly preserved enclosure (no. 4).

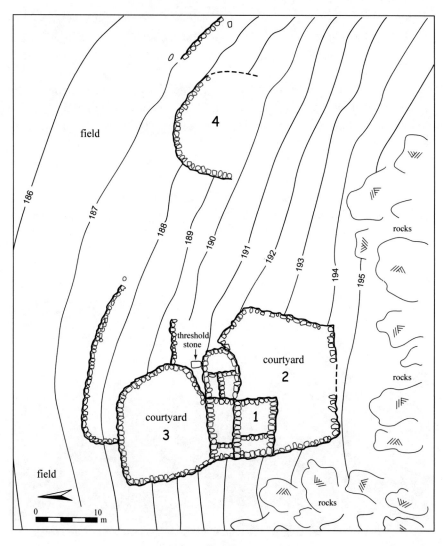

200. Plan of **Wadi Zamor (8)**.

The location of the site might be related to the Roman road (C50) passing along Wadi Ahmar linking Kh. Juraish with Sahl Afjam and the Sartaba ridge.

Pottery: Late Roman – 60%; Byzantine – 20%; Medieval – 12%; Modern – 8%.
Other surveys: none.

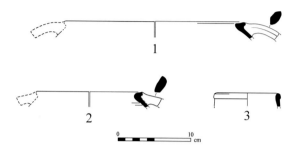

201. Pottery from **Wadi Zamor (8)**: 1. CP (?), lt brn, Rom-Byz; 2. Jar (?), lt brn, Med; 3. Jug, lt brn, Rom-Byz.

◆ ◆ ◆

Site 105: 18-17/60/4

ELEVATION POINT 432 (4)

Israel grid: 18619/17019
UTM grid: 7246/5568
Elevation: 320 m a.s.l., 110 m a.s.a.
Name: nearest place
Site type: cave and courtyard
Area: 100 sq. m (0.1 dunam)
Topography: slope of spur
Rock type: Judea Group
Soil: terra rossa, quality: 6

Cultivation: none
Cisterns: none
Water source: 'Ein Juheir (no. 189), 1.3 km distant
Road: 'Ein Hafireh-Wadi Zamor (C50), 400 m distant
Visit: November 2014; 3 surveyors; 14 sherds

Site on a slope of a spur south and above the channel of Wadi Ahmar, 3 km east from Aqraba.

Collapsed cave. In the surviving parts the ceiling is charred. Inside are built partitions enabling continuous use of the cave spaces after its collapse.

At the front of the cave is a semicircular courtyard about 10 m in diameter.

Pottery: Late Roman (body sherds) – 36%; Medieval – 64%.
Other surveys: none.

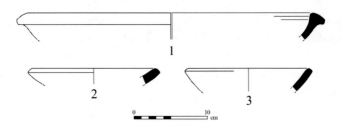

202. Pottery from E.P. 432 (4): 1-3. Bowls, lt colour, Med.

♦ ♦ ♦

Site 106: 18-16/59/1

WADI ZAMOR (2)

Israel grid: 18518/16938
UTM grid: 7237/5560
Elevation: 350 m a.s.l., 60 m b.s.a.
Name: nearest place
Site type: courtyard
Area: 1000 sq. m (1 dunam)
Topography: slope
Rock type: Judea Group
Soil: terra rossa, quality: 4

Cultivation: none
Cisterns: none
Water source: 'Ein Juheir (no. 189), 1.7 km distant
Road: 'Ein Hafireh-Wadi Zamor (C50), 100 m distant
Visit: February 2015; 8 surveyors; 100 sherds

Site on a steep slope in a rocky area east and above Wadi Zamor, 2.5 km east-south-east of Aqraba.

Medium-sized courtyard: north-eastern side 30 m long and the south-western side 28 m. The courtyard wall is built mainly of one row of unworked medium-sized stones, and is preserved up to a height of 1 m. Three of the courtyard corners are right-angled and the north-western one is rounded. Two openings have been traced in the north and south. In the south-west corner is a room, 8×6 m, containing a square stone with a circular basin cut in it.

In the valley east of the site are remains of numerous terraces.

Pottery: Early Roman – 30%; Late Roman – 70%.
Other surveys: none.

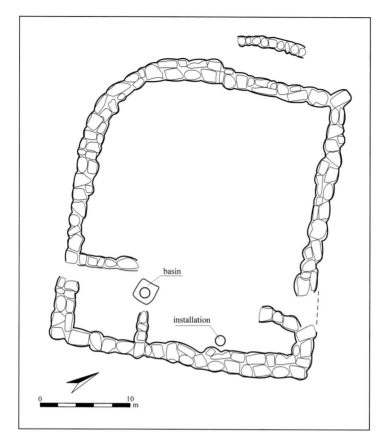

203. Plan of **Wadi Zamor (2)**.

204. Pottery from **Wadi Zamor (2)**: 1. Jar, lt colour, LR; 2. Jar, lt colour, Rom; 3. Jug, reddish, ER; 4. Jug, reddish, Rom.

Site 107: 18-16/59/2
ELEVATION POINT 432 (8)

Israel grid: 18569/16989
UTM grid: 7242/5566
Elevation: 375 m a.s.l., 0 m a.s.a.
Name: nearest place
Site type: enclosure
Area: 1,500 sq. m (1.5 dunams)
Topography: spur
Rock type: Judea Group

Soil: terra rossa, quality: 8
Cultivation: field crops by the site
Cisterns: none
Water source: 'Ein Juheir (no. 189), 1.3 km distant
Road: 'Ein Hafireh-Wadi Zamor (C50), 200 m distant
Visit: May 2014; 4 surveyors; 50 sherds

Site on a very moderate slope descending westwards to Wadi Zamor, 2.5 km east of Aqraba. Site E.P. 432 (5) is close to it in the east.

Elliptical enclosure, 26×24 m, built of large stones. The eastern part is missing. In the western part are four built cells, on average 3×2 m, with walls one medium-sized stone thick. The three southern cells adjoin, while the northern

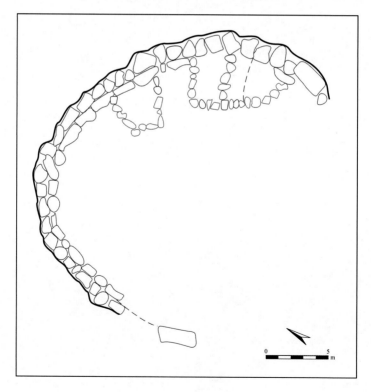

205. Plan of E.P. 432 (8).

one is separate.

There is a moderate sherd scatter; evidence of prolonged dwelling or sojourn.

Pottery: Late Roman – 20%; Medieval (body sherds) – 30%; Ottoman – 50%.
Other surveys: none.

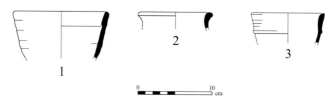

206. Pottery from **E.P. 432 (8)**: 1. Bowl (?), lt brn, Ott (?); 2. Jar, gr, Ott; 3. Jar, lt brn, LR.

207. Aerial photo looking east at **E.P. 432 (8)** (A. Solomon).

Site 108: 18-16/59/3

WADI ZAMOR (3)

Israel grid: 18527/16983
UTM grid: 7238/5565
Elevation: 345 m a.s.l., 40 m b.s.a.
Name: nearest place
Site type: structure, installations and caves
Area: 500 sq. m (0.5 dunam)
Topography: saddle
Rock type: Judea Group

Soil: terra rossa, quality: 4
Cultivation: none
Cisterns: none
Water source: 'Ein Juheir (no. 189), 1.3 km distant
Road: 'Ein Hafireh-Wadi Zamor (C50), 200 m distant
Visit: March 2015; 4 surveyors; 45 sherds

Site on a saddle west and above Wadi Zamor, 2 km east of Aqraba and 1.4 km south of Kh. Jureish. From the site is a view of the confluence of Wadi Ahmar with Wadi Zamor, at Kh. Jureish and at Kh. er-Risa (1) and to the ridges east of Aqraba.

A structure, 6×6 m, built of large stones. Other walls are scattered in the area, but do not form a plan.

25 rock-cut installations 20 m east of the structure, mostly cup marks 20 to 40 cm in diameter. Also, pressing facilities, which include a collecting vat, a threshing surface and rock-cut levelled surfaces.

At least two plundered caves; the front of one of them rock-cut in the form of an arch.

Relatively little pottery was collected, mostly LR.

Pottery: Iron I (body sherds) – 2%; Late Roman – 76%; Byzantine (body sherds) – 20%; Medieval (body sherds) – 2%.
Other surveys: none.

Site 109: 18-16/59/4
ELEVATION POINT 432 (5)

Israel grid: 18586/16983
UTM grid: 7243/5565
Elevation: 385 m a.s.l., 10 m a.s.a.
Name: nearest place
Site type: farm and cisterns
Area: 1,000 sq. m (1 dunam)
Topography: edge of valley
Rock type: Judea Group

Soil: stony desert, quality: 3
Cultivation: none
Cisterns: 2
Water source: 'Ein Juheir (no. 189), 1.4 km distant
Road: 'Ein Hafireh-Wadi Zamor (C50), 400 m distant
Visit: May 1998; 5 surveyors; 40 sherds

Small site at the edge of a spur in a hilly zone by the confluence of Wadi Zamor and Wadi Ahmar, 2.7 km east of Aqraba.

In the western part of the site is a farm containing a dwelling structure and a courtyard.

The structure consist of three rooms, each about 5×3 m. The room openings face east to the courtyard. In the outer wall and the walls between the rooms are secondary divisions. The construction is of small stones strengthened with clay.

Large rectangular courtyard about 20×15 m is attached to the structure in the east. The walls are 2 m high. The courtyard is divided by an inner wall.

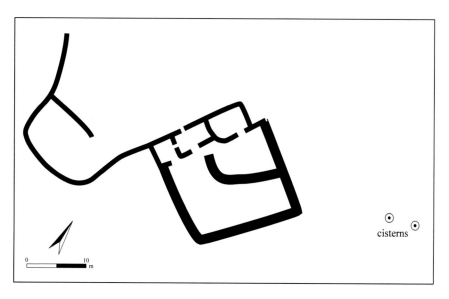

208. Plan of E.P. 432 (5).

Long curving wall starts from the south-west corner of the structure to the south-west, forming an enclosure open to the north.

20 m east of the farm are openings of cisterns.

The structure is dated to the Medieval period or even later, but is built over an earlier site, apparently LR, not now visible on the surface.

Pottery: Iron II (body sherds) – 5%; Late Roman – 70%; Medieval – 20%; Ottoman (body sherds) – 5%.
Other surveys: none.

209. Aerial photo viewing west of E.P. 432 (5).

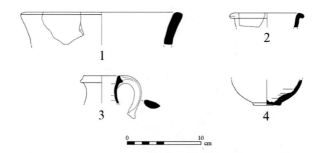

210. Pottery from E.P. 432 (5): 1. Jar, lt brn, Med; 2. Bowl, buff, LR; 3. Jug, org, LR; 4. Bowl/jug base, lt brn, LR.

Site 110: 18-16/59/5
EL-GURFEH (2)

Israel grid: 18574/16962
UTM grid: 7242/5564
Elevation: 400 m a.s.l., 30 m a.s.a.
Name: local
Site type: cave, courtyards, installations and cistern
Area: 500 sq. m (0.5 dunam)
Topography: spur slope
Rock type: Judea Group

Soil: terra rossa, quality: 8
Cultivation: plantations (nearby)
Cisterns: 1
Water source: 'Ein Juheir (no. 189), 1.5 km distant
Road: 'Ein Hafireh-Wadi Zamor (C50), 400 m distant
Visit: November 2014; 4 surveyors; 130 sherds

Site on a slope of a spur, 2.5 km east of Aqraba and 100 m south of the site of el-Gurfeh (1) (Site 111).

Cave, 20×6 m divided by built walls. In the walls of the cave are hewn niches which served for storage. The ceiling is charred.

Two courtyards outside the cave. The lower one is 20×5 m and the upper one is 12×5 m: apparently the courtyards served also as agricultural terraces.

On the northern slope of the spur are several rock cuttings including a trough 60×40 cm lined with cement, a rectangular 2×1.5 m trough blocked with

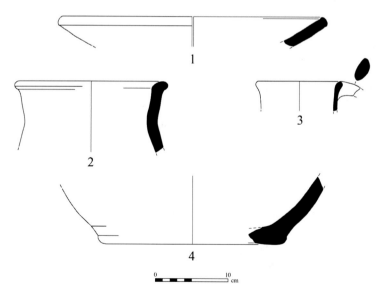

211. Pottery from **el-Gurfeh (2)**: 1. Bowl, lt colour, Med; 2. Jar, lt brn Med; 3. Jug, lt colour, LR; 4. Base, lt colour, Med.

soil, and a plastered cistern, the depth of which is not clear. The cistern opening is nearly 2 m diameter, and has a metal lid.

North of the site are more terraces.

Pottery: Late Roman – 23%; Medieval – 77%.
Other surveys: none.

Site 111: 18-16/59/6

EL-GURFEH (1)

Israel grid: 18580/16967
UTM grid: 7243/5564
Elevation: 385 m a.s.l., 40 m b.s.a.
Name: local
Site type: cave, courtyards, walls and cistern
Area: 5,000 sq. m (5 dunams)
Topography: slope at a valley edge
Rock type: Judea Group

Soil: terra rossa, quality: 7
Cultivation: field crops near the site
Cisterns: 1
Water source: 'Ein Juheir (no. 189), 1.5 km distant
Road: 'Ein Hafireh-Wadi Zamor (C50), 400 m distant
Visit: November 2014; 9 surveyors; 135 sherds

Site on the northern slope of E.P. 432 hill, 2.5 km north-west of Gittit and 2.5 km east of Aqraba. The site is on the north side of the Wadi el-Gurfeh valley.

In the central upper part of the site is a dwelling cave, 17×7.5 m. The entry to the wide part of the cave is from a low cliff to the north. The inner space of the cave is sub-divided by walls into three areas.

Above the cave is an array of anti-erosion support walls.

In the slope below the cave is a series of levelled courtyards and terraces. The support walls survive up to a maximum height of 2 m. Residues of plaster remain on sections of the walls.

North and below the central part of the site is another array of terraces and support walls. East of it are several walls.

Near the site are a cistern and two rock-cut troughs (not in plan).

This is a typical residence site which existed on plots of fertile land and plantations and field crops in the area.

Pottery: Late Roman – 30%; Byzantine (body sherds) – 7%; Medieval – 59%; Unidentified – 4%.
Stone: three fragments of basalt grinding vessels.
Other surveys: none.

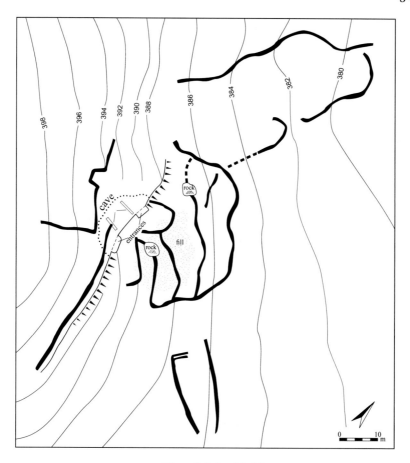

212. Plan of **el-Gurfeh (1)**.

213. Aerial photo view west of **el-Gurfeh (1)** (A. Solomon).

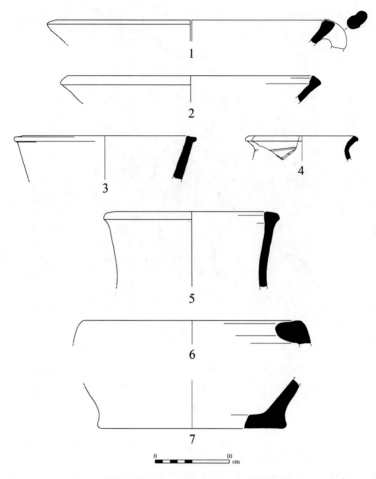

214. Pottery from **el-Gurfeh (1)**: 1. Krater/bowl, lt brn, Med; 2-3. Bowls, lt brn, Med; 4. Jar, lt brn, LR; 5. Jar, lt brn, Med; 6. Pithos, lt brn, Med, 7. Base, lt brn, Med.

Site 112: 18-16/59/7
WADI ZAMOR (6)

Israel grid: 18547/16946
UTM grid: 7240/5562
Elevation: 405 m a.s.l., 100 m a.s.a.
Name: nearest place
Site type: hamlet
Area: 1 ha (10 dunams)
Topography: spur
Rock type: Judea Group
Soil: terra rossa, quality: 4

Cultivation: field crops near the site
Cisterns: 4
Water source: 'Ein Juheir (no. 189),
   1.6 km distant
Road: 'Ein Hafireh-Wadi Zamor (C50),
   300 m distant
Visit: March 2015; 4 surveyors;
   40 sherds

Site at a very high spot above Wadi Zamor, 2 km east of Aqraba. East of it is a cultivated plateau, and further, on the plateau of E.P. 432, are more large cultivated areas.

There are well preserved remains of a small hamlet, comprising at least five structures, apparently representing nuclear families: it can be assumed that all were related to a single paternal family.

The structures are:

- Modern structure, 5×5 m, the best preserved in the village. The 80 cm thick walls are well-built of worked stones, strengthened with cement and plastered inside.

  The structure has a concrete roof with a gutter to collect rainwater. The 80 cm wide entrance is in the east. A bench is built along the inside of the southern wall. In each of the walls is a window or narrow hatch, as are for all the other structures of the village (no. 1 in plan).

- Round courtyard, built of small stones, 25 m diameter. The courtyard wall is 80 cm thick. The entrance is from the north-eastern corner. A round structure 4 m in diameter is attached to the outside of the north wall of the courtyard. This structure has its own entrance from outside the courtyard and a hatch in the wall (no. 2).

- Round structure built of small stones. Sections of the walls are plastered on the inside. The entrance is in the east. A built bench and a niche are preserved inside the structure, made of stone and clay. The surviving roofing has a layer of thick branches, crosswise above it thin branches, and the finish is a layer of clay for waterproofing. The clay mortar has recently been replaced by concrete (no. 3).

- Large complex consisting of three parts (no. 4) in the northern part of the site: below structure no. 1 a plastered coarsely built dwelling house of a

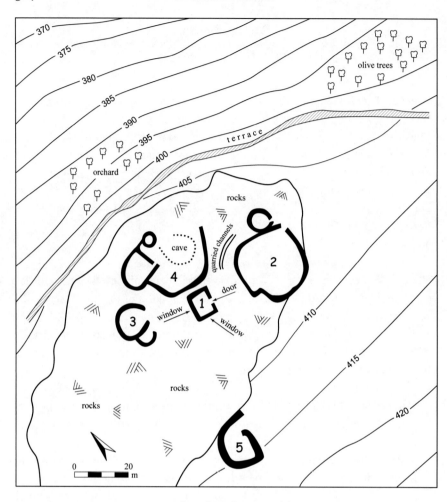

215. Plan of **Wadi Zamor (6)**.

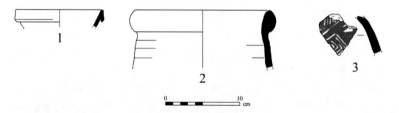

216. Pottery from **Wadi Zamor (6)**: 1. Bowl, reddish, Rom; 2. Jar, lt colour, Mod; 3. Sherd, lt brn, dark orn on white, Med.

large room with a round kitchen attached to it; a round courtyard built of fieldstones attached to the dwelling house in the south (the courtyard is incomplete in the north); and a cave inside the courtyard with a 4 m wide opening. The cave is 6 m deep with a partition wall inside.
- Elliptical structure, 6×5 m, simply built of fieldstones. The entrance is on the north-east (no. 5).

The village is built on a large rocky surface. A long terrace wall borders it in the north-east. On the rocky surface are rock-cut water collecting channels.

A small olive grove with about 30 trees and a hedge of cactus plants are adjacent to the village in the north-east.

It appears that the village has been inhabited continuously since Medieval times at least, until it was abandoned only during the last few decades.

The ancient road C50 which passes near the village is seen clearly on the wadi bank below the site.

This is a fine example of a well-preserved Ottoman hamlet typical of Samaria.

Pottery: Iron I (?) (body sherds) – 5%; Late Roman – 12%; Early Moslem (body sherds) – 5%; Medieval (Mamluk) – 20%; Ottoman-Modern – 58%.
Other surveys: none.

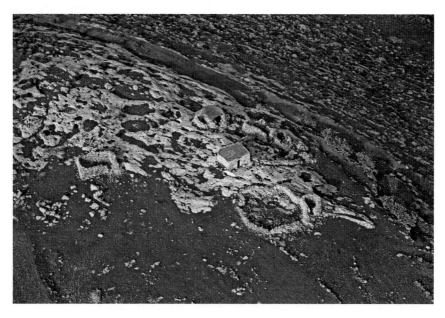

217. Aerial photo of **Wadi Zamor (6)**, looking west (A. Solomon).

Site 113: 18-16/59/8
EL-GURFEH (3)

Israel grid: 18591/16947
UTM grid: 7244/5562
Elevation: 420 m a.s.l., 0 m a.s.a.
Name: ancient nearest place
Site type: structure
Area: 2,500 sq. m (2.5 dunams)
Topography: rocky plateau
Rock type: Judea Group
Soil: terra rossa, quality: 5

Cultivation: none
Cisterns: none
Water source: 'Ein Juheir (no. 189), 1.8 km distant
Road: 'Ein Hafireh-Wadi Zamor (C50), 500 m distant
Visit: November 2014; 5 surveyors; 100 sherds

Site located on a rocky plateau of E.P. 432, 2.3 km north-west of Gittit.

Ruined structure, built of very large stones; but due to its derelict state it is impossible to construct the original plan. Beside one of the walls there is a bench built of one row of stones. On top of the ancient structure is a *maq'ad* built of a single row of small stones.

The original structure stood on the summit of the plateau, serving as an observation guard post or a watchtower during the Roman and Byzantine periods.

Sherds were collected near the structure and in an adjacent field.

Pottery: Roman-Byzantine – 94%; Medieval – 4%; Ottoman (body sherds) – 2%.
Other surveys: none.

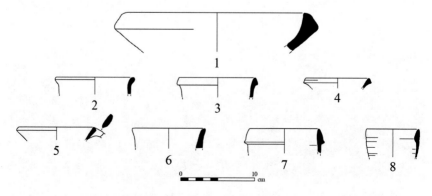

218. Pottery from **el-Gurfeh (3)**: 1. Bowl, lt brn, Med; 2. Bowl, lt brn, Rom-Byz; 3. Bowl (?), lt brn, Rom-Byz; 4-5. Jugs, lt brn, Rom-Byz; 6-8. Jugs (?), lt brn, Rom-Byz.

Site 114: 18-16/59/9
ELEVATION POINT 432 (7)

Israel grid: 18579/16905
UTM grid: 7243/5557
Elevation: 425 m a.s.l., 0 m a.s.a.
Name: nearest place
Site type: sherd scatter
Area: 2,000 sq. m (2 dunams)
Topography: plain
Rock type: Judea Group
Soil: terra rossa, quality: 7

Cultivation: none
Cisterns: none
Water source: 'Ein Juheir (no. 189), 2.2 km distant
Road: Gittit Valley (C58), 500 m distant
Visit: February 2014; 4 surveyors; 120 sherds

Sherd scatter spread over an area of about 2000 sq. m in a stone-cleared plain on the spur of E.P. 432, 2.2 km north-west of Gittit.
Many sherds. Apparently several structures existed during the LR period, dismantled during fieldstone clearance.

Pottery: Late Roman-Byzantine – 100%.
Other surveys: none.

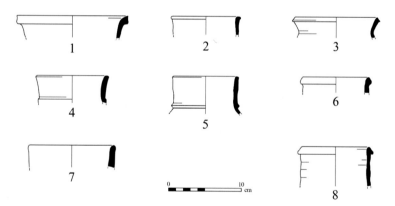

219. Pottery from E.P. 432 (7) (all LR-Byz): 1-2. Bowls, lt brn; 3. CP, reddish; 4-5, 8. Jars, lt brn; 6. Jar, reddish; 7. Jar (?), lt brn.

Site 115: 18-16/69/1
ELEVATION POINT 432 (3)

Israel grid: 18615/16988
UTM grid: 7246/5566
Elevation: 335 m a.s.l., 60 m a.s.a.
Name: nearest place
Site type: sherd scatter, cisterns and structure
Area: 5 ha (50 dunams)
Topography: spur slope
Rock type: Judea Group
Soil: terra rossa, quality: 6
Cultivation: 2
Cisterns: none
Water source: 'Ein Juheir (no. 189), 1.4 km distant
Road: Gittit Valley (C58), 400 m distant
Visit: March 2014 and more; 5 surveyors; 550 sherds

Site on a slope of a spur above a ravine which empties into Wadi Ahmar, 3 km east of Aqraba.

Two cisterns in the centre of the spur 50 m apart. The cisterns are cemented, covered by iron lids, and apparently modern. Stone-built drainage channels lead to them; one is attached to a round 2 m diameter stone structure – perhaps a watchtower.

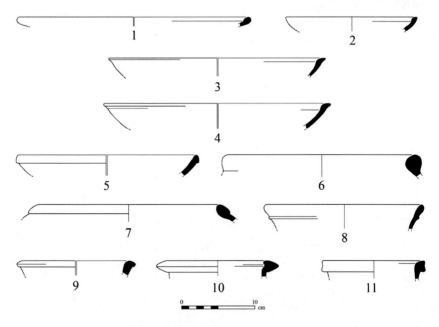

220. Pottery from E.P. 432 (3) (all MB II except nos. 3-4): 1-2, Bowls, lt brn; 3-4. Bowls, dk brn, LR-Byz (?); 5. Bowl, lt brn; 6. CP, lt brn; 7. Krater, lt brn; 8, 10-11. Jars, lt brn; 9. Jar, dk brn.

In the south, on the slope further up on the spur, are numerous terraces.

Up the slope is a 50 cm diameter semicircular rock-cutting whose purpose is unknown.

A few ancient walls were discovered, evidence of an ancient settlement whose building stones were used for constructing the terraces.

There is a large sherd scatter.

This is one of the cluster of MBA II sites at E.P. 432 (2) and el-'Urqan (1) (Sites 118 and 117 respectively) in the fringes of Samaria.

Pottery: Middle Bronze II – 75%; Iron I-II (body sherds) – 1%; Late Roman-Byzantine – 15%; Medieval (body sherds) – 9%.
Flint: 15 items: 6 flakes, 5 blades, 1 borer and 3 scrapers.
Other surveys: none.

◆ ◆ ◆

Site 116: 18-16/69/2

MUGHARET ET-TINEH

Israel grid: 18604/16979
UTM grid: 7245/5565
Elevation: 380 m a.s.l., 0 m a.s.a.
Name: local
Site type: cave, courtyards, sherd scatter and cistern.
Area: 7,000 sq. m (7 dunams)
Topography: slope
Rock type: Judea Group

Soil: terra rossa, quality: 4
Cultivation: none
Cisterns: 1
Water source: 'Ein Juheir (no. 189), 1.5 km distant
Road: Gittit Valley (C58), 400 m distant
Visit: November 2014 and more; 9 surveyors; 1,500 sherds

Broad site on a moderate slope descending eastwards from E.P. 432 to the dwelling caves above Wadi Ahmar, 500 m west of the unpaved road which descends to Wadi Ahmar and 2.5 km north-west of Gittit.

The site consist of four parts:
- Plundered medium-size deeply dug cave 6 m wide and 6 m deep (no. 1 in plan). There are almost no sherds in the excavated spill from the cave. Above and beside it are several walls. A wall stretching north from the cave forms a porch 24×2 m. This wall conducts water to a cistern. At the front of the cave is a round room, 3 m in diameter. This complex of walls is linked to the peripheral walls and terraces (see below).
- Large cistern, about 10 m deep, with an opening 2 m diameter, 32 m north of

the cave. The cistern opening is surrounded by numerous heaps of excavated chalky material-limestone dug from within. The excavated spill is supported by a wall. Apparently the cistern was the main water source for the entire site (no. 2).

- Ramp or a large levelled terrace, 20×7 m, down and a short distance northwards from the cave. The terrace, the function of which is unknown, is supported by a high wall built of large stones (no. 3).

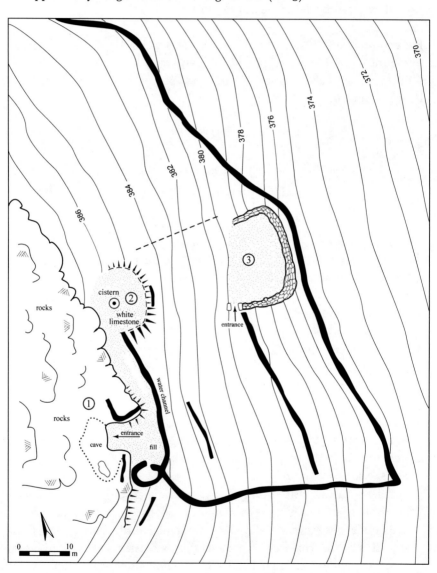

221. Plan of **Mugharet et-Tineh**.

- Two large courtyards supported by terrace walls on the slope, below the cave and the cistern. The upper courtyard, 38×28 m, contains a grey spilled material and many Medieval painted and decorated sherds, possibly a pottery workshop. It is difficult to substantiate this without excavation, but if the assumption is correct this is a significant discovery contributing to the research of the Medieval period.

Pottery: Late Roman-Byzantine – 8%; Medieval – 90%; Ottoman – 2%.
Ceramic notes: Some of the Medieval sherds are coloured dark chocolate brown over a yellowish-cream background; red over white; black over yellowish cream; and black over glazed green. The commonest ornamentation patterns are piercing and incisions – mainly on handles; and many coarse storage vessels. Three Ottoman pipes were also found.
Flint: 11 items: 7 flakes, 3 blades and a scraper.
Other finds: glass bracelets and a worn round copper pendant.
Other surveys: none.

222. Aerial photo viewing west of **Mugharet et-Tineh** (A. Solomon).

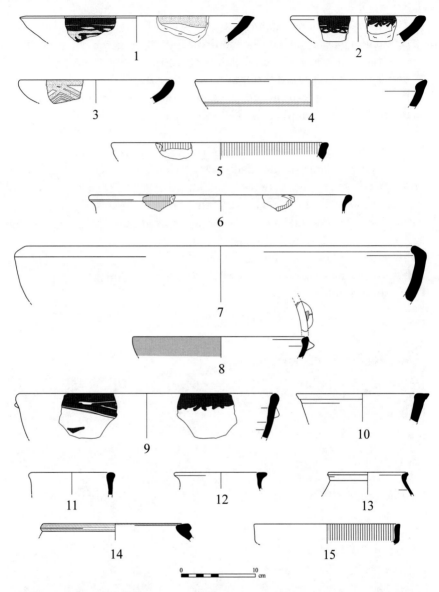

223. Pottery from **Mugharet et-Tineh** (all except nos. 12-13 are Med): 1-2. Bowls, greyish, blk orn over white; 3. Bowl, dk brn, white orn over red; 4. Bowl, lt brn, burnished remnants outside; 5. Bowl, lt brn, green glaze; 6. Bowl, reddish, green glaze; 7, 10. Bowls, lt brn; 8. Bowl, lt brn, red slip; 9. Bowl, lt brn, blk orn over white; 11. Bowl, lt brn; 12. Bowl (?), lt brn, Rom-Byz; 13. Bowl, lt brn, Rom-Byz; 14. Bowl (?), lt brn, yellowish slip on the rim; 15. Bowl, greyish, green glaze inside.

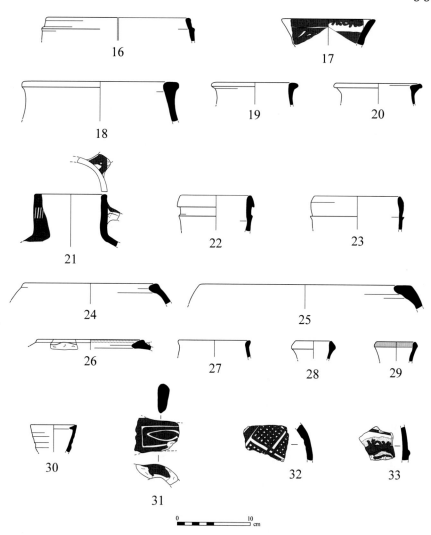

224. Pottery from **Mugharet et-Tineh** (continued): 16. CP, reddish, Rom-Byz (?); 17. Jar, greyish, blk orn over white, Med; 18. Jar, lt brn, Med; 19. Jar, lt brn, Rom-Byz; 20. Jar, blk, Rom-Byz; 21. Jar/jug, lt brn, blk orn over white, Med; 22-23. Jars, lt brn, Rom-Byz; 25. Holemouth Jar, lt brn, Med; 26. Holemouth jar, lt brn, yellow burnish outside and on rim, Med; 27. Jug, lt brn, Rom-Byz (?); 28. Jug, lt brn, Rom-Byz; 29. Jug, lt brn, red slip, Rom-Byz; 30. Cup (?), lt brn, Rom-Byz; 31. Handle, greyish, blk orn over white, Med; 32-33. Body sherds, greyish, blk orn over white, Med.

Site 117: 18-16/69/3
EL-'URQAN (1)

Israel grid: 18626/16969
UTM grid: 7248/5564
Elevation: 316 m a.s.l., 90 m a.s.a.
Name: local
Site type: cave, structures, courtyard and walls
Area: 1,000 sq. m (1 dunam)
Topography: slope
Rock type: Judea Group

Soil: terra rossa, quality: 3
Cultivation: none
Cisterns: none
Water source: 'Ein Juheir (no. 189), 1.7 km distant
Road: Gittit Valley (C58), 300 m distant
Visit: June 2014; 4 surveyors; 300 sherds

Site 2 km north-west of Gittit and 3 km east of Aqraba, on a rocky slope descending eastwards to the road leading to the el-'Urqan caves. There is a very good view of deep Wadi Ahmar.

The site extends along two natural steps, 20×50 m.
- Lower southern terrace: built on a north-south 25 m long wall of large stones. Another wall starts at the south end of the wall, going west. Apparently the lower terrace was originally subdivided by walls into several segments on the west side, but only poor remains survive.
- Upper northern terrace – also built on massive north-south wall about 40 m long, built of large stones. A hall and rooms, with straight well-built walls of medium-sized stones, at its southern part.

Remains of structures or enclosures in the eastern lower part (out of plan).

This site is one of many MBA II sites of fine construction in the region. The many sherds are evidence of permanent habitation.

Pottery: Middle Bronze II – 80%; Late Roman (body sherds) – 10%; Medieval – 10%.
Flint: 4 items: 3 hammer stones and a retouched blade.
Other surveys: none.

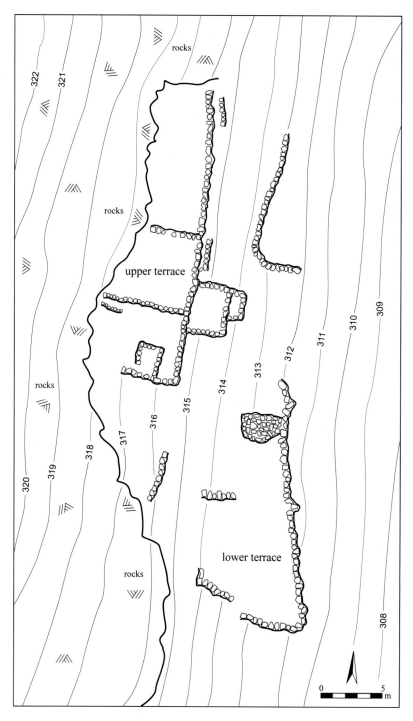

225. Plan of el-'Urqan (1).

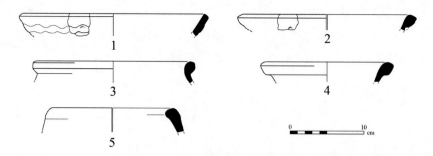

226. Pottery from **el-'Urqan (1)**: 1. Bowl, dk brn, plastic orn, MB II; 2. Bowl, dk brn, MB II; 3. Krater, lt brn, MB II; 4. Jar, lt brn, MB II; 5. Holemouth jar, lt brn, Med.

◆ ◆ ◆

Site 118: 18-16/69/4

ELEVATION POINT 432 (2)

Israel grid: 18666/16964
UTM grid: 7252/5564
Elevation: 290 m a.s.l., 100 m a.s.a.
Name: nearest place
Site type: sherd scatter, cisterns and installations
Area: 1,500 sq. m (1.5 dunams)
Topography: moderate slope
Rock type: Judea Group

Soil: terra rossa, quality: 7
Cultivation: none
Cisterns: 5
Water source: 'Ein Juheir (no. 189), 2 km distant
Road: Gittit Valley (C58), 200 m distant
Visit: March 2014; 4 surveyors; 260 sherds

Site on a moderate slope in the plateau of E.P. 432, 2 km north-north-west of Gittit.

Two arable terraces, built one above the other. The upper terrace, about 50×15 m, is built of medium-large stones. In the western part is a rectangular 2.5×2 m cell open to the west. The walls are built of medium-sized stones, and are preserved up to 6 courses (1 m high). The cell is apparently modern.

Five cisterns surround the site in the north and south at a maximum distance of 300 m from the terraces. This is an outstanding grouping of cisterns in the area.

Beside the cisterns are: rock-cut cup marks, a basin and concrete troughs.

At the top of the spur is a modern house.

Many sherds were collected in the furrows ploughed in the terraces and on the slope below them.

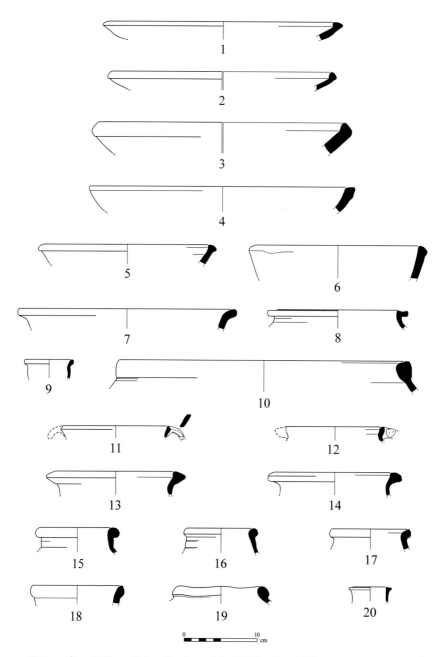

227. Pottery from **E.P. 432 (2)**: 1. Bowl, greyish, MB II; 2. Bowl, lt brn, MB II; 3-4, 6. Bowls, lt brn, Med; 5. Bowl, lt brn, LR (?); 7. Krater (?), lt brn, MB II (?); 8. Bowl, reddish, LR; 9. Bowl, greyish, LR; 10. Krater, lt brn, Med; 11. CP, lt brn, LR; 12. CP (?), reddish, LR; 13. Jar, lt brn, MB II; 14. Jar, dk brn, MB II; 15. Jar, dk brn, MB II (?); 16-17. Jars, lt brn, MB II (?); 18. Jar, lt brn, IA I (?); 19. Jar, lt brn, IA I; 20. Jug, reddish, LR.

Pottery: Middle Bronze II – 31%; Iron I – 12%; Late Roman – 50%; Medieval – 7%.
Flint: 4 items: 1 flake core and 3 blades.
Other surveys: none.

♦ ♦ ♦

Site 119: 18-16/69/5

EL-'URQAN (2)

Israel grid: 18643/16935
UTM grid: 7249/5561
Elevation: 340 m a.s.l., 60 m b.s.a.
Name: local
Site type: courtyards and road
Area: 3,000 sq. m (3 dunams)
Topography: edge of valley
Rock type: Judea Group

Soil: terra rossa, quality: 5
Cultivation: none
Cisterns: none
Water source: 'Ein Juheir (no. 189), 2.1 km distant
Road: Gittit Valley (C58), at the site
Visit: June 2014; 3 surveyors; 200 sherds

Site at the bottom of the slope of E.P. 432 ridge, 300 m south of the caves of 'Urqan and 2 km north-west of Gittit. Nearby is a road descending to Wadi Ahmar.

The site consist of three parts:
- Central courtyard, 20×18 m, built of very large stones; some sections built of two rows of stones. In the eastern side of the yard is a retaining glacis (no. 1 in plan).
- Rectangular courtyard. Only the southern and eastern walls survive. In the east, near the courtyard is a 3×2.5 m modern *maq'ad*, built of small stones. Above the courtyard is an elevated platform, 16 m diameter, supported by two rows of stones (no. 2).
- North of courtyard no. 1 is a built road leading in the direction of Wadi Ahmar (no. 3). Apparently this is a section of a Roman road (C58) which passed at the bottom of the entire ridge, linking the sites at its foot.

Pottery: Middle Bronze II (?) (body sherds) – 2%; Iron I-II – 9%; Late Roman – 63%; Byzantine – 15%; Medieval (body sherds) – 11%.
Other surveys: none.

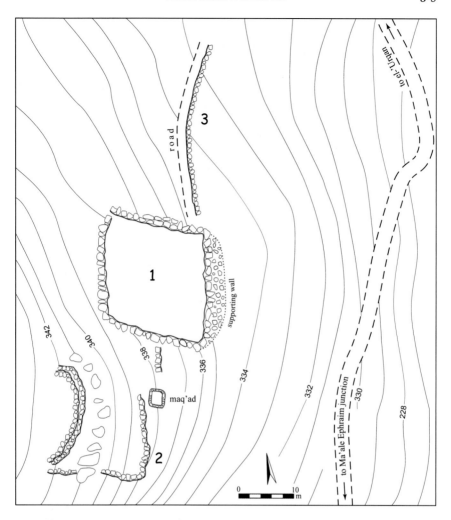

228. Plan of **el-'Urqan (2)**.

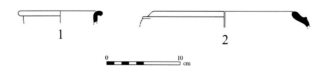

229. Pottery from **el-'Urqan (2)**: 1. Bowl (?), lt brn, LR-Byz; 2. CP, dk brn, IA II.

230. Aerial photo looking west of **el-'Urqan (2)** (A. Solomon).

Site 120: 18-16/69/6
EL-KAUKAB (1)

Israel grid: 18647/16926
UTM grid: 7250/5560
Elevation: 350 m a.s.l., 50 m b.s.a.
Name: local
Site type: courtyards, enclosure and road
Area: 3,000 sq. m (3 dunams)
Topography: edge of valley

Rock type: Judea Group
Soil: terra rossa, quality: 8
Cultivation: field crops by the site
Cisterns: none
Water source: 'Ein Juheir (no. 189), 2.2 km distant
Road: Gittit Valley (C58), at the site
Visit: April 2014; 4 surveyors; 25 sherds

Agricultural site on the eastern side of the E.P. 432 ridge, 100 m south of the site of el-'Urqan (2) and 100 m north of the site of el-Kaukab (2). From the site is a view to Wadi Ahmar and Kh. Jureish. Nearby is a large area of cultivated land.

Two circular courtyards and a square enclosure. On average the courtyards and enclosure are 10 m across. The walls are built of medium-sized stones and are 60 cm thick.

LANDSCAPE UNIT 35

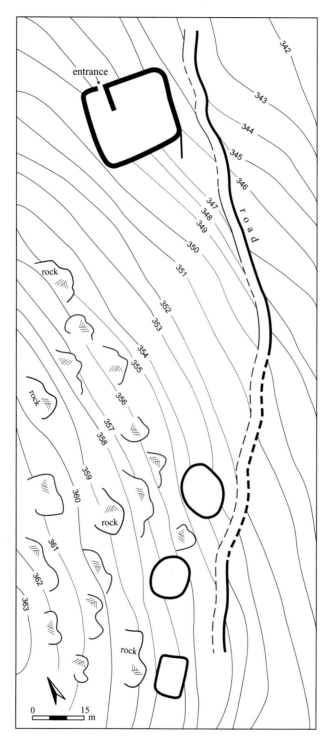

231. Plan of **el-Kaukab (1)**.

Apparently, the courtyards were for storage of crops.

East of the courtyards and along them are remains of an ancient road (C58) which connected all the sites at the sides of the valley at the bottom of the ridge.

There is a new concrete structure 300 m north-east of the site.

Small pottery find.

Pottery (body sherds): Late Roman – 80%; Byzantine – 20%.
Other surveys: none.

◆ ◆ ◆

Site 121: 18-16/69/7

EL-KAUKAB (2)

Israel grid: 18648/16910
UTM grid: 7250/5558
Elevation: 365 m a.s.l., 5 m a.s.a.
Name: local
Site type: courtyard, cistern, cave and road
Area: 500 sq. m (0.5 dunam)
Topography: slope at edge of valley

Rock type: Judea Group
Soil: terra rossa, quality: 8
Cultivation: field crops by the site
Cisterns: 1
Water source: 'Ein Juheir (no. 189), 2.3 km distant
Road: Gittit Valley (C58), at the site
Visit: July 2015; 5 surveyors; 20 sherds

Large courtyard, 1.7 km north-west of Gittit, next to the unpaved road descending from Mras ed-Din to Wadi Ahmar.

The courtyard is 35×22 m, built of one row of stones; with some sections of the perimeter wall built from two rows. The wall is about 1-1.5 m thick. The western wall turns slightly inside, forming an entrance passage into the courtyard.

Opening of a small rock cut cave in the north-eastern corner faces the courtyard.

Cistern at the south of the site, encircled currently by a modern concrete surface.

Remains of an ancient road (C58) lead south from near the cistern. The road has the same features as the road linking between the various sites in the edge of the valley at the foot of the ridge. It is probable that the road is earlier than the cistern.

This is an agricultural Roman –Byzantine site typical of those along the ridges and boundary of the cultivated valley.

Pottery (body sherds): Late Roman – 80%; Byzantine – 15%; Medieval – 5%.
Other surveys: none.

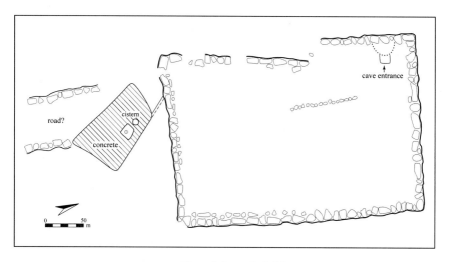

232. Plan of **el-Kaukab (2)**.

233. Aerial view south at **el-Kaukab (2)** (A. Solomon).

Site 122: 18-16/79/1
ELEVATION POINT 242

Israel grid: 18711/16950 (centre of the site)
UTM grid: 7256/5562
Elevation: 235 m a.s.l., 30 m a.s.a.
Name: nearest place
Site type: farm, courtyards and installations
Area: 3 ha (30 dunams)
Topography: saddle
Rock type: Avdat Group

Soil: terra rossa, quality: 6
Cultivation: none
Cisterns: none
Water source: 'Ein Juheir (no. 189), 2.5 km distant
Road: 'Ein Hafireh-Wadi Zamor (C50), 400 m distance
Visit: February 1998 and more; 4 surveyors; 70 sherds

Site extending westwards from the saddle above Wadi Ahmar to an inner valley, south of E.P. 242, 2 km north of Gittit.

Two courtyards in the centre of the site:
- Eastern courtyard, 25×25 m, located on a moderate slope (no. 1 in plan). The perimeter wall about 1 m thick is well built of two rows of slightly worked stones. The western part of the courtyard is divided into a series of rooms. West of the courtyard are ancient remains, earlier than the courtyard, apparently from the IA. West of the courtyard is a cave.
- Western courtyard, 10×10 m, located at the west of the saddle, overlooking a small valley which descends to the wadi. The perimeter wall is built of very large stones, and is two courses high (no. 2).

The courtyards represent a typical farm. Apparently, Iron Age houses were dismantled, and the farm was built with their stones in the Roman period.

On top of E.P. 242 hillock are several rock-cut craters (no. 3).

The small valley is now cultivated, and is surrounded by a modern terrace wall. Several small square courtyards are attached to the wall (no. 4).

In the northern part of the site, on the slope, is a deserted 20th century modern farm with two houses and a baking oven (*tabun*). The houses are built of small stones affixed with clay. Tree trunks and metal sheeting were used for roofing (no. 5).

In the southern part of the site is a courtyard, 25×25 m. Two inner walls inside form two narrow spaces: northern and western (no. 6).

The entire complex is a very advanced agricultural array, beginning in the Iron Age; and functioning mainly during the Roman period, with some parts continuing to function in the 20th century.

Pottery: Iron II – 25%; Late Roman – 60%; Medieval (body sherds) – 10%; Ottoman/Modern – 5%.
Flint: 2 items: 1 bladelet core and a blade.
Other surveys: none.

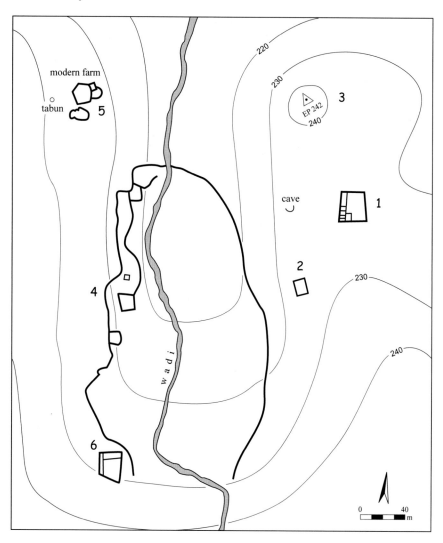

234. Plan of E.P. 242.

235. Aerial photo looking north-west at **E.P. 242** (A. Solomon).

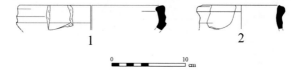

236. Pottery from E.P. 242: 1. Bowl, lt brn, Ott/Mod; 2. Jar, gr, IA II.

Site 123: 18-16/89/1

WADI ZAMOR (7)

Israel grid: 18848/16919
UTM grid: 7270/5559
Elevation: 100 m a.s.l., 20 m a.s.a.
Name: nearest place
Site type: courtyards, threshing floors, cistern, cave and installations
Area: 1 ha (10 dunams)
Topography: spur and valley edges
Rock type: Mount Scopus Group

Soil: brown lithosol, quality: 8
Cultivation: none
Cisterns: 1
Water source: 'Ein Abu Daraj (no. 177), 2.5 km distant
Road: 'Ein Hafireh-Wadi Zamor (C50), near the site
Visit: December 1994; January 2014; 4 surveyors; 56 sherds

Site at the south-western edges of the valley of Wadi Zamor, at the bottom of a steep spur descending from E.P. 338, 1.8 km north-east of Gittit.

Three built courtyards; at least one of them serving as a farm and residence.
- Northern courtyard, 30×15 m, is well built of large stones (no. 1 in plan). Various annexes are attached to both sides of the surrounding wall, inside and outside. In the northern part of the courtyard is a dwelling structure with a threshold stone. Two threshing floors and a cave are adjacent to the courtyard in the west. Beside the courtyard and the northern threshing floor are more walls.

  About 30 m north-east from the courtyard is another round threshing floor 20 m in diameter.
- Southern courtyard similar to the northern one in its construction, but larger, 40×15 m, with entrance in the eastern side (no. 2).
- Upper courtyard built on the summit of the spur, 200 m south-west of the northern courtyard and 65 m above it. This courtyard is irregular, 30×10 m, and has two openings (no. 3). Near the courtyard are a cistern with a water supply channel, basins and rock-cut troughs.

In a repeat visit to the site in January 2014, we found that the southern courtyard had been totally destroyed by a quarry.

The three courtyards and the other structures are documented here as one site because of their proximity to each other, but it is difficult to determine if indeed they belonged to the same socio-economic unit (farm?).

Pottery: Hellenistic-Early Roman – 5%; Late Roman – 95%.
Other surveys: none.

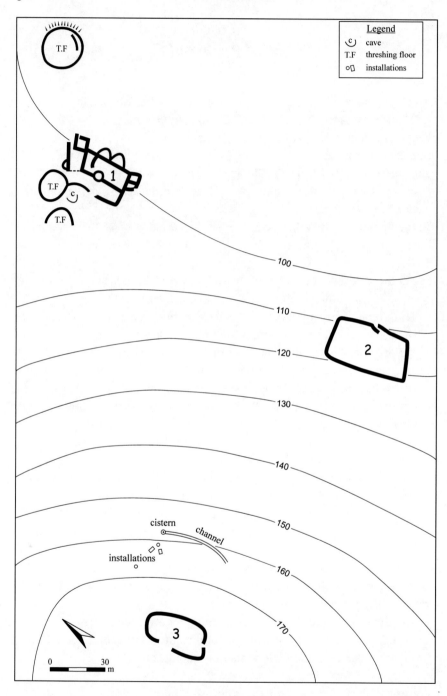

237. Plan of **Wadi Zamor (7)**.

238. Aerial photo view west at the northern courtyard at **Wadi Zamor (7)** (A. Solomon).

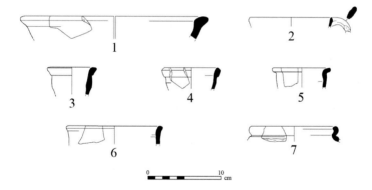

239. Pottery from **Wadi Zamor (7)**: 1. Krater (?), dk brn, LR (?); 2-5. Jugs, lt brn, LR; 6. Jug, dk brn, LR; 7. CP, lt brn, Hel-ER.

Site 124: 18-16/89/2
GITTIT QUARRY

Israel grid: 18857/16917
UTM grid: 7271/5559
Elevation: 100 m a.s.l., 0 m a.s.a.
Name: given by the 2009 excavation team
Site type: pen/corral, tower, cave, cistern, and flint scatter
Area: 5,000 sq. m (5 dunams)
Topography: valley edges
Rock type: Judea Group

Soil: terra rossa, quality: 8
Cultivation: fields by the site
Cisterns: 1
Water source: 'Ein Abu Daraj (no. 177), 2.5 km distant
Road: 'Ein Hafireh-Wadi Zamor (C50), near the site
Visit: 1999; salvage excavation under the auspices of Judea and Samaria Archaeology Staff Officer

Site scattered over the northern slope of a hill, 1.7 km north-east of Gittit.

Three areas were dug as part of a salvage excavation before starting a quarry at the site (summary of Kagan 2009):

Area A: An array of walls was exposed with a rectangular 30×26 m pen at its centre, built of one row of large fieldstones. In the south-eastern corner is an entrance 3 m wide. The north-eastern wall of the corral also functions as a terrace retaining wall. No dating finds.

Area B: Byzantine remains 220 m south-east of area A. Terraces and walls connect both areas. A tower, 5.8×2.1 m, on a rocky step, built of large fieldstones and paved with flat fieldstones. The entrance was not found. 4th and 5th centuries CE sherds were collected.

Area C: Early Moslem remains 240 m north-east of area B. Ancient rock-cut bell-shaped cistern, 2.25 m deep and 5-8 m at bottom, blocked with stones beneath modern structures. A rock-cut shaft, currently blocked by stones, leads into the cistern. The shaft opening is 2 m by 85 cm. The cistern connects to a natural cave through an opening in its eastern side. The cave area is 30 sq. m. In the eastern side of the cave is another natural opening. The cave is divided by several partition walls. It was used for dwelling from the Early Moslem period until modern times. No datable finds in the cistern, but it is reasonable that it was in use before the use of the cave. Some time later the cistern was closed and served as a dwelling.

Neolithic flint artefacts scattered over the entire three areas.

Pottery (in the salvage excavation): Neolithic, Byzantine, Early Moslem, Medieval, Ottoman, Modern.
Other surveys: none.

Site 125: 18-16/48/1
KHALET EL-KHASHABEH

Israel grid: 18483/16852
UTM grid: 7234/5552
Elevation: 350 m a.s.l., 0 m a.s.a.
Name: nearest place
Site type: village
Area: 5,000 sq. m (5 dunams)
Topography: valley edges
Rock type: Judea Group
Soil: terra rossa, quality: 6

Cultivation: none
Cisterns: 2
Water source: 'Ein Juheir (no. 189), 2.4 km distant
Road: 'Ein Hafireh-Wadi Zamor (C50), near the site
Visit: February 2014; 3 surveyors; no sherds collected

Site on both sides of unpaved road ascending from the Gittit valley to Aqraba, 2.5 km southeast of the town centre.

Remains of a deserted Ottoman village of about 20 structures built of stones and plastered with clay. Some of the structures have stone-built courtyards attached. The structures are preserved to a height of up to one storey.

Near the village are two cisterns.

In the slope north of the structures are cave openings and various constructed remains, probably part of the village.

Bedouin settled in modern clay houses built between the deserted structures; and a mosque has been built in the centre of the deserted village by the UN.

Grossman (1977) notes that in the late stages of the Ottoman period small villages were built in Samaria by farmers who had left the larger villages and settled closer to arable areas. Grossman calls them 'daughter villages'. This village could have been an example of a daughter village of the nearby town of Aqraba.

Pottery: not collected, the village is from the Ottoman period.
Other surveys: none.

Site 126: 18-16/58/1
ELEVATION POINT 432 (6)

Israel grid: 18523/16893
UTM grid: 7237/5556
Elevation: 395 m a.s.l., 50 m a.s.a.
Name: nearest place
Site type: structures and caves
Area: 2,000 sq. m (2 dunams)
Topography: slope
Rock type: Judea Group
Soil: terra rossa, quality: 7

Cultivation: none
Cisterns: none
Water source: 'Ein Juheir (no. 189), 2 km distant
Road: 'Ein Hafireh-Wadi Zamor (C50), 300 m distance
Visit: February 2014; 3 surveyors; 20 sherds

Site on a terraced slope above a cultivated valley, on the western side of E.P. 432 ridge, 2.5 km north-west of Gittit.

Terrace, 10 m wide and 200 m long, apparently to support a surface for construction. On the terrace are two collapsed structures and two caves. The structures are built of two rows of medium-sized stones with a cemented small stone infill. The walls are plastered with clay on both faces.

Western structure, about 6×4 m, partially preserved to a height of 1.5 m. The maximum thickness of the walls is 80 cm. The 70 cm wide entrance is in the north wall.

Elliptical eastern structure 5×4 m. In the southern side there is a window. The northern side of the structure rests on a rock. In the lower part of the rock is the entrance of a blocked cave. East of the structure is a rock shelter.

Between the two structures is a cave, about 8×3 m and 1.1 m high, with an entrance 70 cm wide. On both sides of the entrance are short walls. The cave possibly served as shelter and for dwelling.

Other terraces exist along the slope.

Pottery (body sherds): Late Roman-Byzantine – 20%; Medieval – 80%.
Other surveys: none.

Site 127: 18-16/58/2
WADI 'URQAN ES-SABA

Israel grid: 18532/16863
UTM grid: 7239/5553
Elevation: 345 m a.s.l., 10 m a.s.a.
Name: nearest place
Site type: structures, courtyards and installations
Area: 1 ha (10 dunams)
Topography: valley edge
Rock type: Judea Group

Soil: terra rossa, quality: 6
Cultivation: field crops by the site
Cisterns: none
Water source: 'Ein Juheir (no. 189), 2.5 km distant
Road: 'Ein Hafireh-Wadi Zamor (C50), 300 m distance
Visit: May 1998; February 2014; 4 surveyors; 47 sherds

Site in the extremity of Wadi Zamor valley, 2.3 km north-west of Gittit. West and south of the site are several small modern villages.

Four structures arranged in a triangle; three in the southern side of the triangle about 30 m apart. The structures are similar, about 7×5 m. They are divided inside and are built of unworked large stones.

Remains of a courtyard adjacent to the middle of the three structures. Next to the courtyard is a rock-cut basin.

About 150 m north of the structures is another courtyard with a rock-cut basin within.

There are numerous terrace walls in the area; some of them connect the structures (not in plan).

During a return visit to the site, in February 2014, we learnt that the site had been dismantled and cleared completely as land preparation for cultivation, and only the rock-cut basin survived.

Pottery: Iron I-II (body sherds) – 16%; Late Roman-Byzantine – 84%.
Other surveys: none.

240. Pottery from **Wadi 'Urqan es-Saba**: 1.bowl, lt brn, blk red slip outside, Rom-Byz; 2. Jug (?), lt brn, Rom-Byz.

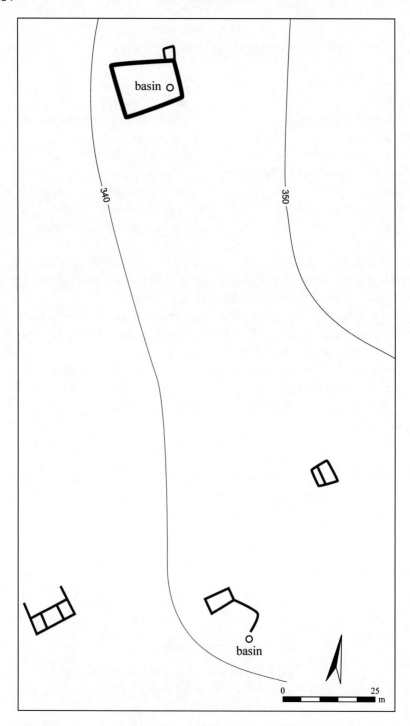

241. Plan of **Wadi ʿUrqan es-Saba**.

Site 128: 18-16/58/3
RAS ER-RAHIB

Israel grid: 18599/16861
UTM grid: 7245/5553
Elevation: 395 m a.s.l., 10 m a.s.a.
Name: local and not on map
Site type: courtyard, enclosure and structures
Area: 1,000 sq. m (1 dunam)
Rock type: Judea Group
Soil: terra rossa, quality: 8
Cultivation: none
Cisterns: 1
Water source: 'Ein Juheir (no. 189), 2.6 km distant
Road: Gittit Valley (C58), 400 m distance
Visit: May 1998; 4 surveyors; 50 sherds

Small site, 1.8 km north-west of Gittit and 200 m north-west of E.P. 419.

The main feature at the site is a courtyard, 18×10 m. In the south-eastern corner of the courtyard is a small newly-built cell, 5×4 m.

North and around the courtyard are three small rooms identical in size.

Elliptical enclosure, 15×10 m, is attached to the eastern wall of the courtyard.

All structures are of medium-sized stones preserved to a height of up to three courses.

Pottery: Late Roman – 96%; Modern (body sherds) – 4%.
Flint: 7 items: 4 flakes, 2 blades and a scraper.
Other surveys: none.

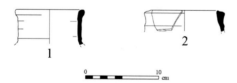

242. Pottery from **Ras er-Rahib**: 1-2. Jars, lt brn, LR.

Site 129: 18-16/58/4
ES-SIREH (2)

Israel grid: 18546/16845
UTM grid: 7240/5551
Elevation: 355 m a.s.l., 60 m b.s.a.
Name: Given by the Survey
Site type: courtyard
Area 500 sq. m: (0.5 dunam)
Topography: valley edge
Rock type: Judea Group
Soil: terra rossa, quality: 7

Cultivation: field crops by the site
Cisterns: none
Water source: 'Ein Juheir (no. 189), 2.6 km distant
Road: 'Ein Hafireh-Wadi Zamor (C50), 500 m distance
Visit: November 2014; 4 surveyors; 100 sherds

Site at the edge of a valley between the ridge of E.P. 472 and the ridge of E.P. 393, 400 m north of the fortress in es-Sireh (1) and 2.3 km north-west of Gittit. From the site there is a lookout to Aqraba and its ridges and to Nebi Noon.

Small courtyard, 16×15 m, with rounded corners. The surrounding wall is built of one row of medium-sized and large stones. In the north-eastern corner are remains of an entrance and a small corridor leading to the centre of the courtyard.

Outside the courtyard, parallel to its western side, is a wall protecting against erosion; west of it, several metres away, is another badly built wall, with the same function.

Close by, a fragment of a round stone with a column drum with holes in its side – identified as a tool to flatten plaster on roofs and threshing floors.

The site belongs to the type of courtyard designed for storing crops, typical of the Roman-Byzantine period in the region.

Pottery: Early Roman – 25%; Late Roman – 75%.
Other surveys: none.

243. Pottery from **es-Sireh (2)**: 1-2. CPs, lt brn, LR; 3. Bowl, lt brn, Rom; 4-5. Jugs, lt brn, Rom.

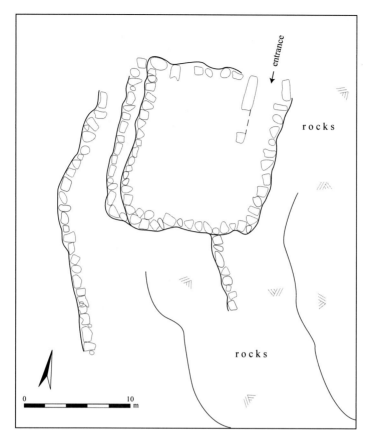

244. Plan of **es-Sireh (2)**.

♦ ♦ ♦

Site 130: 18-16/58/5

ES-SIREH (3)

Israel grid: 18553/16837
UTM grid: 7241/5551
Elevation: 360 m a.s.l., 70 m b.s.a.
Name: Given by the Survey
Site type: courtyard and dams
Area: 1,500 sq. m (1.5 dunams)
Topography: valley edge
Rock type: Judea Group
Soil: terra rossa, quality: 7

Cultivation: field crops by the site
Cisterns: none
Water source: 'Ein el-Majdal (no. 185), 2.6 km distant
Road: 'Ein Hafireh-Wadi Zamor (C50), 600 m distance
Visit: November 2014; 4 surveyors; 70 sherds

Site at the eastern edge of the valley, along which passes the unpaved road from Aqraba-Gittit, 100 m south of es-Sireh (2) and 300 m north of the fortress in es-Sireh (1).

Small, round sloping courtyard, 16 m diameter. Its wall is built from two to three rows of medium-sized and large stones. The eastern part of the wall is built from a row of very large upright stones, about 1×1 m in average.

A wadi channel 20 m south of the courtyard is dammed by several stone walls with a conducting wall along it. Possibly there was a linkage between the dams and the courtyard.

This courtyard belongs also to the type of crop storage courtyards in the region.

Pottery (body sherds): Late Roman – 50%; Medieval (Mamluk) – 50%.
Other surveys: none.

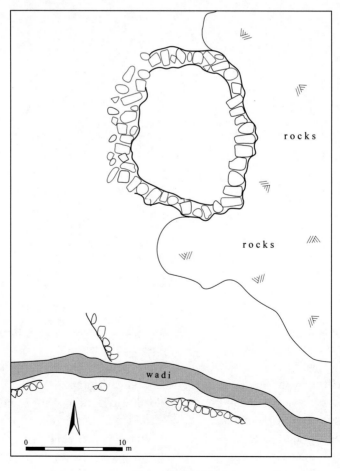

245. Plan of **es-Sireh (3)**.

Site 131: 18-16/58/6
ELEVATION POINT 419 (6)

Israel grid: 18575/16829
UTM grid: 7243/5550
Elevation: 410 m a.s.l., 70 m a.s.a.
Name: nearest place
Site type: courtyard, cave, winepress and cistern
Area: 2,000 sq. m (2 dunams)
Topography: flat summit
Rock type: Judea Group

Soil: terra rossa, quality: 8
Cultivation: none
Cisterns: 1
Water source: 'Ein el-Majdal (no. 185), 2.4 km distant
Road: Gittit Valley (C58), 600 m distance
Visit: March 2014; 4 surveyors; 250 sherds

Site on a summit in the ridge of E.P. 419, 2 km west-north-west of Gittit and 3.5 km south-east of Aqraba. The site is a good lookout to the valleys east of Aqraba and the valley in the ridge of E.P. 419.

Courtyard, 20×19 m, built of one row of large stones. The western wall did not survive. A wall, most of which did not survive, starts from the south corner, possibly in the past forming a small enclosure.

Rock-cut winepress, 6×3 m, attached to the western wall of the courtyard.

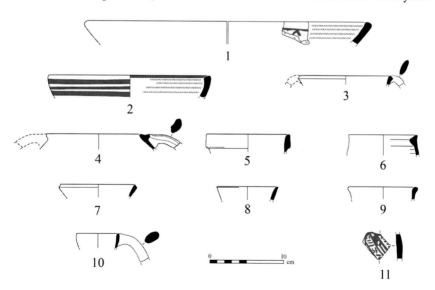

246. Pottery from E.P. 419 (6): 1. Bowl, lt brn, lt colour burnish, dk orn inside, Med; 2. Bowl, greyish, greyish burnish inside, dk red bands painted outside, Med; 3. CP, lt brn, Rom; 4. CP, lt brn, LR-Byz; 5. Jar, lt brn, Rom; 6. Jar (?), lt colour, LR-Byz; 7-8. Jugs, reddish, Rom; 9-10. Jugs, lt colour, Rom-Byz; 11. Body sherd, lt colour, dk colour orn over white, Med.

The location of the must pit is putative only.

Below and north of the courtyard are an operating cistern and a trough. Two drainage channels lead to the cistern.

About 20 m south-west of the courtyard is a large cave about 12 m diameter, with two openings.

The courtyard was probably the ancient hub of the site.

Pottery: Middle Bronze II (body sherds) – 8%; Early Roman – 12%; Late Roman – 40%; Byzantine – 20%; Medieval – 20%.
Stone: threshing sledge stones.
Other surveys: none.

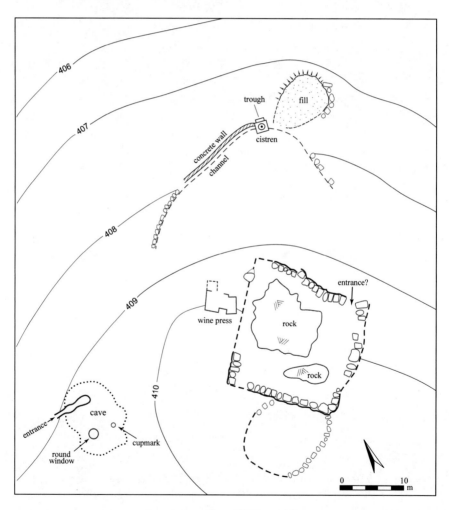

247. Plan of E.P. 419 (6).

LANDSCAPE UNIT 35

Site 132: 18-16/58/7

ELEVATION POINT 393 (1)

Israel grid: 18526/16817
UTM grid: 7238/5549
Elevation: 350 m a.s.l., 0 m a.s.a.
Name: nearest place
Site type: courtyard
Area: 200 sq. m (0.2 dunam)
Topography: valley edge
Rock type: Judea Group

Soil: terra rossa, quality: 8
Cultivation: field crops nearby
Cisterns: none
Water source: 'Ein el-Majdal (no. 185), 2.4 km distant
Road: 'Ein Hafireh (C50), 400 m distance
Visit: July 2015; 5 surveyors; 12 sherds

Small site at the edge of a valley on the northern slope of E.P. 393, 2.5 km west of Gittit and 2.6 km north-north-east of Majdal Bani Fadil.

Rectangular courtyard, 17×14 m, built of a double row wall of medium-sized stones, 1.1 m thick, preserved up to a height of three courses (0.5 m).

This is another LR site which belongs to the advanced agricultural array in the inner valleys west of Gittit.

Pottery (body sherds): Late Roman – 100%.
Other surveys: none.

Site 133: 18-16/58/8

ES-SIREH (1)

Israel grid: 18564/16811
UTM grid: 7242/5548
Elevation: 350 m a.s.l., 40 m b.s.a.
Name: ancient
Site type: fortress (?)
Area: 2,000 sq. m (2 dunams)
Topography: valley edge
Rock type: Judea Group
Soil: terra rossa, quality: 8

Cultivation: field crops nearby the site
Cisterns: none
Water source: 'Ein el-Majdal (no. 185), 2.3 km distant
Road: Gittit Valley (C58), 500 m distance
Visit: April 2014 and more; 3 surveyors; 80 sherds

Site east and next to the unpaved road Aqraba-Ma'ale Ephraim junction, between the ridges of E.P. 419 and E.P. 393, 3.3 km south-east of Aqraba and 2 km west-north-west of Gittit. There is a view of some of the valleys around the site and to the sheer ridge in the west.

Fortress with two parts:
- Eastern main part is trapezoidal: east side – 28 m, west side – 20 m, south side – 25 m, and north side – 22 m. The encircling wall is built of two rows of very large stones. The largest stones are 1.5-2 m long; they weigh half a ton and more. The walls are preserved up to a height of 3-4 courses (about 2 m).

  Along the north-western wall is a corridor, external width 4-5 m, and internal width 2-3 m. Large stone slabs roofed the corridor and fell in an earthquake: they can still be seen placed together.

  The possible entrance 1.5 m wide is in the southern wall.

  The quality of construction, sizes of the stones and their unique arrangement testify that this structure is a fortress defending the nearby road.

  The fortress interior is free of all construction.
- Western part, 15×9 m, annexed to the fortress. The surrounding wall is built of small and medium-sized irregularly-shaped stones, surviving up to a height of 80 cm, and has collapsed in many places.

  It is difficult to decide whether this annex is from the same period as the fortress, or a later addition, but according to the different quality of construction this part is not an original part of the fortress construction phase.

Guérin (1874: chapter 30), who travelled in the region on his way from Aqraba to the Jordan Valley, noted the road and the fortress, and proposed that its location is strategically intended for the protection of the road.

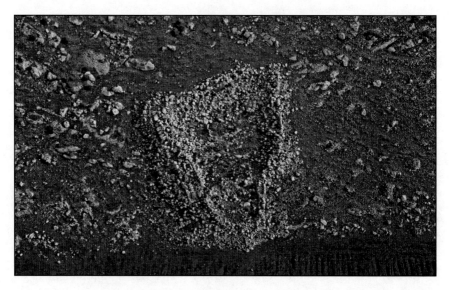

248. Aerial photo looking east at **es-Sireh (1)** (A. Solomon).

According to the pottery, it is apparent that the site functioned from the Late Roman period until the Byzantine period. It is reasonable to assume that the fortress was built on an Iron Age I site, but the ancient structures (if they indeed existed) did not survive. The site was in secondary use (although not as a fortress) during the Mamluk period.

Pottery: Iron I – 13%; Late Roman – 50%; Byzantine – 31%; Medieval (Mamluk) (body sherds) – 6%.
Other surveys: none.

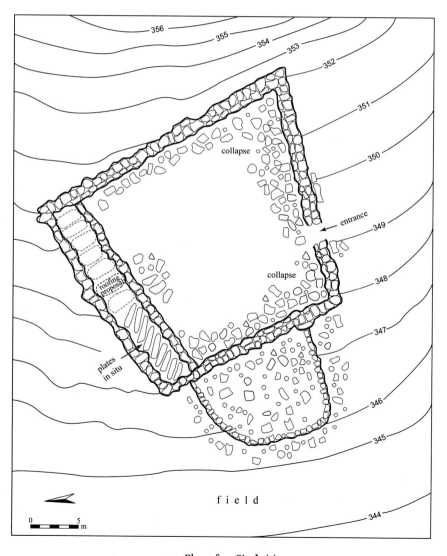

249. Plan of es-Sireh (1).

250. Pottery from **es-Sireh (1)**: 1. Bowl, reddish, IA I; 2. Jug (?), lt brn, black slip outside and over rim inside, LR-Byz.

◆ ◆ ◆

Site 134: 18-16/58/9

ELEVATION POINT 432 (1)

Israel grid: 18575/16883
UTM grid: 7243/5555
Elevation: 420 m a.s.l., 15 m a.s.a.
Name: nearest place
Site type: enclosures
Area: 1,000 sq. m (1 dunam)
Topography: slope in edge of valley
Rock type: Judea Group
Soil: terra rossa, quality: 8

Cultivation: field crops by the site
Cisterns: none
Water source: 'Ein Juheir (no. 189), 2.2 km distant
Road: Gittit Valley (C58), 600 m distance
Visit: March 2014; 4 surveyors; 60 sherds

Site on a slope descending east to the internal wadi of E.P. 432, 2.2 km northwest of Gittit and 3.4 km south-east of Aqraba.

Round enclosure, 24 m in diameter, built from a single row of very large stones. The original layout of the perimeter wall has been preserved mainly in the north and south; elsewhere there are breaches or construction with smaller stones. In one section, a massive wall survived to a height of three courses.

Much debris within the enclosure indicates the previous existence of a high wall of several courses.

Smaller round enclosure, 6 m diameter, is located 5 m east of the above enclosure. The interrelation between the enclosures is not clear.

Apparently the site was built during Middle Bronze Age II. The size of the stones, which do not fit later periods, indicate the ancient time. The original enclosure was damaged, and its stones collapsed inwards.

Pottery: Chalcolithic-Early Bronze (?) (1 body sherd) – 1.5%; Middle Bronze II – 33%; Iron I (body sherds) – 8%; Late Roman – 24%; Byzantine – 16%; Medieval (?) (1 body sherd) – 1.5%; unidentified – 16%.
Other surveys: none.

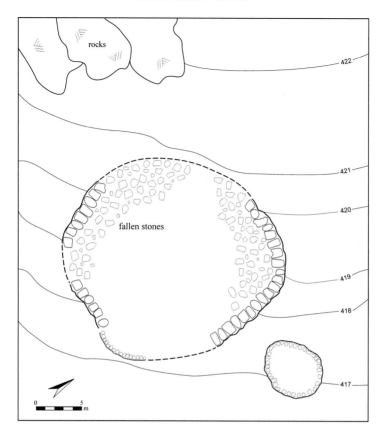

251. Plan of E.P. 432 (1).

252. Aerial photo, looking north-west at E.P. 432 (1) (A. Solomon).

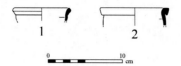

253. Pottery from E.P. 432 (1):
1-2. Bowls, lt brn, LR-Byz.

◆ ◆ ◆

Site 135: 18-16/68/1
ELEVATION POINT 419 (5)

Israel grid: 18615/16895
UTM grid: 7247/5557
Elevation: 410 m a.s.l., 0 m a.s.a.
Name: nearest place
Site type: courtyard
Area: 1,500 sq. m (1.5 dunams)
Topography: plateau
Rock type: Judea Group
Soil: terra rossa, quality: 8

Cultivation: field crops by the site
Cisterns: none
Water source: 'Ein Juheir (no. 189), 2.3 km distant
Road: Gittit Valley (C58), 200 m distance
Visit: April 2014; 4 surveyors; 40 sherds

Site on the eastern side of E.P. 419 plateau. From the site is a view of the Sartaba ridge and the vicinity of Kh. Juraish. Around the site are wide areas of cultivated land.

Large irregular courtyard: south 27 m, north 33 m, east 20 m and west 24 m, was found. The encircling wall is built mostly of one row of large stones. Several sections are built in two rows, and in many other sections the two rows of stones are laid with headers up to 1.5 m long.

In the eastern corner of the courtyard is a space 7×5 m. In the southern corner of the space is a cell built of large stones, the function of which is unknown. The entrance to the courtyard was probably in the north-western corner.

This site is one of many other MBA II sites in the region, which excel in fine construction.

Pottery: Middle Bronze II – 95%; Late Roman (body sherds) – 5%.
Other surveys: none.

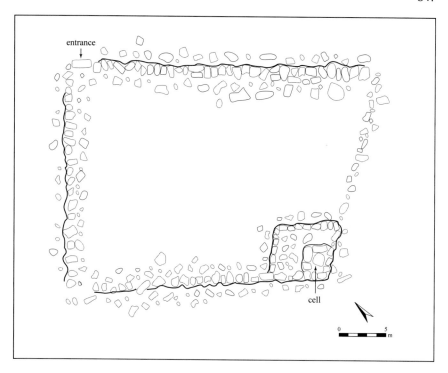

254. Plan of E.P. 419 (5).

255. Aerial photo, looking east at E.P. 419 (5) (A. Solomon).

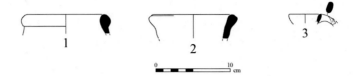

256. Pottery from E.P. 419 (5): 1. Jar, lt brn, MB II (?); 2. Jar (?), lt brn, MB II (?); 3. Jug, lt brn, MB II.

♦ ♦ ♦

Site 136: 18-16/68/2

ELEVATION POINT 419 (3)

Israel grid: 18639/16894
UTM grid: 7249/5557
Elevation: 395 m a.s.l., 0 m a.s.a.
Name: nearest place
Site type: farm, stronghold and road
Area: 5,000 sq. m (5 dunams)
Topography: valley edge
Rock type: Judea Group

Soil: terra rossa, quality: 8
Cultivation: field crops by the site
Cisterns: none
Water source: 'Ein Juheir (no. 189), 2.4 km distant
Road: Gittit Valley (C58), by the site
Visit: February 2014; 4 surveyors; 225 sherds

Site on a strip of land 250 m long by 50 m wide, 1 km north of Kh. Tawil (2), on the north-western edge of Gittit Valley, along a new unpaved road leading southwards to Ma'ale Ephraim junction.

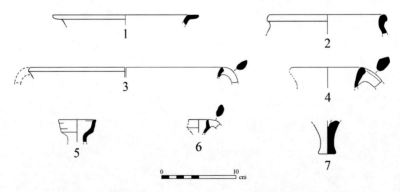

257. Pottery from E.P. 419 (3): 1. Bowl, red, Rom; 2. Bowl, dk brn, IA II; 3. CP, red, Rom; 4. Jug, dk brn, IA II; 5. Flask, lt brn, Rom; 6. Juglet, lt brn, Hell-ER; 7. Unguentarium base, lt brn, Hel-ER.

The components of the site are:
- Two courtyards, 10×10 m, on a 120 m long strip of land linked by terraces. (no. 1 in plan).
- Old road about 4 m wide, bordered on both sides with rows of medium-sized stones (no. 2). The road starts eastwards from the modern north-south unpaved road along the valley.

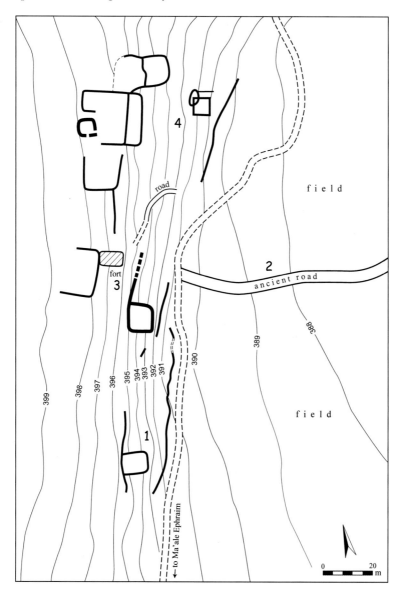

258. Plan of E.P. 419 (3).

- Structure built of large stones, 10×4 m, possibly a fort or tower. In the western side is a courtyard 15×10 m (no. 3).
- Complex of courtyards of various dimensions, connected to an array of terraces and to remains of a curving road (no. 4).

The site is probably built over the arable area of a farm.

Pottery: Iron II – 2%; Hellenistic-Early Roman – 13%; Late Roman – 67%; Medieval (body sherds) – 18%.
Flint: 5 items: 1 flake, 2 blades, and 2 retouched blades.
Other surveys: none.

Site 137: 18-16/68/3

ELEVATION POINT 432 (9)

Israel grid: 18619/16876
UTM grid: 7247/5555
Elevation: 408 m a.s.l., 0 m a.s.a.
Name: nearest place
Site type: fortress
Area: 1,000 sq. m (1 dunam)
Topography: moderate slope
Rock type: Judea Group

Soil: terra rossa, quality: 2
Cultivation: none
Cisterns: none
Water source: 'Ein Juheir (no. 189), 2.5 km distant
Road: Gittit Valley (C58), 100 m distance
Visit: June 2014; 4 surveyors; 70 sherds

Site at the centre of E.P. 432 on moderate slope descending eastwards to the valley of Kh. Tawil (2), 1.7 km north-west of Gittit.

Fortress, initially well-built of large partially worked stones, currently now mostly in ruins due to plundering of stones, was found. The north-western wing and two watchtowers survive. The whole of the eastern side is in ruins, and there are piles of plundered stones.

The north-western wall is 17 m long and 1 m thick.

The northern tower, 5×4 m, is massively built with walls 1.5 m thick. It appears to have been the principal element of fortification.

The smaller south-eastern tower, about 4×3 m, projecting from the southern wall of the fortress and connected to a central wall exposed by plundering.

It is likely that the fortress was built in the Late Roman period over remains of a small Middle Bronze Age site to guard the agricultural area. The site continued to function through the Byzantine and Medieval periods.

Pottery: Middle Bronze II (body sherds) – 8%; Late Roman – 74%; Byzantine – 12%; Medieval (body sherds) – 6%.
Other surveys: none.

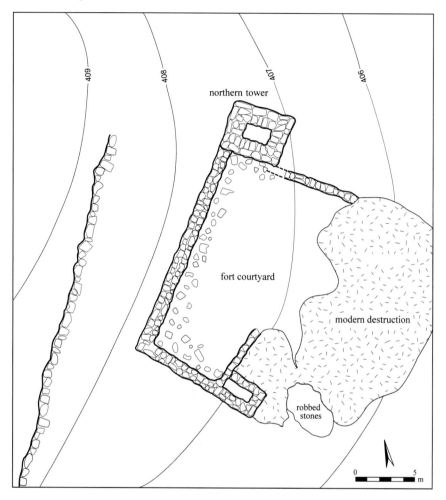

259. Plan of E.P. 432 (9).

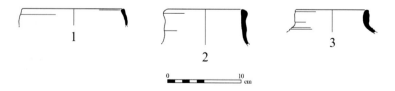

260. Pottery from E.P. 432 (9): 1. Bowl, reddish, LR-Byz; 2. Jar, lt colour, LR; 3. Jar, reddish, LR.

Site 138: 18-16/68/4
ELEVATION POINT 419 (1)

Israel grid: 1863/1684
UTM grid: 7249/5552
Elevation: 385 m a.s.l., 0 m a.s.a.
Name: nearest place
Site type: courtyard, structure and cistern
Area: 2,000 sq. m (2 dunams)
Topography: slope at edge of valley
Rock type: Judea Group

Soil: terra rossa, quality: 8
Cultivation: field crops by the site
Cisterns: 1
Water source: 'Ein Juheir (no. 189), 2.9 km distant
Road: Gittit Valley (C58), by the site
Visit: February 2014; 3 surveyors; 200 sherds

Site at edge of cultivated valley, 700 m north-north-west of Kh. Tawil (1) and 1.3 km north-west of Gittit.

Square courtyard, 15×15 m, built of a single row of very large stones. Near the

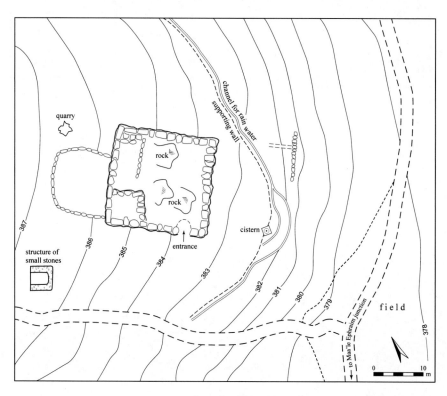

261. Plan of **E.P. 419 (1)**.

southern corner is an entrance. There is a room in the western corner, 5×4 m.

A horseshoe-shaped courtyard, 11 m in diameter, built of small stones, is attached to the west side of the large courtyard.

10 m west of the courtyards is a small ruined structure built of small stones.

South-east of the courtyard are drainage channels leading water to a cistern in current use.

The site is a Late Roman-Byzantine agricultural farm, one of many similar sites along the valley. It was probably built over an earlier Iron Age site.

Pottery: Iron II – 25%; Late Roman – 35%; Byzantine – 20%; Medieval – 20%.
Other surveys: none.

262. Aerial photo, looking north-west at **E.P. 419 (1)** (A. Solomon).

Site 139: 18-16/68/5
GITTIT (1)

Israel grid: 1869/1684
UTM grid: 7255/5552
Elevation: 344 m a.s.l., 0 m a.s.a.
Name: nearest place
Site type: courtyards, walls and cistern
Area: 1,000 sq. m (1 dunam)
Topography: plateau
Rock type: Judea Group
Soil: terra rossa, quality: 6
Cultivation: field crops by the site
Cisterns: 1
Water source: 'Ein Juheir (no. 189), 3 km distant
Road: Wadi Kamoneh-Gittit Valley (C54), 400 m distant
Visit: January 2014; 3 surveyors; 71 sherds

Site on a flat plateau near the modern industrial zone of Gittit, 1 km north-west of the settlement. From the site there is a view of the Sartaba ridge.

Two adjacent courtyards, built of medium-sized stones. The southern one is 15×12 m, and the northern one is 18×15 m. The courtyards enclose a surface level about 1 m higher than the surroundings. The walls are preserved to a height of 1 m.

In the west both courtyards abut a very thick wall, which was built in two phases. The wall's lower part, about 1 m above the level of the courtyards, is built of medium-sized stones, on top of which is a row of 10 boulders. The northernmost boulder is the largest, measuring 5×2 m. The construction of the wall raises queries: it is not clear in which phase the boulders were laid, and for what purpose. Judging by the patina the boulders are not ancient.

In the northern courtyard a drainage channel leads to a cistern with a metal cover.

30 m south-east of the site is another courtyard, and 30 m south of the site is another wall built of very large rocks (out of plan).

Pottery: Iron I (body sherds) – 2%; Late Roman – 70%; Byzantine – 20%; Medieval (body sherds) – 8%.
Other surveys: none.

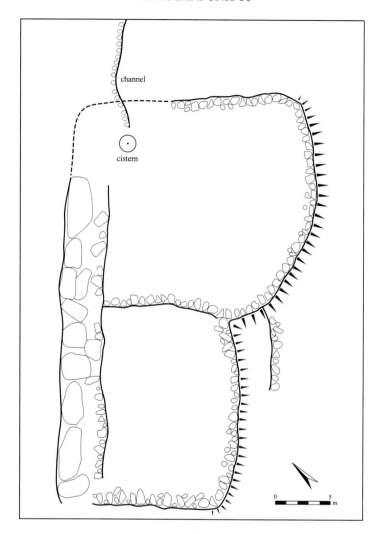

263. Plan of **Gittit (1)**.

264. Pottery from **Gittit (1)** (all LR-Byz): 1. Bowl, greyish; 2. Bowl, reddish; 3. Jar (?), greyish; 4. Jug, reddish.

Site 140: 18-16/68/6
GITTIT (2)

Israel grid: 1869/1684
UTM grid: 7255/5551
Elevation: 340 m a.s.l., 0 m a.s.a.
Name: nearest place
Site type: courtyard
Area: 1,000 sq. m (1 dunam)
Topography: plateau
Rock type: Judea Group
Soil: terra rossa, quality: 6

Cultivation: field crops by the site
Cisterns: none
Water source: 'Ein Juheir (no. 189), 3 km distant
Road: Wadi Kamoneh-Gittit Valley (C54), 400 m distant
Visit: January 2014; 4 surveyors; 12 sherds

Site on a partially cultivated plateau, 1 km north-west of Gittit and 700 m north-east of Kh. Tawil (1).

Irregular courtyard, 18×15 m. The encircling wall, 1.5 m high on the eastern side, is built of medium-sized stones. The interior of the courtyard is levelled, and is 1.5 m higher than the surroundings.

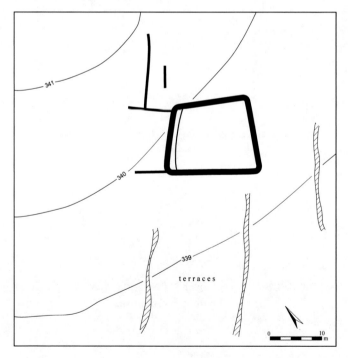

265. Plan of **Gittit (2)**.

In the west and north are remains of walls abutting the courtyard, perhaps parts of other structures.

South and west of the courtyard are terrace walls.

There are very few Roman and Medieval body sherds.

Apparently the courtyard was founded in the Roman period, and the site was reused during Medieval times.

The courtyard appears to have been used for storage of crops, like other similar courtyards in the Gittit Valley.

Pottery (body sherds): Late Roman – 50%; Medieval – 50%.
Other surveys: none.

♦ ♦ ♦

Site 141: 18-16/68/7

ELEVATION POINT 419 (2)

Israel grid: 18639/16862
UTM grid: 7249/5553
Elevation: 373 m a.s.l., 0 m a.s.a.
Name: nearest place
Site type: courtyard and structure
Area: 1,000 sq. m (1 dunam)
Topography: valley edge
Rock type: Judea Group

Soil: terra rossa, quality: 8
Cultivation: field crops by the site
Cisterns: none
Water source: 'Ein Juheir (no. 189), 2.7 km distant
Road: Gittit Valley (C58), by the site
Visit: February 2014; 4 surveyors; 200 sherds

Site on the western edge of Gittit Valley, 600 m north of Kh. Tawil (1). East of the site and close to it passes the unpaved road to the Ma'ale Ephraim junction.

Courtyard, 21×19 m, built of one row of large stones. The encircling wall has been preserved to a maximum height of three courses. There is a modern *Maq'ad* in the courtyard.

Structure, 11×6 m, of medium-sized stones, with walls 1 m high; partly paved with stones, attached to the east of the courtyard, possibly a room with an opening in the southern corner. The room appears to be later than the courtyard.

From the courtyard two walls go eastwards, hinting at the existence of another room or structure.

The courtyard is one of a number of Roman-Byzantine courtyards characteristic of the Gittit valley.

Pottery: Early Roman – 15%; Late Roman – 60%; Byzantine – 25%.
Flint: 6 items: 3 flakes, 2 blades and a retouched blade.
Other surveys: none.

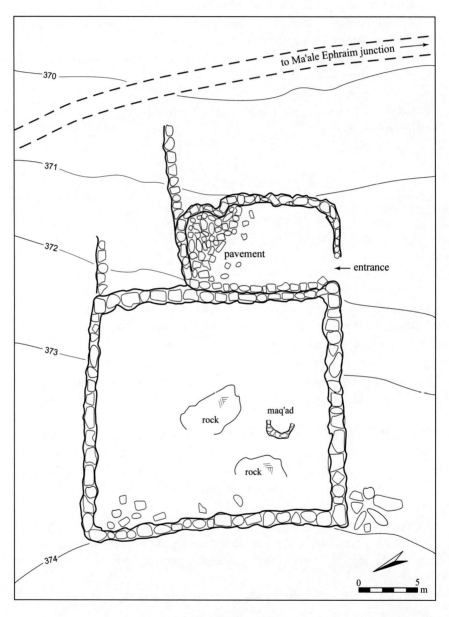

266. Plan of E.P. 419 (2).

LANDSCAPE UNIT 35

267. Aerial photo viewing west at **E.P. 419 (2)** (A. Solomon).

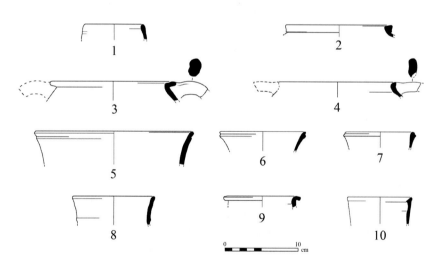

268. Pottery from **E.P. 419 (2)**: 1. Bowl (?), lt brn, LR-Byz; 2-4. CPs, lt brn, LR-Byz; 5. Jar (?), lt brn, LR-Byz; 6-8, 10. Jugs, lt brn, Rom; 9. Jug (?), lt brn, LR-Byz.

Site 142: 18-16/68/8
KHIRBET TAWIL (2)

Israel grid: 18624/16805 (site centre)
UTM grid: 7248/5548
Elevation: 370 m a.s.l., 40 m b.s.a.
Name: nearest place
Site type: strongholds, road and water system
Area: 7,000 sq. m (7 dunams)
Topography: valley edge
Rock type: Judea Group

Soil: terra rossa, quality: 8
Cultivation: field crops by the site
Cisterns: 1
Water source: 'Ein el-Majdal (no. 185), 2.5 km distant
Road: Gittit Valley (C58), at the site
Visit: April 2014; 3 surveyors; 105 sherds (north stronghold) and 400 sherds (south stronghold).

Site at the edge of a valley west of Gittit, north-west of Kh. Tawil (1) and close to it. West and above the site is the ridge of E.P. 419. From the site there is a good lookout to the Gittit area and the region of the Sartaba ridge. The linkage to Kh. Mras ed-Din, 500 m south of the site, is significant.

Three main components in this Iron Age II-III site:
- Two forts built 70 m apart alongside the edge of the field south to north. The northern fort is 10×10 m, and the southern one is 7×7 m. Both are built of large stones.

    Scanty remains of a courtyard are attached to the northern fort.

    A courtyard attached to the southern fort, 15×15 m, is built of two rows of stones. The stones of the outer row are well worked.

    Many sherds were collected in the vicinity of the forts, evidence of prolonged dwelling.
- Rock cut and built road (C58), 2 m wide, are beside the forts. The visible section of the road is at least 250 m long. The road is bounded by two rows of stones. The builders took into account the rocky topography. In two locations along the road are constructed steps.
- Sophisticated water system, apparently designed to provide water to the inhabitants and passers-by, that includes three components:
    1. Large cistern at the end of the water supply system; its opening nearly 1 m diameter. The capacity of the cistern exceeds by far the capacity of a domestic cistern. Next to the cistern there is a large basin.
    2. Rock-cut pool, 18×8 m and 2 m deep, attached to the cistern in the west. The pool was filled by several rock-cut channels.
    3. Up the slope are two passages cut in the rock 30 m from the pool and the northern fort. Both are 20 m long and 1 m wide, and the height of a man.

The rock cuts were made to conduct water to the pool and the northern fort. They possibly also served for passage from the vicinity of the forts to the summit. Two rock-cut channels descend from the end of the rock cut passages: one to fill the pool and the other to supply water to the fort.

Such a water system, which makes intelligent use of rock cuttings in order to collect and divert rainwater, is rare in the Iron Age. The reasons for building such an unusual water system for the region and the period should be investigated further.

About 200 m north of the northern fort are scanty remains of a courtyard (out of plan).

Pottery: Northern fort: Iron II-III – 72%; Late Roman (body sherds) – 14%; Byzantine (body sherds) – 14%. Southern fort: Iron I (body sherds) – 6%; Iron II-III – 75%; Late Roman – 19%.

Other surveys: Finkelstein et al. 1997: 801.

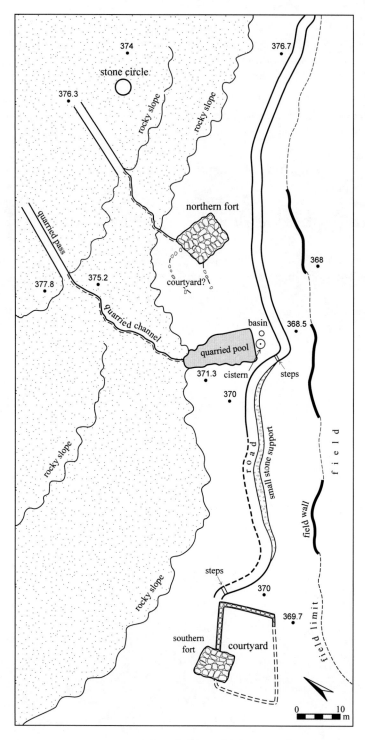

269. Plan of **Kh. Tawil** (2).

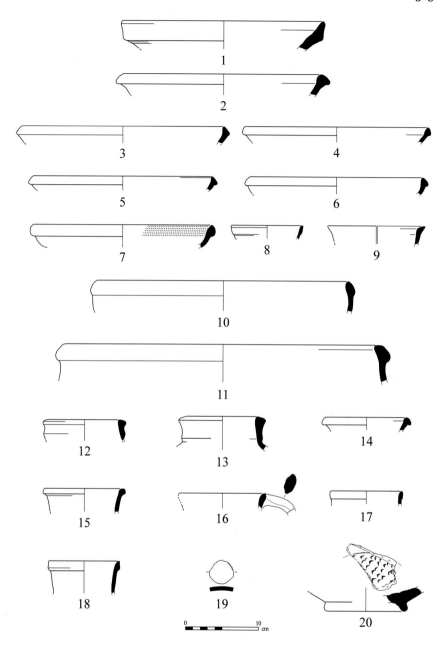

270. Pottery from **Kh. Tawil (2)**, Southern stronghold: 1. Bowl/Krater, lt brn, LR; 2-4, 10. Bowls, lt brn, IA II; 5. Bowl, dk brn, IA II; 6. Bowl, lt colour, IA II; 7. Bowl, lt brn, burnish remains inside, IA II; 8. Bowl (?), dk brn, LR; 9. Bowl, lt brn, IA II (?); 11. Krater, lt brn, IA II; 12. Jar, lt brn, IA II; 13. Jar, dk brn, IA II; 14. Jug, lt brn, IA II; 15, 18. Jugs, lt brn, LR; 16. Jug (?), lt brn, LR; 17. Jug (?), lt colour, LR; 19. Lid, lt brn, LR; 20. Bowl base, lt brn, cuneate dec, IA III.

271. Pottery from **Kh. Tawil (2)**, Northern stronghold: 1. Bowl, lt brn, red burnish inside and on rim outside, IA II; 2. Jug, lt brn, IA II.

◆ ◆ ◆

Site 143: 18-16/78/1

ELEVATION POINT 338

Israel grid: 18782/16899
UTM grid: 7263/5557
Elevation: 305 m a.s.l., 180 m a.s.a.
Name: nearest place
Site type: structures and sherd scatter
Area: 500 sq. m (0.5 dunam)
Topography: slope
Rock type: hard karstic chalk
Soil: terra rossa, quality: 6

Cultivation: none
Cisterns: none
Water source: 'Ein Abu Daraj (no. 177), 3.2 km distant
Road: Wadi Kamoneh-Gittit Valley (C54), 600 m distant
Visit: January 2014; 3 surveyors; 50 sherds

Site on a slope in the northern part of a saddle between E.P. 338 and E.P. 335, 1.4 km north of Gittit. From the site is a lookout northwards to Wadi Zamor and Sahl Afjam Valley.

There is a sherd scatter and scanty wall remains - not enough to produce a plan.

Pottery: Late Roman – 80%; Byzantine – 20%.
Other surveys: none.

Site 144: 18-16/78/2
SIRT ET-TURMUS (1)

Israel grid: 18706/16886 (site centre)
UTM grid: 7256/5556
Elevation: 310 m a.s.l., 30 m a.s.a.
Name: nearest place
Site type: large village
Area: 10 ha (100 dunams)
Topography: spur and valley edge
Rock type: Judea Group
Soil: terra rossa, quality: 7
Cultivation: none
Cisterns: none
Water source: 'Ein Juheir (no. 189), 3 km distant
Road: Gittit Valley (C58), 600 m distant
Visit: March 1999 and more; 7 surveyors; 150 sherds

Large site on a moderate slope sloping eastwards to a broad field north of Wadi Ahmar, 1.3 km north of Gittit.

Numerous complexes and structures, scattered over an area of about 400×300 m along the spur. It seems that in the past, areas which are currently vacant were settled. The construction is very good – an impressive laying of very large, slightly worked stones on top of thick retaining walls on the slope. An average stone is 80×40×30 cm. The walls, 80 cm to 2 m thick, are built of one or two rows of stones.

There are two principal complexes and other structures:

- Eastern complex situated in the lower part of the spur (no. 1 in plan); 40×40 m in area, consisting of a large courtyard with rooms around it. The construction is of very large stones. Some of the original openings and lintels survive. North and west around the courtyard are more rooms.

    Tower-like structure projecting westwards from the complex.

    In the eastern infrastructure of the building is a very thick wall, apparently a retaining wall or terrace. At a later stage, possibly Medieval, small stones added to the building raised the infrastructure and around the courtyard. This was apparently the principal complex.

- The western, 110×80 m, complex is situated on the upper part of the slope (no. 2 in plan). The complex has a podium based on thick support walls built of two or three rows of large stones. On the podium is an array of interconnected courtyards and rooms of various types.

    The walls, particularly those in complex no. 2, survive to a height of up to 4 courses (3 m).

    Both main complexes probably served as public buildings.

- Many different structures are scattered over the slope, mostly single rooms built of very large stones. These rooms are rather small, 3×3 m, although larger ones and courtyards were also found.

Sirt et-Turmus (1) is a well preserved Middle Bronze Age II rural site. Some planning is evident in the layout of complexes of rooms and courtyards founded on thick retaining walls in the slope. The obvious resemblance to other MB II settlements in the vicinities of Gittit-Mekhora in the Samaria fringes is surprising, and attests to the advanced rural settlement array in the region.

Pottery: Middle Bronze II – 68%; Late Bronze (?) – 2%; Iron I-II – 10%; Late Roman – 15%; Medieval – 5%.
Flint: 28 items: 1 blade core, 13 flakes, 9 blades, 1 burin, 2 retouched blades, and 2 scrapers. Although the find is not sufficiently indicative, it is reasonable to assume that it is mostly from the MB II.
Other surveys: Finkelstein et al. 1997: 802.

272. Aerial view west at **Sirt et-Turmus (1)** (A. Solomon).

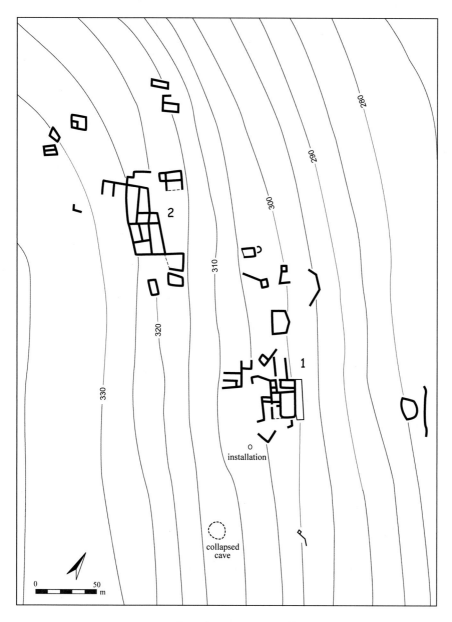

273. Plan of **Sirt et-Turmus (1)**.

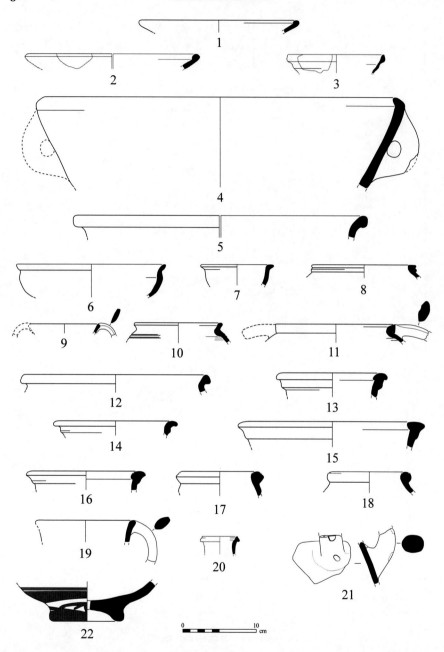

274. Pottery from **Sirt et-Turmus (1)**: 1-2. Bowls, lt brn, MB II; 3, 7-8. Bowls, lt brb, LR; 4. Krater, lt brn, Med; 5. Krater, lt brn, MB II; 6. Bowl, lt brn, LBA (?); 9. CP, reddish, LR; 10. CP/cooking jug, dk brn, LR; 11. CP, dk brn, LR; 12. CP, lt brn, LBA/IA I; 13-16. Jars, lt brn, MB II; 17. Jar, dk brn, IA I-II; 18. Jar, lt brn, IA I-II; 19. Jug, lt brn, IA I-II; 20. Juglet, lt brn, LR; 21. Jar handle, lt brn, two defaced seal impressions, MB II/LBA; 22. Base, lt brn, blk orn over white, Med.

Site 145: 18-16/78/3
SIRT ET-TURMUS (2)

Israel grid: 18730/16864
UTM grid: 7258/5554
Elevation: 307 m a.s.l., 10 m a.s.a.
Name: nearest place
Site type: courtyard and cave
Area: 2,000 sq. m (2 dunams)
Topography: valley edge
Rock type: Judea Group
Soil: terra rossa, quality: 8

Cultivation: field crops by the site
Cisterns: none
Water source: 'Ein Juheir (no. 189), 3.2 km distant
Road: Wadi Kamoneh-Gittit Valley (C54), 400 m distant
Visit: January 2014; 4 surveyors; 70 sherds

Site at the western edge of a fertile cultivated valley, 400 m south of Sirt et-Turmus (1) and 1 km north of Gittit.

The site consists of two main parts:
1. Cave, 10 m in diameter. The cave collapsed down the slope, and now only a rock shelter remains. In front of the cave down the slope is a large courtyard or levelled elevated earth surface, 45×10 m. The surface is encircled by a retaining wall, part of which is thick and built of small stones, and the rest is built of one row of large stones.
2. At the bottom of the site is another courtyard, 10×8 m, built of one row of stones.

Presumably the site was agricultural, in use from the Late Roman period and onwards.

Pottery: Late Roman – 57%; Byzantine (body sherds) – 21%; Medieval (body sherds) – 14%; Modern (body sherds) – 8%.
Stone: a basalt threshing sledge stone.
Other surveys: none.

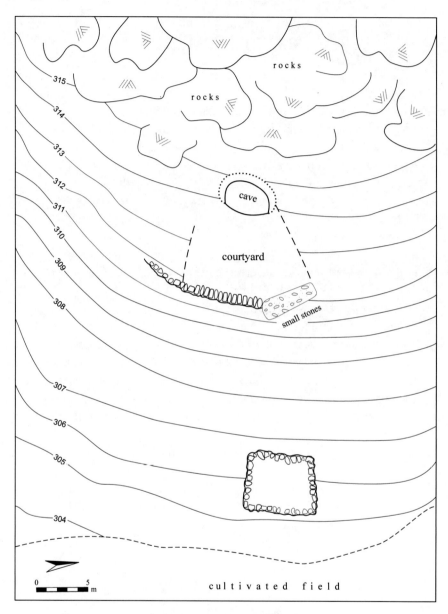

275. Plan of **Sirt et-Turmus (2)**.

LANDSCAPE UNIT 35

Site 146: 18-16/78/4
ELEVATION POINT 335

Israel grid: 18767/16869
UTM grid: 7262/5554
Elevation: 299 m a.s.l., 0 m a.s.a.
Name: nearest place
Site type: enclosure
Area: 1,000 sq. m (1 dunam)
Topography: valley edge
Rock type: Judea Group
Soil: terra rossa, quality: 8

Cultivation: field crops by the site
Cisterns: none
Water source: 'Ein Juheir (no. 189), 3.4 km distant
Road: Wadi Kamoneh-Gittit Valley (C54), 500 m distant
Visit: January 2014; 4 surveyors; 60 sherds

Site on the eastern edge of a fertile valley, 1.2 km north of Gittit.

A single round enclosure, 15 m diameter. The surrounding wall is built of one row of large stones. The wall is strengthened by a ramp elevating the level by nearly 1 m above the surroundings.

The site was possibly built in more than a single construction phase.

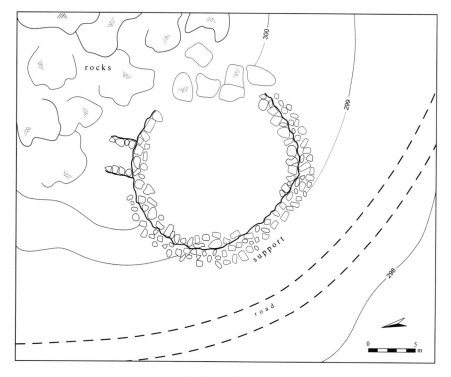

276. Plan of E.P. 335.

The enclosure is one of many Roman-Byzantine agricultural sites characteristic of the Gittit valley and its vicinity.

Pottery: Late Roman – 91%; Byzantine (body sherds) – 9%.
Stone: a threshing sledge stone.
Other surveys: none.

277. Pottery from E.P. 335: 1. CP (?), reddish, LR; 2. Jug, reddish, LR.

◆ ◆ ◆

Site 147: 18-16/78/5
SIRT ET-TURMUS (3)

Israel grid: 18741/16849
UTM grid: 7260/5552
Elevation: 290 m a.s.l., 10 m a.s.a.
Name: nearest place
Site type: sherd scatter
Area: 4,000 sq. m (4 dunams)
Topography: valley edge
Rock type: Judea Group
Soil: terra rossa, quality: 9

Cultivation: cereals
Cisterns: none
Water source: 'Ein Juheir (no. 189), 3 km distant
Road: Wadi Kamoneh-Gittit Valley (C54), by the site
Visit: January 2014; 3 surveyors; 75 sherds

Site on a slope of a hill on the western edge of a fertile valley, 500 m north of Gittit.

The site contains a moderate number of sherds, perhaps related to the terraces spread along the slope. The sherds were collected from the denser concentrations.

Pottery: Late Roman-Byzantine – 100%.
Other surveys: none.

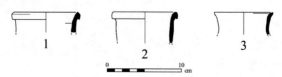

278. Pottery from **Sirt et-Turmus (3)** (all LR-Byz):
1-2. Jars, lt brn; 3. Jug, lt brn.

Site 148: 18-16/88/1
WADI ZAMOR (1)

Israel grid: 18891/16888
UTM grid: 7274/5556
Elevation: 92 m a.s.l., 150 m b.s.a.
Name: nearest place
Site type: farm, threshing floor and caves
Area: 2,000 sq. m (2 dunams)
Topography: valley edge
Rock type: Judea Group

Soil: terra rossa, quality: 8
Cultivation: field crops by the site
Cisterns: none
Water source: 'Ein Abu Daraj (no. 177), 2.3 km distant
Road: Wadi Kamoneh-Gittit Valley (C54), 500 m distant
Visit: January 2014; 4 surveyors; 30 sherds

Site on the western edge of Sahl Afjam Valley, 300 m west of Alon road and 2 km north-east of Gittit.

There are two main parts to the site:
- Farm, 19×10 m, with a rectangular courtyard, built on a slope. The support wall is built of one row of large stones. In the north-western corner is a small room built on the surface. In the courtyard is a large dwelling cave with a rock-cut arched opening. The maximum length of the cave is 9 m; inside are three rock-cut rooms and constructions.
- Round threshing floor, 14 m diameter, is about 40 m north of the farm. The encircling wall retains earth filling, 1 m deep, used for farm activities.

    Roughly-built terrace which retains a levelled soil filling, west and above the threshing floor.

Cave with two natural openings, with a wall inside (not in plan), about 50 m south of the courtyard. Below and parallel passes an unpaved road which is in now use.

There are very few sherds.

Pottery (body sherds): Late Roman – 50%; Byzantine – 33%; Medieval – 17%.
Other surveys: none.

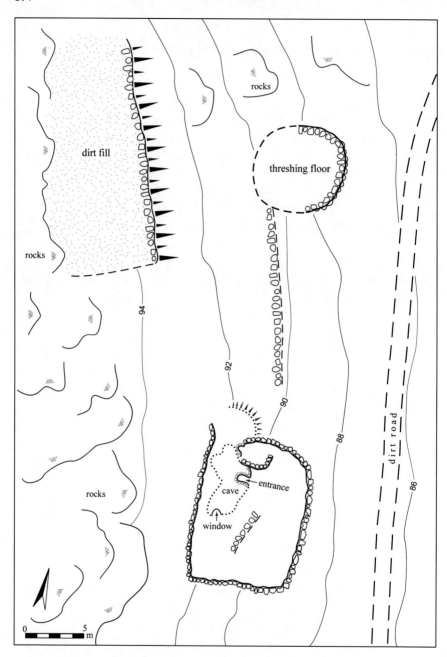

279. Plan of **Wadi Zamor (1)**.

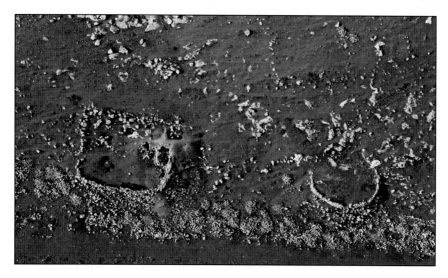

280. Aerial photo, viewing west at **Wadi Zamor (1)** (A. Solomon).

Site 149: 18-16/88/2
WADI KAMONEH (2)

Israel grid: 18889/16848
UTM grid: 7274/5552
Elevation: 110 m a.s.l., 5 m a.s.a.
Name: nearest place
Site type: courtyards, caves and a flint scatter
Area: 4,000 sq. m (4 dunams)
Topography: valley edge
Rock type: Judea Group

Soil: terra rossa, quality: 3
Cultivation: none
Cisterns: none
Water source: 'Ein Hafireh (no. 174), 2.4 km distant
Road: Wadi Kamoneh-Gittit Valley (C54), 300 m distant
Visit: November 1994; 2014; 5 surveyors; 60 sherds

Site on a slope descending from the north to the valley of Wadi Kamoneh close to the exit of Wadi Kamoneh into an inner fertile valley, 1.6 km north-east of Gittit.

Built complex between two long upper and lower support walls. The walls are built east-west along the slope 40 m apart.

The complex consists of three main parts:
- Large courtyard, 24×24 m, adjacent to the upper support wall (no. 1 in plan). The surrounding wall is 80 cm thick, built of one row of medium-sized stones. Two openings are close to the north-eastern and north-western

corners. Inside the courtyard are remains of an internal division and a cave.
- About 30 m west of courtyard no. 1 western wall, a frame wall goes down from north to south. Attached to it is a small courtyard, 15×15 m (no. 2). The small courtyard is joined by walls to the large one. Between the two courtyards is another cave.
- Well-built structure abutting the western part of the upper support wall (no. 3). The walls of the structure are about 1 m thick. The structure has two rooms, with openings facing south. A lintel and a small window survive in one of the rooms.

East of the complex is a small courtyard and remains of walls (no. 4).

The site was built in the Late Roman period, and continued in use until the last century, with several interruptions. The chronological construction order in relation to the courtyards and the structure is not clear.

Many flint items were collected, some dated to the Pre-Pottery Neolithic B period.

Pottery: Iron II – 3%; Late Roman – 50%; Byzantine – 20%; Medieval (body sherds) – 12%; Ottoman – 12%; Modern – 3%.
Flint: 78 items: 1 flake core, 3 blade cores, 3 bladelet cores, 1 naviform core, 1 naviform core waste, 50 flakes, 5 blades, 4 bladelets, 3 retouched flakes, 2 retouched bladelets, 4 scrapers and a burin. At least part of the assemblage belongs to the Pre-Pottery Neolithic B.
Other surveys: none.

281. Aerial photo view north at **Wadi Kamoneh (2)** (A. Solomon).

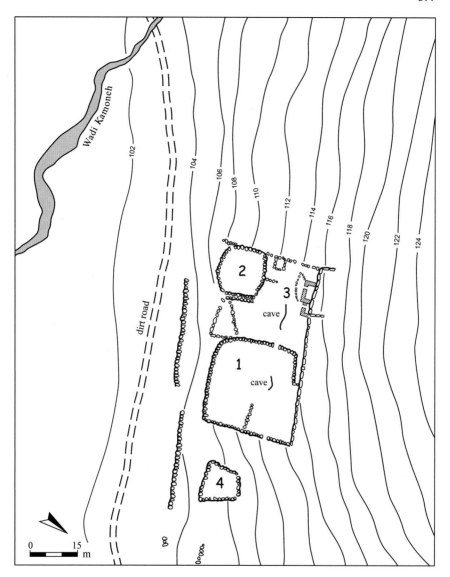

282. Plan of **Wadi Kamoneh (2)**.

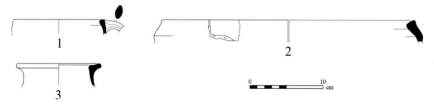

283. Pottery from **Wadi Kamoneh (2)**: 1. Jug, org, LR-Byz; 2. Bowl, lt brn, IA II; 3. Jar, blk, Ott/Mod.

Site 150: 18-16/98/1
WADI KAMONEH (5)

Israel grid: 18909/16873
UTM grid: 7276/5555
Elevation: 85 m a.s.l., 5 m a.s.a.
Name: nearest place
Site type: courtyard, and prehistoric
Area: 200 sq. m (0.2 dunam)
Topography: valley edge
Rock type: Judea Group
Soil: terra rossa, quality: 8

Cultivation: field crops by the site
Cisterns: none
Water source: 'Ein Abu Daraj (no. 177), 2.2 km distant
Road: Wadi Kamoneh-Gittit Valley (C54), 500 m distant
Visit: January 2014; 3 surveyors; 50 sherds

Site on the western edge of Sahl Afjam, above a cultivated field at the bottom of the slope of E.P. 338, 2 km north-east of Gittit centre.

Elliptical courtyard, 20×10 m, built of medium-sized stones.

Flint artefacts are scattered over the slope above the courtyard, probably dated to the Epipalaeolithic period.

Pottery (body sherds): Late Roman-Byzantine – 100%.
Flint: 141 items: 2 bladelet cores, 3 core waste, 80 flakes, 27 blades, 19 bladelets, 1 microlith burin, 1 burin, 4 scrapers and 3 retouched blades. Despite the low number of indicative items, the bladelets and the microlith burin point to a possible Upper Palaeolithic date, and with higher probability to the Epipalaeolithic period.
Other surveys: none.

Site 151: 18-16/98/2
WADI KAMONEH (3)

Israel grid: 18908/16859 (site centre)
UTM grid: 7276/5554
Elevation: 100 m a.s.l., 20 m a.s.a.
Name: nearest place
Site type: structures and threshing floors
Area: 2 ha (20 dunams)
Topography: slope and valley edge
Rock type: Dolomite chalk

Soil: terra rossa, quality: 8
Cultivation: fields by the site
Cisterns: none
Water source: 'Ein Abu Daraj (no. 177), 2.2 km distant
Road: Wadi Kamoneh-Gittit Valley (C54), 300 m distant
Visit: December 1994; 2005 and more; 4 surveyors; 76 sherds

Broad site at the edge of a spur descending to Kamoneh Wadi from the west, 500 m south-west of the Alon road.

Complex of five structures and numerous threshing floors, apparently from at least two phases of activity.

- Square structure, 8×5 m, built of large stones, some of which are worked (no. 1 in plan). The structure is divided into two cells. A few Roman sherds were collected.

  Round threshing floor, 14 m diameter, built of medium-sized stones, to west close to the structure. Mainly the eastern part has been preserved.

- Structure, 6×5 m, built of large fieldstones, 40 m south of structure no. 1 (no. 2). The eastern wall has been preserved 2-3 courses high. The structure is divided to two cells.

  Semicircular threshing floor, 12 m diameter, nearby the structure and facing the exposed rock surface. The threshing floor is apparently later than the structure.

- Rectangular structure, 8×5 m, divided in two cells, 20 m east of structure no. 2. The walls have been preserved nearly 1.8 m high (no. 3). The structure seems late in date, but is probably founded on ancient foundations of larger stones.

- Semicircular threshing floor, 12 m diameter, built of medium-sized stones, north-west of structure no. 3, facing exposed rock surface (no. 4).

- Structure divided into two cells (no. 5), east of the structures and threshing floors (nos 1-4). The eastern cell is 5×4 m and the western one is 4×3 m. The walls survived up to nearly 2 m high.

  Two later threshing floors north of the structure and a little west of it.

- Remains of structure, 5×4 m, built of large stones (no. 6), north of the main concentration of structures at the site, across the spur. Abutting it to the

west are two small cells, and a larger one in the east.
The entire site was an advanced multi-period agricultural system, which took advantage of the fertile fields in the valleys of Sahl Afjam and Wadi Kamoneh.

Pottery: Middle Bronze II (body sherds) – 2%; Iron II-III – 10%; Hellenistic – 10%; Early Roman – 12%; Late Roman – 33%; Byzantine – 12%; Medieval – 6%; Ottoman – 10%.
Flint: 36 items: 1 flake core, 1 bladelet core, 2 ridged blades, 14 flakes, 8 blades, 3 bladelets, 3 retouched blades, 1 scraper and a borer.
Stone: two basalt items and a whetstone.
Other surveys: none.

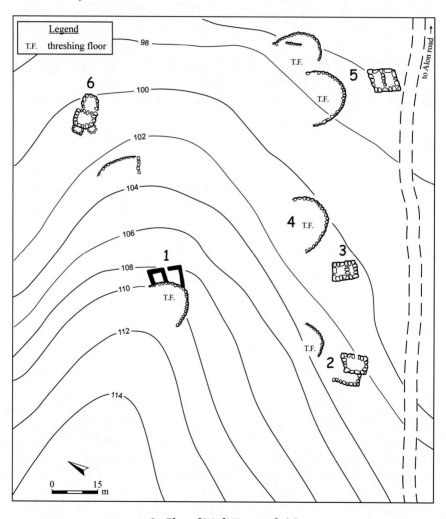

284. Plan of **Wadi Kamoneh (3)**.

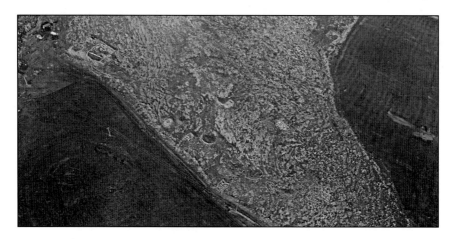

285. Aerial photo, looking west at **Wadi Kamoneh (3)** (A. Solomon).

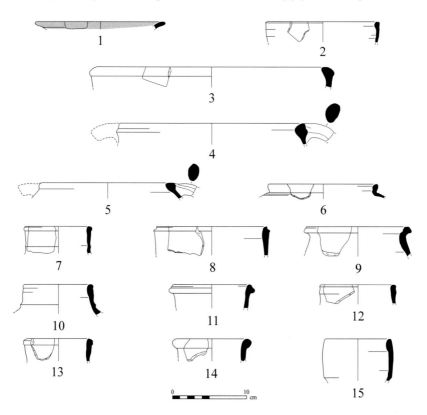

286. Pottery from **Wadi Kamoneh (3)**: 1. Bowl, org, red slip in and out, LR-Byz; 2. Bowl, lt brn, LR-Byz; 3. Bowl, lt brn IA II-III; 4. CP, dk brn, IA II; 5. CP, lt brn, Byz; 6. Bowl, lt brn, LR-Byz; 7. Jar, lt brn, LR; 8. Jar, lt brn, Ott (?); 9. Jar, gr, Med (?); 10. Jar, gr, LR; 11. Jug, lt brn, IA II (?); 12. Jug, dk brn, LR-Byz; 13. Jug, lt brn, LR-Byz; 14. Jug, lt brn, IA II (?); 15. Jug, red, Mod.

Site 152: 18-16/98/3
WADI KAMONEH (4)

Israel grid: 18961/16862
UTM grid: 7281/5554
Elevation: 85 m a.s.l., 10 m a.s.a.
Name: nearest place
Site type: enclosures and installations
Area: 2,000 sq. m (2 dunams)
Topography: hillock
Rock type: Judea Group
Soil: Mediterranean brown, quality: 3

Cultivation: none
Cisterns: none
Water source: 'Ein Hafireh (no. 174), 1.6 km distant
Road: 'Ein Hafireh-Wadi Zamor (C50), by the site
Visit: November 2005; 5 surveyors; 56 sherds

Site located 2.2 km north-east of Gittit, on a low flat hillock at the edge of the Kamoneh valley, between the Alon road in the north and an old asphalt road in the south. During the construction of the Alon road an artificial tall cliff was formed in the east-northern part of the site.

Remains of two enclosures, built of large stones.

Partially preserved wall of large stones at the edge of the slope descending to the south-west is the southern boundary of the site.

A partially preserved curved enclosure wall built of large stones projects from the western section of the wall. The diameter of this enclosure is 25 m.

At the centre of the site is another round enclosure, 13 m diameter.

Two rock-cut basins west of the site.

287. Aerial view west at **Wadi Kamoneh (4)** (A. Solomon).

The site is one of many Roman-Byzantine agricultural sites characteristic of the Gittit valley and its vicinity.

Pottery: Middle Bronze II (body sherds) – 4%; Iron II (body sherds) – 8%; Late Roman – 78%; Byzantine – 10%.
Other surveys: none.

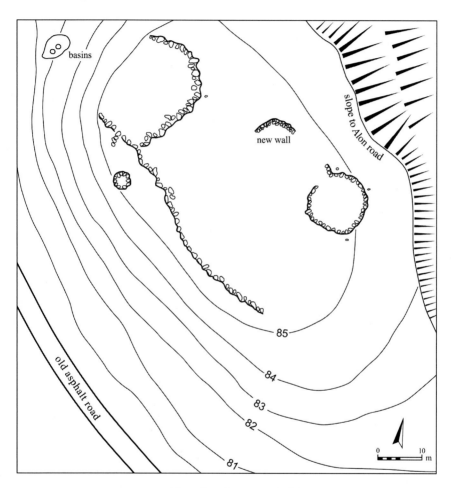

288. Plan of **Wadi Kamoneh (4)**.

289. A sherd from **Wadi Kamoneh (4)**: jar, gr, LR-Byz.

Site 153: 18-16/98/4
WADI KAMONEH (9)

Israel grid: 18980/16834
UTM grid: 7284/5552
Elevation: 90 m a.s.l., 20 m a.s.a.
Name: nearest place
Site type: rock-cuttings, sherd and flint scatters
Area: 200 sq. m (0.2 dunam)
Topography: moderate slope
Rock type: Judea Group

Soil: terra rossa, quality: 7
Cultivation: none
Cisterns: none
Water source: 'Ein Hafireh (no. 174), 1.5 km distant
Road: Wadi Kamoneh-Gittit Valley (C54), by the site
Visit: January 2014; 2 surveyors; 61 sherds

Small site at the eastern edge of Kamoneh Valley, 2.5 km east-north-east of Gittit.

Three rock-cuttings; one about 60 cm diameter and the other two about 40 cm: all are about 20 cm deep.

Scatters of sherds and flint items around the cuttings.

Pottery: Iron II – 10%; Late Roman-Byzantine – 44%; Medieval – 16%; Modern – 20%; Unidentified – 10%.
Flint: 18 items: 10 flakes, 6 blades, 1 scraper and a retouched blade.
Stone: three threshing sledge stones.
Other surveys: none.

290. Pottery from **Wadi Kamoneh (9)**: 1. Bowl, dk brn, IA II; 2. Jug, reddish, Med (?).

Site 154: 18-16/98/5
WADI KAMONEH (8)

Israel grid: 18928/16814
UTM grid: 7278/5549
Elevation: 110 m a.s.l., 20 m a.s.a.
Name: nearest place
Site type: cistern and sherd scatter
Area: 400 sq. m (0.4 dunam)
Topography: slope
Rock type: Judea Group
Soil: terra rossa, quality: 9

Cultivation: none
Cisterns: 1
Water source: 'Ein Hafireh (no. 174), 2 km distant
Road: Wadi Kamoneh-Gittit Valley (C54), by the site
Visit: January 2014; 4 surveyors; 126 sherds

Site on the southern edge of Wadi Kamoneh valley, on the northern slope of E.P. 162, 1.8 km east-north-east of Gittit.

Quarried bell-shaped cistern at least 5 m deep, with an opening 1 m in diameter on the slope of the spur, fed from the east by a rock-cut channel. Next to it is a rock-cut trough.

Late Roman-Byzantine period sherd scatter, on the slope below the cistern.

Pottery: Roman-Byzantine – 100%.
Other surveys: none.

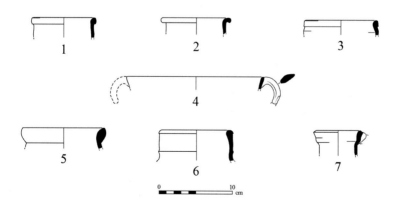

291. Pottery from **Wadi Kamoneh (8)** (all Rom-Byz): 1, 3. Bowls, lt brn; 2. Bowl (?), lt brn; 4. CP. Reddish; 5. Jar, lt brn; 6. Jar, dk brn; 7. Jug, lt brn.

Site 155: 18-16/98/6
WADI KAMONEH (1)

Israel grid: 18938/16803
UTM grid: 7279/5548
Elevation: 160 m a.s.l., 50 m a.s.a.
Name: nearest place
Site type: farm house and courtyards
Area: 1,000 sq. m (1 dunam)
Topography: hillock
Rock type: Judea Group
Soil: terra rossa, quality: 5

Cultivation: none
Cisterns: none
Water source: 'Ein Hafireh (no. 174), 1.9 km distant
Road: Wadi Kamoneh-Gittit Valley (C54), 300 m distant
Visit: January 2014; 7 surveyors; 100 sherds

Site on the upper part of the eastern slope of E.P. 162, 2 km east of Gittit. From the site is a lookout east and north to Sahl Afjam and to the Alon road.

Complex of a well-preserved farmhouse and three courtyards.

Structure, 6×3.5 m, with walls 1.3 m thick, built shoddily of small stones. The structure has two openings, in the south and east, leading into two courtyards.

Courtyard, 10×8 m, built of a mixture of large and small stones (no. 1 in plan), abutting south side of structure.

Larger irregular courtyard, about 15×12 m, adjacent to both the structure and courtyard no. 1 (no. 2). The encircling wall is built alternately of small and medium-sized stones. In the north part of the courtyard is a rock-cut cupmark.

Another courtyard, 16×9 m does not join the structure, but abuts courtyard no. 2 (no. 3).

Apparently the farm is Medieval, possibly on Roman structure foundations.

Pottery; Late Roman – 15%; Medieval – 85%.
Flint: 6 items: 2 flakes and 4 blades.
Metal: a long nail, a needle for repair of nets (?), and two Roman sandal nails.
Other surveys: none.

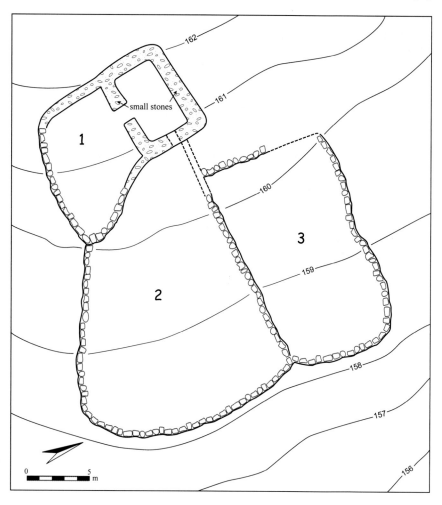

292. Plan of **Wadi Kamoneh (1)**.

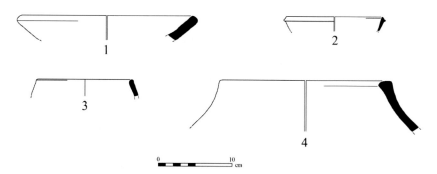

293. Pottery from **Wadi Kamoneh (1)**: 1. Bowl, lt brn, Med; 2. Bowl, reddish, LR; 3. Bowl, lt brn, LR; 4. Jar/pithos, lt brn, Med.

294. Aerial photo looking east at **Wadi Kamoneh (1)** (A. Solomon).

◆ ◆ ◆

Site 156: 18-16/88/7

WADI KAMONEH (7)

Israel grid: 18882/16809
UTM grid: 7274/5549
Elevation: 130 m a.s.l., 150 m b.s.a.
Name: nearest place
Site type: strongholds, road and cistern
Area: 3,000 sq. m (3 dunams)
Topography: slope
Rock type: Judea Group

Soil: terra rossa, quality: 5
Cultivation: none
Cisterns: none
Water source: 'Ein Hafireh (no. 174), 2.4 km distant
Road: Wadi Kamoneh-Gittit Valley (C54), 300 m distant
Visit: January 2014; 3 surveyors; 40 sherds

Site on a slope overlooking the valley of Wadi Kamoneh from the west, which is part of Sahl Afjam, 500 m north-west of E.P. 162 and 1.5 km north-east of Gittit.

Two forts, similar in construction, but not in dimensions.

The upper and larger, 8×4 m, fort is built of very large stones. The eastern wall survives up to three courses high. A constructed road leads south sets out from the fort (no. 1 in plan).

The lower fort, 4×4 m, is 12 m below the upper one and 30 m away, and is also built of large stones (no. 2).

The slope is meticulously terraced, but is not now cultivated.

About 300 m north of the lower fort is a cistern (Bir Afjam) (out of plan).

Both forts apparently guarded the fertile valley of Wadi Kamoneh. The dating of these structures is problematic.

Pottery (body sherds): Iron I-II – 50%; Late Roman – 50%.
Other surveys: none.

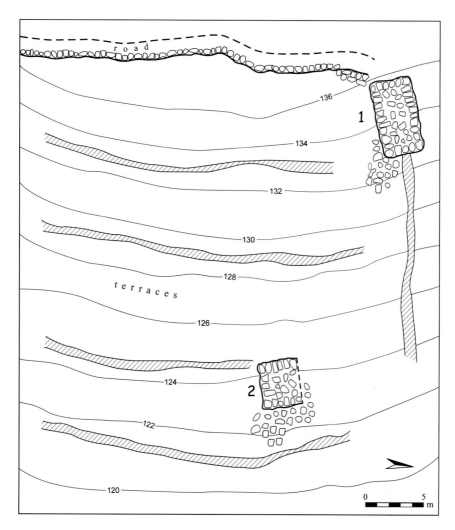

295. Plan of **Wadi Kamoneh (7)**.

Site 157: 18-16/47/1
KHIRBET ISYAR

Israel grid: 18491/16773
UTM grid: 7235/5545
Elevation: 340 m a.s.l., 30 m b.s.a.
Name: local but not on map
Site type: fortified site
Area: 1 ha (10 dunams)
Topography: small valley
Rock type: Judea Group
Soil: terra rossa, quality: 6

Cultivation: field crops by the site
Cisterns: 3
Water source: 'Ein el-Majdal (no. 185), 1.8 km distant
Road: Kh. Bani Fadel-Khalet el-Khashabeh (C53), by the site
Visit: January 1999; 2005; 6 surveyors; 120 sherds

Fortified site in a small valley between two low ridges in the western part of Gittit Valley, 2.3 km north of the village of Majdal Bani Fadil.

Well-preserved curving wall encircles the west, north and a small part of the south of the site. The eastern side and most of the southern side were apparently demolished by modern agricultural cultivation and the construction of the Roman road (C53). The wall, 1.5-2 m thick, is built of two rows of large stones. The original extent of the site is unknown.

Remains of about 15 to 20 structures with squarish rooms and walls one stone thick at the west of the site.

296. Aerial photo looking west at **Kh. Isyar** (A. Solomon).

Terrace walls on the hill above the site.

Remains of Medieval structures on the slope. Above them are dwellings of Bedouin and caves (not in plan).

Rock-cut installations and cisterns in the large rocky surfaces, probably connected to the ancient site.

Many sherds are scattered over the site.

The site was first settled in the Middle Bronze Age, became a regional hub in IA I, and we presume that the arable IA activity around it was related to its

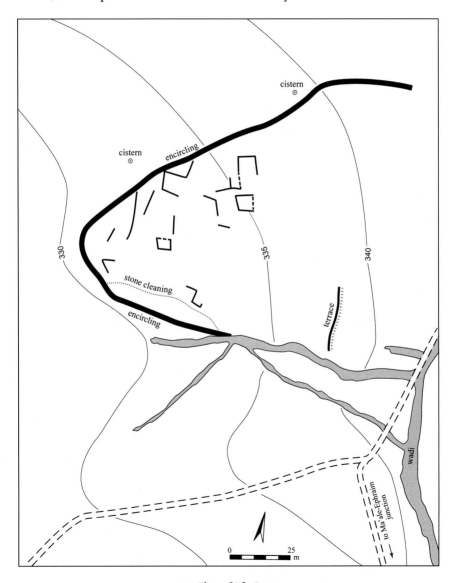

297. Plan of **Kh. Isyar**.

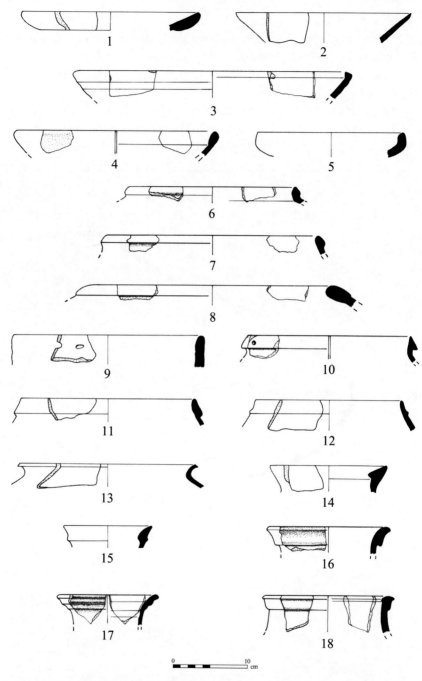

298. Pottery from **Kh. Isyar**: 1. Bowl, buff, Per.; 2. Bowl, buff, MB II; 3. Bowl, lt brn, MB II; 4. Bowl, dk brn, MB II; 5. Bowl, brn, IA I; 6-7. CPs, dk brn, MB II; 8-9. CPs, lt brn, MB II; 10, 12. CPs, dk brn, IA I; 12, 13. CPs, lt brn, IA I; 14. Jar, brn, MB II; 15. Jar, buff, MB II; 16. Jar, lt brn, MB II; 17. Jar, lt gr, MB II; 18. Jar, dk brn, MB II.

inhabitants. An intriguing question is why the site was deserted during the IA I and did not continue into the flourishing IA II period.

Pottery: Middle Bronze II – 25%; Iron I – 65%; Persian-Hellenistic – 3%; Late Roman – 3%; Medieval – 4%.
Flint: 5 items: 1 core waste, 1 flake, 2 blades, and a scraper.
Other surveys: none.

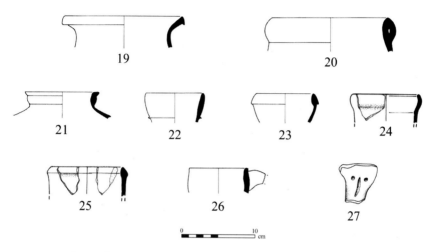

299. Pottery from **Kh. Isyar** (continued): 19. Jar, buff, Per-Hel; 20. Pithos, dk brn, IA I; 21. Jar, pink, MB II; 22. Jar, lt brn, LR; 23. Jar, brn, IA I; 24. Jug, gr, IA I (?); 25. Jug, lt brn, IA I; 26. Jug, brn, IA I; 27. Handle with indentation, brn, IA I.

Site 158: 18-16/47/2
ISYAR (1)

Israel grid: 18460/16744
UTM grid: 7231/5541
Elevation: 405 m a.s.l., 15 m a.s.a.
Name: nearest place
Site type: courtyard
Area: 1,000 sq. m (1 dunam)
Topography: slope
Rock type: Judea Group
Soil: terra rossa, quality: 7

Cultivation: field crops by the site
Cisterns: none
Water source: 'Ein el-Majdal (no. 185),
  1.5 km distant
Road: Kh. Bani Fadil-Khalet
  el-Khashabeh (C53), 400 m distant
Visit: March 2015; 5 surveyors;
  no sherds found

Site on a slope, 400 m south-west of Kh Isyar (Site 157) and 3 km west of Gittit. East of the site there is a fertile cultivated valley.

Courtyard with two linked parts, both 20×15 m. The construction is of one row of arranged large fieldstones.

No dateable sherds found.

Other surveys: none.

Site 159: 18-16/47/3
ISYAR (2)

Israel grid: 18493/16750
UTM grid: 7235/5542
Elevation: 375 m a.s.l., 30 m a.s.a.
Name: nearest place
Site type: fortified complex
Area: 2 ha (20 dunams)
Topography: flat hill
Rock type: Judea Group
Soil: terra rossa, quality: 5

Cultivation: field crops by the site
Cisterns: 3
Water source: 'Ein el-Majdal (no. 185),
  1.5 km distant
Road: Kh. Bani Fadel-Khalet
  el-Khashabeh (C53), by the site
Visit: March 2015; 5 surveyors;
  120 sherds

Large complex site on a flat hill in the cluster of the Isyar sites, south of Kh. Isyar (Site 157), 2.5 km west of Gittit.

At least two complexes:
- Western complex, 95×45 m, on the western slope of the hill. The construction is of medium-sized stones and is very meticulous. The complex is fortified and encircled by a wall, 2.5 m thick; the western and southern sides of which appear to be casements. At the northern end of the casement wall is a round tower (?), 5 m diameter. A 1 m thick wall built of small stones encloses the complex in the east. In the northern part of the wall is a rock-cut entrance. At the northern end is an inner room, 12×9 m.

  In light of the considerable destruction it is difficult to define the exact plan of the complex.

  In the northern part of the area bounded by the wall is a built cave which appears to be a burial cave. Inside the cave is a rock-cut corridor at least 4 m long, 1.5 m wide and 2.5 m high. Above the entrance to the cave is a lintel stone, 2 m long, 1 m wide and 1 m high.

  The connection between the complex and the burial cave is not clear.
- Round structure or courtyard, 20 m diameter, built of very large stones in the north-eastern complex. A large squarish structure preceded the courtyard, but only a small part of it survived. A wall sets out eastward from the structure, and apparently turns south.

Three large cisterns. The southern cistern is partially surrounded by a new earth rampart draining water to the cistern. The north-eastern cistern is situated on a slope with a dug and built channel leading to it. A trough is attached to the western cistern.

At the centre of the hill, over wide exposed and cleared rocky surfaces are many cup marks and rock-cuttings to collect rain water.

On the hill is a modern Arab structure, and next to it a sheepfold.

The site was probably established in the Iron Age I, perhaps connected with the nearby fortified site of Kh. Isyar (Site 157). Unlike the site at Kh. Isyar, the site continued to the Iron Age II, during which it was deserted. A new settlement at the site was established in the Roman period. Because of the poor preservation of the fortified structure it is hard to suggest the date of its construction and use (Iron Age or Roman period).

Pottery: Iron I – 32%; Iron II – 8%; Early Roman – 17%; Late Roman – 17%; Byzantine – 13%; Medieval – 13%.
Stone: threshing sledge stones.
Other surveys: none.

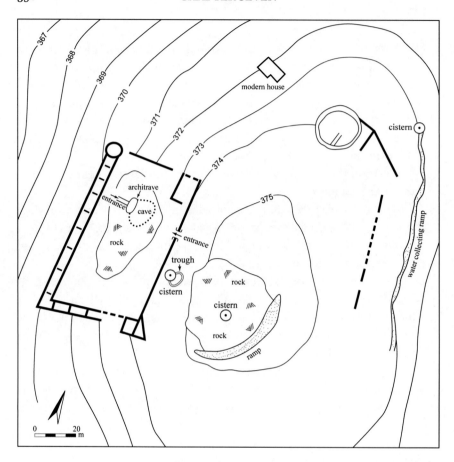

300. Plan of **Isyar (2)**.

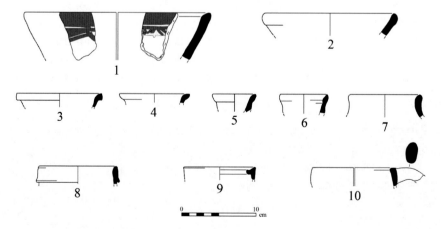

301. Pottery from **Isyar (2)**: 1. Bowl, lt brn, blk orn over white, Med.; 2. Bowl, lt brn, Med; 3-6, 8. Jugs, lt brn, LR-Byz; 7, 10. Jugs, lt brn, IA I-II; 9. Jug, blk, LR-Byz.

Site 160: 18-16/57/1
ELEVATION POINT 390 (5)

Israel grid: 18570/16747
UTM grid: 7242/5542
Elevation: 375 m a.s.l., 5 m a.s.a.
Name: nearest place
Site type: courtyards
Area: 1,000 sq. m (1 dunam)
Topography: edge of valley
Rock type: Judea Group

Soil: terra rossa, quality: 8
Cultivation: field crops by the site
Cisterns: none
Water source: 'Ein el-Majdal (no. 185), 1.6 km distant
Road: Gittit Valley (C58), 400 m distant
Visit: July 2015; 5 surveyors; 30 sherds

Site on the slope of the spur of E.P. 390, 400 m west of Kh. Mras ed-Din and 1.8 km west of Gittit.

Large square complex courtyard, 20.5×20.5 m. The courtyard is well built of large and medium-sized boulders. The walls have been preserved to a maximum height of 3 courses (about 1.5 m). In the northern corner is a rectangular cell, 9×2.5 m. The face of the rock is exposed in the southern part of the courtyard.

Smaller courtyard, 14×10 m, identical in masonry, abutting the north-eastern wall of the large courtyard. A wall crosses the smaller courtyard from north-east to south-east, dividing it into two: a cell, 10×4 m, adjacent to the large courtyard, and a cell, 10×10 m north-east of it.

Scanty stone collapses are attached to the walls of the various courtyards, evidence that the walls did not originally exceed much more than their present height.

The site is a part of the advanced agricultural array on the slopes of E.P. 390 and E.P. 393. It is hard to ascertain its date of construction, though it most probably mainly functioned during the Roman and Byzantine periods.

Pottery: Iron II – 10%; Roman-Byzantine (body sherds) – 80%; Medieval (body sherds) – 10%.
Other surveys: none.

302. A sherd from E.P. 390 (5): Bowl, lt brn, lt burnish in and out, IA II.

Site 161: 18-16/57/2
ELEVATION POINT 393 (3)

Israel grid: 18537/16739
UTM grid: 7239/5541
Elevation: 370 m a.s.l., 5 m a.s.a.
Name: nearest place
Site type: structure and sherd scatter
Area: 300 sq. m (0.3 dunam)
Topography: slope of spur at edge of valley
Rock type: Judea Group
Soil: terra rossa (in the valley),
quality: 8
Cultivation: cereals, in the valley
Cisterns: none
Water source: 'Ein el-Majdal (no. 185), 1.5 km distant
Road: Kh. Bani Fadil-Khalet el-Khashabeh (C53), 100 m distant
Visit: June 2014; 5 surveyors; 120 sherds

Site on a spur with a moderate slope, 2 km west of Gittit and 1.2 km north-north-west of Ma'ale Ephraim junction.

Rectangular structure, 7×4 m, built of large and medium-sized stones.

Many Roman-Byzantine sherds were collected, mainly from the slope between the structure and the valley north of it. A few earlier Middle Bronze Age II sherds perhaps originate from nearby sites, and therefore cannot substantiate the period of the structure.

The structure and the activity around it are linked to the cultivation of the arable areas in Classical periods.

Pottery: Middle Bronze II (body sherds) – 3%; Roman-Byzantine – 97%.
Flint: 3 items: 1 flake, 1 bladelet and a scraper.
Other surveys: none.

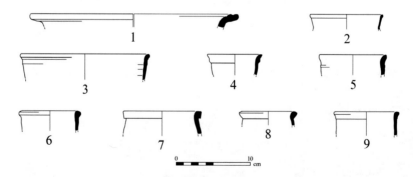

303. Pottery from E.P. 393 (3) (all Rom-Byz): 1. Krater, lt brn; 2. Bowl (?), greyish; 3-5. Bowls, reddish; 6. Bowl, dk brn; 7. Bowl (?), reddish; 8. Bowl (?), reddish; 9. Jug, reddish.

Site 162: 18-16/57/3
ELEVATION POINT 390 (2)

Israel grid: 18578/16732 (centre of the site)
UTM grid: 7243/5540
Elevation: 385 m a.s.l., 10 m a.s.a.
Name: nearest place
Site type: scattered structures and courtyards
Area: 3 ha (30 dunams)
Topography: spur and edge of valley
Rock type: Judea Group

Soil: terra rossa, quality: 6
Cultivation: field crops by the site
Cisterns: none
Water source: 'Ein el-Majdal (no. 185), 1.6 km distant
Road: Gittit Valley (C58), 500 m distant
Visit: April 1997; 4 surveyors; 950 sherds

Large site at the southern edge of Gittit Valley, 400 m south-west of Mras ed-Din and 1.5 km west of Gittit.

Ten structures and courtyards, the exact nature of which is not clear. Since there seems to be an architectonic linkage between them, they are introduced here as one site.

- Small rectangular structure built of large stones (structure no. 1 in plan).
  Pottery (70 body sherds): Middle Bronze II – 90%; Late Roman – 10%.
- Courtyard, 25×25 m, built of very large stones. In the north-eastern corner is a small room (no. 2).
  Pottery (90 sherds): Middle Bronze II – 86%; Iron II-III – 4%; Late Roman – 6%; Medieval (body sherds) – 2%.
- Courtyard slightly smaller than no. 2, similar in masonry, with rooms in its northern part (no. 3).
  Pottery (80 sherds): Middle Bronze II – 90%; Iron II-III – 5%; Late Roman (body sherds) – 5%.
- Large complex, 3,000 sq. m, on a slope, with rooms joining a large terrace wall. The rooms are large and rectangular, 8×6 m on average. The walls are one or two stones thick (no. 4).
  Pottery (200 sherds): Middle Bronze II/Late Bronze – 100%.
  Flint: 10 items: 6 flakes and 4 blades.
- Densely built three-roomed structure (no. 5), 7×7 m, without small finds.
- Rectangular structure with a courtyard (no. 6), and a large sherd scatter.
  Pottery (250 sherds): Middle Bronze II – 80%; Late Roman – 20%.
  Flint: 8 items: 1 flake core, 4 flakes, and 3 blades.
- Large structure with rooms and a courtyard beside it on the slope, built of large stones (no. 7).

Pottery (100 sherds): Middle Bronze II – 95%; Late Roman – 5%.
- Square structure with rectangular inner courtyard, both built of large stones (no. 8).
  Pottery (120 body sherds): Middle Bronze II – 100%.
- Rectangular structure (no. 9).
  Pottery (9 body sherds): Middle Bronze II – 100%.
- Round enclosure, 20 m diameter, divided by east-west wall. A wall starts eastwards from the east side of the enclosure (no. 10).
  Pottery (90 sherds): Middle bronze II – 80%; Late Roman – 20%.

The site belongs to a group of sites spread along the edge of the valley.

The bulk of the pottery is dated to the Middle Bronze Age II period, hence the site was established and used in this period. Structures were built on its remains during the Late Roman period.

Other surveys: none.

304. Aerial photo view west at **E.P. 390 (2)** (A. Solomon).

LANDSCAPE UNIT 35

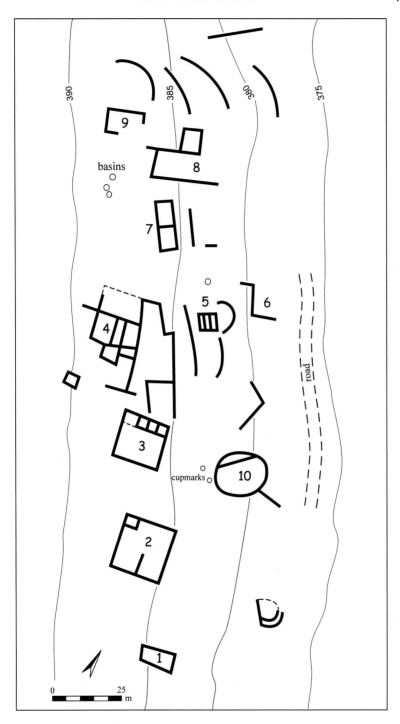

305. Plan of E.P. 390 (2).

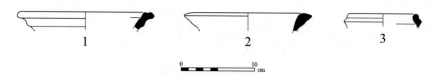

306. Pottery from **E.P. 390 (2)**, structure no. 2: 1. Bowl (?), lt brn, LR (?); 2. Jar, lt colour, MB II; 3. Jug, dk brn, IA II-III.

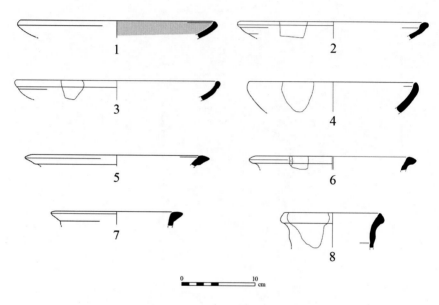

307. Pottery from **E.P. 390 (2)**, structure no. 3: 1. Bowl, lt brn, red slip inside, MB II; 2. Bowl, lt brn, MB II; 3. Bowl, lt brn, IA II-III; 4. Bowl, gr, IA II-III; 5, 7. Jars, lt brn, MB II; 6, 8. Jars, gr, MB II.

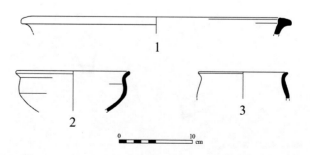

308. Pottery from **E.P. 390 (2)**, structure no. 4 (all MB II/LB): 1. Krater, greyish; 2. Bowl, lt brn; 3. CP, lt brn.

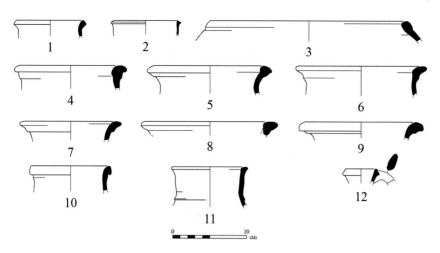

309. Pottery from **E.P. 390 (2)**, structure no. 6: 1-2. Bowls (?), reddish, LR; 3. Krater, greyish, MB II; 4. Jar, reddish, MB II; 5-7, 9. Jars, greyish, MB II; 8. Jar (?), lt brn, MB II; 10. Jar, gr, MB II (?); 11. Jar, lt brn, LR; 12. Jug, reddish, LR.

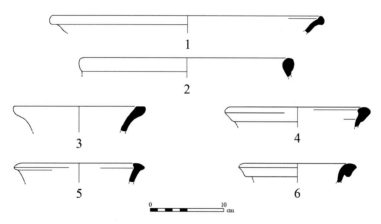

310. Pottery from **E.P. 390 (2)**, structure no. 7: 1. Bowl, lt brn, LR (?); 2. CP, dk brn, MB II; 3. Jar, lt brn, MB II (?); 4-6, Jars, lt brn, MB II.

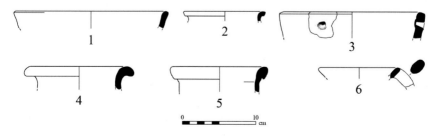

311. Pottery from **E.P. 390 (2)**, structure no. 10: 1. Bowl, dk brn, MB II; 2. Bowl, dk brn, LR; 3. CP, lt brn, MB II; 4. Jar, lt colour, MB II; 5. Jar, dk brn, MB II; 6. Jug, dk brn, MB II.

Site 163: 18-16/57/4
ELEVATION POINT 390 (7)

Israel grid: 18573/16722
UTM grid: 7243/5539
Elevation: 390 m a.s.l., 0 m a.s.a.
Name: nearest place
Site type: structures, enclosures, cisterns and installations
Area: 1 ha (10 dunams)
Topography: flat plateau
Rock type: Judea Group

Soil: terra rossa, quality: 3
Cultivation: field crops by the site
Cisterns: none
Water source: 'Ein el-Majdal (no. 185), 1.5 km distant
Road: Kh. Bani Fadil-Khalet el-Khashabeh (C53), 400 m distant
Visit: June 2014; 4 surveyors; 350 sherds

A site on a flat plateau (E.P. 390) in the centre of a large area of fields, 1.7 km west of Gittit and 4.5 km south-east of Aqraba.

There are at least four parts to the site:
- Structure, 20×15 m, in the northern part of the site, built of large boulders (no. 1 in plan). The walls survived up to 1-1.5 m high. Thinner walls divide the inner space into at least three rooms. In the south is an opening with two jamb stones. Various phases of construction are visible in the structure, among them relatively new ones. A round courtyard is attached to the structure in the west.
- Three enclosures or threshing floors built of large stones (no. 2) south of structure no. 1. The northern enclosure is 15 m diameter, the central one is 26 m, and the southern one, very little of which is preserved, is about 15 m. At the centres of the three enclosures are cleared rock surfaces suggesting that they served as threshing floors.
- Structure, 10×10 m, built of large stones (no. 3) about 75 m south-south-west of structure no. 1. Close to and north of the structure are seven cup marks on a flat rock. Adjacent to the eastern wall is a modern *maq'ad*.
- Two large cisterns (no. 4) in the eastern and western parts of the site. A large concrete surface has been laid in the western cistern. Near the eastern cistern is a modern *maq'ad*.

According to the diversity of pottery, it is likely that the site was in use for a long period.

The site is one of a considerable number of sites spread along a 2 km stretch on the plateau of E.P. 390. Apparently some of the owners of the fields in the area used some of the structures as dwellings.

Pottery: Iron II – 57%; Late Roman – 23%; Byzantine – 11%; Medieval – 9%.
Other surveys: none.

312. Plan of E.P. 390 (7).

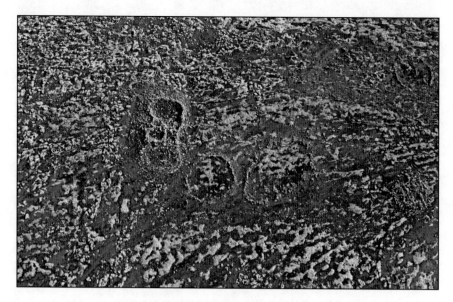

313. Aerial photo looking east at **E.P. 390 (7)** (A. Solomon).

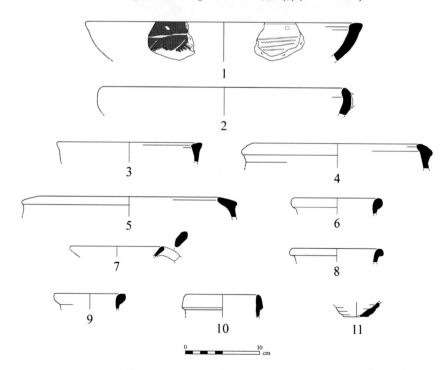

314. Pottery from **E.P. 390 (7)**: 1. Bowl, lt brn, lt burnish inside, painted white over black outside, Med; 2. Bowl, greyish, IA II; 3. Bowl, reddish brn, IA II; 4. Krater (?), lt brn, IA II; 5. Krater, lt brn, IA II; 6. Jar/jug, dk brn, IA II; 7. Jug (?), reddish brn, LR-Byz; 8. Jug, lt brn, LR-Byz; 9. Jug, lt brn, IA II; 10. Jug, dk brn, LR-Byz; 11. Base, lt brn, LR-Byz.

Site 164: 18-16/57/5
ELEVATION POINT 390 (6)

Israel grid: 18583/16725
UTM grid: 7244/5540
Elevation: 365 m a.s.l., 5 m a.s.a.
Name: nearest place
Site type: courtyard
Area: 500 sq. m (0.5 dunam)
Topography: valley edge
Rock type: Judea Group

Soil: terra rossa, quality: 8
Cultivation: field crops by the site
Cisterns: none
Water source: 'Ein el-Majdal (no. 185), 1.6 km distant
Road: Kh. Bani Fadil-Khalet el-Khashabeh (C53), 500 m distant
Visit: July 2015; 5 surveyors; 50 sherds

Site on the north-eastern slope of the ridge of E.P. 390, 400 m south-west of Mras ed-Din and 1.7 km west of Gittit.

Remains of a courtyard, built of large boulders, some based on bedrock. Only 18 m of the western wall and 10 m of the north-western wall survive. There is a plundered cell, 3×3 m, built of boulders, at the meeting point of the walls in the western corner of the courtyard.

The site is one of the Roman-Byzantine agricultural sites on the north-eastern slope of E.P. 390 and E.P. 393.

Pottery: Late Roman-Byzantine 60%; Medieval (body sherds) – 30%; Unidentified – 10%.
Other surveys: none.

315. Pottery from **E.P. 390 (6)**: 1. Jar (?), lt brn, Rom-Byz (?); 2. Jug (?), lt brn, Rom-Byz.

Site 165: 18-16/57/6
KH. TAWILEH

Israel grid: 18526/16717 (site centre)
UTM grid: 7238/5539
Elevation: 420 m a.s.l., 30 m a.s.a.
Name: local, but not on map
Site type: structures, courtyards and road
Area: 2.7 ha (27 dunams)
Topography: spur
Rock type: Judea Group
Soil: terra rossa, quality: 7
Cultivation: field crops by the site
Cisterns: none
Water source: 'Ein el-Majdal (no. 185), 1.3 km distant
Road: Kh. Bani Fadil-Khalet el-Khashabeh (C53), by the site
Visit: February 1999 and more; 6 surveyors; 95 sherds

Vast site on the summit of a spur next to and on the north-eastern slope of an inner valley, 2 km west of Gittit.
Two separate complexes, an additional enclosure and a road.
- Southern upper complex is well built of large stones (no. 1 in plan). Large upright standing stones are embedded in the outer faces of the boundary walls. There are a structure and three courtyards in the complex.

  Structure, 15×8 m, with interior divided into three equal rooms, 8×5 m. Two interlocked courtyards are attached to the structure. The southern, larger, courtyard is subdivided.

  South of the structure is a round courtyard, 25 m diameter; next to it are remains of another courtyard or enclosure.
- Northern lower complex located at the centre of the slope, 40 m north of complex no. 1 (no. 2). It is about 50×50 m, and its construction is similar to that of complex no. 1. There are several spaces and structures with adjacent rooms attached to them.
- Round enclosure, 20 m diameter (no. 3) 150 m south-east of complex no. 2.
- Wall, nearly 140 m long, between the complexes.
- Constructed Roman road (C53) leads from the junction near Kh. Bani Fadil to Aqraba and Neapolis, and passes at the bottom of the slope (no. 4).

The Middle Bronze Age II settlement in Kh. Tawileh has been preserved almost intact, representing a rare example of a rural village of the period.

Pottery: Intermediate Bronze – 2%; Middle Bronze II – 78%; Late Roman (body sherds) – 20%.
Other surveys: none.

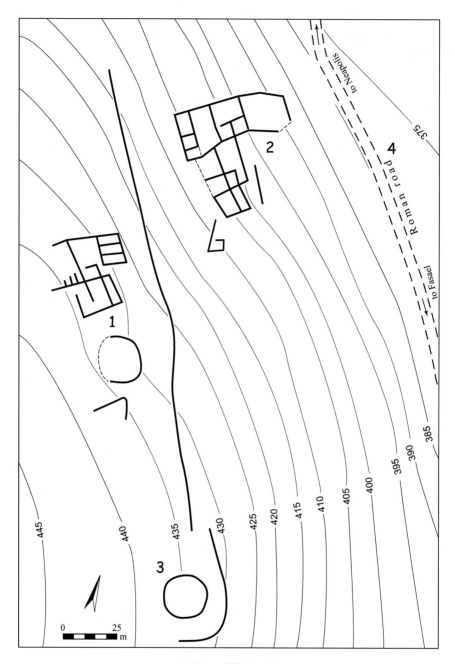

316. Plan of **Kh. Tawile**.

317. Aerial photo looking west at **Kh. Tawile** (A. Solomon).

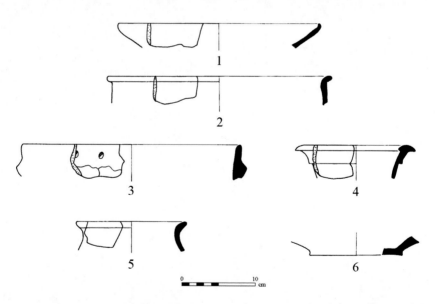

318. Pottery from **Kh. Tawile** (all except no. 5 are MB II): 1. Bowl, gr; 2. Krater, pink; 3. CP, lt brn; 4. Jar, buff; 5. Amphoriskos, brn, IBA (?); 6. Bowl base, pink.

Site 166: 18-16/57/7
ELEVATION POINT 393 (2)

Israel grid: 18557/16729
UTM grid: 7241/5540
Elevation: 385 m a.s.l., 10 m a.s.a.
Name: nearest place
Site type: cistern, installations and sherd scatter
Area: 1,000 sq. m (1 dunam)
Topography: slope of spur in edge of valley

Rock type: Judea Group
Soil: terra rossa, quality: 8
Cultivation: field crops by the site
Cisterns: 1
Water source: 'Ein el-Majdal (no. 185), 1.6 km distant
Road: Kh. Bani Fadil-Khalet el-Khashabeh (C53), 200 m distant
Visit: June 2014; 2 surveyors; 53 sherds

Site on the southern slope of the spur of E.P. 393, 2 km south-west of Gittit.

Cistern, with opening 30×30 cm, covered by a metal lid with a hole in it, for use with small containers. The walls are lined with medium-sized stones with modern cement.

Channels drain water from the upper part of the spur to the cistern. On the west and south the cistern is bounded by a stone wall, apparently remains of a courtyard preceding the cistern.

At least three rock-cut cup-marks on a rock surface, 50 m north of the cistern, two of them 20 cm diameter.

Sherd scatter on the slope below the cistern.

Pottery (body sherds): Late Roman-Byzantine – 36%; Medieval – 58%; Unidentified – 6%.
Other surveys: none.

Site 167: 18-16/57/8
WADI ES-SAYAD (1)

Israel grid: 18503/16715
UTM grid: 7236/5538
Elevation: 390 m a.s.l., 10 m a.s.a.
Name: nearest place
Site type: structure
Area: 100 sq. m (0.1 dunam)
Topography: edge of valley
Rock type: Judea Group
Soil: terra rossa, quality: 8

Cultivation: field crops by the site
Cisterns: none
Water source: 'Ein el-Majdal (no. 185), 1.2 km distant
Road: Kh. Bani Fadil-Khalet el-Khashabeh (C53), 400 m distant
Visit: June 2014, April 2015; 5 surveyors; 42 sherds

Site on a slope of a spur on edge of valley, 2.5 km west of Gittit and 1.5 km north-north-east of Majdal Bani Fadil.

Structure, 10×10 m, built of very large stones, maybe a stronghold. Walls, 1.5 m thick, survive to a height of up to 3 courses (1 m). Inside the structure and on the slope are stone collapses, proof that the whole structure was built of stones.

Pottery: Middle Bronze II – 3% (a single rim); Late Roman-Byzantine – 94%; Medieval – 3% (a single body sherd).
Other surveys: none.

319. Pottery from **Wadi es-Sayad (1)**: 1. Jar (?), dk brn, MB II; 2. Jar, lt brn, LR-Byz.

Site 168: 18-16/57/9
ELEVATION POINT 419 (4)

Israel grid: 18597/16780
UTM grid: 7245/5545
Elevation: 370 m a.s.l., 0 m a.s.a.
Name: nearest place
Site type: sherd scatter and walls
Area: 2,000 sq. m (2 dunams)
Topography: edge of valley
Rock type: Judea Group

Soil: terra rossa, quality: 8
Cultivation: field crops by the site
Cisterns: none
Water source: 'Ein el-Majdal (no. 185), 2.3 km distant
Road: Gittit Valley (C58), by the site
Visit: February 2014; 5 surveyors; 160 sherds

Site on the southern slope of E.P. 419, 1.5 km west of Gittit and 300 m north of Kh. Mras ed-Din.

Sherd scatter and a small number of wall remains which do not yield a plan.

It is likely that the site was linked to the nearby central Iron Age site at Kh. Mras ed-Din.

Pottery: Iron II-III – 75%; Late Roman (body sherds) – 19%; Medieval (body sherds) – 6%.
Other surveys: none.

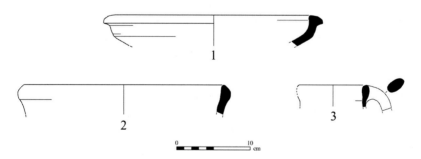

320. Pottery from **E.P. 419 (4)** (all IA II-III): 1. Bowl, lt brn; 2. Krater (?), lt brn; 3. Jug, lt brn.

Site 169: 18-16/57/10

EN-NAQURAH

Israel grid: 18544/16764
UTM grid: 7240/5543
Elevation: 390 m a.s.l., 50 m a.s.a.
Name: local
Site type: structure, courtyards and road
Area: 2,000 sq. m (2 dunams)
Topography: flat plateau
Rock type: Judea Group

Soil: terra rossa, quality: 2
Cultivation: none
Cisterns: none
Water source: 'Ein el-Majdal (no. 185), 1.8 km distant
Road: Kh. Bani Fadil-Khalet el-Khashabeh (C53), 300 m distant
Visit: June 2014; 4 surveyors; 23 sherds

Site on a flat plateau south-east of E.P. 393, 700 m west of Mras ed-Din and 2 km west of Gittit.
Site has three parts:
- Large structure, 16×12 m, built of large regularly shaped stones (no. 1 in plan). The construction is typical of the Middle Bronze Age II period in the region. There is a cell at the south-eastern corner. A courtyard abuts the eastern side of the structure.
- Two partially preserved courtyards (no. 2) about 50 m south-south-east of the structure. The masonry is identical to that of the large structure.
- Road remains close by and west of the structure (no. 3).

It appears that the site was established in the Middle Bronze Age II period, a part of a characteristic settlement momentum in the desert fringes of Samaria, where many similar farm houses of the period were found.

The settlement was renewed in the Late Roman Period after a long interval.

Pottery (body sherds): Middle Bronze II – 45%; Late Roman – 55%.
Other surveys: none.

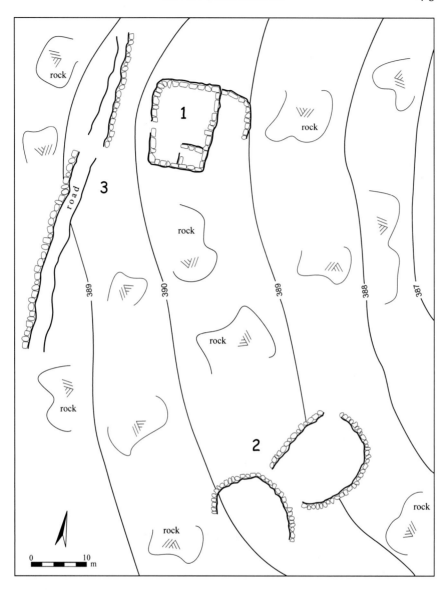

321. Plan of **en-Naqurah**.

Site 170: 18-16/57/11
ELEVATION POINT 390 (8)

Israel grid: 18560/16771
UTM grid: 7241/5544
Elevation: 360 m a.s.l., 20 m b.s.a.
Name: nearest place
Site type: courtyards
Area: 2,000 sq. m (2 dunams)
Topography: valley edge
Rock type: Judea Group
Soil: terra rossa, quality: 8

Cultivation: field crops by the site
Cisterns: none
Water source: 'Ein el-Majdal (no. 185), 2 km distant
Road: Gittit Valley (C58), 600 m distant
Visit: November 2014; 4 surveyors; 19 sherds

Site on the ridges of E.P. 390 and E.P. 393, on a low slope bordering the arable areas west of Mras ed-Din.

Two courtyards, built parallel along and close to the unpaved road from Ma'ale Ephraim junction to Aqraba.
- Courtyard, 12×12 m, walls built of one row of large stones (no. 1 in plan). Considerable sections of the walls are ruined.
- Trapezoidal courtyard (no. 2), 60 m north-west of courtyard no. 1. The longest, northern, wall is 15 m long and the shortest, southern, wall is 10 m long. The walls are built of one row of large stones. An extra row of stones was added to some sections of the walls. A new *maq'ad*, 3×2 m, using stones for its construction from the ancient courtyard, is attached to the centre of the southern wall.

Pottery: Middle Bronze II – 60%; Iron I (body sherds) – 10%; Iron II – 6%; Roman (body sherds) – 10%, Unidentified – 14%.
Flint: 4 items: 1 bladelet core, 1 blade, and 2 bladelets.
Other surveys: none.

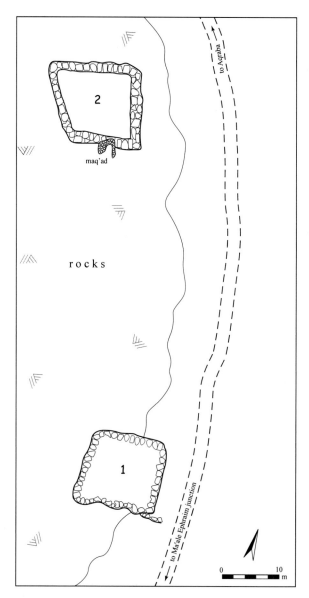

322. Plan of E.P. 390 (8).

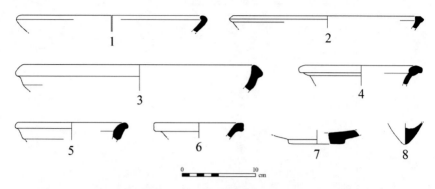

323. Pottery from E.P. 390 (8): 1. Bowl, lt brn, MB II; 2. Bowl, dk brn, MB II (?); 3. Bowl, lt brn, IA II; 4-6. Jars, dk brn, MB II; 7. Base, lt brn, MB II; 8. Juglet base, lt brn, MB II.

◆ ◆ ◆

Site 171: 18-16/67/1

KHIRBET TAWIL (1)

Israel grid: 18665/16780
UTM grid: 7252/5545
Elevation: 399 m a.s.l., 40 m a.s.a.
Name: on the map
Site type: structures and sherd scatter
Area: 8,000 sq. m (8 dunams)
Topography: hillock
Rock type: Judea Group
Soil: terra rossa, quality: 6

Cultivation: none
Cisterns: 1
Water source: 'Ein el-Majdal (no. 185), 2.5 km distant
Road: Gittit Valley (C58), 400 m distant
Visit: March 1997, March 2015; 4 surveyors; 120 sherds

Site on the hill where the Gittit water reservoir is situated, 1 km west of the settlement centre.

There are numerous heaps of stones on the hillock from structures totally demolished during the modern construction of the reservoir.

Few remains are left on the eastern slope of the hill, among them a round enclosure built of very large stones. The surrounding wall has been preserved up to six courses high (2.5 m). Around the enclosure many tesserae were collected, indicating the presence of white and coloured mosaic floors.

At the bottom of the eastern slope is a single structure, 8×5 m, built of medium-sized stones; a Mamluk sherd was found inside it.

Additional structural items were discovered on the slopes outside the water reservoir fence.

There are sherd scatters from the Hellenistic to Early Moslem periods.

Porath (1968, site 166) visited the site prior to the construction of the reservoir describing it: "This is a large rectangular structure at the top of a high hillock. The outer dimensions are about 34 m x 21 m. The outside walls have been preserved up to 1.6 m high (three courses). An inner division into rooms and courtyards is noticeable. The construction is with dressed stones and a few ashlars. Some of the corner stones are drafted. Apparently, this is a large farmhouse or a small fort. There are rock-cut cisterns in the slopes of the hill. There are pottery finds from the periods: (Israelite II), Byzantine. It appears that the find from the Israelite II Period are from Kh. Mras ed-Din".

The Southern Samaria Survey (Finkelstein et al. 1997: 799) visited the site describing it thus: "Remains of a wall built of large stones. It is preserved up to 2 m. Tesserae. The site has been damaged since Porath's survey by the construction of a water reservoir".

Pottery: Late Roman-Byzantine – 98%; Medieval (body sherds) – 2%.
Other finds: glass fragments, mosaic stones.
Other surveys: Conder and Kitchener 1882: 395; Porath 1968, sites 165-166; Finkelstein et al. 1997: 799.

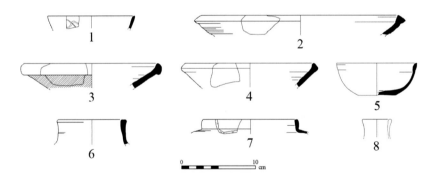

324. Finds from **Kh. Tawil (1)**: 1. Bowl, lt brn, incised dec, Byz; 2, 4-5. Bowls, lt brn, LR-Byz; 3. Bowl, red, painted red outside, LR-Byz; 6. Jar, gr, LR-Byz; 7. CP, red, LR-Byz; 8. Bottle, green glass, Byz (?).

Site 172: 18-16/67/2
MRAS ED-DIN (NORTHERN COMPLEX)

Israel grid: 18612/16754
UTM grid: 7247/5543
Elevation: 375 m a.s.l., 20 m a.s.a.
Name: local, and on the map
Site type: courtyards, cistern and installations
Area: 5,000 sq. m (5 dunams)
Topography: hillock
Rock type: Judea Group

Soil: terra rossa, quality: 9
Cultivation: none
Cisterns: 5
Water source: 'Ein el-Majdal (no. 185), 2 km distant
Road: Gittit Valley (C58), 300 m distant
Visit: April 2014 and more; 8 surveyors; 600 sherds

Site at the edge of the northern hillock of the Mras ed-Din ridge, at the highest point of the ridge, 1 km west of Gittit. There is a convenient lookout over the area from the site.

Two large courtyards:
- Southern courtyard, 20×20 m, built of large dressed stones (no. 1 in plan). The northern wall is built of two rows of stones, and the other walls of one row. In the north-western corner of the courtyards are two narrow rooms, 6 m long. The south-eastern corner is missing and there is a depression in the ground in its place.
- Northern courtyard (no. 2), 26×20 m, is also built of large dressed stones abutting the southern courtyard on the northern slope of the ridge. Inside the courtyard is a wall which appears to be later than the original construction. A very large erect stone, 1.5×1 m, was found at the centre of the northern wall. The entrance to the courtyard is next to the south-western corner.

Cistern, a built water channel and cup marks are located in the large rock surfaces east of the northern courtyard.

The entire complex is supported in the east by a cliff and part of it was strengthened by a wall.

To the east of the courtyards and water supply cisterns is much quarrying, including a burial cave and installations.

A residential cave, enclosed by a high wall, was found on the north-eastern slope of the ridge (not on plan). Pottery from the Medieval period was collected at the cave entrance.

Another well-built structure with masonry of large boulders located on the south-western slope of the ridge, close to the fertile fields, was possibly a guard tower for the fields. No datable finds near the structure, and the date is not known. The masonry and size partly resemble the Middle Roman period tower excavated in the south-eastern complex in Mras ed-Din (Site 173) (and see Appendix A for a detailed report on the excavation of this tower); and this might be a similar structure.

The northern complex of Mras ed-Din is mainly dated to the Roman-Byzantine and Medieval periods. The impressive courtyards are part of the developed agricultural array in the Gittit Valley during Roman-Byzantine times. The courtyards were probably also reused during the Medieval period when the nearby dwelling cave was active.

Pottery: The pottery collected from both Mras ed-Din complexes (Sites 172 and 173) has been collected as one site: Middle Bronze II – 3%; Iron II-III – 70%; Persian – 3%; Roman-Byzantine – 10%; Medieval – 14%.

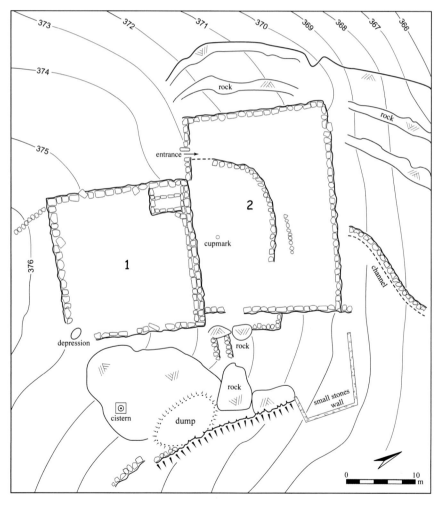

325. Plan of **Mras ed-Din (northern complex)**.

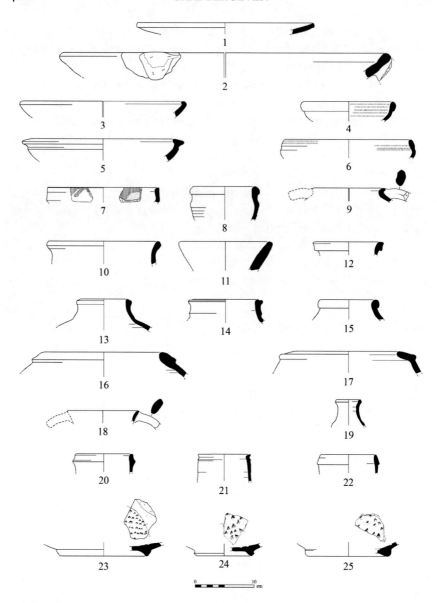

326. Pottery from **Mras ed-Din (northern and south-eastern complexes, Sites 172 and 173)**: 1. Platter, lt brn, Med (?); 2. Platter, lt colour, Med; 3. Bowl, lt brn, MB II; 4. Bowl, reddish, red burnish inside, IA II-III; 5. Bowl, dk brn, IA II-III; 6. Bowl, reddish, red burnish in and out, IA II-III; 7. Bowl, reddish, green glaze in and out, Med; 8. Bowl, greyish, Rom-Byz (?); 9. CP, lt brn, Rom-Byz; 10. Jar, dk brn, IA II-III; 11. Jar (?), greyish, Med; 12. Jar, lt brn, MB II; 13. Jar, reddish, Rom (?); 14. Jar, gr, IA II-III; 15. Jar, lt colour, Pers; 16. Holemouth jar, greyish, IA II-III; 17. Holemouth jar, lt brn, IA II-III; 18. Jug, lt brn, Rom-Byz; 19. Jug, lt brn, IA II-III; 20. Jug, reddish, IA II-III; 21. Jug, reddish, Rom-Byz; 22. Jug (?) dk brn, Rom-Byz; 23-25. Bowl bases, lt brn, cuneated dec, IA III.

Flint: 10 items: 4 flakes, 3 blades, 1 retouched flake and 2 retouched blades.
Other surveys: Porath 1968, site 167; Finkelstein et al. 1997: 800.
Bibliography: Conder and Kitchener 1882: 394; GL: 118.

Site 173: 18-16/67/3

MRAS ED-DIN (SOUTH-EASTERN COMPLEX)

Israel grid: 18624/16740
UTM grid: 7248/5541
Elevation: 370 m a.s.l., 0 m a.s.a.
Name: local, and on the map
Site type: fortress and courtyards
Area: 4,000 sq. m (4 dunams)
Topography: moderate slope and valley edge
Rock type: Judea Group

Soil: terra rossa, quality: 9
Cultivation: field crops by the site
Cisterns: 1
Water source: 'Ein el-Majdal (no. 185), 2 km distant
Road: Gittit Valley (C58), 300 m distant
Visit: February 2014 and more; excavation 2017-2019

Site at the south-eastern edge of the Mras ed-Din ridge, close to large cultivated fields, 1 km west of Gittit and 600 m south-west of Gittit water reservoir.

Two complexes, part of a fortified farm or a local administrative centre from the Iron Age III. The complexes were destroyed at the end of the Iron Age (probably in the 6th Century BCE). A long-term excavation project at the site was inaugurated in 2017 (Bar 2018) with the aim of understanding the function of the site and its abrupt demise. Middle Roman agricultural structures, mainly towers, were erected using the stones of the destroyed Iron Age III site. The excavation report of one of these towers is in Appendix A.

The construction of both the Iron Age and the Roman structures is very good, with large slightly dressed stones.

1. Northern complex: Tower, 6×6 m, in the centre, built of large stones. This is probably a Roman tower similar to that excavated in 2017 in the southern complex (additional data in Appendix A).

   Courtyard with a colonnade to the east of the tower. A small probe in the courtyard near the columns dated the courtyard to the Iron Age III (Bar 2018). North of the courtyard are more undated walls, possibly remains of other courtyards or other agricultural structures.

   The entire array is enclosed by a long wall stretching down eastwards.

2. Southern complex, 35×26 m: In the lower part is a structure, 24×20 m, enclosed by a large stone wall. In the north-western corner is a room, 12×6

m, with a massive stone collapse. Inside an inner large courtyard are rooms along the eastern wall. In the north-eastern corner is a Middle Roman period tower excavated in 2017 (Appendix A). It seems that a Roman farm and other agricultural structures used the stones, and sometimes even the walls still projecting above the surface, of the long-abandoned Iron Age site.

In the upper western part, on a step 1 m high, is another structure with size and masonry similar to the lower structure. This was the main focus of

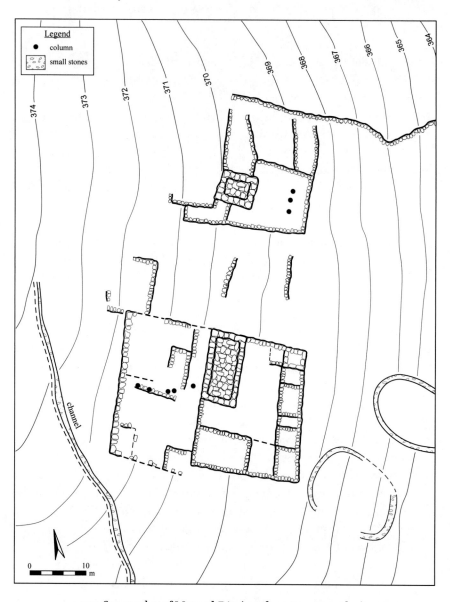

327. Survey plan of **Mras ed-Din (south-eastern complex)**.

the excavations, since no Roman remains were found here, and all the finds were dated to the Iron Age III.

The excavation of the upper part of the site exposed large sections of a very well-built Iron Age III structure. It seems to have been a very large four-room house. Abutting the structure to the north is a large stone-paved courtyard about 15 m wide, the full dimensions of which are still not known. Additional rooms abutted the four-room house to the east.

A massive destruction with many crushed pottery vessels in situ was found in most of the excavated rooms. The date of the pottery is 7th-6th Century BCE, and at least some of the pottery is Judaite (Fig. 330).

Additional structures and construction on the slope of the ridge, west of the southern complex, including a modern water diversion channel and two undated elliptical enclosures east of it.

There is abundant Iron Age III pottery throughout the site, including more than 20 cuneated bowls. The abundance of such bowls indicates the likelihood that some of the site's inhabitants were Cuthean or interacted with the deported Cuthean population of Samaria (Zertal 1989; Itach 2015).

Apparently the site functioned as a local administrative centre guarding the area and transit routes in the region, probably under Assyrian rule.

The site is very important in understanding the latest phases of the Assyrian

328. Aerial view of **Mras ed-Din (south-eastern complex)** during the 2019 excavation season, showing the area excavated in the upper southern complex (upper part of picture and see also a detailed plan below, Fig. 329), the lower southern complex covered with vegetation (lower part of picture, and note the Roman tower protruding from the vegetation at the bottom centre), and parts of the northern complex (to the right of the picture, completely covered with vegetation) (A. Lipkin).

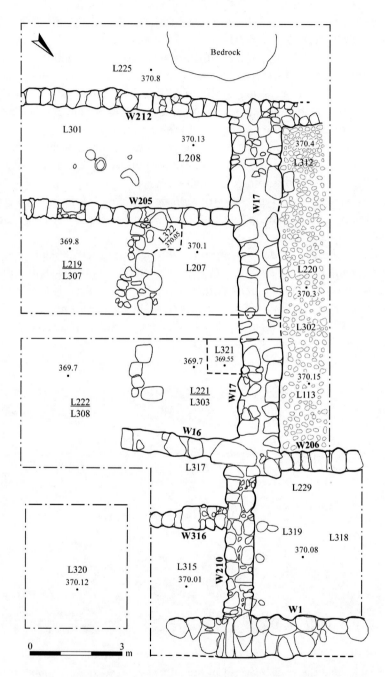

329. Plan of the 2019 excavations at the upper part of the southern complex at **Mras ed-Din (south-eastern complex)**. Note the well-built rooms of the four-room house, the rooms abutting to the north-east, and sections of the paved courtyard in the north-west.

control of Samaria on the eve of the dramatic changes of the 6th Century BCE, with the Babylonian and later the Persian conquests of the region.

Pottery and flint: the pottery and flint were collected from both sites in Mras ed-Din and combined without separation (see summary of finds in Site 172, fig. 326).
Other surveys: none.
Additional bibliography: Conder and Kitchener 1882: 394; GL: 118.

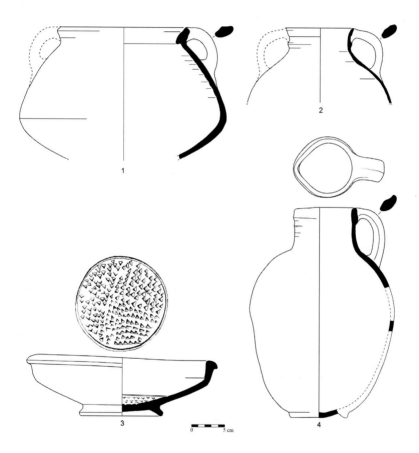

330. Typical Iron Age III pottery from the excavation of the destruction stratum at the southern complex at **Mras ed-Din (south-eastern complex)**. Note the complete cuneated bowl and the Judaite cooking pot.

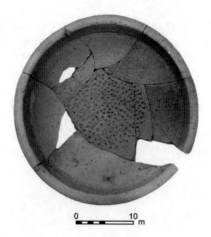

331. Iron Age III cuneated bowl from **Mras ed-Din (south-eastern complex)** (R. Shaffir).

◆ ◆ ◆

Site 174: 18-16/87/1

WADI KAMONEH (6)

Israel grid: 18898/16795
UTM grid: 7275/5547
Elevation: 145 m a.s.l., 100 m b.s.a.
Name: nearest place
Site type: courtyards
Area: 1,500 sq. m (1.5 dunams)
Topography: slope
Rock type: Judea Group
Soil: terra rossa, quality: 7

Cultivation: none
Cisterns: none
Water source: 'Ein Hafireh (no. 174), 2.3 km distant
Road: Wadi Kamoneh-Gittit Valley (C54), 200 m distant
Visit: January 2014; 4 surveyors; 40 sherds

Site on a rocky slope at the western edge of Wadi Kamoneh valley, 400 m west of E.P. 162 and 1.5 km east-north-east of Gittit.

Courtyard complex, built of large stones. The walls are one stone thick.

Central courtyard is large and irregular, 25×10 m. The walls are preserved to heights of 1 to 2 m (the eastern wall). The entrance to the courtyard is along a constructed path from the north. On both sides of the entrance are large piles of stones.

Array of structures, most of them dismantled, in the east, connected to the central courtyard.

Scanty remains of another courtyard in the south, and below it are terraces on the slopes.

The central courtyard and many other ones like it apparently served for strorage of crops and was part of the farm setup in E.P. 162.

Pottery (body sherds): Iron II – 7%; Late Roman – 93%.
Other surveys: none.

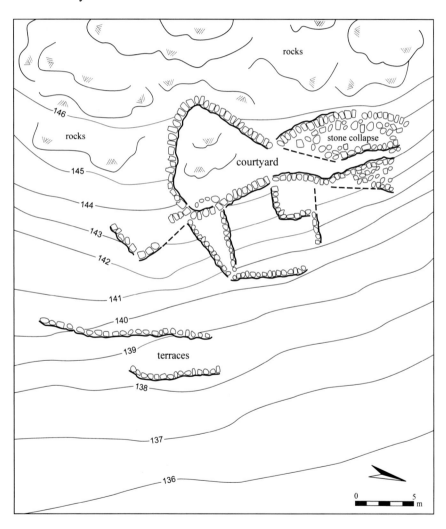

332. Plan of **Wadi Kamoneh (6)**.

Site 175: 18-16/97/1
ELEVATION POINT 162

Israel grid: 18922/16788
UTM grid: 7278/5547
Elevation: 150 m a.s.l., 40 m a.s.a.
Name: nearest place
Site type: farm, enclosures and threshing floors
Area: 2 ha (20 dunams)
Topography: spur and slope
Rock type: Judea Group

Soil: brown forest, quality: 2
Cultivation: none
Cisterns: 1
Water source: 'Ein Hafireh (no. 174), 2 km distant
Road: Wadi Kamoneh-Gittit Valley (C54), 300 m distant
Visit: December 1994; 4 surveyors; 50 sherds

Composite site on top and northern slope of a spur, 300 m north of the Alon road and 1.7 km east of Gittit. The Kamoneh valley is visible from the site.

Site has three parts:
- Central courtyard, 40×40 m, built of large stones. The wall thickness is 1.5 m. There are constructed entrances in the northern and southern walls. An elongated structure abuts the north-western corner and the western wall, with a room at the north end. In the south-western corner of the courtyard is a quarried and plastered water pool. At the centre of the courtyard is an elliptical structure. A wall starts from the northern wall of the courtyard towards the elliptical structure, next to the opening of a quarried cave and a cupmark. Several construction stages are evident in the walls.
- Two threshing floors and the remains of a third one, up the slope, about 25 m east of the courtyard. An 8×5 m rectangular structure, built of medium-sized stones, is 10 m east of the threshing floors. The structure is preserved up to 1.8 m high. A lintel was identified above the entrance. The structure is apparently modern.
- Two constructed enclosures at the top of the hillock, next to E.P. 162, one inside the other: an enclosure, 10 m diameter, and under it the remains of an earlier enclosure. A short wall starts from the upper enclosure.

The well-preserved courtyard is part of the developed agricultural array in the region during the Roman-Byzantine periods. The courtyard was probably reused during the Medieval period. The enclosures on E.P. 162 are typical of shepherds' structures in the region during the Iron Age.

LANDSCAPE UNIT 35

Pottery: Courtyard and threshing floors: Late Roman – 40%; Byzantine – 30%; Medieval – 20%; modern – 10%. Enclosures: Iron I-II – 100%.
Flint: 3 items: 1 flake, 1 blade and a retouched blade.
Other surveys: none.

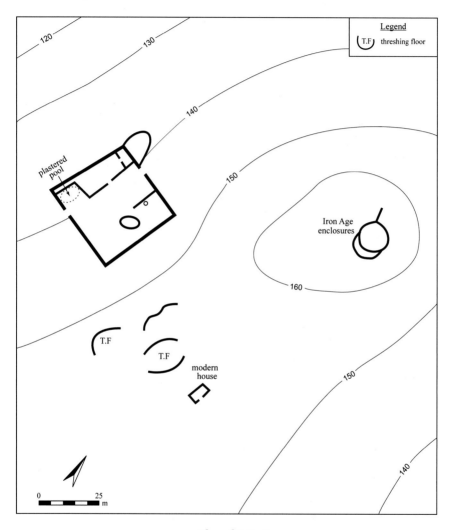

333. Plan of E.P. 162.

334. Aerial view east at E.P. 162 (A. Solomon).

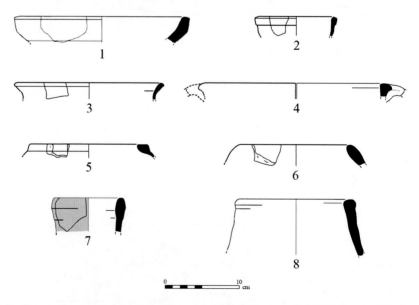

335. Pottery from E.P. 162: 1. Bowl/jar, red, Mod; 2. Bowl, red, LR-Byz; 3. Bowl, lt brn, LR-Byz; 4. Krater, dk gr, IA I-II; 5. Bowl, dk brn, LR-Byz; 6. Holemouth jar, lt brn, Med; 7. Jar, dk brn, black slip outside, Med; 8. Jar, lt brn, Mod.

Site 176: 18-16/66/2
ELEVATION POINT 390 (4)

Israel grid: 18611/16674 (site centre)
UTM grid: 7247/5535
Elevation: 380 m a.s.l., 10 m a.s.a.
Name: nearest place
Site type: structures
Area: 5,000 sq. m (5 dunams)
Topography: spur
Rock type: Judea Group
Soil: terra rossa, quality: 7

Cultivation: none
Cisterns: none
Water source: 'Ein el-Majdal (no. 185), 1.4 km distant
Road: Kh. Bani Fadil-Khalet el-Khashabeh (C53), 600 m distant
Visit: April 1997, November 2013; 7 surveyors; 40 sherds

Site spread around E.P 390 at the south-eastern edge of a rocky spur in Gittit Valley on both sides of the Alon road and south-west of Gittit.
Site has two parts:
- Small structures and courtyards, built of very large stones, among the rocks on the top of the hillock; between them are scattered Middle Bronze Age II sherds.
- Rectangular structure, east of the Alon road, and near it Iron Age I pottery was collected.

The site is linked to a large group of sites, dated to the Middle Bronze Age II and the Iron Age, in the north-eastern slope of E.P. 390.

Pottery: Middle Bronze II – 100% (in the west); Iron I – 100% (in the east).
Other surveys: Finkelstein et al. 1997: 798-799.

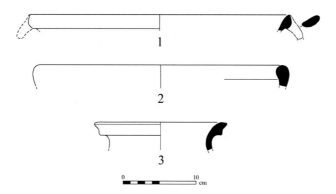

336. Pottery from **E.P. 390 (4)**: 1. Bowl/platter, lt brn, MB II; 2. Bowl, dk brn, IA I; 3. Jar, lt brn, MB II.

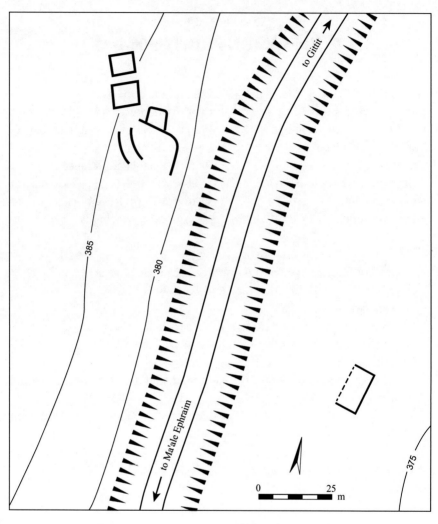

337. Plan of E.P. 390 (4).

Site 177: 18-16/66/1
ELEVATION POINT 390 (3)

Israel grid: 18608/16682
UTM grid: 7246/5535
Elevation: 377 m a.s.l., 10 m a.s.a.
Name: nearest place
Site type: courtyard and structure
Area: 5,000 sq. m (5 dunams)
Topography: valley edge
Rock type: Judea Group
Soil: terra rossa, quality: 8

Cultivation: field crops by the site
Cisterns: none
Water source: 'Ein el-Majdal (no. 185), 1.4 km distant
Road: Kh. Bani Fadil-Khalet el-Khashabeh (C53), 600 m distant
Visit: December 2014; 8 surveyors; 330 sherds

Site in the southern part of E.P. 390 ridge, on a slope descending eastwards to Gittit Valley, 1.6 km south-west of Gittit and 5 km south-east of Aqraba. The Alon road passes 60 m east of the site.

Site has two parts:
- Large courtyard, 35×35 m, built of one row of large stones. A bulldozer damaged the courtyard, removing the south-western corner. In the northern side is a 1 m wide opening. The courtyard probably belongs to the later periods of habitation at the site in the Roman and Byzantine periods. The courtyard is part of the agricultural array in the region during the Roman-Byzantine periods.
- Rectangular structure, 9×4.5 m, west of the courtyard, built of very large partially dressed stones. This was probably an earlier Middle Bronze Age II structure connected to the large sites from this period on the ridge of E.P.390.

In the Southern Samaria Survey (Finkelstein et al. 1997: 798-799) a sherd scatter and two corrals were mentioned at coordinates 18610/16695, and the sherds were dated to the MBA II, LBA, IA II/Pers and EM periods. As the location is in a field east of the current site, it is possible that the site described by us is the same one (with several descriptive and dating mismatches between the surveys).

Pottery: Middle Bronze II – 33%; Iron I-II – 1%; Late Roman – 40%; Byzantine (body sherds) – 5%; Medieval – 3%; Unidentified – 18%.
Flint: 6 items: 1 blade, 1 retouched flake and 4 sickle blades.
Other surveys: Finkelstein et al. 1997: 798-799 (?).

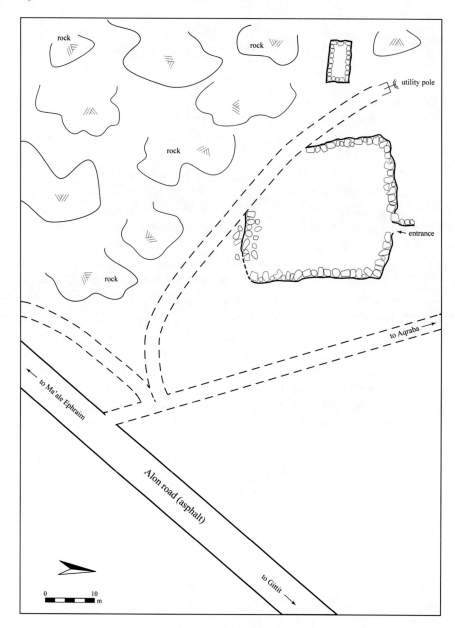

338. Plan of E.P. 390 (3).

339. Aerial photo looking east at E.P. 390 (3) (A. Solomon).

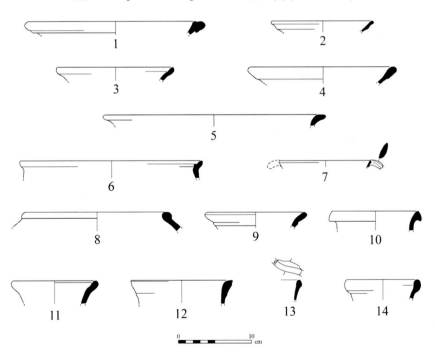

340. Pottery from E.P. 390 (3): 1. Bowl (?), reddish, MB II (?); 2-3. Bowls, lt brn, LR; 4. Bowl, lt brn, Med; 5. Krater, reddish, LR; 6. Krater, lt brn, Unidentified; 7. CP, reddish, LR; 8. CP, dk brn, MB II; 9. Jar, greyish, Unidentified; 10. Jar, greyish, MB II; 11. Jar, lt brn, Med; 12. Jar, lt brn, LR; 13. Jug, lt brn, IA I-II; 14. Jar, lt brn, IA II (?).

Site 178: 18-16/56/3
ELEVATION POINT 390 (1)

Israel grid: 18599/16656
UTM grid: 7246/5533
Elevation: 390 m a.s.l., 0 m a.s.a.
Name: nearest place
Site type: courtyard and sherd scatter
Area: 1,000 sq. m (1 dunam)
Topography: plain
Rock type: Judea Group
Soil: terra rossa, quality: 7

Cultivation: field crops by the site
Cisterns: none
Water source: 'Ein el-Majdal (no. 185), 1.2 km distant
Road: Kh. Bani Fadil-Khalet el-Khashabeh (C53), 300 m distant
Visit: February 2008; 4 surveyors; 38 sherds

Site in a cultivated field south of E.P. 390 ridge, 400 m north of Ma'ale Ephraim junction.

Rectangular courtyard, 36×22 m, built of two rows of medium-sized field stones. The thickness of the surrounding wall is 1.5 m. The courtyard is vacant except for a room, 5×4 m, in the south-western corner, totally covered by collapsed stones.

Remains of another completely dismantled structure, possibly a courtyard, 30 m to the south-east of the courtyard.

In a field south of the courtyard is an abundant sherd scatter, mostly from the Iron Age III: apparently structures or tents stood there, or it was a gathering place. The site was probably connected to the important nearby Iron Age III site at Kh. Mras ed-Din (Site 173).

The construction of the courtyard is probably from the Late Roman period, when a developed agricultural array was established in the region.

Pottery: Iron I – 10%; Iron II-III – 66%; Late Roman – 17%; Byzantine (body sherds) – 2%; Medieval (body sherds) – 5%.
Other surveys: none.

LANDSCAPE UNIT 35

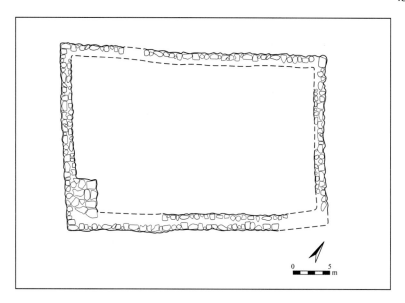

341. Plan of **E.P. 390 (1)**.

342. Aerial photo looking west at **E.P. 390 (1)** (A. Solomon).

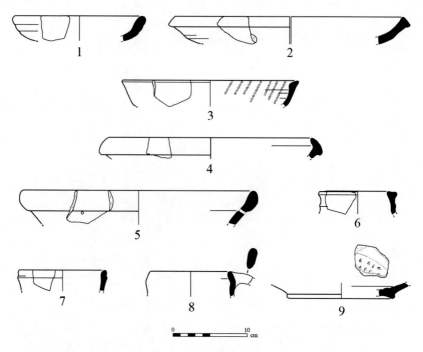

343. Pottery from E.P. 390 (1): 1-2, 4-5. Bowls, lt brn, IA II-III; 3. Bowl, dk gr, inside burnish traces, IA II-III; 7. Jug, lt brn, IA II-III; 8. Jug, lt brn, IA I; 9. Bowl, lt brn, cuneated dec inside base, IA III.

Site 179: 18-16/56/2

WADI ES-SAYAD (2)

Israel grid: 18549/16642
UTM grid: 7240/5531
Elevation: 400 m a.s.l., 5 m a.s.a.
Name: nearest place
Site type: sherd scatter
Area: 2,000 sq. m (2 dunams)
Topography: slope of spur at valley edge
Rock type: Judea Group

Soil: terra rossa, quality: 8
Cultivation: field crops by the site
Cisterns: none
Water source: 'Ein el-Majdal (no. 185), 700 m distant
Road: Kh. Bani Fadil-Khalet el-Khashabeh (C53), by the site
Visit: June 2014; 5 surveyors; 250 sherds

Abundant sherd scatter on a moderate slope at the edge of a spur, 2.2 km south-west of Gittit.

The sherds were collected in a field area of about 50×40 m, at the edge of a cultivated valley where cereals are now grown. The field is divided into plots by modern walls.

Pottery: Iron II (body sherds) – 12%; Late Roman – 24%; Byzantine – 16%; Medieval (Crusader and Mamluk) – 48%.
Flint: 6 items: 3 flakes, 1 blade and 2 scrapers.
Stone basalt bowl.
Other surveys: none.

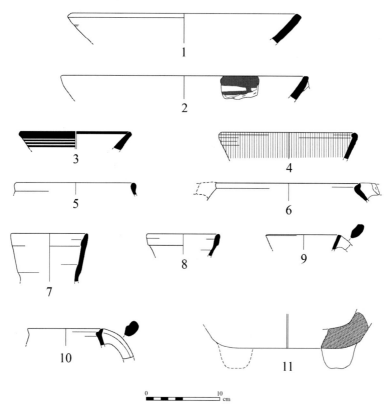

344. Finds from **Wadi es-Sayad (2)**: 1. Bowl, lt brn, Med; 2. Bowl, reddish, black dec over white, Med; 3. Bowl, lt colour, black dec over white, Med; 4. Bowl, lt brn, green glaze in and out, Med; 5. Bowl (?), lt brn, LR-Byz; 6. CP (?), lt brn, LR-Byz; 7. Jar, lt brn, Med (?); 8. Jug, lt brn, LR-Byz; 9. Jug, lt brn, LR; 10. Jug (?), lt brn, LR-Byz; 11. Bowl, basalt.

Site 180: 18-16/56/1
MA'ALE EPHRAIM JUNCTION

Israel grid: 18558/16621
UTM grid: 7242/5529
Elevation: 418 m a.s.l., 0 m a.s.a.
Name: given by the Survey
Site type: courtyard and flint scatter
Area: 1,000 sq. m (1 dunam)
Topography: moderate slope
Rock type: Judea Group
Soil: terra rossa, quality: 8
Cultivation: field crops by the site
Cisterns: none
Water source: 'Ein el-Majdal (no. 185), 600 m distant
Road: Kh. Bani Fadil-Khalet el-Khashabeh (C53), 200 m
Visit: April 2014; 3 surveyors; 75 sherds

Site in the western edge of a large field at the foot of the high Majdal Bani Fadil ridge, 500 m west of Ma'ale Ephraim Junction. There is a lookout from the site to Aqraba, the Gittit water reservoir, Kh. Mras ed-Din and Ma'ale Ephraim Junction.

Courtyard, 18×18 m, built of one row of large stones. Some of the stones, especially the corner stones, have slight dressing. Most of the encircling wall is preserved up to three courses high (1-1.5 m). The southern side survived less than the other ones, but a probable jamb was identified in it; and it is possible that the entrance was from that side. In the north-western corner of the courtyard is a room, 8×8 m, built in the same way as the courtyard.

Around the courtyard is a scanty scatter of sherds and flint.

The courtyard probably served for storage of crops. It was possibly also connected to the nearby Roman roads (C41, C53).

Pottery: Middle Bronze II – 20%; Iron I-II – 27%; Late Roman – 33%; Byzantine – 20%.

Flint: 32 items: 3 flake cores, 1 bladelet core, 1 core waste, 16 flakes, 8 blades, 2 bladelets, and a scraper.

Other surveys: none.

LANDSCAPE UNIT 35

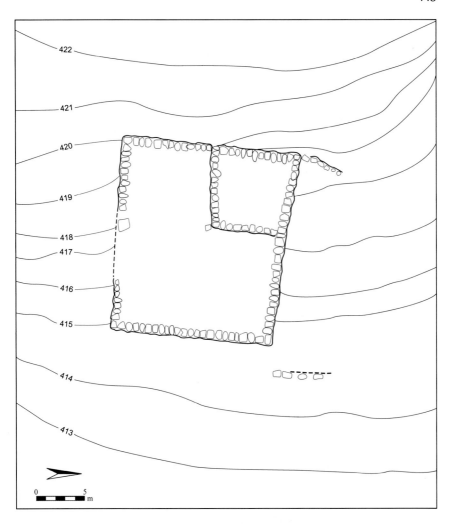

345. Plan of **Ma'ale Ephraim Junction**.

Site 181: 18-16/55/1
KHIRBET BANI FADIL

Israel grid: 18594/16564 (centre of the site)
UTM grid: 7245/5523
Elevation: 420 m a.s.l., 15 m a.s.a.
Name: ancient and on map
Site type: large and composite site
Area: 2 ha (20 dunams)
Topography: spur
Rock type: Judea Group
Soil: terra rossa, quality: 7

Cultivation: field crops by the site
Cisterns: 1
Water source: 'Ein el-Majdal (no. 185), 1 km distant
Roads: Kh. Bani Fadil-Khalet el-Khashabeh (C53) and Phasaelis-Neapolis (C41), by the site
Visit: May 1994, November 2005 and more; 8 surveyors; 200 sherds

Broad site on a spur of the rocky hillock of E.P. 444 and its slope, next to the abandoned asphalt road from Phasaelis-Ma'ale Ephraim to Aqraba, 600 m south of Ma'ale Ephraim Junction.

The location of the site in the 1:50,000 maps is incorrect, and is marked 250 m south of its correct location.

The site contains four parts (below from south to north):
- Rock-cut installations, terrace walls and remains of structures (no. 1 in plan) next to a pinewood near a curve in the old asphalt road (no. 1 in plan).
- North of no. 1, on the slope descending eastwards, are rock surfaces 300-400 m long and 50-70 m wide (no. 2), ending in the south at a line of fractured cliffs 2-3 m high containing several quarried caves. Bedouin now inhabit some of the caves.

    Several built courtyards opposite the caves in the eastern part of the cliffs.
    Remains of a constructed aqueduct, along the western part of the cliffs, the date of which is unknown.
- Completely terraced strip of land about 100 m wide, north of the rocky area. The terraces are connected to each other and some of them form inner courtyards. The majority of the collected sherds come from this part of the site. The centre of the ancient settlement was probably here (no. 3).
- Three constructed courtyards, rock cuttings and remains of structures built of very large stones survive north of the terraces in an area of exposed rocks. The construction is typical of that of the Middle Bronze Age II in the region (no. 4).

Porath (1968) found here: "A large rectangular structure composed of a large courtyard and several rooms south of it, on the step descending to the Jordan Valley, near the road from Tell Sheikh Diyab to Majdal Bani Fadil. The structure is built of large fieldstones and dressed stones. Pottery artefacts: Israelite I-II; Persian".

Ilan (1973: 291) observed here: "A daughter settlement of Majdal Bani Fadil".

The Southern Samaria Survey (Finkelstein et al. 1997: 797) describes: "A group of caves. Islamic pottery on the terraces in front of them. Some 150 m to the north, broad terraces with early pottery. The site is apparently connected to the caves, which served as shelter for shepherds and their flocks. The identification of the Early Bronze Age sherds is questionable".

Peleg (2012: 24-25) describes: "About ten large dwelling caves. All the caves are natural, some containing signs of rock-cutting. The openings of most of the caves, which are situated on one level of rock and slope down from south to north, face eastwards, except one cave, the opening of which faces north. Some of the caves served as flock pens for the shepherds of the area until recently. Fragments of Iron Age III ceramic artefacts were discovered…typical of Judea region in the seventh century BCE".

It seems that all the previous researchers at the site noted only some of the components of this important site, strategically located at one of the main routes and crossroads from the Jordan Valley to the Samaria region. The site was mainly settled in the MBA and Iron Ages, probably connected to its important strategic location.

Pottery: Middle Bronze II – 17%; Late Bronze (?) – 3%; Iron I – 30%; Iron II-III – 20%; Early Roman – 5%; Late Roman – 5%; Byzantine – 5%; Medieval – 10%; Ottoman – 10%.

346. Aerial photo looking west at **Khirbet Bani Fadil** (A. Solomon).

Flint: 250 items: 4 flake cores, 2 blade cores, 5 bladelet cores, 4 ridged blades, 2 core wastes, 107 flakes, 38 blades, 30 bladelet, 1 retouched flake, 27 retouched blades, 20 side scrapers, 4 geometric sickle blades, 4 scrapers and 2 borers. The geometric sickle blades testify highly reasonably that at least part of the find is from the MBA II.

Other surveys: Porath 1968, sites 182 and 183; Finkelstein et al. 1997: 796-798.
Additional bibliography: Conder and Kitchener 1882: 392; GL: 118.

347. Plan of **Khirbet Bani Fadil**.

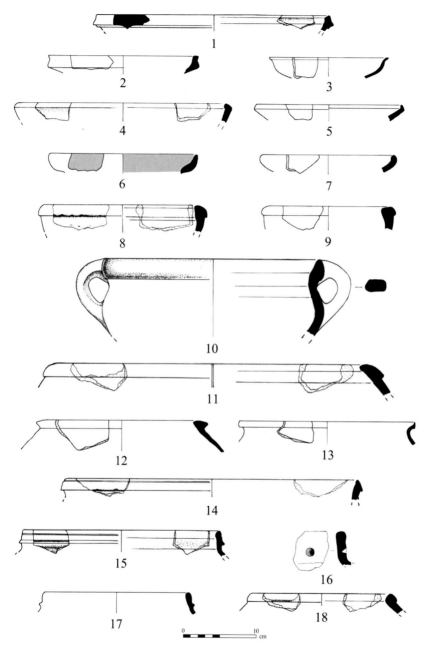

348. Pottery from **Khirbet Bani Fadil**: 1. Bowl, red, Rom-Byz; 2. Bowl, lt brn, LR; 3. Bowl, lt colour, LB (?); 4-5. Bowls, lt brn, MB II; 6. Bowl, brn, cream colour slip, IA II; 7. Bowl, brn, IA I; 8. Bowl, brn, IA II; 9. Bowl, gr, IA II; 10. Krater, brn, IA I; 11. Krater, lt brn, IA II; 12. Krater, brn, IA II; 13. CP, brn, LB/IA I; 14. CP, gr, LB/IA I; 15. CP, brn, IA I; 16. CP, brn, MB II; 17. CP, brn, IA I; 18. CP, dk brn, MB II.

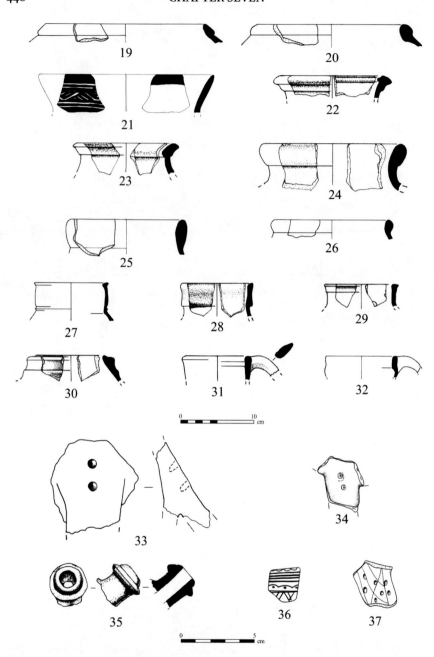

349. Pottery from **Khirbet Bani Fadil** (continued): 19-20. CPs, brn, MB II; 21. Krater/jar, reddish, black dec over white slip, Med; 22-23. Jars, lt brn, MB II; 24-25. Pithoi, lt brn, IA I; 26. Jar, lt brn, IA I; 27. Jar, black, Byz; 28. Jar, gr, ER; 29. Jar, lt colour, Rom (?); 30. Jar, dk brn, IA II-III; 31. Jug, lt brn, IA I-II; 32. Jug, lt brn, IA II; 33-34. Handles, brn, incised dec, IA I; 35. Pipe, lt brn, Ott; 36. Body sherd, violet dec over cream colour, Med; 37. Handle, lt colour, incised dec, Med.

BIBLIOGRAPHY

ABBREVIATIONS

ANET = Pritchard, J. B., (ed.), 1969. *Ancient Near Eastern Texts Related to the Old Testament* (3rd edition), Princeton.

GL = 1976. *Department of Antiquities, Geographical list of the Records Files, 1918-1948*, Jerusalem.

War = *Josephus, The Jewish War*, with an English translation by Thackeray, H. St. J., (*Loeb Classical Library*), London 1967-1968.

LITERATURE

Abel, F. M., 1935. *La Géographie de la Palestine*, seconde partie, Paris.

Avi-Yonah, M., 1953. "The Madeba Mosaic Map", *Eretz-Israel* 2: 129-156 (Hebrew).

Avi-Yonah, M., 1956. "The Samaritan Revolts against the Roman Empire", *Eretz-Israel* 4: 127-132 (Hebrew).

Avi-Yonah, M., 1962. *Historical Geography of Eretz-Israel*, Jerusalem (Hebrew).

Bagatti, B., 1979. *Antichi villaggi cristiani di Samaria*, Gerusalemme (Italian).

Bar, S., 2010. "Early Bronze Age I 'Um Hammad Ware' – A Study in Regionalism", *Palestine Exploration Quarterly*, 142/2: 82-94.

Bar, S., 2013. "Shifting Settlement Patterns in the Southern Jordan Valley and the Desert Fringes of Samaria during the Early Bronze age I Period", *Palestine Exploration Quarterly*, 145/2: 90-107.

Bar, S., 2014. *The Dawn of the Bronze Age*, Leiden and Boston.

Bar, S., 2015a. "The Settlement Patterns in the Northern Samaria Highlands during the Late Chalcolithic Period", *Palestine Exploration Quarterly*, 147/2: 87-103.

Bar, S., 2015b. "New Aspects of the Intermediate Bronze Age in the Southern Jordan Valley and Eastern Samaria", *Judea and Samaria Research Studies*, 24: 13-25 (Hebrew).

Bar, S., 2015c. "Khirbet el-Meiyiteh, Area A Remains of an Intermediate Bronze Age Fortified Site in Nahal Milcha", *In The Highland's Depth* 7: 207-217 (Hebrew).

Bar, S., 2017. "A new suggestion for the identification of Thena of Eusebius" *The Highland's Depth* 5: 11-22 (Hebrew).

Bar, S., 2018. "Khirbet Mras ed-Din in Eastern Samaria: Evidence of the Assyrian mass deportation system and the settlement of Foreigners in Samaria after the Conquest of the Israelite Kingdom", *Jordan Valley Research Studies* 2: 17-26 (Hebrew).

Bar, S., and Zertal, A., 2019. *The Manasseh Hill Country Survey vol. 7- The South-Eastern Samaria Shoulder, from Wadi Rashash to Wadi 'Aujah*, Haifa (Hebrew).

Bar, S., and Zertal, A., 2020. *The Manasseh Hill Country Survey vol. 8 - The Slopes of Western Samaria, from Nahal Shechem to Wadi Zir*, Haifa (Hebrew).

Bar, S., Cohen, O., and Zertal, A., 2013. "New Aspects of the Intermediate Bronze Age (IB/MBI/EBIV): Khirbet el-Meiyiteh – A Fortified Site on the Eastern Fringe of Samaria", *Revue Biblique* 120:161-181.

Bar-Adon, P., 1972. "The Judaean Desert and Plain of Jericho". In Kochavi, M. (ed.), *Judaea Samaria and the Golan Archaeological survey 1967-1968*, Jerusalem. Pp. 91-149 (Hebrew).

Bayer, G., 1940. "Neapolis (Nablus) und sein Geibet in der Kreuzfahrzeit", *Zeitschrift des Deutschen Palästina – Vereins* 63: 155-209.

Benoit, O. P., Milik, J. T. and de Vaux, R., 1961. *Les Grottes de Murabbaat*, Oxford.

Ben-Aryeh, Y., 1970. *The Rediscovery of the Holy Land in the Nineteenth Century*, Jerusalem (Hebrew).

Ben-Yosef, D., 2007. *The Jordan Valley During Iron Age I: Aspects of its History and the Archaeological Evidence for its Settlement* (Doctoral dissertation). University of Haifa, Haifa (Hebrew).

Ben-Zvi, I., 1976. *The Book of the Samaritans*, Jerusalem (Hebrew).

Borenstein, A., 1993. "Precious Things of Heaven – Ancient Agriculture in Samaria", in Erlich, Z., and Eshel. Y. (eds.), *Judea and Samaria Studies Proceedings of the 3rd Annual Meeting – 1993*. Kedumim-Ariel, 87-115 (Hebrew).

Campbell, E. F., 1968. "The Shechem Area Survey", *Bulletin of the American Schools of Oriental Research* 190: 19-41.

Campbell, E. F., 1991. *Shechem II, Portrait of a Hill Country Vale – The Shechem Regional Survey*, Atlanta.

Cohen, A., 1998. *The History of Eretz Israel under the Mamluk and Ottoman Rule (1260-1804)*, Jerusalem (Hebrew).

Cohen, H., 2013. *The Southern Jordan Rift Valley and the Desert-Frontier Region of Samaria during the Middle Bronze Age II* (Doctoral dissertation). University of Haifa, Haifa (Hebrew).

Conder, C. R. and Kitchener, H. H., 1882. *Survey of Western Palestine II: Samaria*, London.

Dan, J., 1977. "The Soils of Judea and Samaria", in Shmueli, A., Grossman, D., Zeevy, R. (eds.), *Judea and Samaria Studies in Settlement Geography*. Jerusalem. Pp. 14-29 (Hebrew).

Dorsey, D. A., 1991. *The roads and Highways of Ancient Israel*, Baltimore and London.

Drori, J., and Reiner, E., 1981. "The Land of Israel in the Mamluk State", in Shavit, Y., (ed.) *The History of Eretz Israel under the Mamluk and Ottoman Rule (1260-1804)*. Jerusalem. Pp. 9-90 (Hebrew).

Eisenberg, E., Yevin, Z., and Damati, E., 1993. "Khirbet el-Makhruq", in Stern, E. (ed.), *The New Encyclopedia of Archaeological Excavations in The Holy Land*, vol. 3. Jerusalem. Pp. 929-932.

Finkelstein, I., 1986. *The Archaeology of the Period of Settlement and Judges*, Tel-Aviv (Hebrew).

Finkelstein, I., Lederman, Z., and Bunimovitz, S., 1997. *Highlands of Many Cultures – The Southern Samaria Survey*, Tel-Aviv.

Gil, M., 1981. "The Land of Israel during the Moslem Rule (634-1099)", in Prawer, J. (ed.), *The History of Eretz Israel Under Moslem and Crusader Rule 634-1291*, vol. 6. Jerusalem. Pp. 15-160 (Hebrew).

Grintz, Y. M., 1986. *Sefer Yehudith (The book of Judith). A Reconstruction of the Original Hebrew Text with Introduction, Commentary, Appendices and Indices*, Jerusalem (Hebrew).

Grossman, D., 1977. "The founding of Off –Shoot Villages in the Samaria Periphery-Background and Process", in Shmueli, A., Grossman, D., and Zeevy, R. (eds.), *Judea and Samaria Studies in Settlement Geography*, vol. 2. Jerusalem. Pp. 396-410 (Hebrew).

Grossman, D., 1986. "Oscillations in the Rural Settlement of Samaria and Judaea in the Ottoman Period", in Dar, S., and Safrai, Z., (eds.), *Shomron Studies*. Tel-Aviv. Pp. 303-388 (Hebrew).

Guérin, M. V., 1874. *Description Géographique, Historique et Archéologique de la Palestine*, Paris.

Hadashot Arkheologiyot 45 (1973). "Survey Near Nahal Gittit" (P. 19) (Hebrew).

Halperin, C., 1966-1987. *Encyclopaedia of Agriculture*, Tel-Aviv (Hebrew).

Hoter, R., 1971. "Shomron Mountains", in Dar, S., and Ruth, Y. (eds.), *Shomron – A Collection of Articles and Sources*, Tel-Aviv. Pp. 224-235 (Hebrew).

Hovers, E., and Ben-Yosef, O., 1987. "A Prehistoric Survey of Eastern Samaria: Preliminary report", *Israel Exploration Journal*, 37/2-3: 77-87 (Hebrew).

Hutteroth, W. D., and Abdulfattah, K., 1977. *Historical Geography of Palestine, Transjordan and Southern Syria in the Late 16th Century*, Erlangen.

Ilan, Z., 1973. *The Jordan Valley and the Samarian Desert*, Tel-Aviv (Hebrew).

Ilan, Z., and Damati, E., 1975. "Ancient Roads in the Samarian Desert", *Museum Haaretz Yearbook* 17-18: 45-51 (Hebrew).

Itach, G., 2015. "The Wedge-Incised Bowl and the Assyrian Deportation – a Reexamination", *In The Highland's Depth* 5: 71-92 (Hebrew).

Kagan, E. D., 2009. "Remains from the Byzantine and Early Islamic Periods at the Gittit Quarry", in Yezersky, I. (ed.), *Excavations and Discoveries in*

Samaria. Jerusalem. Pp. 225-226.

Kochavi, M., (ed.) 1972. *Judea, Samaria and the Golan Archaeological Survey 1967-1968*, Jerusalem (Hebrew).

Lapp, N., 1993. "Wadi ed-Daliyeh", in Stern, E. (ed.), *The New Encyclopedia of Archaeological Excavations in The Holy Land*, vol. 1. Jerusalem. Pp. 320-323.

Markus, M., 1992. *The Jordan Rift Valley and Eastern Samaria: Landscape Survey and Excursion Routs*, Tel-Aviv (Hebrew).

Mazar, B., 1986. "Pharaoh Shishak's Campaign to the Land of Israel", in Ahituv, S., and Levine, B. A. (eds.), *The Early Biblical Period, Historical Studies*. Jerusalem. Pp. 139-150.

Nebenzahl, K., 1986. *Maps of the Holy Lands: Images of Terra Sancta through two millennia*, Tel-Aviv.

Nobbe, C. F. A. (ed.), 1845. *Claudii Ptolemaei, Geographia*, Lipsiae.

Notley, R. S., and Safrai, Z., 2005. *Eusebius, Onomasticon, The Place Names of Divine Scripture*, Boston, Leiden.

Palmer, E. H., 1881. *The Survey of Western Palestine, Arabic and English Name Lists Collected During the Survey*, London.

Peleg, Y., 2012. "Iron Age Cave Settlements in the Land of Benjamin's Frontier Desert, *Judea and Samaria Research Studies* 21: 23-33 (Hebrew).

Porath, Y., 1968. *The Samaria Survey (B)*, Unpublished Text (Hebrew).

Safrai, Z., 1980. *Frontiers and Rule in Eretz Israel in the Time of the Mishnah and the Talmud*, Tel-Aviv.

Schein, S., 1981. "Eretz Israel in the Time of the Crusaders", in Prawer, Y. (ed.), *The History of Eretz Israel Under Moslem and Crusader Rule (part B), 1099-1291*. Jerusalem. Pp. 177-351 (Hebrew).

Shachar, A., (ed. in chief), 1995. *The New Atlas of Israel*, Jerusalem (Hebrew).

Spanier, Y., 1993. "The Relationship between Nomads and Permanent Settlements in East Samaria – Past and Present", in Erlich, Z. H., and Eshel, Y. (eds.), *Judea and Samaria Research Studies, Proceedings of the 3rd Annual Meeting*. Kedumim-Ariel. Pp. 379-387 (Hebrew).

Tavger, A., 2012. "The Status and Size of the Province of Shamrayn (Samaria) during the Persian Period: A Reexamination", *In the Highland's Depth* 2: 65-89 (Hebrew).

Thomsen, P., 1917. "Die Roemischen Meilensteine der provinzen Syria, Arabia und Palästina", *Zeitschrift des Deutschen Palästina-Vereins* 40: 1-143.

Tsafrir, Y., Di Segni, L., and Green, J., 1994. *Tabula Imperii Romani Judea Palestina: Eretz Israel in the Hellenistic, Roman and Byzantine Periods – Maps and Gazetteer*, Jerusalem.

Van de Velde, C. W. M., 1854. *Narrative of a Journey through Syria and Palestina in 1851 and 1852*. Edinburgh and London.

Wallis, G., 1961. "Thaanath Silo", *Zeitschrift des Deutschen Palastina – Vereins* 77:

38-45.

Yadin, Y., 1964. "The Valley of Succoth in the Campaigns of David and Ahab", in Liver, J. (ed.), *The Military History of the Land of Israel in Biblical Times*. Tel-Aviv. Pp. 170-182 (Hebrew).

Yekutieli, U., 1971. "Samaria during the Moslem Period", in Dar, S., and Ruth, Y., (eds.), *Shomron, a Collection of Articles and Sources*. Tel-Aviv. Pp. 204-218 (Hebrew).

Zertal, A., 1989. "The Wedge-Shaped Decorated Bowl and the Origin of the Samaritans", *Bulletin of the American Schools of Oriental Research* 276: 77-84.

Zertal, A., 2004a. *The Manasseh Hill Country Survey vol. 1 - the Shechem Syncline*, Leiden and Boston.

Zertal, A., 2004b. "Taanath Shiloh (Joshua 16:6)", in Heltzer, M., and Malul, M. (eds.), *Teshurot Lavishur*. Tel-Aviv – Jaffa. Pp. 229-237.

Zertal, A., 2008. *The Manasseh Hill Country Survey vol. 2 - the Eastern Valleys and the Fringes of the Desert*, Leiden and Boston.

Zertal, A., 2009. "The Geographical and Archaeological Reality of the Book of Judith", *Eretz Israel* 29: 111-175 (Hebrew).

Zertal, A., 2018. *A Nation Born, the Altar on Mount Ebal and the Birth of Israel*, Ofra.

Zertal, A., and Bar, S., 2017. *The Manasseh Hill Country Survey vol. 4 - from Nahal Bezeq to the Sartaba*, Leiden and Boston.

Zertal, A., and Bar, S., 2019. *The Manasseh Hill Country Survey vol. 5 – The Middle Jordan Valley, from Wadi Fasael to Wadi 'Aujah*, Leiden and Boston.

Zertal, A., and Mirkam, N., 2016. *The Manasseh Hill Country Survey vol. 3 - from Nahal 'Iron to Nahal Shechem*, Leiden and Boston.

PART THREE

APPENDICES AND INDICES

APPENDIX A

EXCAVATIONS OF A MIDDLE ROMAN PERIOD TOWER IN MRAS ED-DIN

Nofar Shamir and Shay Bar

A. INTRODUCTION

Two stone-built towers were found during the survey of the site and the first excavation season at Mras ed-Din (Site 173). One of these structures in the north-eastern part of the main excavation area was probed (Figs. 1.1-1.2). The pottery from the tower was dated to the Middle Roman period. This Appendix presents the architecture and pottery finds, and discusses the possible reasoning for erecting this structure (and the adjacent unexcavated tower - Figs. 1.3-1.4) on the eastern slope of the Mras ed-Din ridge, above the prosperous fields of the Gittit Valley.

Fig. 1.1: Aerial view of Mras ed-Din. The tower is located at the bottom left.

APPENDIX A

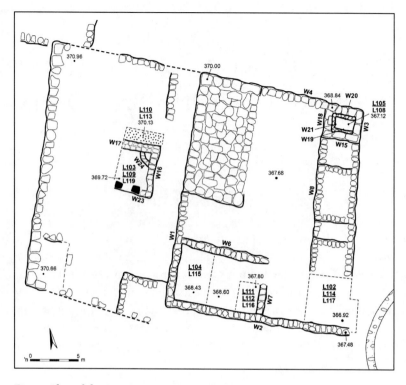

Fig. 1.2: Plan of the 2017 excavation season - main excavation area. The tower is located at the upper right section of the plan.

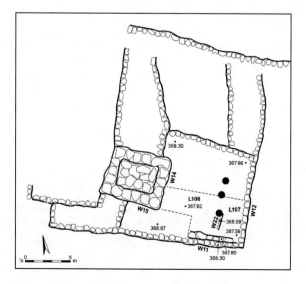

Fig. 1.3: Plan of the 2017 excavation season - northern excavation area. The unexcavated northern tower is clearly visible at the middle of the plan.

Fig. 1.4: The unexcavated northern tower.

B. ARCHITECTURE

The excavated tower (Figs. 1.5-1.8) has two distinct architectonic phases:
1. The foundation of the tower, well-built with small and medium-sized local stones (walls W19-W21; Figs. 1.7-1.8). This foundation was about 1 m wide and 1.3 m deep (five stone courses).
2. The upper structure built of massive boulders (walls W3-W4, W15 and W18; Figs. 1.6-1.7). In the lower course of the boulders, smaller and medium-sized stones were inserted between and below the large stones for stability. This construction was about 0.8 m wide (slightly narrower than the foundations), and up to 1.2 m high (up to two stone courses). These boulders were laid upon the smaller foundation construction.

The inside dimensions of the tower, between the foundation walls, were 1.2×1.4 m, and the outside dimensions were 3.2×3.7 m.

The probable floor level of the tower, at the elevation of the discovered hewn threshold in wall W18, was at the exact level of this change in masonry (Fig. 1.7). A possible 0.8×0.4 m flat stone step was found below the threshold, enabling entrance to the tower from the south.

The floor level itself was probably only a few cm above L101, and did not survive.

According to the survey plan, two poorly preserved walls seem to abut the tower's southern wall, W15. Another wall, W4, the northern wall of the tower, seems to continue to the south. Without further excavations we cannot determine the exact dates and stratigraphic relationship of these walls.

Although two architectonic phases were noted, they were probably built as a single construction activity and belong to a single stratum (as is also supported by the pottery finds - see below).

In the unexcavated northern tower (Fig. 1.4) only two rows of massive boulders are visible, and they are very similar to the upper structure of the excavated tower. Also here, several undated walls seem to abut the tower (Fig. 1.3). It is possible that both towers and at least some of the abutting walls were part of the same Roman stratum at the site.

Locus	Type	Opening elevation	Closing elevation	Baskets
101	Removing stone collapse of tower	368.56	368.39	1001
105	Fill of tower below L101 between walls W19-W21	368.39	368.25	1005, 1009
108	Fill of tower above bedrock; below L105 and between walls W19-W21	368.25	367.12	1012, 1018

Table 1.1: Loci of the excavated tower.

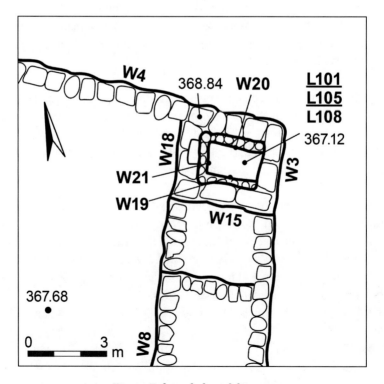

Fig. 1.5: Enlarged plan of the tower.

Fig. 1.6: The tower before excavation.

Fig. 1.7: The tower Locus 101, probably the fill below the tower's original floor. Note the hewn threshold on the right, probably the level of the original floor of the structure.

Fig. 1.8: The tower at the end of the excavation. Note the bedrock (L108), and the different architectural construction phases.

C. POTTERY

A total of 660 sherds were collected from the excavation of the tower. All the pottery was found in the sealed fills below the massive collapse of its upper walls.

Apart from a few Iron Age sherds (about 10% of the total), all the pottery is dated to the Roman period. A detailed study of the few indicative rims presented here suggests a more accurate date in the Middle Roman period (1st-2nd Century CE).

The finds were not found in primary deposition or *in situ*, but some sherds originated from the three loci, suggesting a deliberate fill of the tower foundations before the construction of the floor of the structure. This suggests that the date obtained here is actually a *terminus post quem* date for the construction of the tower.

The Assemblage (Fig. 1.9)

1. Casserole, 24 cm in diameter, with a cut rim. Parallels: Masada Type M-FP2A (Bar-Nathan and Yadin 2006, pl. 31:80) described as a frying pan, and dated between the 1st to the 3rd Centuries CE; Shuafat (Terem 2016, pl. 55-56) dated between the two revolts (70–135 CE); Judean sites (Rapuano 2013, fig. 5:87) dated between the two revolts.
2. Bowl, incurved rim, 13.5 cm in diameter. Parallel: Masada Type M-BL1A (Bar-Nathan and Yadin 2006, pl. 25:2) the commonest bowl at the site with a date range starting during the Hellenistic period and ending in the 2nd Century CE.
3. Cooking pot, everted triangular rim, 12 cm in diameter. Parallel: Masada Type M-CP4 (Bar-Nathan and Yadin 2006, pl. 29:41-42) dated between the 1st Century and the first third of the 2nd Centuries CE.
4. Cooking pot, everted triangular rim, 13 cm in diameter. Parallels: Jerusalem (Geva and Hershkovitz 2006, pl. 4.5:20) 1st Century BCE to 1st Century CE; Samaria (Crowfoot et al 1957, fig. 71.6: 302-303) 3rd Century CE; Shuafat CP type 1 (Terem 2016, pl. 48: 443) dated between the 1st and the 2nd Centuries CE. Terem suggests that this is a cooking pot typical of the villages of Judea between the two revolts.
5. Casserole, everted rim, 14.5 cm in diameter. Parallels: Masada Type M-CS3 (Bar-Nathan and Yadin 2006, pl. 30:65) dated between the end of the 1st Century BCE and the 1st Century CE; Jericho type J-CS1B (Bar-Nathan 2002, pl. 12:159) dated to the 1st Century BCE.
6. Juglet, ridge on the lower part of the rim, 2 cm rim diameter. Parallels: Masada Camp F (Magness 2009, fig. 9:1) dated between the 1st and the early 2nd Centuries CE; Shuafat (Terem 2016, pl. 58: 518) dated to the 1st Century CE; Jericho type J-JT1A1 (Bar-Nathan 2002, pl. 10:86, ill. 39) dated to the

Herodian era; Masada Type M-JT7 (Bar-Nathan and Yadin 2006, pl. 33:24) dated to the last quarter of the 1st Century CE; Jerusalem type 2 (Geva 2010, pl. 4.3:7) dated to the Herodian era.

7. Jar, thickened grooved rim, 8 cm rim diameter. Parallel: Jericho type J-SJ21 (Bar-Nathan and Eisenstadt 2013, pl. 1.1:560) 1st Century BCE to 1st Century CE.
8. Jar, rounded outward rim, high neck with a ridge at its base, rim diameter 8.5 cm. Parallels: Shuafat (Terem 2016, pl. 15: 243) dated between the two revolts (70-135 CE); Masada Type M-SJ12 (Bar-Nathan and Yadin 2006, pl. 11:59) dated between the 1st and the first third of the 2nd Centuries CE; Jerusalem Giv'ati Parking Lot type SJ3d (Tchekhanovets 2013, fig. 5.2:13) dated between the end of the 1st Century BCE and the 1st Century CE.
9. Jar, thickened outward rim, high neck, 8 cm rim diameter. Parallels: Jericho type J-SJ21 (Bar-Nathan and Eisenstadt 2013, pl. 1.9:676) 1st Century BCE to 1st Century CE; Masada Type M-SJ24 (Bar-Nathan and Yadin 2006, pl. 16:101) dated between the end of the 1st and the first quarter of the 2nd Centuries CE.
10. Jar, outward folded rim, ridges on bent neck, 12 cm rim diameter. Parallel: Masada Camp F (Magness 2009, fig. 8:3) 1st Century CE.
11. Jar, outward folded rim, wheel lines on bent neck, 11 cm rim diameter. Parallel: as number 10 above.
12. Jar/jug, triangular rim, outward ridge on rim, high neck, 9.5 cm rim diameter. Parallel: Jericho type J-JT1A1 (Bar-Nathan 2002, pl. 8:55) dated to 31 to 15 BCE.
13. Pithos, thickened rim with an inner ridge, narrow neck, grooved body, 13 cm rim diameter. Parallel: Jericho type J-PT1 (Bar-Nathan 2002, pl. 7:50) dated to the Herodian era.

As is clearly visible from this small assemblage, most of the parallels are dated to the 1st century and the first half of the 2nd Century CE, the period known as the Middle Roman period. No item is dated later than the 2nd Century, and some of the types end during the 1st Century, and therefore, since the pottery from the tower gives a *terminus post quem* date for its construction we can date the activity at the site to the end of the 1st and the first half of the 2nd Centuries CE.

We should also point out the two cooking pots from the assemblage (Fig. 1.9: 3-4), that have a wide ridge on shoulder. These are typical Judean types, also dated to between the two revolts (Terem 2016, pl. 48: 443).

It is interesting to note that albeit small, the assemblage shows no imported pottery, and there is little tableware. This supports a non-domestic activity at the site.

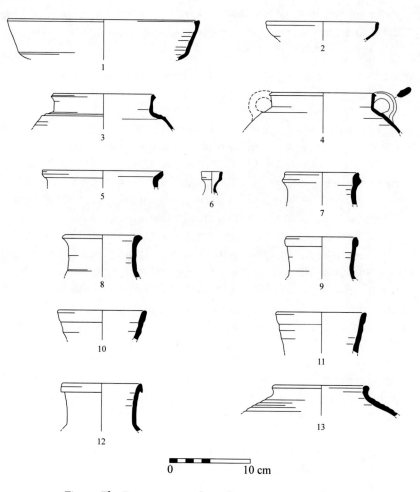

Fig. 1.9: The Roman pottery from the tower at Mras ed-Din.

No.	Locus	Type	Description
1	101+108	Casserole	thin walls; reddish fabric; cut rim; connected with no. 3; 24 cm rim diameter
2	105+108	Bowl	incurved rim bowl. local fabric? thin walls; one groove below the rim outside; 13.5 cm rim diameter
3	108	Cooking pot	orange fabric, red burnish outside; one ridge on the neck; 12 cm rim diameter
4	108	Cooking pot	orange-reddish fabric; large ridge on shoulder; 13 cm rim diameter
5	105	Casserole	red; 14.5 cm rim diameter
6	108	Juglet	grey; 2 cm rim diameter
7	108	Jar	red-orange; 8 cm rim diameter
8	108	Jar	dark grey, white grits; high neck, groove on shoulder; 8.5 cm rim diameter
9	108	Jar	light orange medium white grits; 8 cm rim diameter
10	101	Jar	light brown fabric; white grits; folded rim; 12 cm rim diameter
11	101	Jar	light brown fabric; white grits; folded rim; wheel lines on neck, outward; 11 cm rim diameter
12	105	Jar/jug	light orange; 9.5 cm rim diameter
13	108	Pithos	light orange; 13 cm rim diameter

Table 1.2: Accompanying data to Fig. 1.9.

D. THE TOWERS IN CONTEXT

The tower at Mras ed-Din is a small segment of the very well attested activities in the eastern Samaria shoulder during the Middle Roman period. At the Roman period, this region showed gradual development and settlement increase compared to the earlier Hellenistic period. This is best seen in the intensified agricultural activities in the area (see Chapter 3.11) and the construction of a paved road system transecting many parts of the region (see Chapter 1.4).

The main Roman centre nearby was the village of Aqraba, 4 km to the north-west. During the Second Temple period it was an important town mentioned by Josephus as Akrabbatá, the capital of a district called Akrabbatène (War III, iii: 5). Eusebius called the town Akrabbeim and the district Akrabbatinés (see Chapter 4). The Judean cooking pots in the assemblage possibly represent a glimpse into the lives of the inhabitants or workers of possible Judaite origin in the heartland of the Akrabbatène district. We thus suggest that the valley of Gittit, one of the richest valleys of eastern Samaria, was the agricultural hinterland of Akrabbatène during the Roman period.

Historical sources mention the capture of the Jewish region of Akrabbatá during the First Revolt by Titus Flavius Vespasianus six months before the destruction of the Second Temple in Jerusalem (70 CE; War IV, ix:9). After the end of the revolt, Jewish communities continued to live in the region (the time-span of the Middle Roman period). Hadrian suppressed the Bar Kokhba revolt (135 CE; the end of the Middle Roman period), destroyed most of the Jewish communities, and settled the region with a Samaritan population.

The ridge of Mras ed-Din is rich in agricultural installations, and at least some of the dated features are from the Roman-Byzantine periods. The two very large courtyards at the western part of the ridge, 300 m west of the towers (Site 172), alongside many caves, hewn installations and cisterns, are probably segments of a large agricultural site.

A smaller Roman presence is attested in several sites near Mras ed-Din. Most of them are small agricultural sites (mainly courtyards, enclosures and installations), but some of them are larger. Some examples are the farms at Elevation Point 419 (6), 1 km to the north-west and Elevation Point 419 (3), 1.5 km to the north; and the possible fortresses at es-Sireh (1), 1.1 km to the north-west and Elevation Point 432 (9), 1.3 km to the north. If the two towers at Mras ed-Din are an agricultural phenomenon (stand-alone or part of the larger agricultural site on the ridge) they fit well with the intensive Roman agricultural activities in the valley.

Similar Roman towers were recorded and excavated in many parts of Samaria; e.g. by Dar (1986) in Western Samaria, mainly in the vicinity of Bet Lid (Bar and Zertal 2020, Site 40).

Another explanation for the presence and nature of the towers is their location close to the Roman road system traversing the Gittit Valley. Three roads pass not far from the site (see Fig. 11):
- Regional road C41 from Fasaelis to Neapolis in the small valley, 400 m west of Mras ed-Din;
- Local road C54 ascends from Wadi Kamoneh in the general direction of the site, but has been destroyed by the modern cultivation, and is not visible near the site's vicinity and its route is not clear;
- Local road C58 crosses the Gittit Valley from north to south, and short sections of it are still visible to the north of the site.

While the local roads are probably intended to support agricultural activities in the valley, the regional C41 road is important and needed maintenance all year round. It is possible that these towers were part of the road maintenance and control system.

Further explorations of the site and its vicinity will assist in further understanding the local and regional activities during the Middle Roman period in Eastern Samaria.

REFERENCES

Bar, S., and Zertal, A., 2020. *The Manasseh Hill Country Survey vol 8 - The Slopes of Western Samaria, from Nahal Shechem to Wadi Zir*, vol. 8, Haifa (Hebrew).

Bar-Nathan, R., 2002. *Hasmonean and Herodian Palaces at Jericho: Final Reports of the 1973-1987 Excavations. The Pottery*, Jerusalem.

Bar-Nathan, R. and Eisenstadt, I., 2013. "The Ceramic Corpus from the Roman Estate at Jericho: Late 1st–Early 2nd Centuries CE", in Bar-Nathan, R., and Gärtner, J. (eds.), *Hasmonean and Herodian Palaces at Jericho* 5. Jerusalem. Pp. 3-84.

Bar-Nathan, R. and Yadin, Y., 2006. *Masada VII: The Yigael Yadin Excavations 1963-1965: Final Reports: The Pottery of Masada*, Jerusalem.

Crowfoot, J. W., Crowfoot, G. M. and Kenyon, K. M., 1957. *The objects from Samaria*, London.

Dar, S., 1986. *Landscape and Pattern: An Archaeological Survey of Samaria, 800 B.C.E. – 636 C.E.*, Oxford.

Geva, H. and Hershkovitz, M., 2006. *Jewish Quarter Excavations in the Old City of Jerusalem, Volume III: Area E and Other Studies, Final Report. Chapter Four: Local Pottery of the Hellenistic and Early Roman Periods*. Jerusalem. Pp. 94-144.

Geva, H., 2010. *Jewish Quarter Excavations in the Old City of Jerusalem, Conducted by Nahman Avigad 1969–1982, Vol. IV: The Burnt House of Area B and Other*

Studies, Final Report. Jerusalem. Pp. 118-153.

Magness, J., 2009. "The pottery from the 1995 excavations in Camp F at Masada", *Bulletin of the American Schools of Oriental Research* 353(1), 75-107.

Neser, E., and Bar-Nathan, R., 2002. *Hasmonean and Herodian palaces at Jericho, vol. 3. The pottery*, Jerusalem.

Rapuano, Y., 2013. "The Pottery of Judea between the First and Second Jewish Revolts", *STRATA: Bulletin of the Anglo-Israel Archaeological Society* 31, 57-102.

Tchekhanovets, Y., 2013. *The Early Roman Pottery. Jerusalem: Excavations in The Tyropoeon Valley (Giv'ati Parking Lot) I* (IAA Report 52), Jerusalem. Pp. 109-150.

Terem, V. S., 2016. *Jerusalem and Judaea in the First and Second Century C.E.: Continuity and Change in the Ceramic Culture* (Doctoral dissertation). Bar-Ilan University, Ramat Gan (Hebrew).

INDEX 1

LIST OF SPRINGS AND OTHER WATER SOURCES

No. in Survey	Name in English	Israel Grid	Type
104	Wadi Far'ah (Nahal Tirzah)		stream
173	'Ein el-Foqa	1881/1738	spring
174	'Ein Hafireh	1912/1679	spring
177	'Ein Abu Daraj	1909/1699	spring
185	'Ein el-Majdal	1849/1658	spring
186	El-'Ein et-Tahta	1877/1737	spring
187	'Ein Sha'eb el-Bir	1872/1759	spring
188	'Ein Mta'a	1867/1748	spring (presently dry)
189	'Ein Juheir	1851/1710	spring
190	Bir Mashkara	1855/1717	spring

INDEX 2

LIST OF ROADS

Road no.	Origin and destination	Passing via
C40	Phasaelis-Neapolis	Phasaelis-'Ein Hafireh-Tana-Beit Dajan-Neapolis. In Tana is a short parallel road from the north of the settlement to road C40 south of E.P. 557
C41	Phasaelis-Neapolis	Phasaelis-Kh Bani Fadil-Khalet el-Khashabeh-Aqraba-Neapolis
C50	'Ein Hafireh-Wadi Zamor	'Ein Hafireh-Sahl Afjam-Wadi Ahmar-and then road splits to Wadi Ahmar and Wadi Mashqara
C51	Nahal Tirzah (Wadi Far'ah)-Neapolis	Nahal Tirzah-E.P. 271- at Sheikh Kamel merges with C40- Neapolis
C52	Nahal Tirzah (Wadi Far'ah)-Neapolis	Nahal Tirzah-E.P. 427-at E.P. 506 merges with C40-Neapolis
C53	Kh. Bani Fadil-Majdal Bani Fadil	Kh. Bani Fadil-Majdal Bani Fadil
C54	Wadi Kamoneh-Gittit Valley	Sets out from C40-Wadi Kamoneh-Gittit Valley
C55	Wadi el-Kabi-Yanun	Wadi el-Kabi-E.P. 474-Yanun
C56	Tana et-Tahta-Neapolis	Tana et-Tahta-E.P. 475-at E.P. 557 merges with C40-Neapolis
C57	Tana et-Tahta-Neapolis	Tana et-Tahta-Wadi Tal'ah-Beit Furik-Neapolis
C58	Gittit Valley	Gittit Valley

INDEX 3

AGRICULTURAL INSTALLATIONS AND OTHER FEATURES

As in the previous volumes, a list of installations and other features is included. It has been suggested that settlement sites should be recorded separately from other features (Zertal 2004a). The linkage of a site to its agricultural vicinity is clear, but it is difficult to relate an installation or agricultural area to a particular site with certainty. The difficulty is because of the large number of sites, the conservatism in using the facilities, and the fact that a particular facility could have been in use for centuries, and sometimes for millennia. Hence, relating features and facilities to a site, or dating them to a period, requires separate thorough research.

For a detailed description of the main different type of installations see Zertal and Mirkam 2016: 565-566.

Type	Location	Region	Description
Enclosures	1893/1794	Khalet el-Radadin	An oval 10×4 m enclosure and a 12×12 m square one. No dateable find
Ancient road	1877/1774	Sheikh Kamel	Ancient 4 m wide road, built with two rows of kerb stones, ascending towards E.P. 667
Stone heaps	1880/1750	Wadi Juni	The site is known as Umm er-Rujman (GL: 116)
Ruins	1900/1750	Aqbet el-Butmeh	Watchtower and heap of fieldstones. The ruins are known as Muntar el-Banik (GL: 117)
Encampment	1893/1759	Aqbet el-Butmeh	Remains of Bedouin encampment
Encampment	1894/1758	Aqbet el-Butmeh	Remains of Bedouin encampment
Encampment and corrals	1894/1757	Aqbet el-Butmeh	Remains of Bedouin encampment. East and south of it five corrals, 10 m in diameter
Dams	1893/1754	Aqbet el-Butmeh	Array of 10 dams along a stream channel
Road (?)	1895/1753	Aqbet el-Butmeh	Section of a road (?), east of it are terrace walls built of large stones
Walls	1895/1755	Aqbet el-Butmeh	Wall of large stones. South of it construction remains, terraces and a few Rom-Byz sherds

Type	Location	Region	Description
Flint scatter	1895/1757	Aqbet el-Butmeh	Scatter of flint. In the field north of it there are sherds scatters
Corrals	1896/1764	Aqbet el-Butmeh	Two stone corrals: one rectangular 15×4 m, and round 8 m in diameter. No dateable find
Terraces	1894/1750	Aqbet el-Butmeh	Terraced slope
Wall	1895/1750	Aqbet el-Butmeh	Field partition wall, on both sides sections paved with small stones. In the fields Rom-Byz sherds
Wall	1896/1751	Aqbet el-Butmeh	Double wall built of large stones, serves as terrace
Road	1896/1751	Aqbet el-Butmeh	North-south road remains 4 m wide in field, built of two parallel stone walls
Agriculture	1897/1751	Aqbet el-Butmeh	Agricultural activity - two stone heaps and field walls
Wall	1899/1750	Aqbet el-Butmeh	On Mekhora water reservoir hill, wall of small stones used as runoff water collecting duct
Cupmark	1899/1748	Aqbet el-Butmeh	Rock-cut 10 cm cupmark on slope of Mekhora water reservoir hill
Cistern and road	1893/1750	Aqbet el-Butmeh	Quarried cistern 12 m deep, next to it remains of ancient road and terrace walls
Sherd scatter	1891/1750	Aqbet el-Butmeh	Sherd scatter on moderate slope above the valley east of Mekhora. 30 LR and Med sherds. Terrace walls above scatter
Cave	1889/1749	Aqbet el-Butmeh	Cave with walls and terraces in front, without finds. Cluster of terraces north of the cave
Sherd scatter	1890/1748	Aqbet el-Butmeh	Scanty unidentified sherd scatter and many terraces on slopes east of the valley east of Mekhora
Sherd scatter	1898/1742	Aqbet el-Butmeh	Scanty Roman sherd scatter
Sherd scatter	1896/1742	Aqbet el-Butmeh	Scanty Roman sherd scatter
Sherd scatter	1890/1738	Aqbet el-Butmeh	Rom and Med sherd scatter and many terraces
Terraces	1892/1741	Aqbet el-Butmeh	Terraces and scanty Rom pottery on a slope
Terraces	1890/1746	Mekhora	Group of terraces. No dateable finds
Agricultural structure	1876/1742	Wadi Qard	Agricultural structure and field partition walls. No dateable finds

AGRICULTURAL INSTALLATIONS AND OTHER FEATURES 473

Type	Location	Region	Description
Installations and terraces	1877/1744	Wadi Qard	Group of terraces on a slope towards Wadi Qard, rock-cut oil press (nether millstone) and cup marks nearby
Walls	1886/1744	'Ein el-Foqa	Array of field walls and a few Rom-Byz sherds
Construction	1885/1746	'Ein el-Foqa	Scanty construction remains and Rom-Byz sherds below the road up to Tana
Agriculture	1885/1744	'Ein el-Foqa	Terraces and few Rom-Byz sherds
Enclosure	1885/1742	'Ein el-Foqa	Round 4 m in diameter enclosure, built of large stones on a moderate slope. No finds
Construction	1886/1740	'Ein el-Foqa	Structure remains on a moderate slope. Wall built of two stone rows. No dateable finds
Installation	1882/1736	Tana et-Tahta	Pressing installation and a rock-cut surface next to it
Road	1885/1751	Tana et-Tahta	2-2.5 m wide road section built of two walls of large stones. Cross incised on flat section of bedrock
Structure	1884/1746	Tana et-Tahta	Structure remains on spur north of 'Ein el-Foqa. No dateable finds
Structures	1884/1745	Tana et-Tahta	Two 2×2 m structures of large and medium-sized stones, 80 m apart. No dateable finds
Agriculture	1883/1744	Tana et-Tahta	Terraces, field structures and installations over wide area in the spurs east of Kh. Tana et-Tahta. No dateable finds
Agriculture	1883/1743	Tana et-Tahta	Structure built of large boulders with installations nearby, courtyards and terraces. No dateable find
Tower	1883/1748	Tana et-Tahta	3×2 m field tower with a group of terraces nearby. No dateable finds
Cistern	1872/1738	Tana et-Tahta	
Agriculture and road	1878/1743	Tana et-Tahta	Terraces and 2 m wide road remains (?), with Rom-Byz sherds
Wall	1877/1741	Tana et-Tahta	Wall on slope, built of large stones
Wall	1876/1740	Tana et-Tahta	Wall on slope, built of large stones
Cistern	1873/1737	Tana et-Tahta	Cemented cistern with metal lid
Structure	1870/1739	Tana et-Tahta	4×3 m field tower built of large stones. No dateable finds
Quarry	1870/1739	Tana et-Tahta	Limestone quarry
Quarry	1872/1737	Tana et-Tahta	

Type	Location	Region	Description
Road	1878/1743	Tana et-Tahta	Remains of 5 m wide ancient road from Tana to north via E.P. 395 towards E.P. 475
Installations	1871/1727	Tana et-Tahta	Two rock-cut basins 30 cm in diameter. Aside one of them is another rock cutting, perhaps a quarry
Cistern	1871/1728	Tana et-Tahta	Plastered
Ancient road	1874/1724	Tana et-Tahta	150 m stretch of 5 m wide ancient road
Threshing floor	1876/1725	Tana et-Tahta	No dateable finds
Agriculture	1872/1727	Tana et-Tahta	Threshing floor, field walls and Rom-Byz sherds
Cave	1872/1718	Tana et-Tahta	Cave and modern construction. No dateable finds
Burial cave	1870/1730	Tana et-Tahta	Plundered burial cave. No dateable finds
Wall	1870/1731	Tana et-Tahta	Wall built of very large boulders
Cave	1867/1735	Tana et-Tahta	Cave with a courtyard. No dateable finds
Burial cave	1867/1737	Tana et-Tahta	Plundered burial cave. No dateable finds
Cistern	1885/1721	Iraq ez-Zah	
Cup marks	1894/1702	Jebel el-Mahjarah	Two cup marks in rock near Jebel el-Mahjarah (8). One is 5 cm diameter and depth. Terraces and stones heaps about 50 m north
Corrals	1893/1702	Jebel el-Mahjarah	Two modern rectangular corrals at edge of a valley
Cistern	1892/1705	Jebel el-Mahjarah	Modern cistern on hill slope, fed by a plastic pipe and next to it a concrete trough. Stones wall leads to the opening diverting rainwater to the cistern. Next to the cistern is a natural cave with a medium-sized wall leading to it. The cave entrance is partially built. At the front of the cave is a courtyard enclosed by a double wall
Caves and courtyards	1891/1706	Jebel el-Mahjarah	Cave with courtyard built with a double wall in front. The entrance is partially built. Next to it is another courtyard, and at its eastern side are cave openings. This courtyard has a double wall: the outer one of medium-sized stones and the inner wall of small stones. The jamb stones survive. Terraces nearby
Terraces	1892/1708	Jebel el-Mahjarah	Terraces of large stones over a spur slope above valley. Walls survive up to 1.5 m high

AGRICULTURAL INSTALLATIONS AND OTHER FEATURES 475

Type	Location	Region	Description
Agriculture	1876/1718	Jaffa en-Noon	Terrace walls and two massive walls on slope possibly courtyard frame. No dateable finds
Construction	1880/1719	Jaffa en-Noon	Structure remains, damaged by plunder of stones. Nearby is rock-cut 50 cm diameter round installation. A few Rom-Byz sherds
Cistern	1880/1719	Jaffa en-Noon	Plastered and collapsed cistern, 8×5×4 m deep. Opening survives. Rock cut 50×50 cm installations by the cistern and a few Rom-Byz sherds
Terraces and caves	1877/1731	Jaffa en-Noon	Groups of terraces and caves on a slope west of Tana et-Tahta. No dateable finds
Road	1877/1728	Jaffa en-Noon	150 m section of 4 m wide road
Caves	1883/1727	Jaffa en-Noon	Caves, rock shelter and ruined courtyards. Presently there is a Bedouin encampment. No dateable finds
Road	1884/1726	Jaffa en-Noon	Fragmentarily preserved 300 m ancient road section
Structure	1881/1722	Jaffa en-Noon	10×6 m structure on a slope facing Iraq ez-Zah. No dateable finds
Cistern	1874/1717	Jaffa en-Noon	
Road	1872/1716	Jaffa en-Noon	300 m section of ancient 4 m wide road on a slope. Close by is a group of terraces
Threshing floor	1872/1716	Jaffa en-Noon	Threshing floor and a natural cave. No dateable finds
Agriculture	1875/1719	Jaffa en-Noon	Agricultural walls
Agriculture	1879/1721	Jaffa en-Noon	Agricultural walls on slope
Installations	1879/1714	Jaffa en-Noon	Rock-cut installations
Cave	1879/1716	Jaffa en-Noon	Cave with construction remains. No dateable finds
Cistern	1880/1714	Jaffa en-Noon	
Construction	1878/1710	Jaffa en-Noon	Remains of collapsed square structure. No dateable finds
Cupmark	1883/1714	Farqom cave	Rock-cut cupmark, 15 cm diameter and depth
Threshing floor	1884/1711	Farqom cave	Threshing floor 12 m in diameter on spur. No dateable finds
Installation	1885/1713	Farqom cave	Round installation with flat bottom, 50 cm in diameter and 25 cm deep
Pathway	1888/1709	Wadi el-Afjam	Pathway built of two parallel rows of stones

Type	Location	Region	Description
Cistern and structure	1885/1708	Wadi el-Afjam	Active cemented cistern with iron lid and an iron trough. A collecting duct drains to it the entire plateau above. East of it a dismantled structure remains. No dateable find
Cistern	1882/1706	Wadi el-Afjam	Cemented cistern with metal lid and concrete trough
Cistern	1882/1706	Wadi el-Afjam	Rock-cut cistern
Corral	1883/1708	Wadi el-Afjam	Modern Bedouin square corral on spur slope. South of it a round corral. South of them, on the slope, terraces and stone heaps
Construction	1883/1708	Wadi el-Afjam	Construction (?) remains and stone clearing heaps on spur slope. No dateable finds
Cistern	1885/1703	Wadi el-Afjam	Modern cemented cistern with metal lid. Attached to it a support wall and a concrete trough
Construction	1885/1708	Wadi el-Afjam	Construction remains on a slope. No finds
Construction	1852/1709	'Ein Juheir	Two built rooms on the slope above 'Ein Juheir. No dateable finds
Tombs	1860/1690	Wadi Ahmar	Rock-cut tombs. The site is known as Urqan el-Baker (GL: 117)
Cistern	1870/1697	Wadi Ahmar	Rock-cut cistern of unknown depth. The opening diameter is 1 m
Terraces	1869/1698	Wadi Ahmar	Terraced slope along Wadi Ahmar
Cupmark	1867/1701	Wadi Ahmar	
Wall	1866/1701	Wadi Ahmar	Wall of medium-sized stones at edge of field. Rom-Byz and Med body sherds
Cup marks	1864/1703	Wadi Ahmar	Three cup marks on slope of spur. One is 30 cm diameter and 20 cm deep. The others are 10 cm in diameter and their depth is unknown. Scanty scatter of sherds and flint
Dams	1870/1695	Wadi Ahmar	Dams built of large stones across a wadi channel
Construction	1859/1705	Wadi Ahmar	Constructed road with kerb stones in the southern part of Wadi Ahmar; next to it construction remains. No dateable finds
Construction	1857/1705	Wadi Ahmar	Walls, unidentified sherd scatter and cupmark
Road	1857/1705	Wadi Ahmar	Ancient road along east bank of Wadi Ahmar

AGRICULTURAL INSTALLATIONS AND OTHER FEATURES

Type	Location	Region	Description
Corrals	1863/1701	Wadi Ahmar	Large rock shelter above a ravine descending to Wadi Ahmar, used nowadays as Bedouin corrals
Cisterns	1862/1701	Wadi Ahmar	Two cisterns
Cave	1861/1704	Wadi Ahmar	Collapsed ceiling. In front is an enclosing wall. No dateable finds
Terraces	1864/1703	Wadi Ahmar	Terraces and at least two 40 cm diameter cup marks
Terrace	1860/1702	Wadi Ahmar	Terrace wall built of medium-sized stones on slope
Terraces	1857/1703	Wadi Ahmar	Terraces on slope
Maq'ads	1865/1697	Wadi Ahmar	Two modern *maq'ads* at edge of valley
Wall	1859/1697	Wadi Ahmar	Stone wall and a few Rom-Byz and Med sherds on a rocky hillock. 50 m south is a rock-cut cupmark, 20 cm in diameter
Cistern	1856/1695	Wadi Ahmar	Blocked cistern
Sherd scatter	1847/1706	Khirbet er-Risa	Sherd scatter in area cleared of stones, mainly Rom-Byz and a few IA and Med
Dwelling cave and tumuli (?)	1848/1706	Khirbet er-Risa	Partially collapsed cave in modern use. Inside partition walls built of medium-sized stones. Outside are three cup marks in the rock surfaces; two are 35 cm in diameter and the third is 10 cm. 50 m west of the cave is a row of three 12×5 m heaps of stones, may be tumuli. Around them scanty Rom-Byz sherds
Construction	1846/1706	Khirbet er-Risa	Construction remains on moderate slope. A few Rom-Byz sherds. Up the slope is a massive wall
Agriculture	1846/1707	Khirbet er-Risa	On the eastern slope of Kh. er-Risa (1) are: threshing floor, wall remains built of large stones and two 50 cm diameter cup marks. There are IA and a few Chalc/EBA sherds
Installations and cistern	1846/1706	Khirbet er-Risa	Two basins: 80 cm and 40 cm diameter; between them a slide recess. 20 m north a cemented rim cistern with a metal lid. Next to it are two troughs: one old and rock-cut, the other modern and built

Type	Location	Region	Description
Installations	1846/1707	Khirbet er-Risa	At eastern edge of Kh. er-Risa (1) is an ancient water reservoir with an opening of a water drawing pit. A rock-cut water collecting duct leads to the cistern. Up the slope is a modern cemented cistern with built walls of water collecting duct. In the slope between them are two sets of pressing/treading or grinding surfaces and a receiving basin. There are modern olive plantations
Wall	1876/1697	Wadi Zamor	Wall of medium-sized stones which served as protection against erosion for a plot of arable land
Terraces	1875/1698	Wadi Zamor	Array of terraces on steep northern slope of Wadi Zamor
Road	1884/1698	Wadi Zamor	Section of ancient road 2 m wide
Silages	1884/1698	Wadi Zamor	Two round storage facilities, 2.5 m diameter, modern
Terraces	1883/1698	Wadi Zamor	Built agricultural steps in wadi channel. Terraces scattered over entire spur above channel
Cave	1881/1699	Wadi Zamor	Natural cave with built entrance. At the front is a round courtyard built on a terrace. South of the courtyard is a cemented opening of a cistern. No dateable finds
Road	1879/1694	Wadi Zamor	Remains of road ascending from the valley to the ridges in the west
Wall	1880/1694	Wadi Zamor	Field partition wall
Structure	1881/1694	Wadi Zamor	No dateable finds
Silages	1881/1693	Wadi Zamor	Three dug pits lined with small stones (silos?) built along agricultural road. Above them there is an array of built terraces
Cistern	1889/1687	Wadi Zamor	Partially built cistern at edge of cultivated field
Cistern	1855/1690	Wadi Zamor	
Cisterns	1857/1685	Wadi Zamor	Two cisterns with water collecting ducts
Threshing floor	1855/1702	Wadi Zamor	Threshing floor remains on rocky hillock south of Wadi Ahmar. No dateable finds
Tomb	1856/1700	Wadi Zamor	Late Roman plundered tomb. 20 body sherds collected

AGRICULTURAL INSTALLATIONS AND OTHER FEATURES 479

Type	Location	Region	Description
Enclosure	1859/1692	Wadi Zamor	Remains of rectangular 14×8 m enclosure, built of medium-sized stones. Few Ott and Mod sherds
Watchtower	1851/1707	Wadi Zamor	Modern watchtower 4 m in diameter in a terraced modern agricultural area. The tower wall is preserved 6 courses (2 m) high
Installations	1851/1707	Wadi Zamor	Cluster of installations in agricultural area: cup marks, with diameter up to 50 cm, oil press nether grindstone, many rock cuttings, construction remains and a few Rom-Byz sherds. 80m westwards is a built watchtower, of which remained at least eight stone courses (1.5 m) high
Dwelling cave	1851/1707	Wadi Zamor	Cave containing remains of plaster and soot, a built plastered wall and two rock-cut niches. No dateable finds
Agriculture	1851/1698	Wadi Zamor	Remains of terrace walls on west bank of Wadi Ahmar
Sherd scatter	1850/1700	Wadi Zamor	Sherd scatter on spur slope, mainly MBA II and IA I and a few Rom-Byz
Walls and stones clearing	1887/1704	Wadi Zamor	Remains of several walls and stone clearing heaps. No dateable finds
Terrace	1887/1684	Wadi Kamoneh	Remains of agricultural terrace built of medium-sized and large stones next to wadi channel. Construction remains on slope
Road	1887/1683	Wadi Kamoneh	Remains of road, built of two parallel stone walls, ascending from Wadi Kamoneh towards north-west
Terraces	1891/1678	Wadi Kamoneh	Terraced slope at valley edge. Massive construction
Structures	1894/1682	Wadi Kamoneh	Stone wall on slope, perhaps structure remains. Remains of two square structures 20 m east. No dateable finds
Cistern	1894/1681	Wadi Kamoneh	Collapsed dug cistern at top of spur
Structure	1895/1681	Wadi Kamoneh	Collapsed structure built of large stones on spur slope. A few Rom-Byz sherds and some flint items
Terrace	1895/1681	Wadi Kamoneh	Thin wall built of small stones, perhaps a terrace
Encampment and terraces	1882/1684	Wadi Kamoneh	Encampment and remains of terraces. Round threshing floor near terraces. No dateable finds

Type	Location	Region	Description
Trough	1894/1682	Wadi Kamoneh	Broken rock-cut trough on northern slope of E.P. 162 next to unpaved road at edge of a valley
Road	1895/1681	Wadi Kamoneh	Narrow road enclosed on both sides by rows of stones, on northern slope of E.P. 162
Threshing floor	1856/1702	Wadi 'Urqan es-Sabah	Threshing floor and a few Rom sherds
Agriculture	1857/1698	Wadi 'Urqan es-Sabah	Field partition walls and terraces
Cistern	1849/1693	Wadi 'Urqan es-Sabah	Dug cistern lined with medium-sized stones, 5 m diameter, about 2 m deep
Wall	1850/1692	Wadi 'Urqan es-Sabah	Wall in field, built of fieldstones, up to 6 courses (at least 1.5 m) high
Wall	1850/1690	Wadi 'Urqan es-Sabah	Massive wall enclosing cultivated terraced area. In the area are many cleared stone walls/terraces
Wall	1853/1687	Khalet el-Khashabeh	Wall of medium-sized and large stones on terraced slope of a spur
Cistern	1848/1684	Khalet el-Khashabeh	
Cave	1849/1683	Khalet el-Khashabeh	Cave with terrace wall in front. No dateable finds
Terraces	1859/1684	Khalet el-Khashabeh	A concentration of terraces on a slope
Stones clearing	1860/1684	Khalet el-Khashabeh	Stone clearing heaps
Maq'ad	1859/1683	Khalet el-Khashabeh	Wall of stones collected during field clearing – part of modern *maq'ad*
Stones clearing	1859/1682	Khalet el-Khashabeh	Rounded stone clearing heap 6 m diameter
Wall	1860/1683	Khalet el-Khashabeh	Wall 3 m long, built of two rows of large stones, rock-cut 20 cm in diameter cupmark. A few Rom-Byz sherds
Paving	1860/1682	Khalet el-Khashabeh	Surface 4 m in diameter paved with small stones. No dateable finds
Agriculture	1856/1692	Khalet el-Khashabeh	Field divided into cultivated strips by stone walls
Wall	1855/1691	Khalet el-Khashabeh	Stone wall which serves as a modern *maq'ad*
Maq'ad	1854/1690	Khalet el-Khashabeh	Modern *maq'ad*

AGRICULTURAL INSTALLATIONS AND OTHER FEATURES 481

Type	Location	Region	Description
Enclosure	1853/1690	Khalet el-Khashabeh	Plot of land bounded by wall of large stones. In centre is a rock-cut basin, 30 cm diameter. In the western part of the area is a modern *maq'ad*. A few Rom sherds
Cup marks	1853/1689	Khalet el-Khashabeh	Rock-cut cup marks in bedrock surface
Cistern	1853/1688	Khalet el-Khashabeh	Cistern with concrete trough attached and collecting duct leading to cistern
Wall	1854/1688	Khalet el-Khashabeh	Field partition wall built of two rows of medium-sized stones
Structure	1855/1690	Khalet el-Khashabeh	Remains of a collapsed structure built of large stones. No dateable finds
Stone clearing	1856/1690	Khalet el-Khashabeh	Stone clearing heaps about 1 m high in field
Stone heaps and cisterns	1880/1670	Gittit	Stone heaps and cisterns. Site known as A-Damya (GL: 118)
Terraces	1873/1685	Gittit	Stone clearing heaps and terraces on slope of spur at edge of valley
Courtyard	1882/1689	Gittit	Courtyard 7×7 m with rounded corners, built of medium-sized and large stones, on hill slope at edge of valley. No dateable finds
Courtyard	1864/1670	Gittit	Courtyard 10×7 m on hill slope, built of medium-sized and large stones. No dateable finds
Structure	1874/1692	Gittit	Collapsed structure 3 m diameter on slope of spur. No dateable finds
Structure	1874/1691	Gittit	Collapsed structure 5×5 m, perhaps a tower, built of large stones on slope of spur. No dateable finds
Threshing floor	1875/1689	Gittit	Threshing floor 7 m diameter on slope of spur. No dateable finds
Wall	1876/1688	Gittit	Remains of a large stones wall in a saddle
Courtyard	1877/1685	Gittit	Remains of courtyard built next to cliff. No dateable finds
Courtyard	1875/1687	Gittit	Courtyard 16×8 m. No dateable finds
Courtyard (?)	1874/1688	Gittit	Courtyard (?) remains beside agricultural plot. No dateable finds
Enclosure	1878/1688	Gittit	Enclosure remains 3 m diameter in saddle, built of one row of stones. No dateable finds
Road	1879/1688	Gittit	Remains of 2 m wide road in a saddle

Type	Location	Region	Description
Courtyard (?)	1881/1687	Gittit	Courtyard (?) remains on a slope of spur. No dateable finds
Terraces	1881/1685	Gittit	Terraces on slope of spur
Courtyard/ threshing floor	1881/1685	Gittit	Courtyard or semicircular threshing floor on steep slope. No dateable finds
Terraces	1881/1683	Gittit	
Cup marks	1886/1682	Gittit	Rock-cut cup marks; 50 cm diameter
Threshing floor	1887/1686	Gittit	No dateable finds
Enclosure	1888/1675	Gittit	Remains of enclosure walls. No dateable finds
Watchtower (?)	1890/1677	Gittit	Structure 5×2 m on slope of spur, built of medium-sized stones. Walls survive up to 2 m high. No dateable finds
Terraces and construction	1863/1683	Gittit	Terraces and construction on moderate slope at edge of valley. Scanty Rom-Byz sherd scatter
Structure	1860/1686	Gittit	Dismantled rectangular structure, built of large stones on spur. No dateable finds
Stones clearance	1860/1685	Gittit	Concentration of stones, maybe clearing. No dateable finds
Wall	1862/1683	Gittit	Remains of wall built of medium-sized stones
Courtyard	1862/1685	Gittit	Round courtyard and cleared stones 10 m diameter, built of medium-sized stones and bedrock. A few Rom-Byz sherds
Cup marks	1861/1685	Gittit	Rock surface containing cup marks of various sizes
Enclosure	1864/1678	Gittit	Enclosure containing stone clearing heaps at bottom of Gittit water reservoir hill. No dateable finds
Wall	1861/1679	Mras ed-Din	Massive wall built of large stones used as terrace on slope of spur
Winepress	1860/1679	Mras ed-Din	Rock-cut winepress comprising treading floor and collecting vat. Massive wall described in item above reaches to winepress. Rom body sherds
Stones clearance	1860/1673	Mras ed-Din	Mound of small stones at edge of field - stone clearing

AGRICULTURAL INSTALLATIONS AND OTHER FEATURES

Type	Location	Region	Description
Structure	1856/1677	Mras ed-Din	Tumulus (?), 8 m diameter. No dateable finds
Cistern	1853/1679	Mras ed-Din	
Ruin	1840/1670	Wadi es-Sayad	Structure foundations. Ruin is known as Kh. Sabubah (GL: 118)
Cistern	1855/1673	Wadi es-Sayad	Cistern on slope of spur. Opening diameter 50 cm. Access to cistern on west side. Now cistern is dry and serves as flock corral
Wall	1855/1674	Wadi es-Sayad	Retaining wall 5 m long on spur slope. Lower part built of large stones and upper part of smaller stones
Structure	1852/1674	Wadi es-Sayad	Remains of structure 10×10 m, built of large stones at edge of valley. No dateable finds
Enclosure	1851/1675	Wadi es-Sayad	Enclosure at edge of field. Northern part paved, maybe served as a threshing floor. A few Rom-Byz sherds
Structure	1850/1676	Wadi es-Sayad	Remains of structure 5×3 m at edge of field. Possibly served for storing agricultural produce. No dateable finds
Cistern	1850/1676	Wadi es-Sayad	Cistern at edge of field
Structure	1850/1676	Wadi es-Sayad	Corner of structure built of large stones in field. No dateable finds
Quarried cave	1850/1675	Wadi es-Sayad	Quarried and plastered cave with steps. Quite recent judging by spill in front. Cupmark by the entrance. Close by is blocked entrance of another cave. No dateable finds
Structure	1851/1674	Wadi es-Sayad	Remains of square structure built of large stones. No dateable finds
Caves	1849/1681	Wadi es-Sayad	Two dwelling (?) caves, nearby a deserted structure (Ottoman?)
Threshing floor and structure	1853/1672	Wadi es-Sayad	Remains of threshing floor 15 m diameter. Next to it structure remains. No dateable finds
Wall	1852/1672	Wadi es-Sayad	Stone fence, perhaps agricultural terrace
Structure	1859/1672	Wadi es-Sayad	Remains of fallen structure in edge of field, possibly for storing cereals. A few Rom-Byz sherds
Structure	1851/1670	Wadi es-Sayad	Remains of structure 8×8 m. No dateable finds
Enclosure	1854/1669	Wadi es-Sayad	Corral 25×15 m. No dateable finds

Type	Location	Region	Description
Courtyard	1846/1675	Wadi es-Sayad	Large courtyard with garden inside, at valley edge. No dateable finds
Rock cutting	1845/1674	Wadi es-Sayad	Rock-cutting marks in large rock
Terrace	1847/1670	Wadi es-Sayad	Terrace built of large and medium-sized stones on slope of spur
Terrace	1846/1670	Wadi es-Sayad	Terrace wall 5 courses (1.8 m) high built of large stones and boulders on slope
Structures and cistern	1846/1671	Wadi es-Sayad	Two stone circles 2 m diameter on slope of spur. About 5 m south is rock-cut cistern with opening 1.5 m diameter. No dateable finds
Stones heap	1848/1669	Wadi es-Sayad	Pile of oval stones 15×7 m on slope of spur at edge of valley. Large stones and boulders at periphery and smaller stones in the centre
Structure and terraces	1846/1675	Wadi es-Sayad	Remains of agricultural structure and terraces spread over wide area
Cistern	1846/1674	Wadi es-Sayad	Cistern (utilization of a natural waterhole)
Agriculture	1849/1671	Wadi es-Sayad	Concentration of terraces over large area and agricultural structure
Niche	1849/1669	Wadi es-Sayad	Rock-cut niche, natural caves, terraces and scanty undated sherds
Cistern	1849/1669	Wadi es-Sayad	Cistern and rock-cut trough
Wall	1850/1668	Wadi es-Sayad	Wall 20 m long 2 m thick descending slope between terraces, possibly for field partition
Walls	1855/1667	Wadi es-Sayad	Agricultural walls on slope of spur and edge of field
Walls	1854/1668	Wadi es-Sayad	Boulder-built walls on slope at edge of field and a few Rom-Byz sherds
Threshing floor	1853/1670	Wadi es-Sayad	Stone built threshing floor 20 m diameter. No dateable finds
Structure	1853/1669	Wadi es-Sayad	Structure remains at top of spur. No dateable finds
Maq'ad	1852/1670	Wadi es-Sayad	Modern *maq'ad* 2 m diameter at top of spur
Structure	1847/1672	Wadi es-Sayad	Structure remains and stone clearance heaps in field. No dateable finds
Wall	1860/1667	El-Minyeh	2.5 m wall in a field
Cupmark	1861/1666	El-Minyeh	Cupmark at edge of a field

Type	Location	Region	Description
Structure	1859/1668	Ma'ale Ephraim Junction	Collapsed structure 4×3 m built of medium-sized and large stones at edge of field. Walls preserved 4 courses (1.7 m) high. Structure apparently for cereal storage. Next to structure is wall of cleared stones. No dateable finds
Wall	1858/1670	Ma'ale Ephraim Junction	Boulder-built wall at edge of field
Structure	1858/1671	Ma'ale Ephraim Junction	Collapsed structure 4×2 m, built of large stones. Apparently for storage of cereals. No dateable finds
Threshing floor	1858/1671	Ma'ale Ephraim Junction	Circle of stones 15 m diameter, possibly threshing floor. A few Rom-Byz and Med sherds
Threshing floor and tumulus	1853/1669	Ma'ale Ephraim Junction	Stone wall threshing floor founded on rock. Next to it is semicircle bounded by wall of medium-sized stones 2 courses high. 30 m west is tumulus 15 m diameter. No dateable finds
Maq'ad	1853/1659	Kh. Bani Fadil	*Maq'ad* next to cave entrance
Installation	1852/1659	Kh. Bani Fadil	Rock-cut basin 60 cm diameter and 40 cm deep
Cistern and courtyards	1854/1660	Kh. Bani Fadil	Cistern with a lid and two modern troughs. Built courtyards by the cistern

INDEX 4

SITE INDEX

Site	Number	Page
Ahmar Terrace, Wadi	102	281
Ahmar Valley, Wadi	103	283
Ali, Kom	81	237
Arrar (1), Merah	52	179
Arrar (2), Merah	51	175
Bir, Wadi Sha'eb el-	18	115
Butmeh (1), 'Aqabet el-	22	122
Butmeh (2), 'Aqabet el-	21	121
Din (Northern Complex), Mras ed-	172	420
Din (South-eastern Complex), Mras ed-	173	423
'Ein, Birket Wadi el-	50	173
'Ein (1), Wadi Khallet el-	49	171
'Ein (2), Wadi Khallet el-	32	137
'Ein (3), Wadi Kahllet el-	37	146
E.P. 162	175	430
E.P. 242	122	324
E.P. 271 (West)	15	111
E.P. 293	33	138
E.P. 335	146	371
E.P. 338	143	364
E.P. 363	58	188
E.P. 390 (1)	178	438
E.P. 390 (2)	162	399
E.P. 390 (3)	177	435
E.P. 390 (4)	176	433
E.P. 390 (5)	160	397
E.P. 390 (6)	164	407

SITE INDEX

Site	Number	Page
E.P. 390 (7)	163	404
E.P. 390 (8)	170	416
E.P. 393 (1)	132	341
E.P. 393 (2)	166	411
E.P. 393 (3)	161	398
E.P. 394 (South)	59	190
E.P. 395 (1)	27	130
E.P. 395 (2)	25	128
E.P. 395 (3)	39	149
E.P. 395 (4)	42	153
E.P. 395 (5)	41	152
E.P. 395 (6)	28	132
E.P. 395 (7)	26	129
E.P. 395 (8)	44	158
E.P. 395 (9)	45	160
E.P. 419 (1)	138	352
E.P. 419 (2)	141	357
E.P. 419 (3)	136	348
E.P. 419 (4)	168	413
E.P. 419 (5)	135	346
E.P. 419 (6)	131	339
E.P. 422	23	123
E.P. 427	3	94
E.P. 432 (1)	134	344
E.P. 432 (2)	118	316
E.P. 432 (3)	115	308
E.P. 432 (4)	105	291
E.P. 432 (5)	109	297
E.P. 432 (6)	126	332
E.P. 432 (7)	114	307
E.P. 432 (8)	107	294

Site	Number	Page
E.P. 432 (9)	137	350
E.P. 474	69	213
E.P. 475	29	134
E.P. 557	13	109
E.P. 572	10	102
E.P. 577	1	91
E.P. 667 (1)	6	96
E.P. 667 (2)	7	98
E.P. 708 (South)	4	95
Ephraim Junction, Ma'ale	180	442
Fadil, Khirbet Bani	181	444
Farqom Cave (1)	82	239
Farqom Cave (2)	77	228
Farqom (1), Wadi	83	241
Farqom (2), Wadi	84	243
Farqom (3), Wadi	85	246
Foqa, 'Ein el-	48	170
Gittit (1)	139	354
Gittit (2)	140	356
Gittit Quarry	124	330
Gurfeh (1), el-	111	300
Gurfeh (2), el-	110	299
Gurfeh (3), el-	113	306
Isyar (1)	158	394
Isyar (2)	159	394
Isyar, Kh.	157	390
Juheir (1), 'Ein	95	268
Juheir (2), 'Ein	96	270
Juni, Wadi	12	107
Juraish (Lower)	97	272
Juraish, 'Ein	80	234

SITE INDEX

Site	Number	Page
Juraish, Khirbet	64	201
Kabi, Wadi el-	62	198
Kamel, Sheikh	11	105
Kamoneh (1), Wadi	155	386
Kamoneh (2), Wadi	149	375
Kamoneh (3), Wadi	151	379
Kamoneh (4), Wadi	152	382
Kamoneh (5), Wadi	150	378
Kamoneh (6), Wadi	174	428
Kamoneh (7), Wadi	156	388
Kamoneh (8), Wadi	154	385
Kamoneh (9), Wadi	153	384
Kaukab (1), el-	120	320
Kaukab (2), el-	121	322
Khashabeh, Khalet el-	125	331
Labadeh, 'Iraq	17	114
Loz (1), Khallet el-	30	135
Loz (2), Khallet el-	31	136
Mahjarah (6), Jebel el-	89	254
Mahjarah (7), Jebel el-	93	260
Mahjarah (8), Jebel el-	90	255
Mahjarah (9), Jebel el-	88	253
Mahjarah (10), Jebel el-	87	251
Mahjarah (11), Jebel el-	91	256
Manzal (1), Wadi	53	180
Manzal (2), Wadi	63	199
Mekhora Pool	34	140
Mta'a, 'Ein	24	124
Museif, Zuhur el-	2	93
Najmeh (1), en-	35	142
Najmeh (2), en-	36	145

Site	Number	Page
Naqurah, en-	169	414
Noon (1), Jaffa en-	66	208
Noon (2), Jaffa en-	72	217
Noon (3), Jaffa en-	65	206
Noon (4), Jaffa en-	76	227
Noon (5), Jaffa en-	67	210
Noon (6), Jaffa en-	70	215
Noon (7), Jaffa en-	73	220
Noon (8), Jaffa en-	74	223
Noon (9), Jaffa en-	75	225
Rahib, Ras er-	128	335
Rahman (1), Bir 'Abd el-	16	112
Rahman (2), Bir 'Abd el-	20	118
Ramdat (1), Mughur el-	78	230
Ramdat (2), Mughur el-	79	232
Risa (1), Khirbet er-	94	265
Risa (2), Khirbet er-	100	277
Saba, Wadi 'Urqan es-	127	333
Saiyakh (1), Sha'ab es-	57	187
Saiyakh (2), Sha'ab es-	56	185
Sayad (1), Wadi es-	167	412
Sayad (2), Wadi es-	179	440
Shafa (1), Zuhur esh-	8	99
Shafa (2), Zuhur esh-	5	95
Silem, es-	98	274
Sireh (1), es-	133	341
Sireh (2), es-	129	336
Sireh (3), es-	130	337
Suheil, M'rah Abu	19	116
Tana Cave	43	158
Tana et-Tahta Cemetery (1)	38	148

SITE INDEX

Site	Number	Page
Tana et-Tahta Cemetery (2)	40	151
Tana et-Tahta, Kh.	47	164
Tana et-Tahta (South-West)	54	181
Tana et-Tahta (Western Quarter), Kh.	46	161
Tawil (1), Khirbet	171	418
Tawil (2), Khirbet	142	360
Tawileh, Kh.	165	408
Tineh, Mugharet et-	116	309
Tireh, Mugharet et-	71	216
Tireh, Mughur et-	68	212
Turmus (1), Sirt et-	144	365
Turmus (2), Sirt et-	145	369
Turmus (3), Sirt et-	147	372
'Urqan (1), el-	117	314
'Urqan (2), el-	119	318
Zah (1), 'Iraq ez-	60	193
Zah (2), 'Iraq ez-	61	197
Zah (3), 'Iraq ez-	55	182
Zamor (1), Wadi	148	373
Zamor (2), Wadi	106	292
Zamor (3), Wadi	108	296
Zamor (4), Wadi	86	248
Zamor (5), Wadi	92	257
Zamor (6), Wadi	112	303
Zamor (7), Wadi	123	327
Zamor (8), Wadi	104	289
Zamor (9), Wadi	101	280
Zamor (10), Wadi	99	276
Zrub (1), Wadi Umm ez-	9	101
Zrub (2), Wadi Umm ez-	14	110

INDEX 5

LIST OF SITES BY PERIOD

Prehistory:

48, 59, 75-78, 96, 99, 102-103, 124, 149-150.

Chalcolithic:

47(?), 60, 64, 80, 86, 88, 95-97, 102-103, 134(?).

Early Bronze Age:

24, 43, 47, 60, 64, 80, 86, 88, 94, 100, 134(?).

Intermediate Bronze Age:

24, 28, 44, 72, 100, 165.

Middle Bronze Age II:

10, 28, 31, 39, 43, 47, 51, 56, 59-60, 64, 72, 78-80, 89, 100-101, 115, 117-118, 119(?), 131, 134-135, 137, 144, 151-152, 157, 161-162, 165, 167, 169-170, 172-173, 176-177, 180-181.

Late Bronze Age:

64, 144(?), 162, 181(?).

Iron Age I:

1, 5, 7, 17, 20, 28, 44, 46-47, 51-52, 56, 58-60, 64, 67, 77-79, 86, 94, 100, 108, 112(?), 115, 118-119, 127, 133, 134, 139, 142, 144, 156-157, 159, 170, 175-178, 180-181.

Iron Ages II-III:

3, 5, 9, 14, 16-20, 23, 25-28, 31, 34-38, 39(?), 41-47, 51-52, 56, 58-60, 62-66, 72-73, 77-79, 81-82, 86, 88, 93-95, 100, 103, 109, 115, 119, 122, 127, 136, 138, 142, 144, 149, 151-153, 156, 159-160, 162-163, 168, 170, 172-175, 177-181.

Persian period:

16, 18, 23, 64, 82-83, 157, 172-173.

Hellenistic period:

7-8, 10, 20, 42, 47, 64, 123, 136, 151, 157.

LIST OF SITES BY PERIOD

Early Roman period:

7-8, 10, 17, 20-22, 26, 28, 33, 36, 39, 42, 46-47, 50, 58, 64, 66, 77, 100, 103, 106, 113, 123, 129, 131, 136, 141, 151, 154, 159-161, 170, 172-173, 181.

Late Roman period:

1-23, 25-26, 28-37, 39-42, 44-75, 77-86, 88-94, 98-101, 103-123, 126-157, 159-175, 177-181.

Byzantine period:

2, 6-12, 14-16, 18, 20-29, 33-38, 40-42, 44-48, 53-54, 56-57, 59, 62-67, 69, 75, 77-79, 84, 86, 88-92, 94, 101, 104, 108, 111, 113-116, 119-121, 124, 126-127, 131, 133-134, 137-139, 141-143, 145-154, 159-161, 163-164, 166-167, 171-173, 175, 177-181.

Early Moslem period:

8, 10, 47, 78, 112, 124.

Middle Ages:

3, 7-8, 11-18, 20, 22, 27-28, 33(?), 35, 37, 41-42, 44-47, 49, 56, 58, 62, 64-65, 69-70, 72, 75, 78-79, 84, 86, 88-89, 91, 98, 100-101, 103-105, 107-113, 115-119, 121- 122, 124, 126, 130-131, 133-134(?), 136-140, 144-145, 148-149, 151, 153, 155, 157, 159-160, 162-164, 166-168, 171-173, 175, 177-179, 181.

Ottoman period:

11, 14, 41, 47, 77-79, 82, 84, 86, 92, 94, 107, 109, 112-113, 116, 122, 124-125, 149, 151, 181.

* Sites where the pottery identification is uncertain are marked with a question mark.

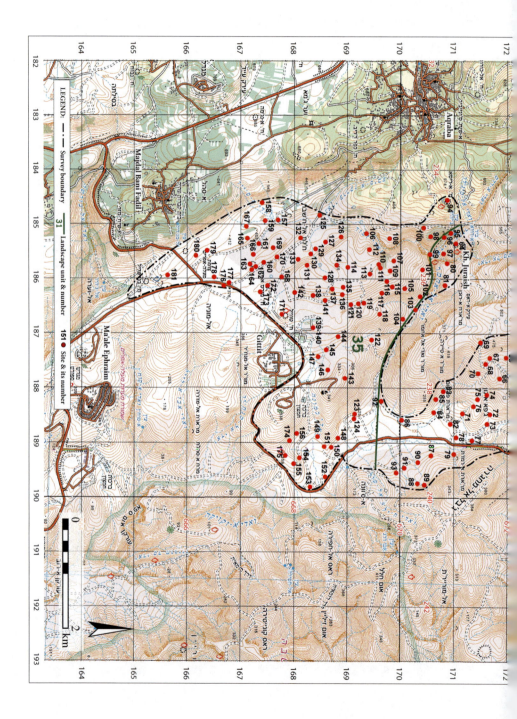

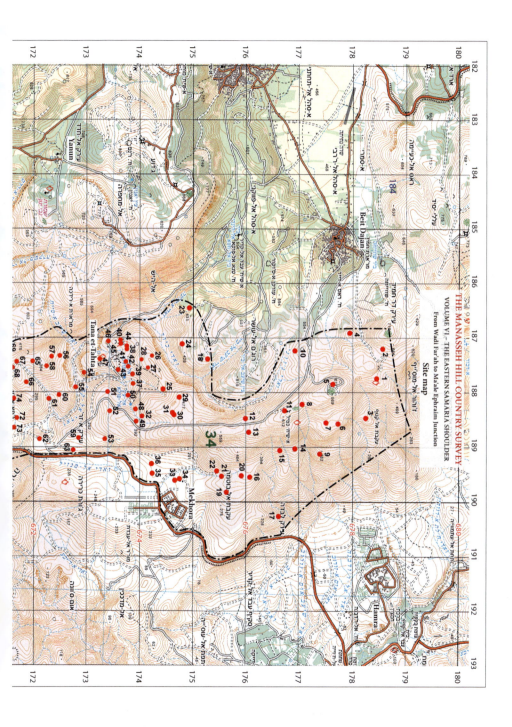

Printed in the United States
by Baker & Taylor Publisher Services